ROBERT A. M. STERN

ROBERT A. M. STERN

Buildings and Projects
1981–1985

Edited by Luis F. Rueda

First published in the United States of America in 1986 by
Rizzoli International Publications, Inc.
597 Fifth Avenue, New York NY 10017

Library of Congress Cataloging-in-Publication Data

Stern, Robert A. M.
Buildings and projects 1981–1985.

Bibliography: p.
1. Stern, Robert A. M. 2. Architecture—
United States—Themes, motives. 3. Interior
architecture—United States. I. Title.
NA737.S64A4 1986a 720′.92′4 85-43484
ISBN 0-8478-0700-2
ISBN 0-8478-0704-5 (pbk.)

Designed by Alessandro Franchini Design, Inc., New York City

Set in type by Roberts/Churcher, Brooklyn, N.Y.;
and A&S Graphics, Inc., Wantagh, N.Y.
Printed and bound in Japan by Dai Nippon Printing Company

Contents

Introduction: Modern Traditionalism
Robert A. M. Stern

Enduring art cannot be founded on a negative statement. Art requires an assertion of belief. Yet the age of architectural ideology is over. There are no rules; only choices and inventions. What is left as a design process is the critical synthesis of what T. S. Eliot has suggested are the twin poles between which creativity oscillates: tradition and individual talent.

Architecture is less an issue of innovation than an act of interpretation; to be an architect is to possess an individual voice speaking a generally understood language of form. To be really articulate as an architect is to raise that voice to heights of lyricism, to make each element, each word, resonate with meaning. So it is for me that the pleasure of architecture lies both in fulfilled memory and in the "play of forms under the light."

Architecture is a narrative art, and architectural style is analogous to poetic diction. Simple writing may literally communicate, but ordinarily does not give much pleasure. Storytellers since the Greek tragedians have therefore embroidered their tales with references to, and even direct quotations from, works of the past in order to connect with tradition. From time to time they have even adopted old forms of expression in toto. The complexity of a narrative, its allusiveness, its resonance, its aggrandizement of the reader's own experience, raises the statement of a simple theme, whether literary or architectural, to the realm of art.

I do not accept the argument that modern technology inevitably gives rise to a universal international style, nor that industrial technology dictated the overthrow of traditional architecture. No one style is appropriate to every building and every place. Believing as I do in the continuity of tradition, I try to create order out of the chaotic present by entering into a dialogue with the past, with tradition. The depth of that dialogue is, I believe, the essence of architecture and, in fact, of all culture. I do not believe that the past offers a cure for the ills of the present; I do believe it offers standards for evaluation. The study of history helps me sort out the enduring values from the transitory phenomena of the present. Architecture is a dialogue with the past carried on in the present with an eye cast toward the future. Rather than breaking with the past, we must all try to root ourselves more deeply in it, because a knowledge of the past can nourish us and a familiarity with its lexical subtleties can help reestablish a sense of decorum to our stridently individualistic present.

By embracing tradition, I don't throw out innovation. But an innovation that is based not on an improvement of what exists but on a radical imposition of something new for its own sake is a form of totalitarianism. The idea that material progress is its own reward—a preoccupation of architects in the late nineteenth century—can no longer be accepted on faith. We know that some kinds of material progress bring almost as many problems as possibilities. Modernism failed to recognize the retrogressive implications of material progress. I prefer to measure progress relative to its absence.

In 1923 Le Corbusier offered the challenge "architecture or revolution." For our moment I would propose a different challenge, in a more conciliatory tone: tradition *and* modernity.

Given the diversity inherent in this methodology, with its insistence on a direct response to particularities of place and program, one might well wonder whether any common threads can exist to connect individual buildings within an architect's oeuvre; or, to put it differently, given the return to traditional formal language, is the thread of intention the only one to establish a continuity and personality in the work of a particular architect and his atelier? Equally one can wonder whether such identification is particularly relevant, except to some historians. Certainly the work my office has produced over the past five years, though it does not have that immediately recognizable stamp of a subsuming personal style (that so quickly renders work by many artists tiresomely familiar), cumulatively expresses the process of intellectual and emotional transformation, or maturation, which is the distinguishing mark of an individual's search for meaning. Architecture should be more than bricks and mortar, ego and id. The public is entitled to buildings that do not, by their very being, threaten the aesthetic and cultural values of the buildings around them. Architecture is not a form of autobiography; it is not a lonely process of self-revelation. Architecture is a public act—a commemorative celebration of place and of culture. Yet architecture is not merely a kind of constructed evidence of events that happen in the culture as a whole; it is not merely a dance to the music of cultural time. Architecture has its own inner clock. Despite the chaos that rages everywhere around us, each building still presents an opportunity to affirm and reestablish the inherent order of things.

Architects should stop worrying about self-expression and zeitgeist, which leads to an obsession with saying things *differently* as opposed to saying them *clearly* or *meaningfully*. Art is, and therefore art evolves. It is not a linear process, it is an eddying process. It sometimes goes backward to go forward. Obviously each artist dreams of making a contribution, but we shouldn't be obsessed with our individuality; we must dream, but we must wake up and go on. . . .

An artist cannot choose his themes; they become his by virtue of what he knows and feels. In a curious way mine were chosen for me before my formal education in architectural design began. I grew up on the proto-modernist architecture which Henry-Russell Hitchcock labeled as "New Tradition"—shingled cottages of New England resorts and the New York skyscrapers of Raymond Hood and Ralph Walker, both examples of a new-old architecture that transcended a particular moment in time. I have only recently come to realize how very much was said to me later by teachers and fellow students about what architecture was and should be that ignored or disparaged what I admired, that tended to sever me from the roots of my early experience. As I studied architecture, the implicit lessons in the buildings and places I had grown up with were virtually disregarded by many of my teachers and my fellow students, for whom the frame of reference was not H. H. Richardson's New England or Raymond Hood's New York, but Walter Gropius's Cambridge and Mies van der Rohe's Chicago. I was surprised that so many of my teachers did not share my enthusiasm. This is not to say that they did not have much to offer me; they taught me to respect the craft of architecture, but I was forced to discard the earlier part of my architectural experience in order to become a "modern" architect.

From my first house in 1966, I have striven to break with the conventionalized late modernism of the 1950s and 1960s and to root my work in a contextually meaningful tradition. At first I thought it was enough to rely on the palette of building materials used in traditional buildings, to establish a continuity with the place. Seldom in my early work did I embrace the forms of the local tradition, preferring instead to attempt to devise new ones (that is, to innovate). Thus my early work was somewhat schizophrenic, struggling to be sympathetic to the place yet breaking the historical code in order to be "original," "interesting," and most especially "modern." In this process of code breaking, I suppressed my natural instincts to see architecture in traditional terms.

It was not by chance that the first volume of my complete works was published in 1980. By the late 1970s I found my way as an architect; I had recovered from the denouement of modernism and discovered the vitality of forms rooted in tradition. Since 1980 I have probed the meaning of the past in a series of buildings that demonstrate the depth and the scope of the new-old approach I call Modern Traditionalism.

The buildings and projects in this volume represent the work of five very fruitful years—a time that has been very kind to me, bringing with it ample opportunities to build not only the houses that formed the bedrock of my early practice but also a wide variety of other building types, which encourage me to widen and deepen my ideas. The buildings seen here are not a reproduction of what went before; they are the further development of an attitude, ongoing steps in a career.

I would like to thank Luis Rueda not only for so patiently and thoughtfully undertaking to compile the text and illustrations but also for preparing many of the drawings used in the book and for supervising the work of others in this task. Eileen Emmet labored tirelessly preparing the bibliographic materials.

Alessandro Franchini has designed the book with great sensitivity, building upon the work of Peter Arnell and Ted Bickford in the first volume, yet making the second one distinctly fresh and his own. Without Roger Seifter and John Ike, my Senior Associates, so much work could not have been undertaken with such consistent quality; together with the other architects who have shepherded the work over the past five years, especially the Associates who are key to the successful resolution of a design, I am grateful. And without Robert Buford, Managing Associate, the growth of the practice from what was once described as a cottage industry to a substantial office would not have been undertaken so smoothly.

Buildings and Projects

Residence
Llewellyn Park, New Jersey
1979–1981

This project consists of two components: the renovation of a fifty-year-old Georgian house designed by Edgar Williams and the addition of a tennis court and a new indoor swimming pool.

Additional space for the family was carved out of former servants' bedrooms; the principal living rooms were reconfigured with space-defining screen walls threaded within a grid of columns. Thus the traditional house of 1929 was modernized through a historical approach drawing on the strategies and decorative elements of the International Style that had flourished in the 1920s.

The pool house is deliberately complex in its formal references—a relaxed setting cloaked in an envelope that responds to the character of the original house, while at the same time taking on the character of a landscape feature; it is a kind of grotto or nymphaeum that marks a transition between the house, its terraces, and the garden. By virtue of its massive columns and thick masonry walls, as well as the proto-classical inspiration of its forms, the pool house dips back deep into time to provide a setting that is both primordial and sophisticated.

1

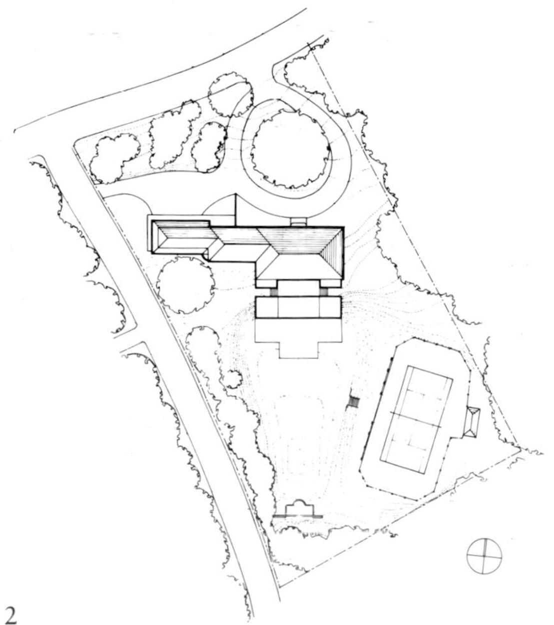

2

1.South elevation and section 2.Site plan 3.View from the south 4.Poolhouse entrance 5.Interior of poolhouse facing southeast

3

4

5

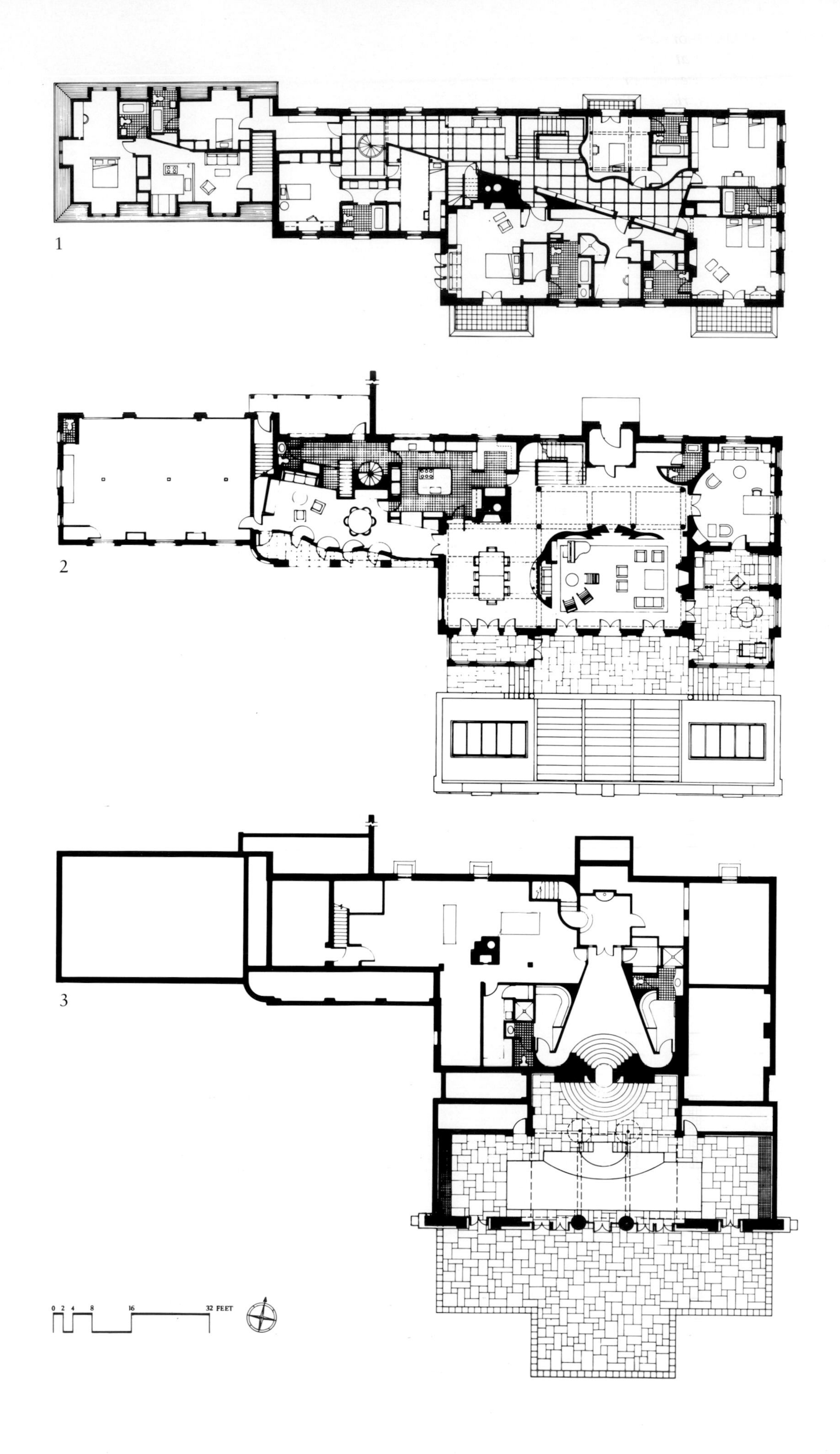
1
2
3
0 2 4 8 16 32 FEET

1.Second floor plan 2.Ground floor plan 3.Pool level plan 4.Vestibule elevations 5.Hallway elevations 6.Poolhouse interior south elevation 7.Poolhouse exterior south elevation

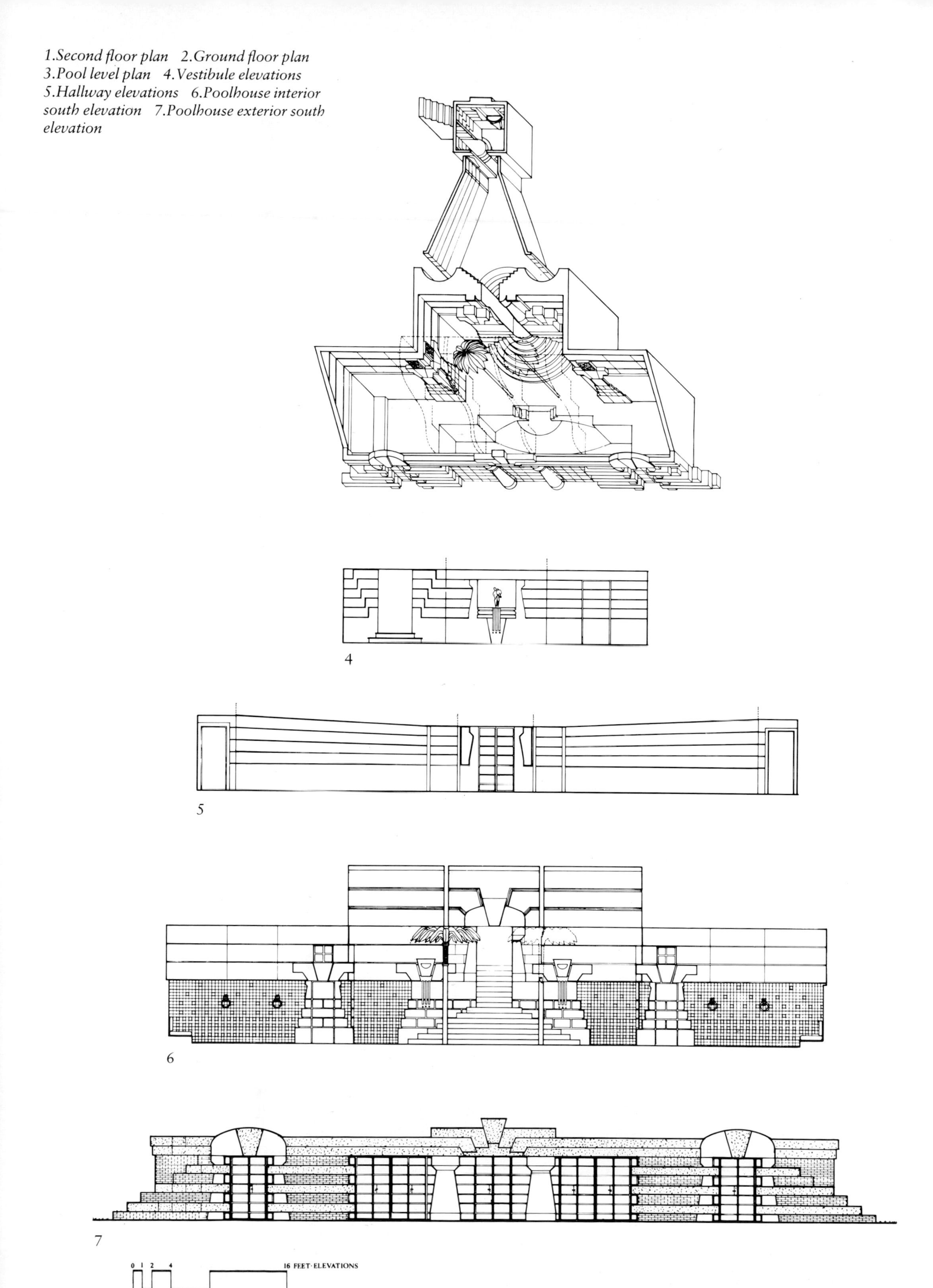

1.View of living room   2.Front door and entrance vestibule   3,4.Study   5,6.Second floor hallway   7.Spiral stair landing at second floor   8.Poolhouse vestibule

1

2

3

4

5

6

7

8

1. Living room 2. Dining room 3,4. Views of poolhouse interior

1

2

3

4

1.Interior of poolhouse from the south 2.Detail of poolhouse stair 3.View of the vestibule from the poolhouse 4.View of the poolhouse from the vestibule

1

2

3

4

Residence at Chilmark
Martha's Vineyard, Massachusetts
1979–1983

Set on one of the island's highest sites, commanding water views in three directions, this shingled house with its gently flared hipped roof, dormers, bay windows, and subsumed porches continues the language of traditional seaside architecture that emerged in the 1870s and has ever since defined for many summertime living along the New England shore. At the entrance, the roofline is interrupted by a large gable containing the asymmetrically located front door and circular window lighting the generously proportioned stair behind. On the opposite side, the hipped roofs are distended to provide a second-story balcony overlooking the principal view.

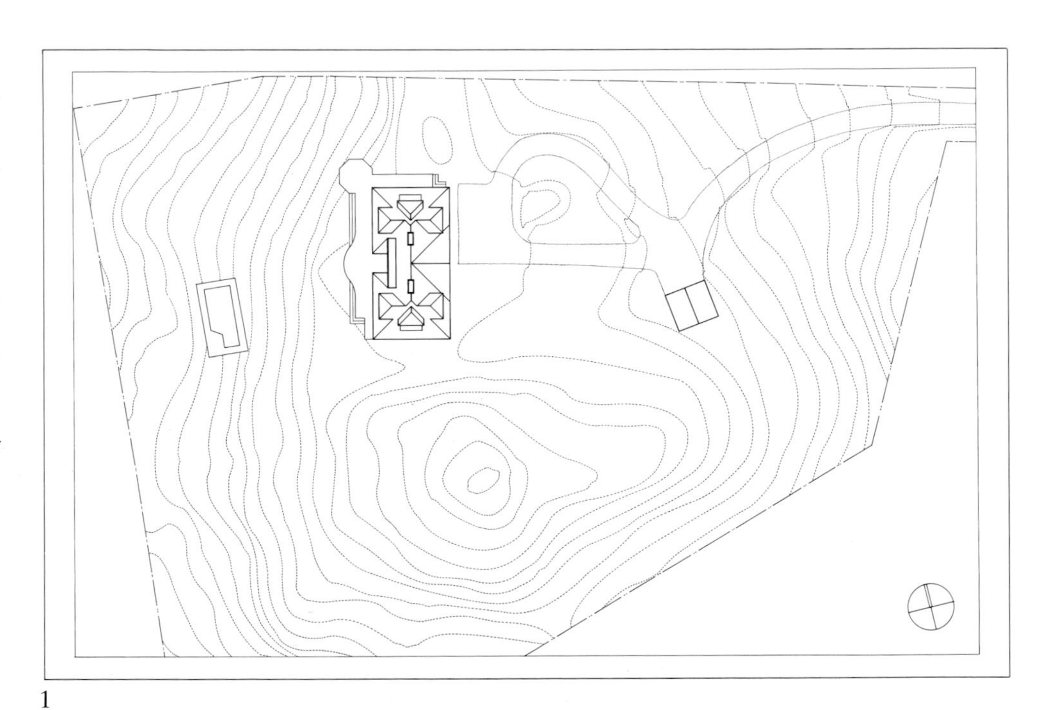

1

2

3

1.Site plan 2.Detail of entrance 3.West facade 4.Second floor plan 5.Ground floor plan 6.West elevation 7.South elevation 8.East elevation 9.Living room elevations 10.Entry hall elevation 11.Stair hall and dining room elevations 12.East facade

4

6

5

7

8

32 FEET - PLANS & ELEVATIONS
16 FEET - INTERIOR ELEVATIONS

9

10

11

12

1. Detail of entrance facade 2. Partial view of west facade 3. South facade 4. View facing north 5. View from the southwest 6. Outdoor sitting area

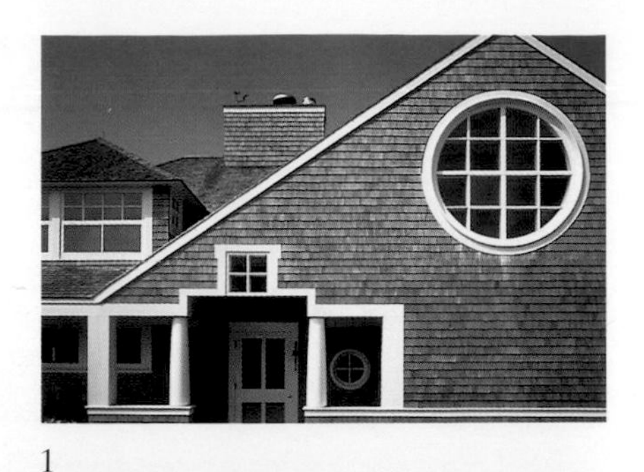

1

2

3

4

5

6

1

2

3

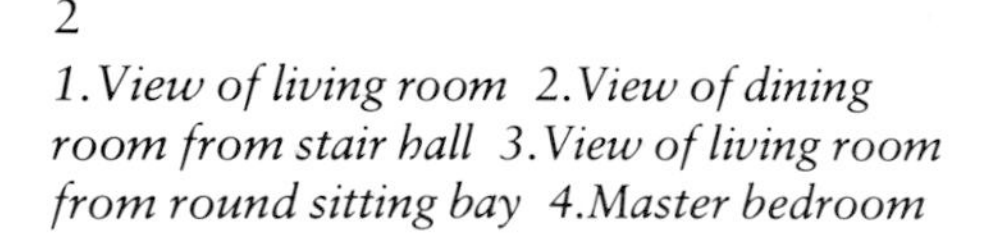

1. View of living room 2. View of dining room from stair hall 3. View of living room from round sitting bay 4. Master bedroom

4

5

6

7

5. View of stair hall and entrance hall
6. Detail of second floor stair landing
7. View of stair hall from second floor landing

House at Farm Neck

Martha's Vineyard, Massachusetts
1980–1983

This house is located on a virtually flat site bordered at one edge by high trees, but otherwise open to neighboring houselots, a golf course, and the water beyond. Our design, in response to the vast site and to the particularly complex program, uses an archetypal gable form, looking back to McKim, Mead and White's Low House and Grosvenor Atterbury's Swayne House in the Shinnecock Hills. The clarity of the gable form lends an imposing scale which is enhanced by the near symmetry of the principal facade and the pronounced silhouette of the chimneys and dormers. On the entrance side, the projection of a smaller gabled wing serves to imply an entrance court while making the scale more intimate. The projecting bay windows open the interior to the view, while the extensive use of mullioned windows helps to enrich the impact of the vast site from within by framing it.

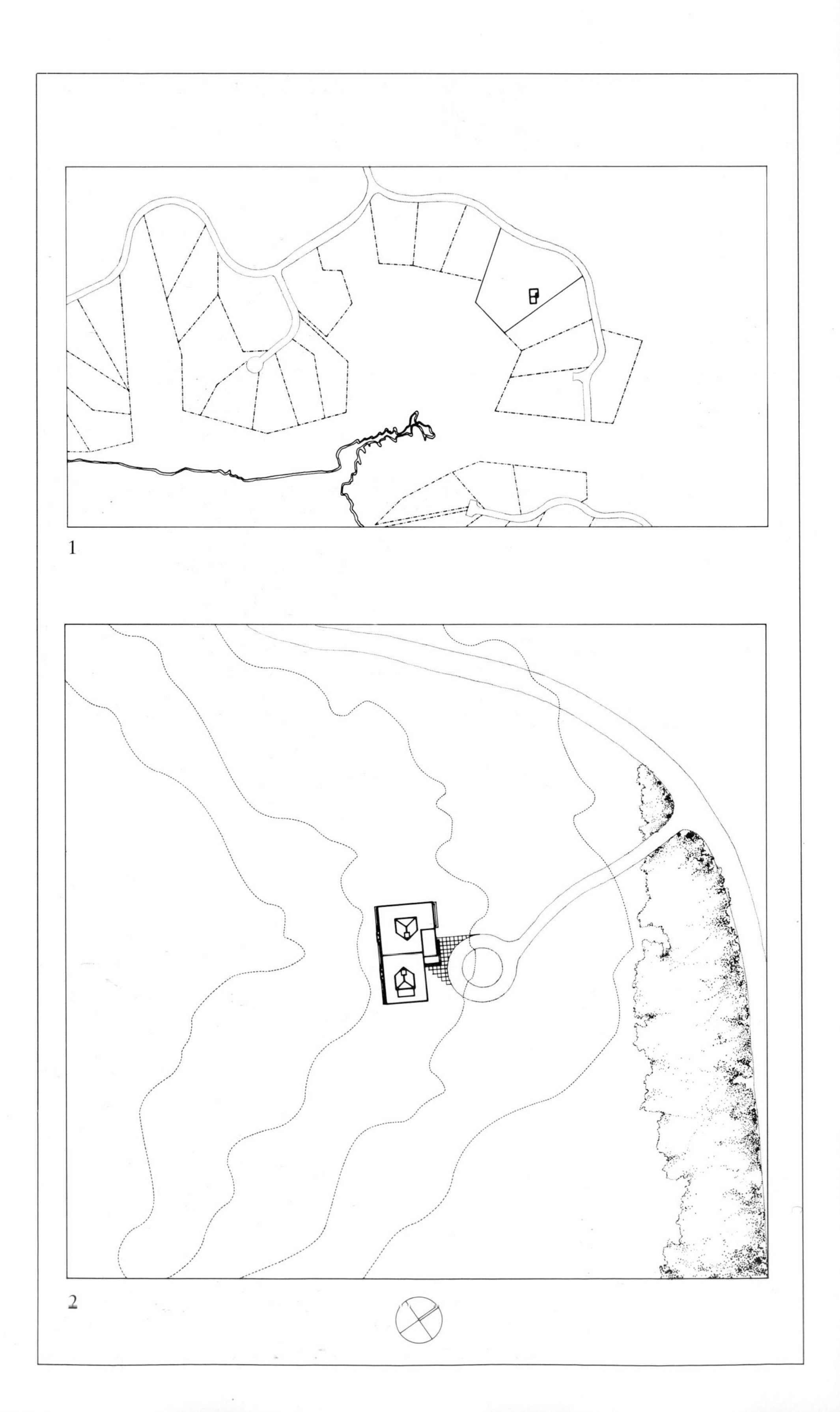

1

2

1.Plan of development 2.Site plan 3.View from the south 4.View from the north 5.Family room 6.View into family room bay window from the second floor 7.Living room

3

4

5

6

7

1

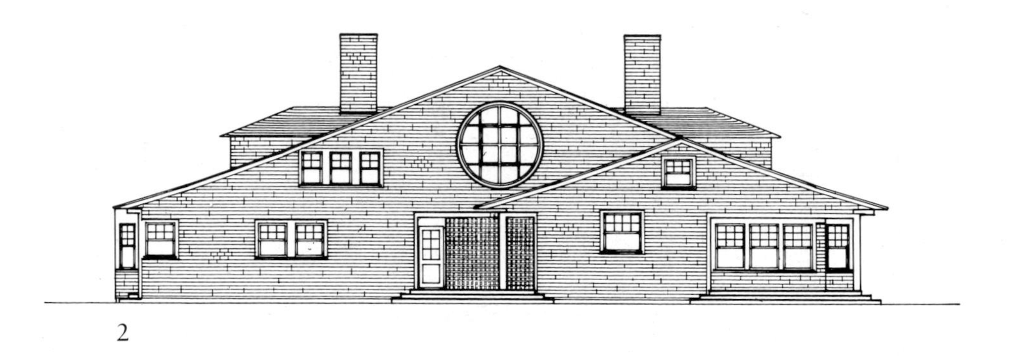
2

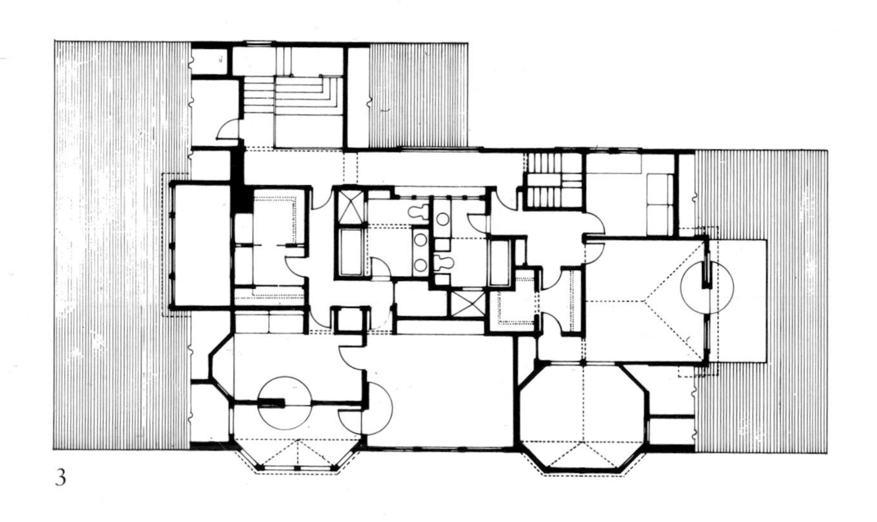
3

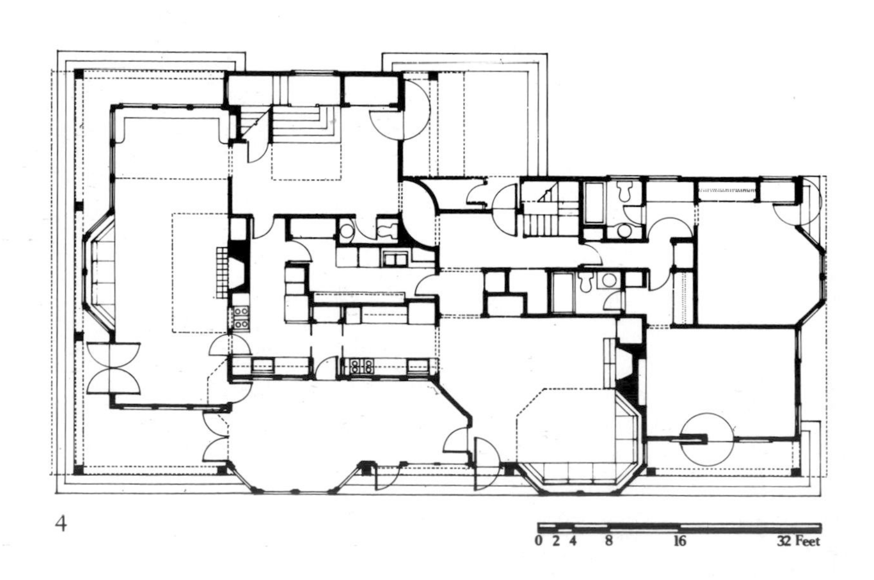

4

1.South elevation 2.North elevation
3.Second floor plan 4.Ground floor plan
5,6.Master bedroom 7.The stairhall
8.View of outdoor deck and porch beyond

5

6

7

8

Residence in Quogue
Long Island, New York
1979–1981

Set along the ocean beach on a typical, narrow seaside lot, this design seeks to connect with the traditions of the Shingle Style and more particularly with the "beach cottages" that proliferated along the East Coast in the 1910s and 1920s. The position of the house at the edge of a high dune made it possible to tuck three small guest bedrooms at grade behind the dune. Thus, the overscaled stoop leads up to the principal floor just below the level of the dune. It also provides an inviting porch from which to observe the sunset across the bay. The master bedroom is located in the attic, lit by a boldly arched window at the seaside that gives the house a big scale and connects it with the high architecture of Classicism, just as the eyelid dormer in the master bath pays its respect to H. H. Richardson. Though the eroded configuration of the principal floor responds to the particular considerations of site, view, and solar orientation, the fundamentally symmetrical organization of the mass is intended to give the house a dignity and iconic clarity of its own—an object of calm amidst helter-skelter.

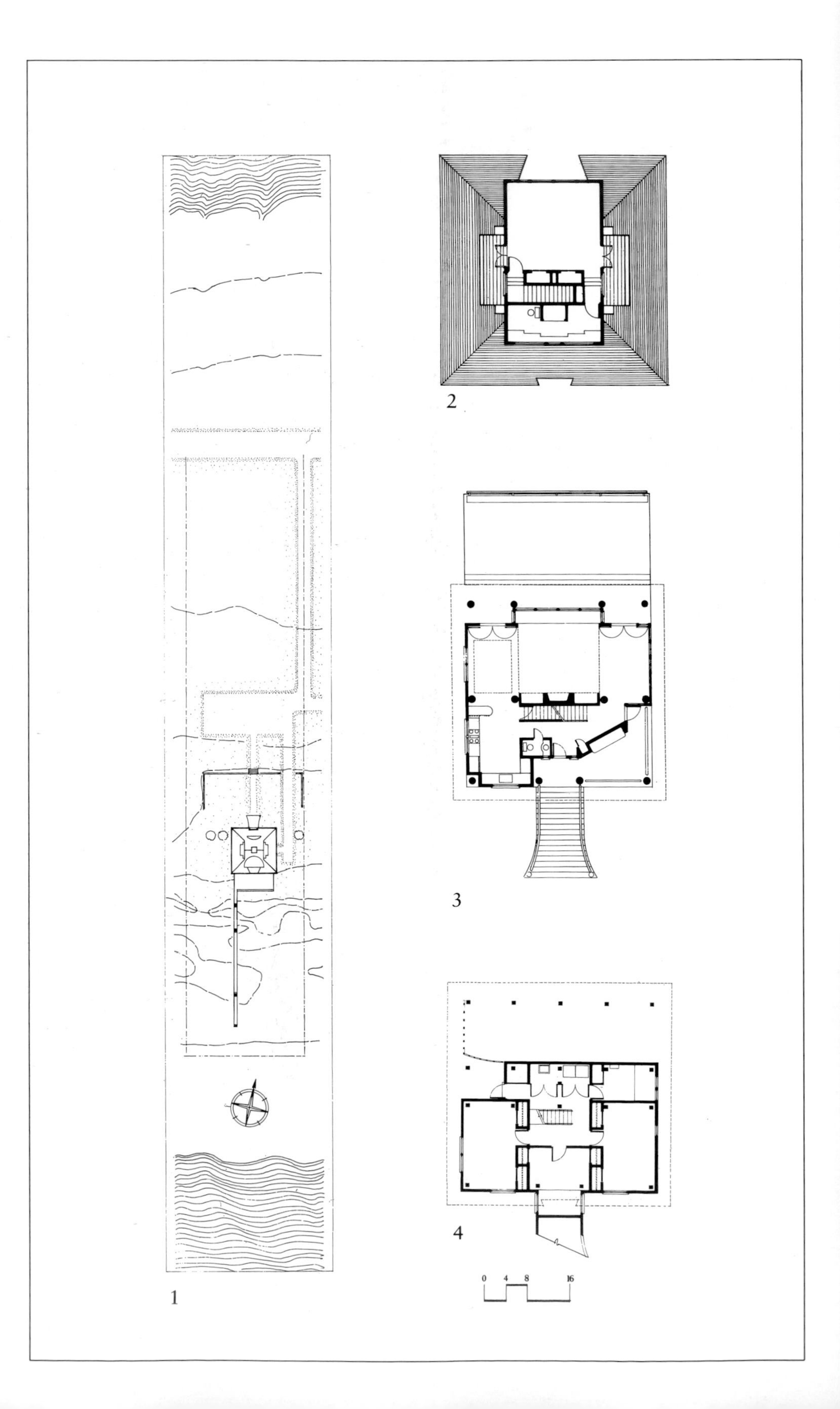

1.Site plan 2.Third floor plan 3.Second floor plan 4.Ground floor plan 5.North facade 6.South elevation 7.East elevation 8.North elevation

5

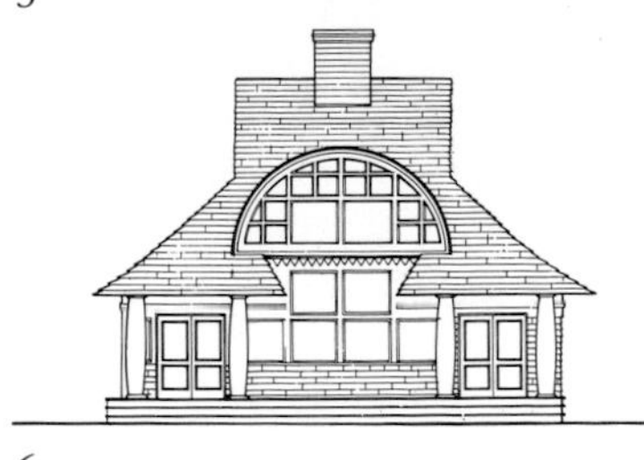

6

7

8

1. View of bedroom 2. View of kitchen from the dining room 3. View from the southwest 4. View from the southeast 5. View from the beach

1

2

3

4

5

Residence

East Hampton, New York
1980–1983

This residence is a contemporary essay in the Shingle Style, which flourished in the coastal resorts of northeastern America in the 1880s and 1890s. In the heart of East Hampton's traditional summer colony, the house takes its cues from the imposing Shingle Style "cottages" characteristic of the neighborhood, which were in turn interpretations by nineteenth-century architects of the houses built in the seventeenth century by East Hampton's first English settlers. One of the primary obligations of any work of architecture is to create a sense of place, to respect and enhance a building's physical and cultural context. Another responsibility is to work within a tradition in a scholarly manner—to be succored but not smothered by the values of architectural culture.

In plan, detail, and massing this house recaptures the Shingle Style's hybridization of Classical and vernacular elements—a synthesis that at once ennobles the rituals of everyday life with memories of cultural traditions inherited from abroad, and creates an architectural statement not so much of its time as of its place. The house declares but does not flaunt its modernity; traditional forms are subtly modified, but their representational character is retained and the massing of the house intensified by the geometrical clarity of its predecessors. The iconic elements of the facades—the entrance porch, the eyebrow dormers, and the turret overlooking the garden—are applied to the relatively straight forward mass of the house, their slightly inflated scale accentuating the dialogue between the mundane and the meaningful, between a specific place and the memory of grander places long since left behind.

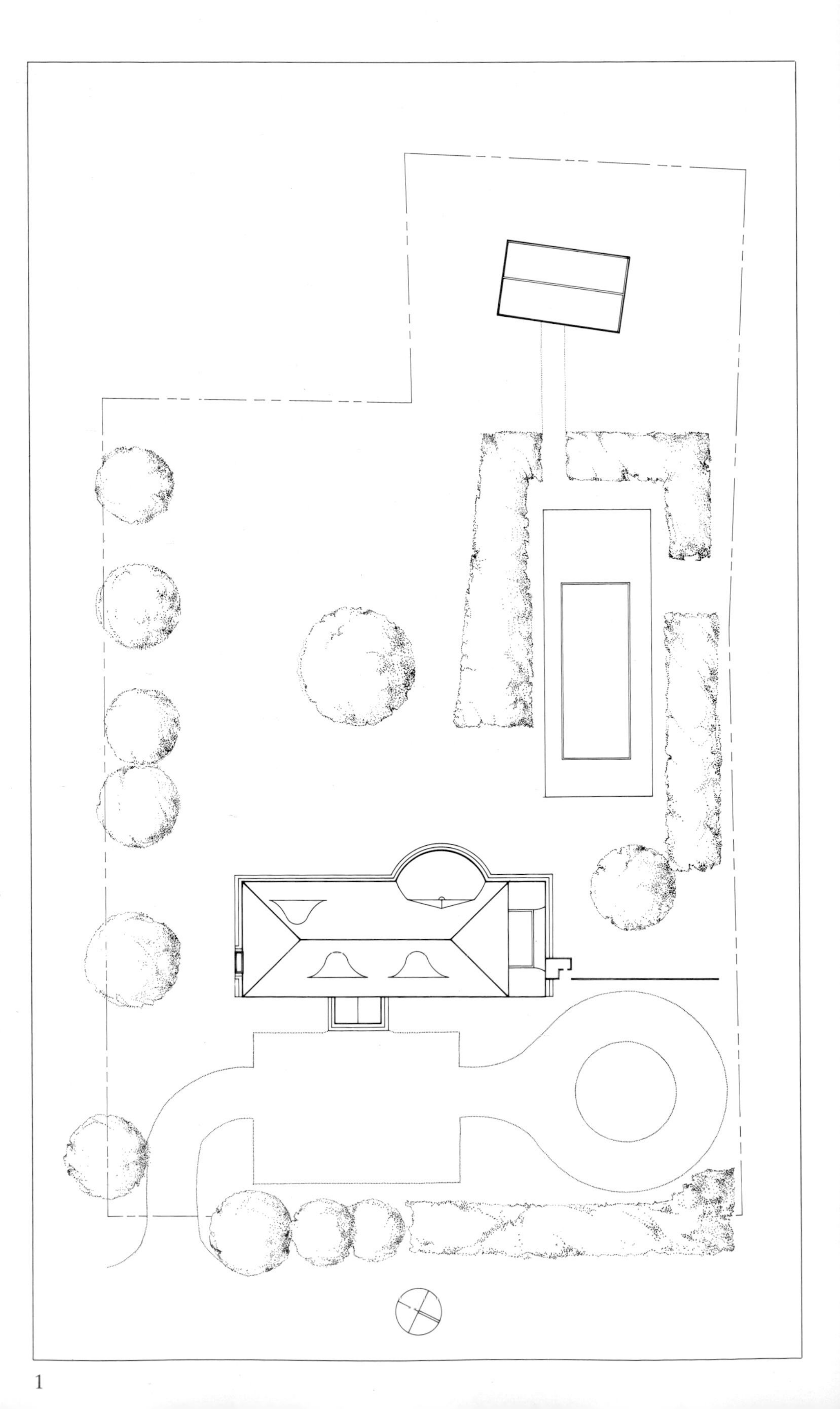

1

1.Site plan 2.East facade 3.East elevation
4.West elevation 5.Second floor plan
6.Ground floor plan

2

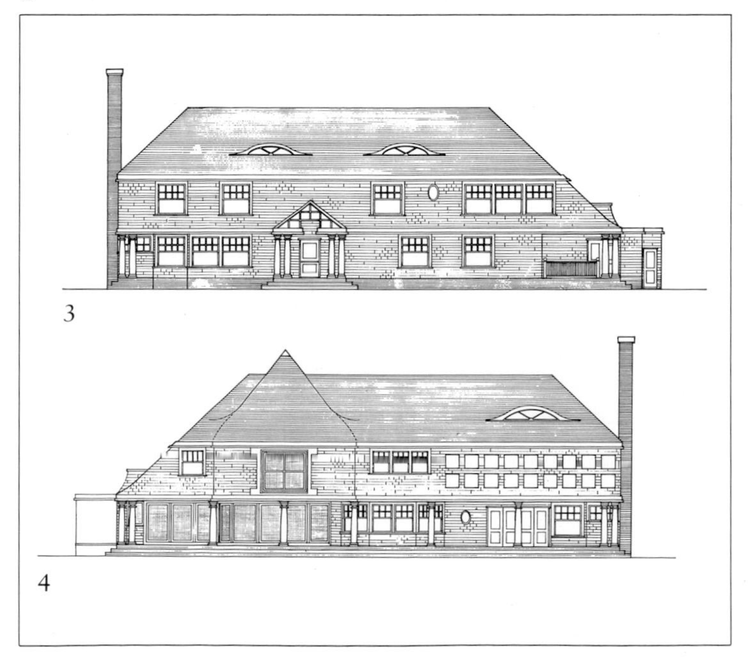

3

4

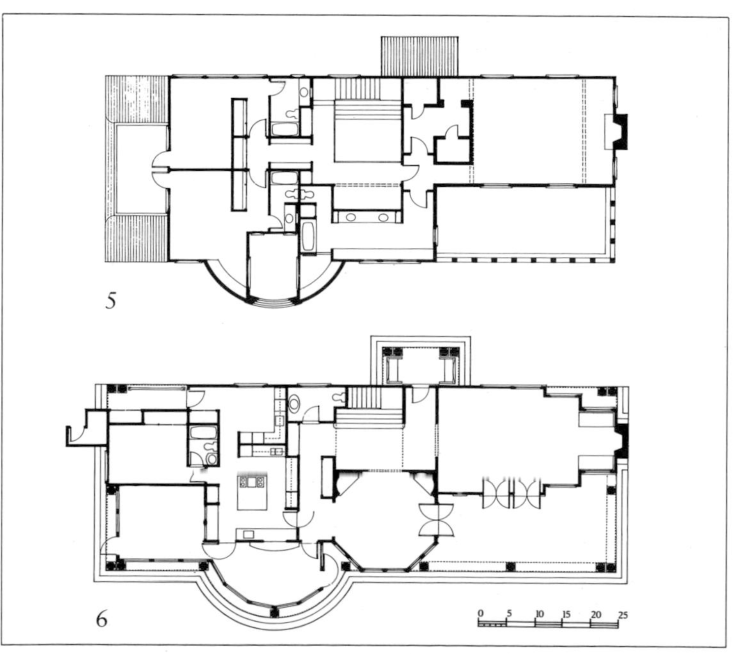

5

6

1.Oblique view of east facade 2.Detail of entrance portico 3.Entrance vestibule and stair hall 4.View of living room from stair hall 5.Partial view of living room and stair hall 6.View of dining room from stair hall 7.Dining room 8.Living room 9.Detail of tower

1

2

3

4

5

6

7

8

9

1
2
3
0 5 10 15 20
0 5 10
4
5
6

1.Section through tower 2.Elevation of tower 3.North elevation 4,5.Elevation and section of screen wall 6.Section of tower wall 7.View of screen wall and porch from second floor window 8.View of inglenook 9.View of underside of tower

7

8

9

Lincoln Squash Club
One Harkness Plaza
New York, New York
1981

Lincoln Squash Club is a public squash and fitness facility occupying the two basement floors of a twenty-eight story apartment house adjacent to Lincoln Center in New York City. On the upper level are a cafe and lounge that overlook the eight squash courts, as well as a pro shop and office. The lower level is given over to the courts and to locker rooms, a fitness center, and additional lounge facilities adjacent to the exhibition court.

The scheme derives its power through the tension created by the contrast between a *moderne* classicism suggestive of a 1920s *boîte* and the no-nonsense detailing of the physical fitness equipment. Streamlined moldings, sconces, and neon lighting combine with the reflective ceiling to heighten the visual excitement of the upper-level cafe.

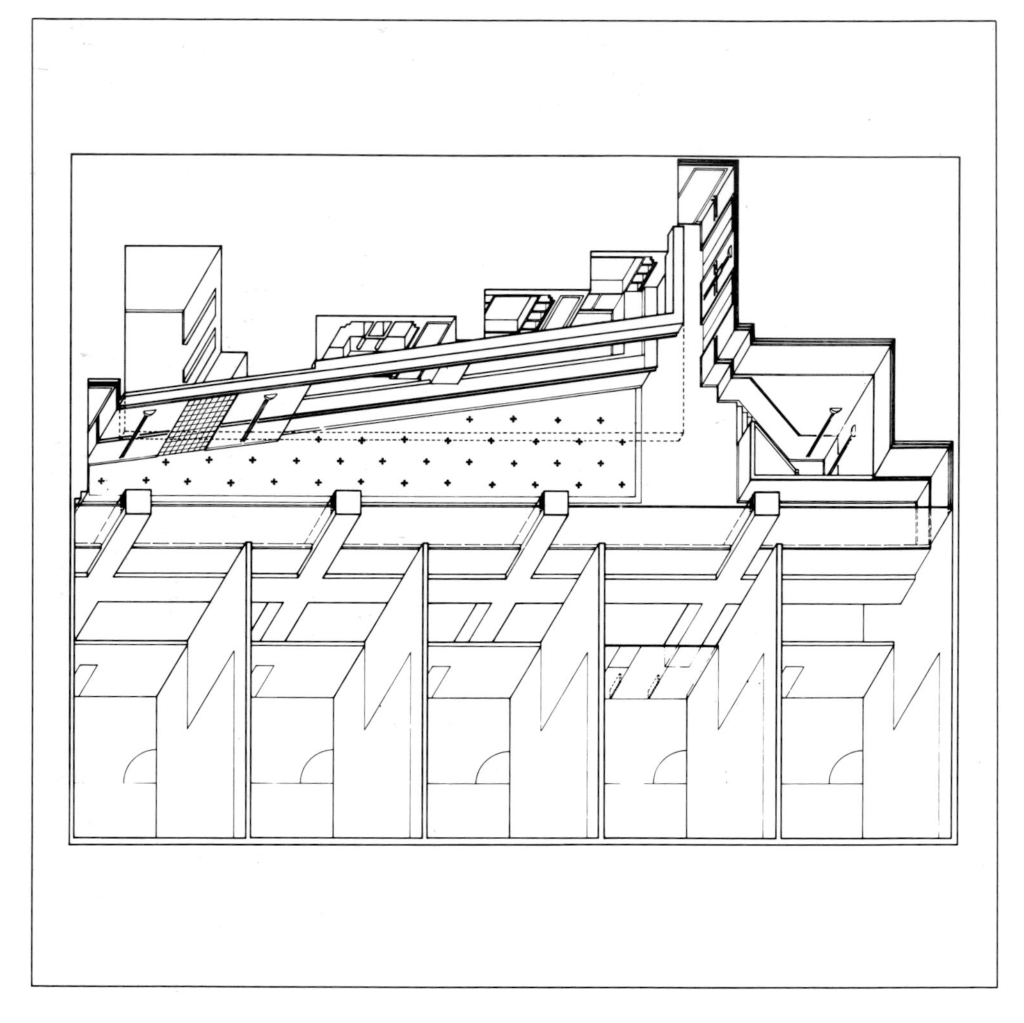

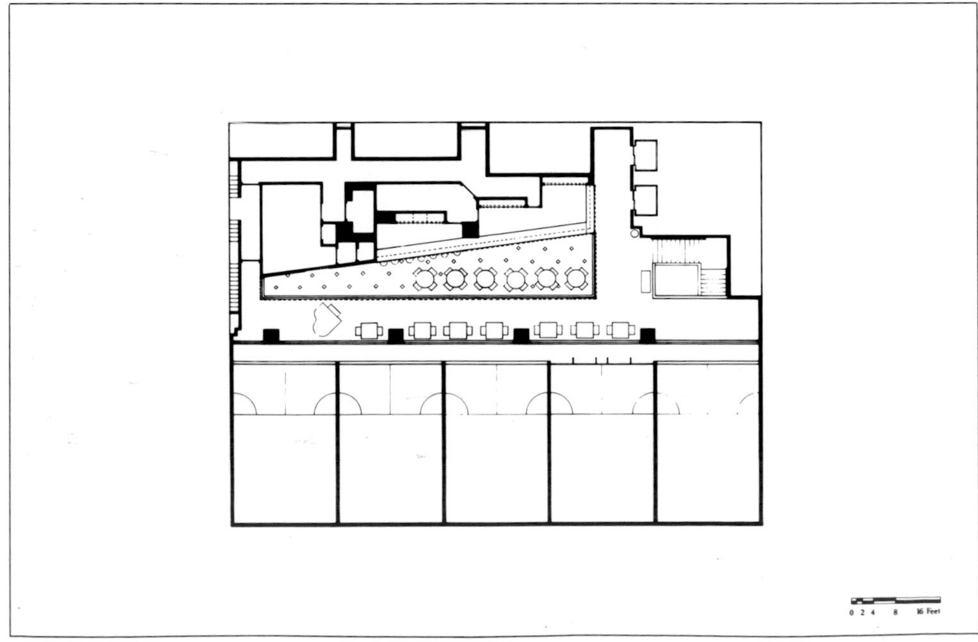

1

1.Floor plan 2.View of cafeteria from entrance 3.View of cafeteria and service counter 4.Cafeteria 5.Detail of cafeteria 6.Detail of light sconce 7.Shower stalls

2 3 4 5 6 7

Offices for Obstetric and Gynecologic Associates

New York, New York
1981

This suite of new offices for a rapidly growing group medical practice contains waiting, examination, and consultation rooms as well as a library-conference room, kitchenette for staff, and a private office for the office manager.

The plan is organized around an apsidal entry hall. To one side is the waiting room, to the other, the corridor off of which are the examination and consultation rooms. The organizing rhythm of Classically inspired pilasters and expressed beams helps to articulate these spaces in three dimensions, and reinforce their character as public places in the plan. Keystone uplights softly illuminate the hall.

The consultation rooms, which serve as the doctors' private offices, are painted a warm, dignified creamy color. The examining rooms themselves are arranged in suites with two rooms sharing a bath. They are painted more overtly feminine colors than the public spaces, softening the effect of the highly technical equipment used in the rooms without compromising their no-nonsense functionality.

1. View of waiting room from reception room 2. Waiting room 3. View of corridor and offices 4. View of reception room from waiting room 5,6. Detail of reception room 7. Floor plan

5

6

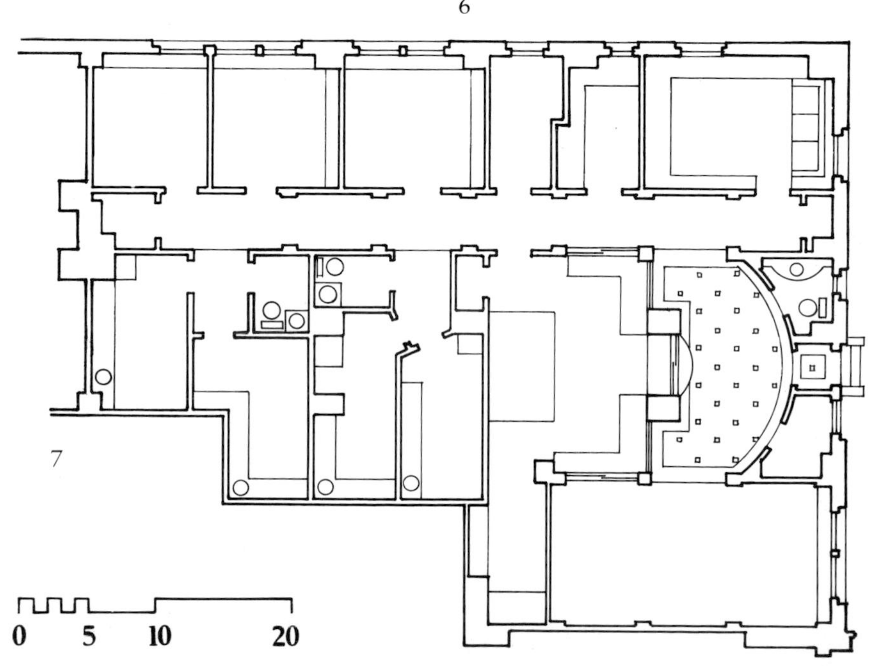

7

1

2

1.Reception desk 2.View of corridor from the reception area 3.Waiting room

3

San Remo Apartment

New York, New York
1981

This apartment occupies the top two floors in the north tower of the San Remo, a distinguished New York apartment building built in 1930. The renovation includes the total reconstruction of the hitherto unused space surrounding the elevator machine room and the transformation of this apartment into a three-level space. The incorporation of the upper floor necessitated the introduction of several new windows in the building's facade, which were detailed to match the existing windows and located to complement the character of the tower. The new windows on the front of the building are trimmed with cast stone which matches the terra-cotta used in the original.

The lower floor includes a large master bedroom suite on the west, while the living room, dining room, and entry hall are arranged en suite along the east end of the apartment, taking advantage of views over Central Park. A stair behind the living room fireplace leads to the upper floor which is designed as an extension of the apartment's entertainment spaces. The stairs from below land in the center of this floor on axis with a smaller stair which leads to the highest interior space in the building—a library balcony. This balcony looks out over the thirteen-foot-high lounge and out through the large new east window to Central Park below. The floor level of the top floor is raised two and a half feet to allow clear views over the terrace parapet. New glass doors on the east and west lead out to the terrace, which wraps around the building on four sides, providing panoramic views of Manhattan.

1

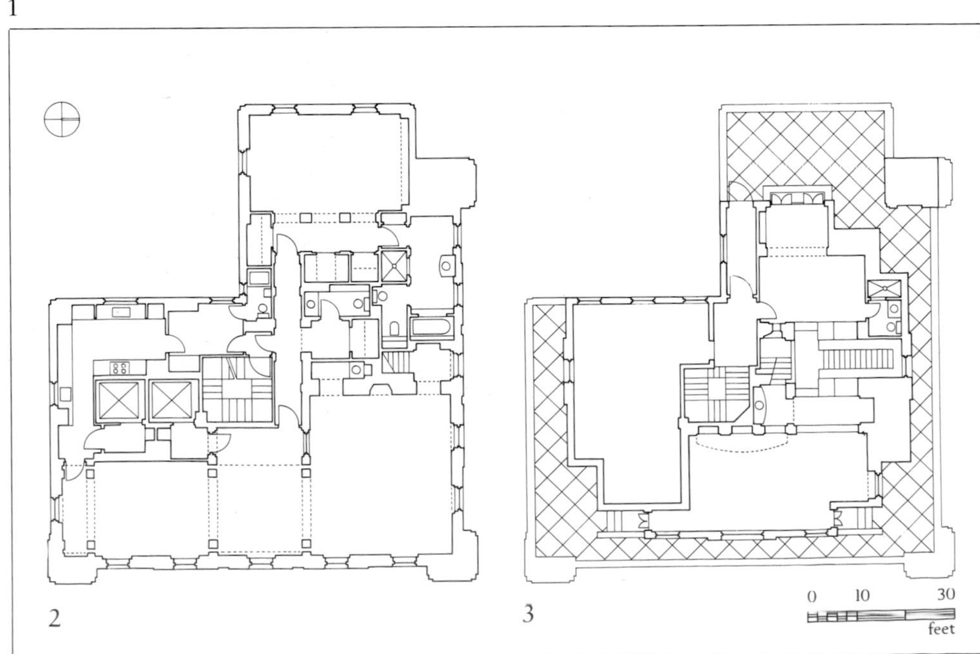

2

3

1. Axonometric of second level 2. First level plan 3. Second level plan 4. Existing condition of tower 5. Tower with proposed new windows 6,7,8. Views of model

4

5

6

7

8

Residence in Mill Neck

Long Island, New York
1981–1983

Located on a bluff overlooking Oyster Bay, this house responds to the complex demands of the site. Its plan is zoned to defend family living spaces from a well-traveled country road. Its entrance is located to maximize the sense of privacy. And its pavilionated massing responds to the conflicting demands of a dramatic east-facing view and the desire for maximum south light. In spirit, the design builds upon Edwin Lutyens' Tigbourne Court, combining a formal entrance facade with a more pavilionated and open aspect towards the garden and the distant landscape.

The plan is organized by a north-south axis that extends from the entrance through the entire length of the house. The major rooms open off it towards the east and west. While the axis continues visually into the garden, a curving glazed wall deflects the plan into a double-height library. A staircase carved into the thickness of the library wall leads to a private study. Throughout the house, French doors open onto terraces, providing a close connection between the interior and the landscape. The Tuscan columns of the exterior are also reiterated inside and generate the proportions of the interior elevations.

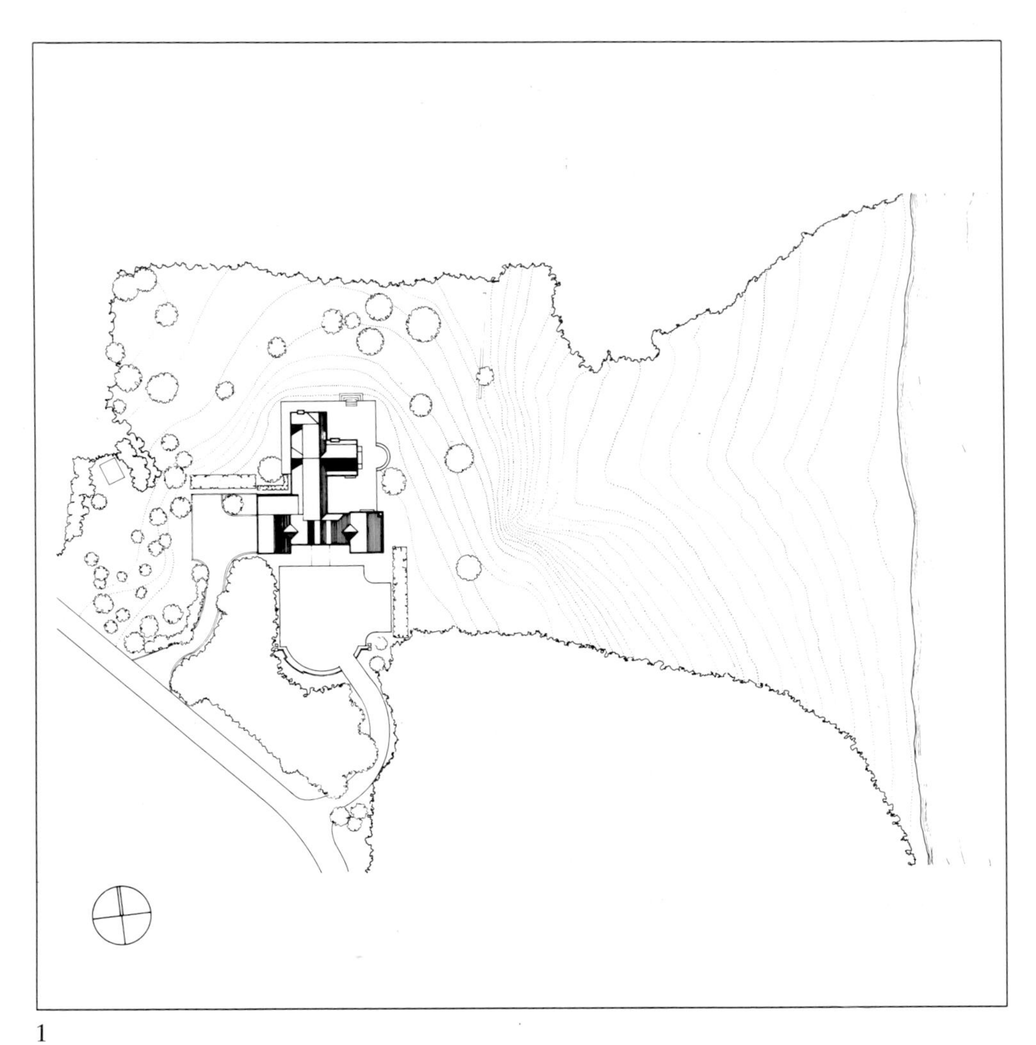

1

2

1.Site plan 2.Partial view from the east 3.South elevation 4.East elevation 5.Longitudinal section 6,7.Sections through the stair hall 8.West elevation 9.Ground floor plan 10.View from the northeast

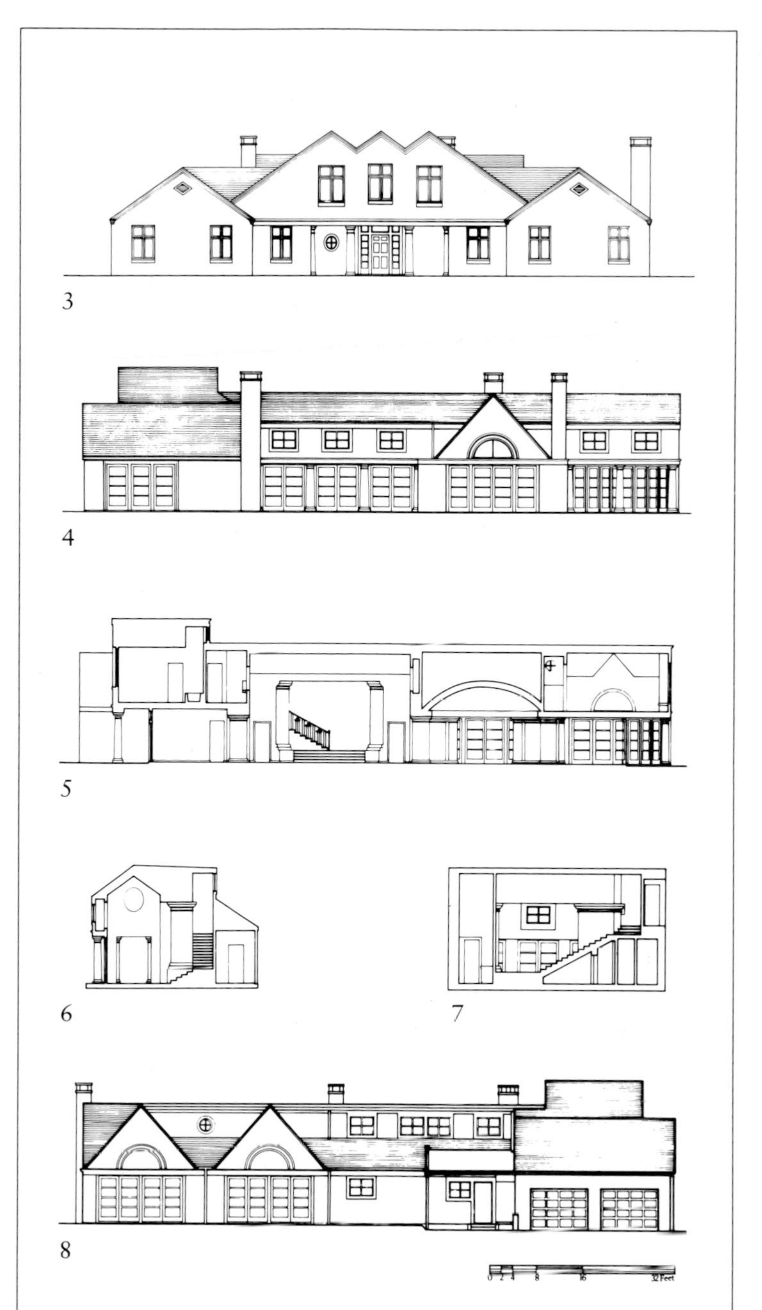

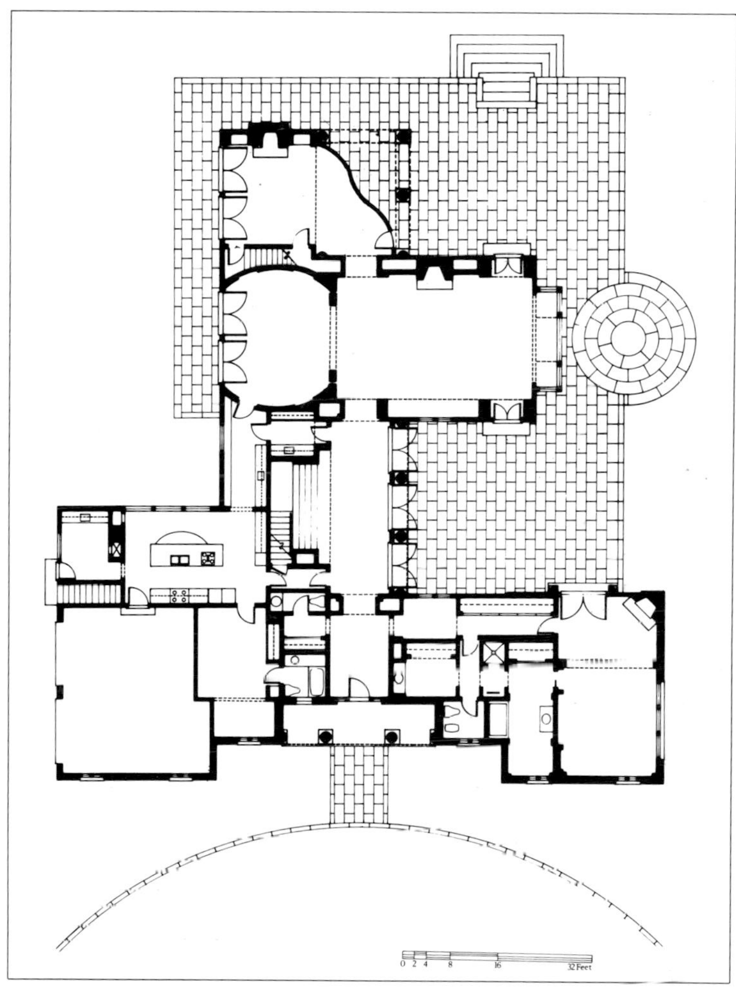

9

10

1.Entrance facade 2.West facade 3.Study
4.Dining room

1

2

3

4

1

2

1.Living room 2.Library 3.Stair hall 4.View of study from the library 5.Living room detail

3

4

5

Kalamazoo Center
Kalamazoo, Michigan
1981

Built in 1958, the open-air, vehicle-free downtown mall in Kalamazoo was the first of its kind in the nation. Since that time, the area's suburban shopping malls have seriously eroded its commercial vitality. Our proposal was designed to revitalize the depressed northern sector of the inner city through a series of linked architectural elements. Rather than merely duplicating suburban malls, Kalamazoo Center proposes a fully articulated urbanism that incorporates a residential enclave, convention and exhibition space, and outdoor recreation facilities.

At the nexus of this revitalization effort is the Winter Garden, a glass-and-metal galleria housing seasonal botanical displays, community events, cafes, and a health club, while providing an exciting visual link between the Hilton Hotel and the railroad station, recently revitalized as a multimodal center. The new convention facility follows the established Kalamazoo practice of "coring" historic buildings, with new construction inserted inside existing blocks to minimize its visual impact on the existing urban fabric.

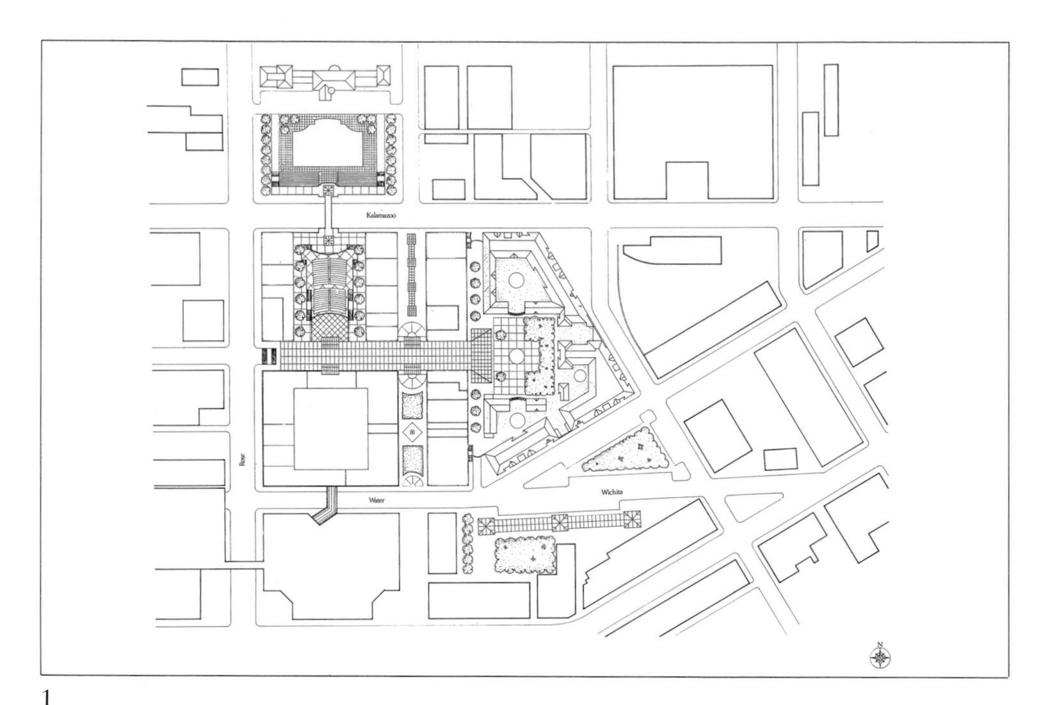

1

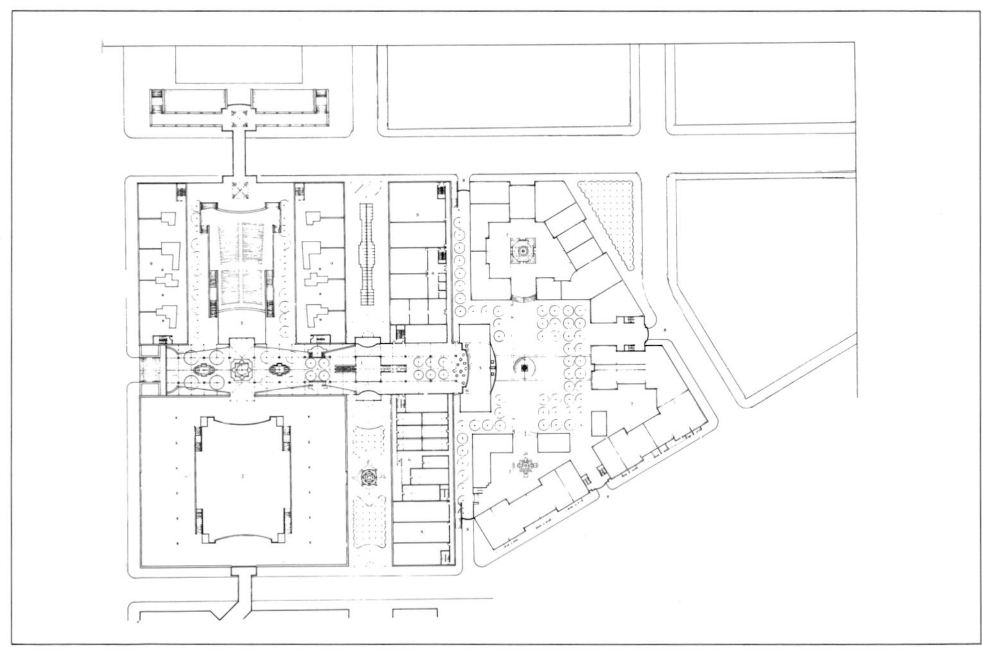

2

1. Site plan 2. Ground floor plan 3. Winter garden from the south 4. Winter garden 5. View of model from the north

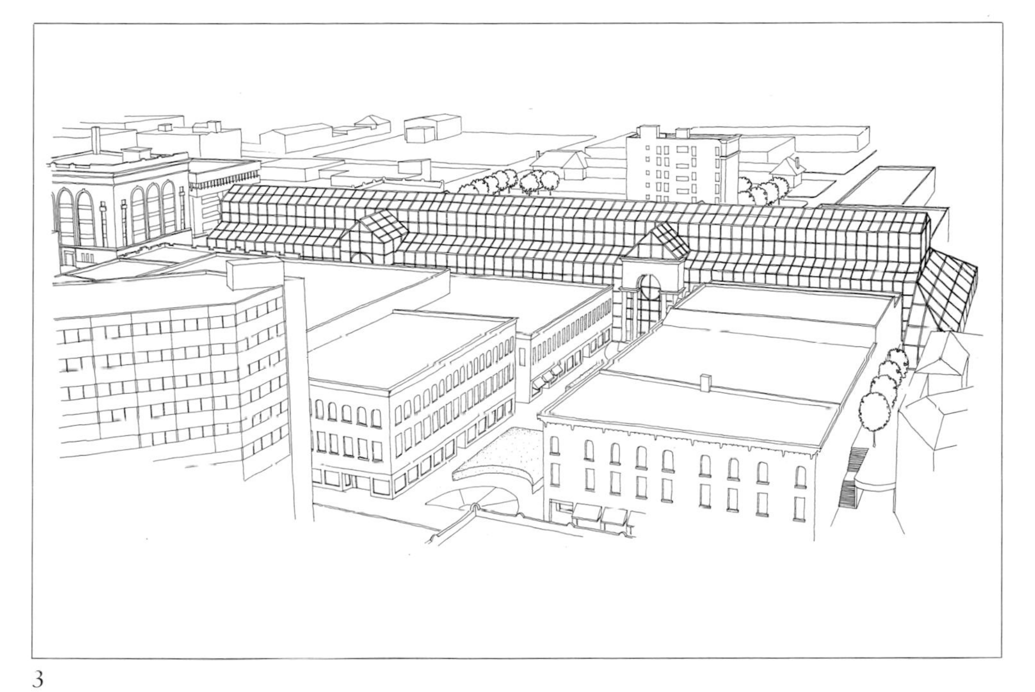

3

4

5

Raymond Hood Exhibit
The Institute for Architecture and Urban Studies
New York, New York
1981

This exhibit was planned for the double-height studio of the Institute for Architecture and Urban Studies. In order to convey the mood of Hood's aesthetic, the design proposed to cover the room's walls in shimmering black plastic, decorated with a stenciled frieze which emulated the exterior cladding of Hood's Ideal Standard Building on Great Marlborough Street in London.

Two Houses
Aspen, Colorado
1981–1982

These two year-round houses, intended for sale by a developer, occupy confined sites with excellent views of the mountains. Sited to achieve maximum privacy for each without sacrificing the view, the houses combine the local pioneer settlers' architectural vocabulary with the discipline of clear planning.

As each house is designed for shared and informal living, the principal rooms are generously sized and open to each other as well as to the rather broad exterior decks. The stair wraps around the fireplace mass and leads to twin master suites in the more private realm of the second floor.

1.West elevation 2.North elevation 3.East elevation 4.South elevation 5.Ground floor plan 6.Second floor plan 7.Site plan showing both houses 8.View of the houses 9.West elevation 10.South elevation 11.East elevation 12.North elevation 13.Ground floor plan 14.Second floor plan

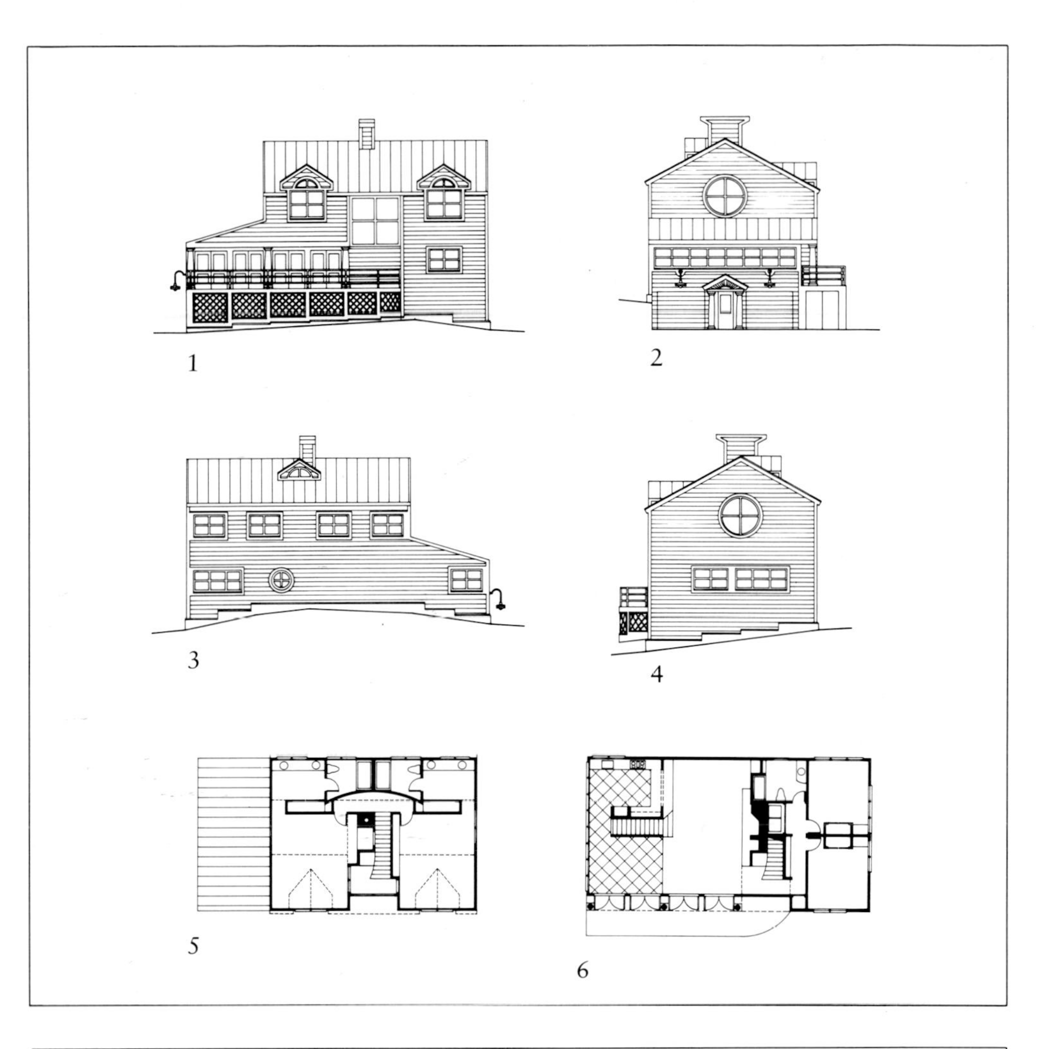

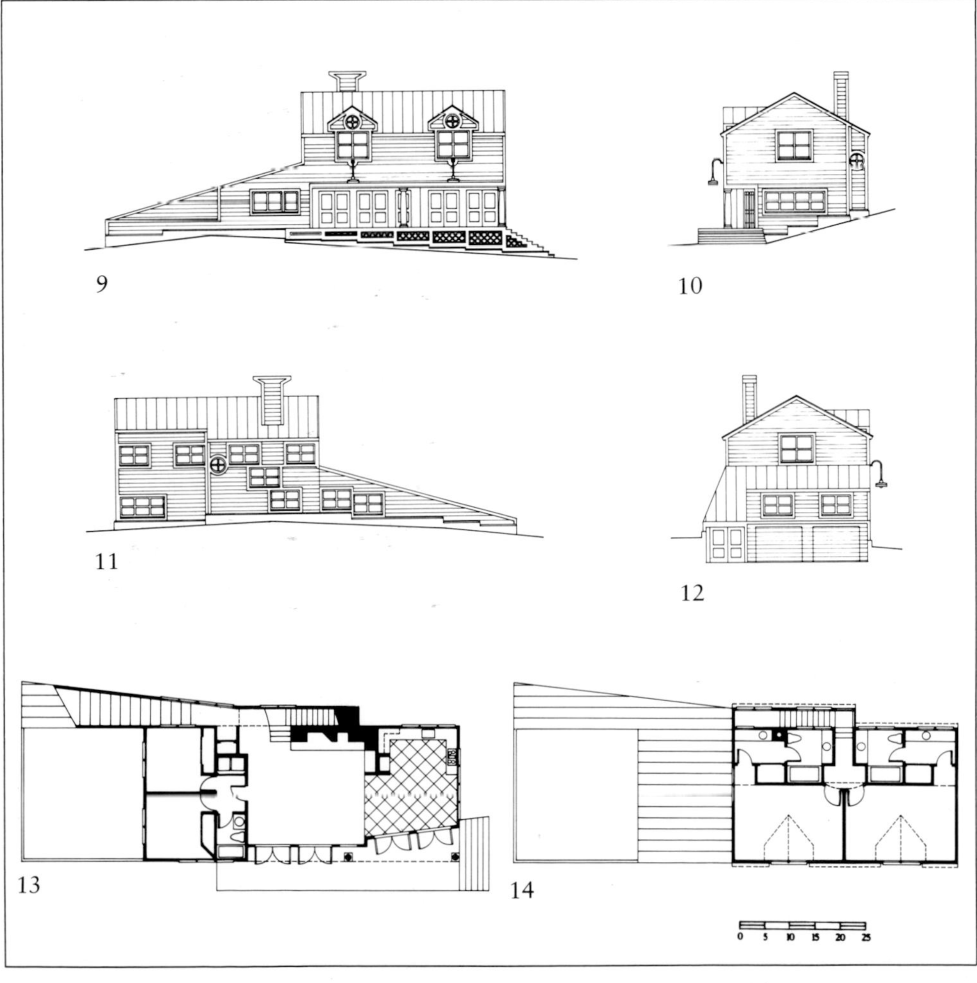

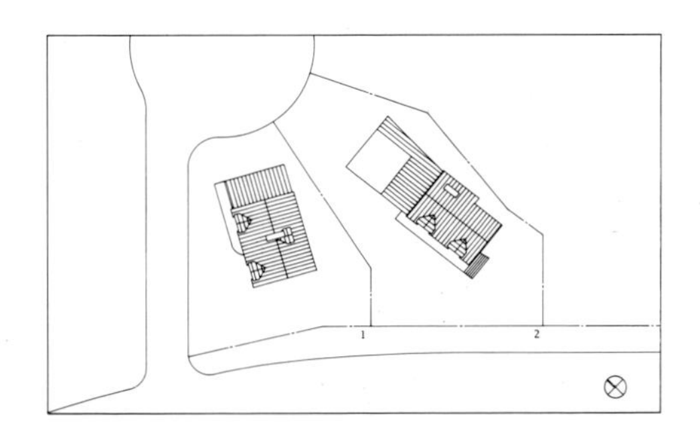

7

8

Mecox Fields
Bridgehampton, New York
1981–

This project occupies fourteen acres of land that has been rezoned from agricultural to residential use. Our responsibilities included the overall site planning, which in the tradition of this area divides the land into regularly proportioned lots, with houses fronting rather closely on the street in order to maximize the view and sense of open space in the rear. Though individual sites are defined by privet hedges, the sense of openness is enhanced for the majority of the houses by our placement of a three-acre reserve area at the northwest corner of the site. This reserve adjoins land that is to remain in farming.

In designing the eight houses, we endeavored to provide the potential buyer with a variety of plans whose individuality is obtained from the placement and layout of such amenities as stair halls, bay windows, and double-height spaces. As we coordinated the planning of each house with the others, we were careful to orient the screened porches to catch prevailing ocean breezes. The exteriors of the houses attempt a similar individualized treatment while working within the common language of the massing; interest arises from the extensive utilization of subsumed porches enveloped by broad hipped and gabled roofs punctuated by dormers, and from four-over-one double-hung windows adapted from stock sash.

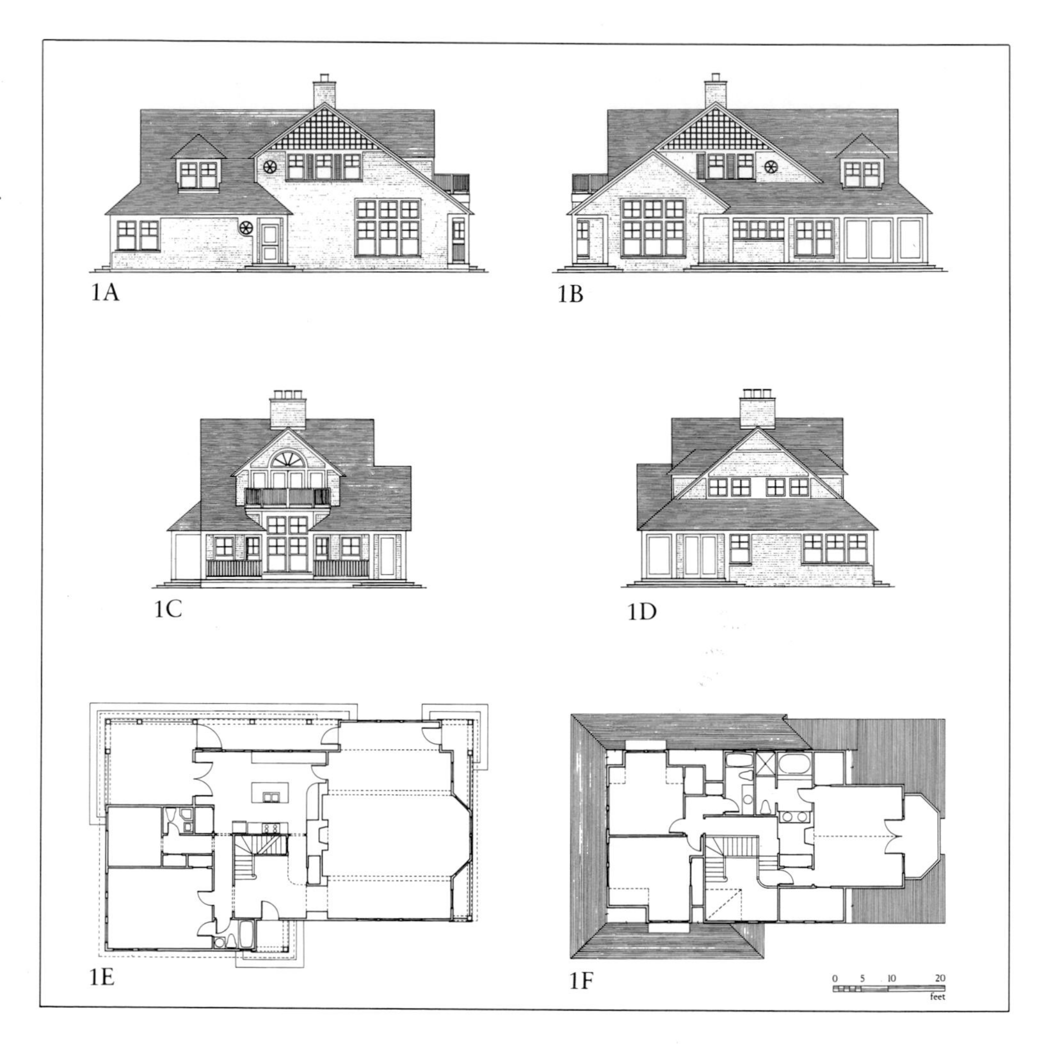

1.House 1: A.West elevation B.East elevation C.South elevation D.North elevation E.Ground floor plan F.Second floor plan 2.Site plan

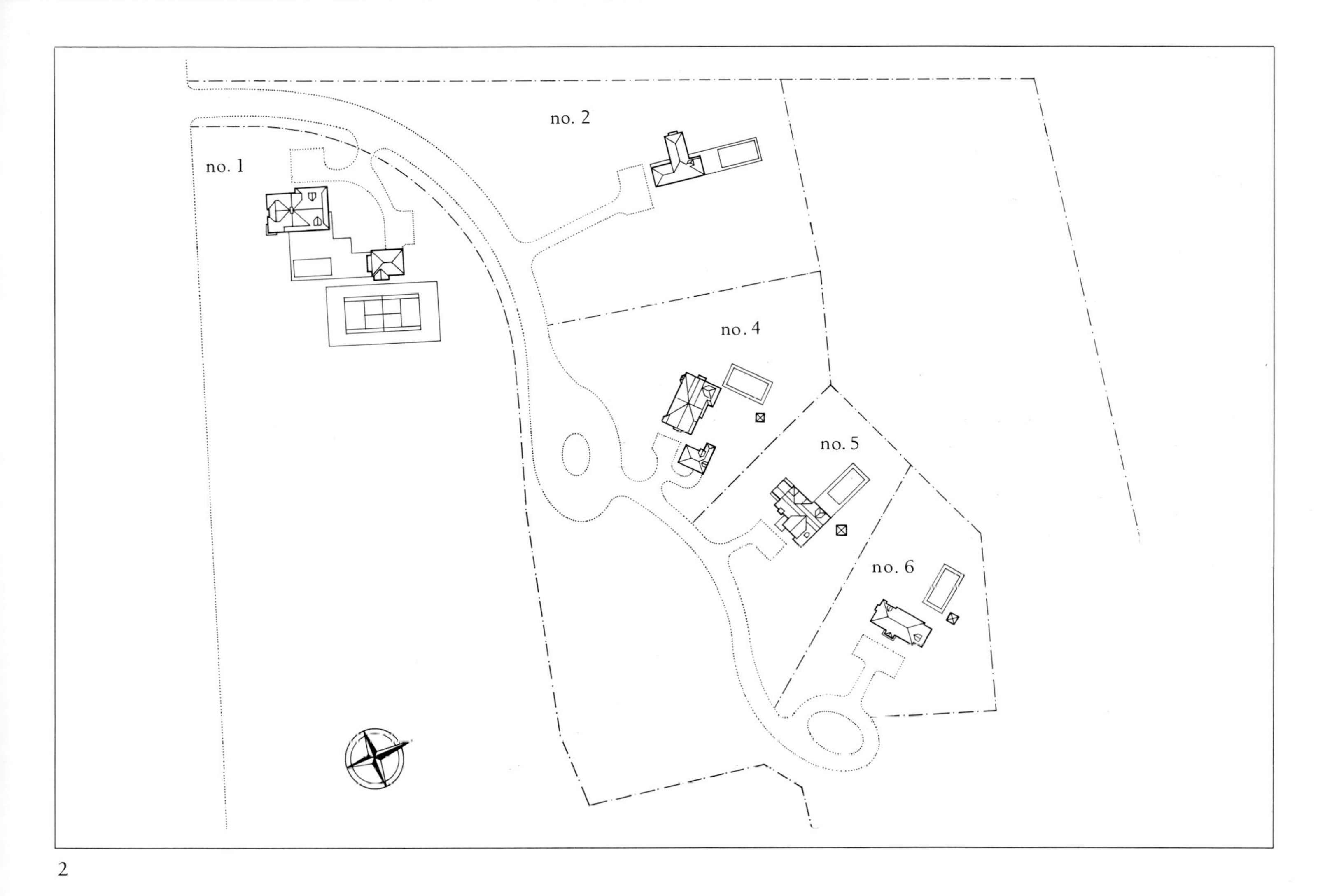

2

1.House 1   2.House 2   3.House 4

1

2

3

4.House 5 5.House 6 6.General view

4

5

6

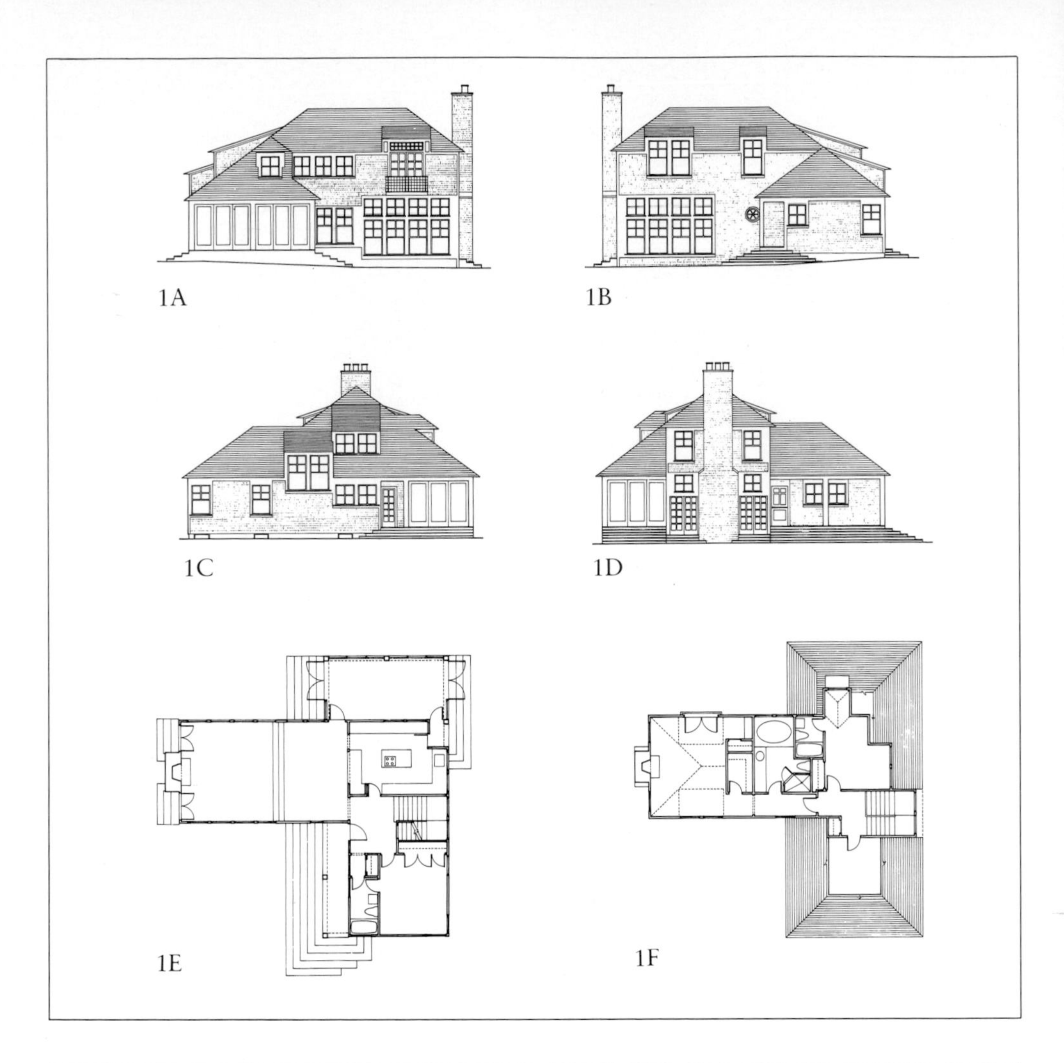
1A
1B
1C
1D
1E
1F

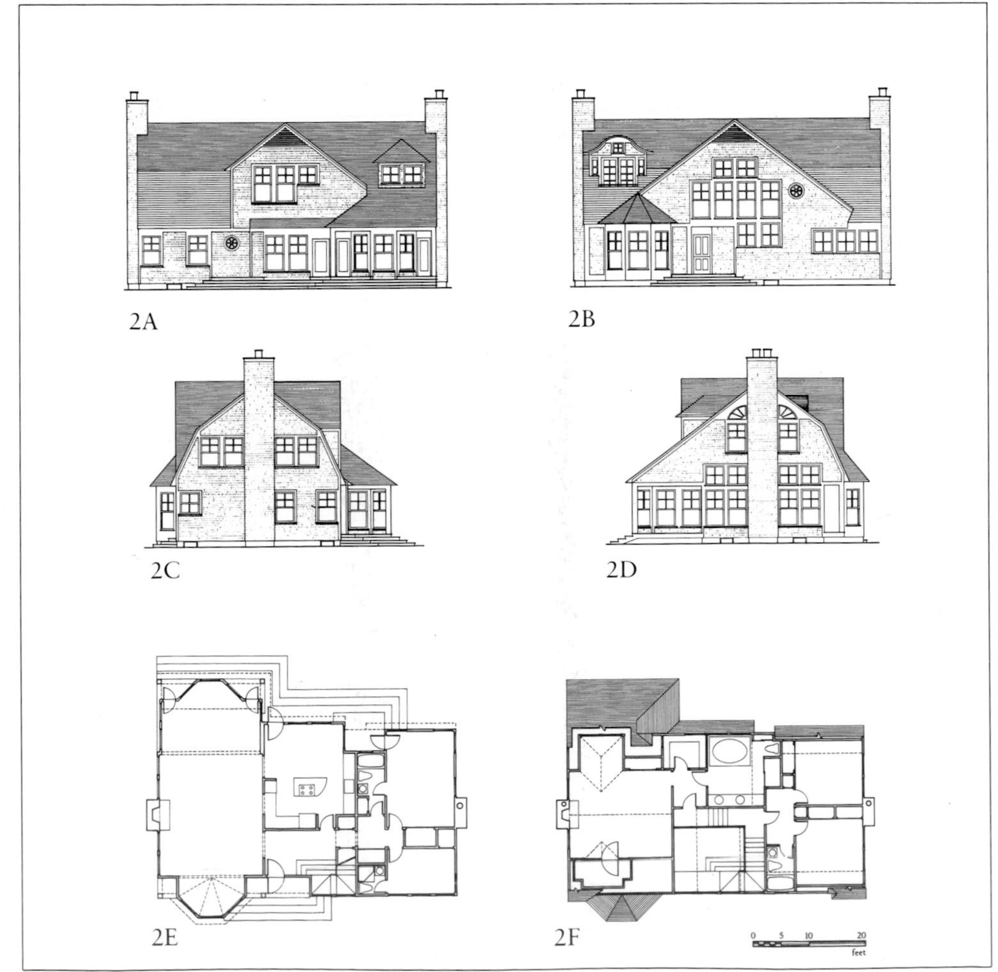
2A
2B
2C
2D
2E
2F
0 5 10 20
feet

1.House 2: A.North elevation B.South elevation C.East elevation D.West elevation E.Ground floor plan F.Second floorplan 2.House 4: A.Northeast elevation B.Southwest elevation C.Southeast elevation D.Northwest elevation E.Ground floor plan F.Second floor plan 3.House 5: A.Northwest elevation B.Southeast elevation C.Northeast elevation D.Southwest elevation E.Ground floor plan F.Second floor plan 4.House 6: A.North elevation B.South elevation C.West elevation D.East elevation E.Ground floor plan F.Second floor plan

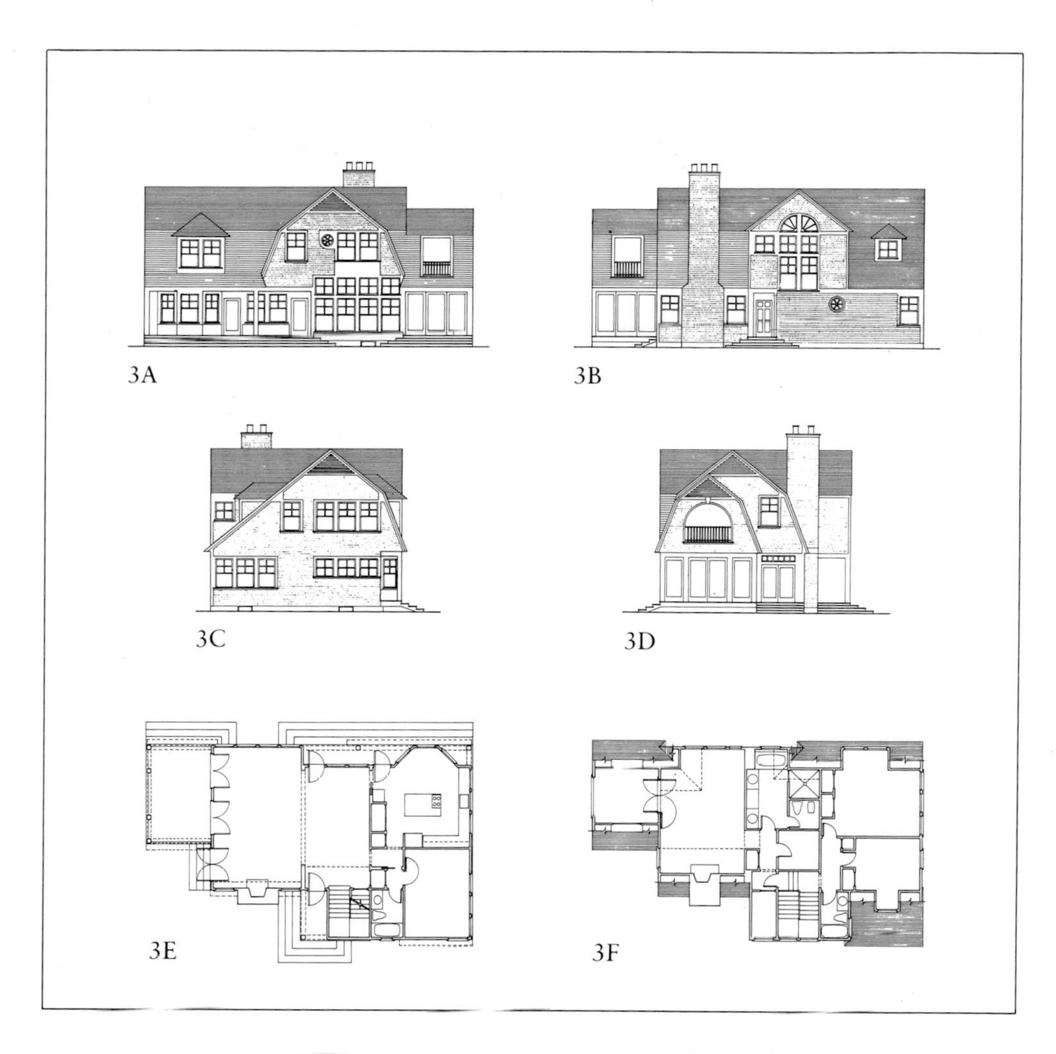

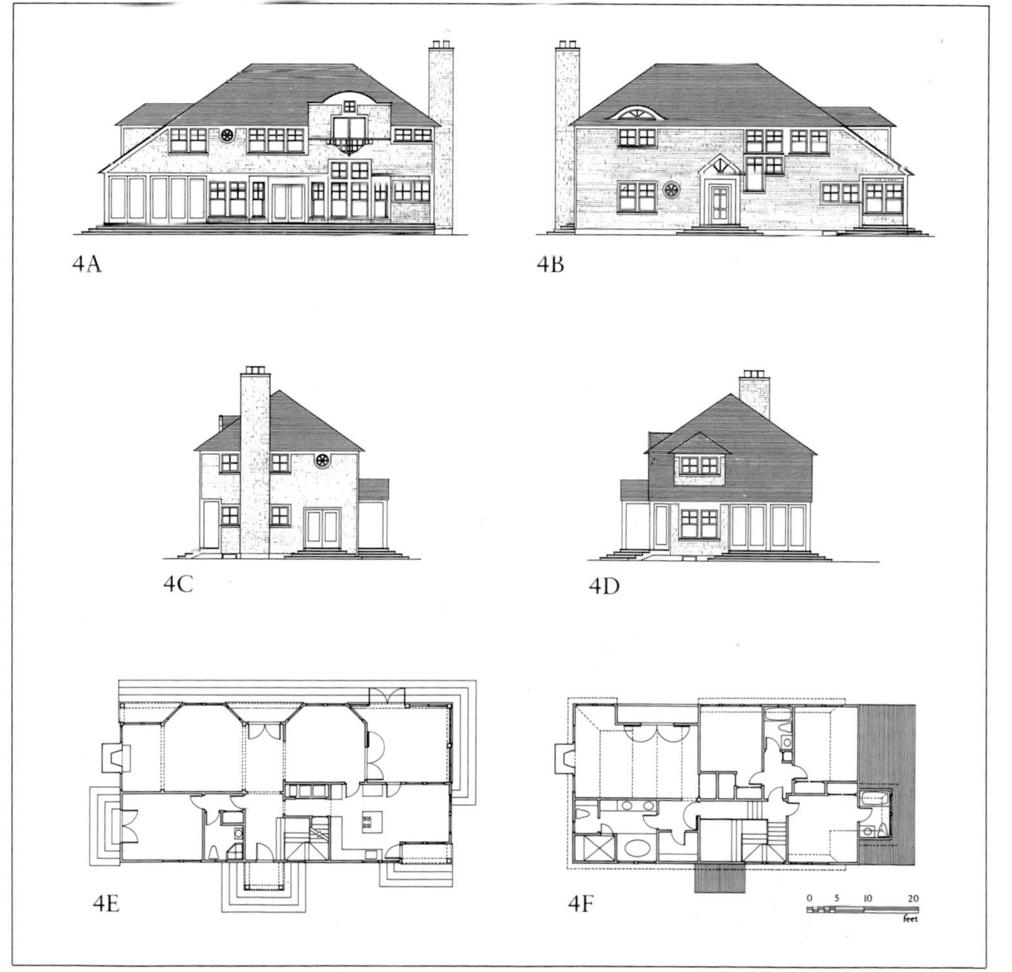

Alterations to the former Woodhouse House
East Hampton, New York
1981

An early example of the Shingle Style architecture of East Hampton's summer colony, this house had been substantially altered during this century, often at the expense of its original character and quality. In undertaking renovations for its present owners, the damages wrought upon the house's garden elevation and interior were principally addressed, with large unshaded plate-glass windows replaced by a more sympathetic combination of glass doors shielded by a vine-covered pergola.

1.Oblique view of garden facade 2.View of pergola and patio 3.Garden facade 4.Detail of pergola 5.Stair hall

1

2

3

4

5

Showroom for Shaw-Walker, Inc.
Merchandise Mart
Chicago, Illinois
1981–1982

The Shaw-Walker Company pioneered the manufacture of steel office furniture and, since its inception in 1899, has been a continuing proponent of such engineering advances as fireproofing, modular systems, and task/ambient lighting.

The showroom occupies 12,000 square feet of loft space in the Merchandise Mart, where existing mechanical systems lower ceilings to 9 feet 4 inches. Within the confines of such a long, low space, the scheme establishes a sense of monumental scale through the use of Classical composition, articulating the plan into bays and heightening its verticality by means of a free interpretation of the Tuscan order.

Its location at the intersection of two principal corridors is signaled by a back- and top-lit version of the Shaw-Walker "jumping man" logo—the company's once world-famous symbol that we have revived. The entrance leads through a reception area to the principal display hall whose basilical plan focuses the viewer's attention equally on the office systems placed in each square central bay and on the individual pieces of furniture isolated within alcoves along the edge. The alcoves are bounded by an assemblage of modulated glazed and opaque walls washed by concealed lighting, which simulate daylight and enhance the sense of a public gathering place.

The use of a Classical ordering system in conjunction with such anti-Classical devices as freely curved walls mirrors the stylistic evolution of the company's products while contributing to a further erosion of the boundaries between so called traditional and modern design.

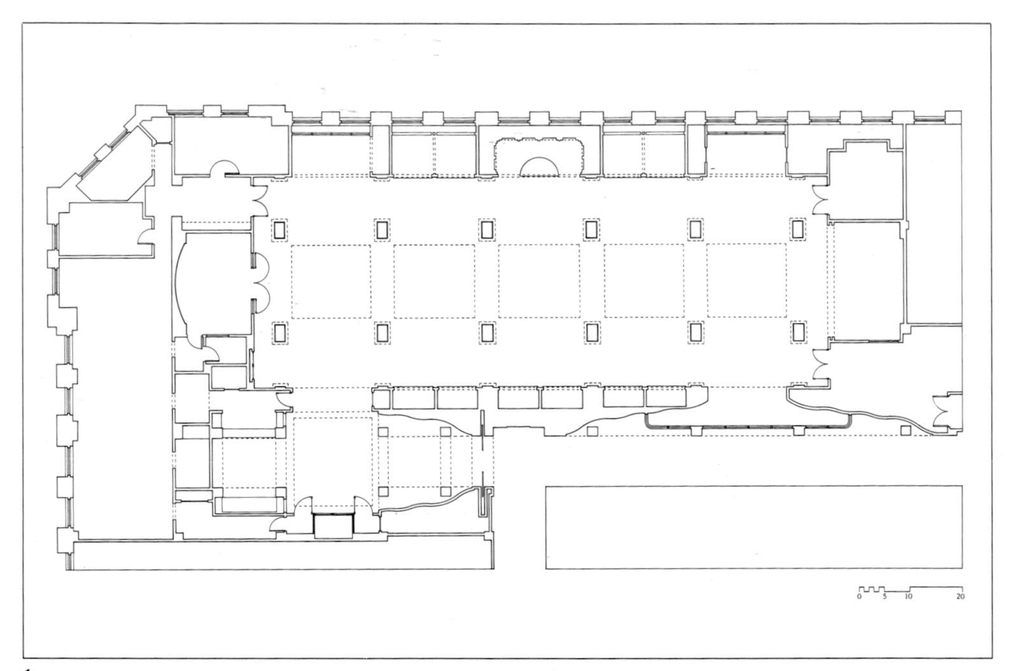

1

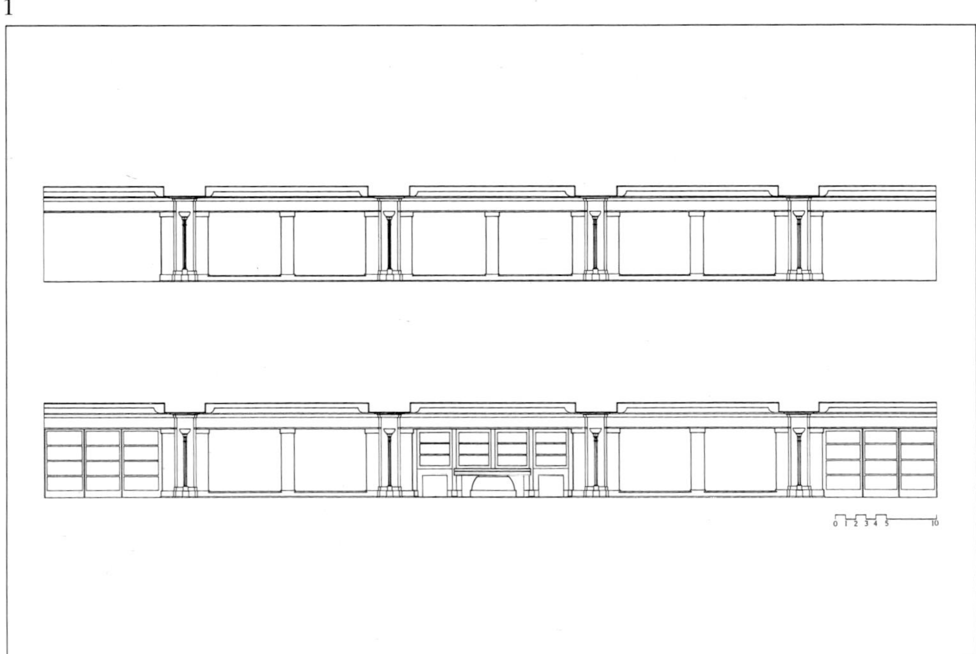

2

1.Floor plan 2.Partial elevations of showroom 3.View of entrance from the hallway 4.Showroom and display bays 5.Detail of pier and light torchere

3

4

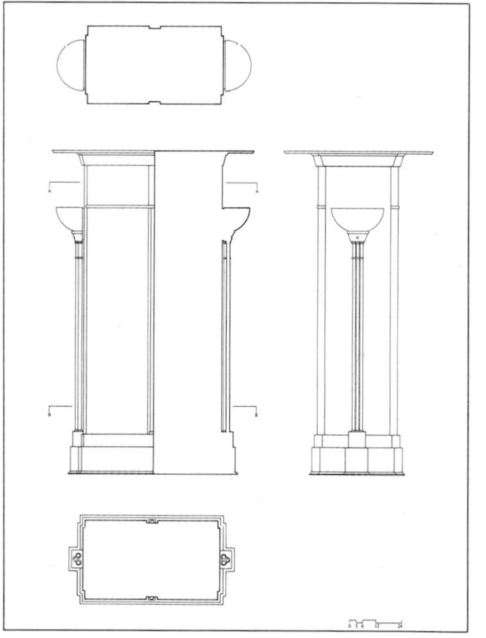

5

1.Entrance 2.Display on window facing the hallway 3,4.Display bays 5.Reception 6,7.Conference room 8,9.Showroom

1

2

3

4

5

6

7

8

9

Showroom for Shaw-Walker, Inc.
Washington, D.C.
1982–1983

The Shaw-Walker Showroom in Washington, D.C., continues themes established in our previous work for the client, while at the same time constituting a specific response to the immediate requirements of the Design Center Building, a former refrigerated meat packing warehouse with low ceilings and massive structural elements, and to the Classical architecture of Washington, D.C.

The preferred sequence through the plan leads the visitor down a forced-perspective entrance gallery to a square, top-lit entrance lobby and a showroom articulated into three bays defined by massive piers and lit by torchères as well as from sources concealed behind coves.

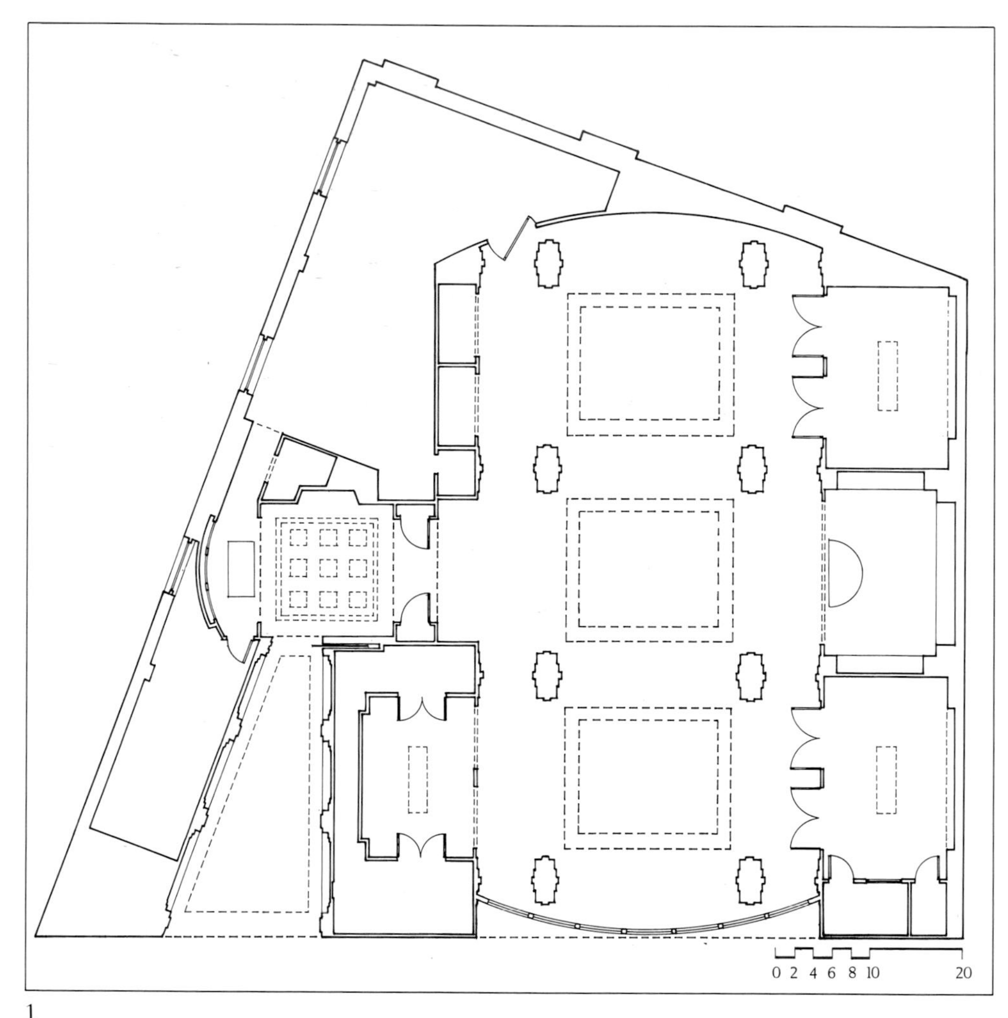

1

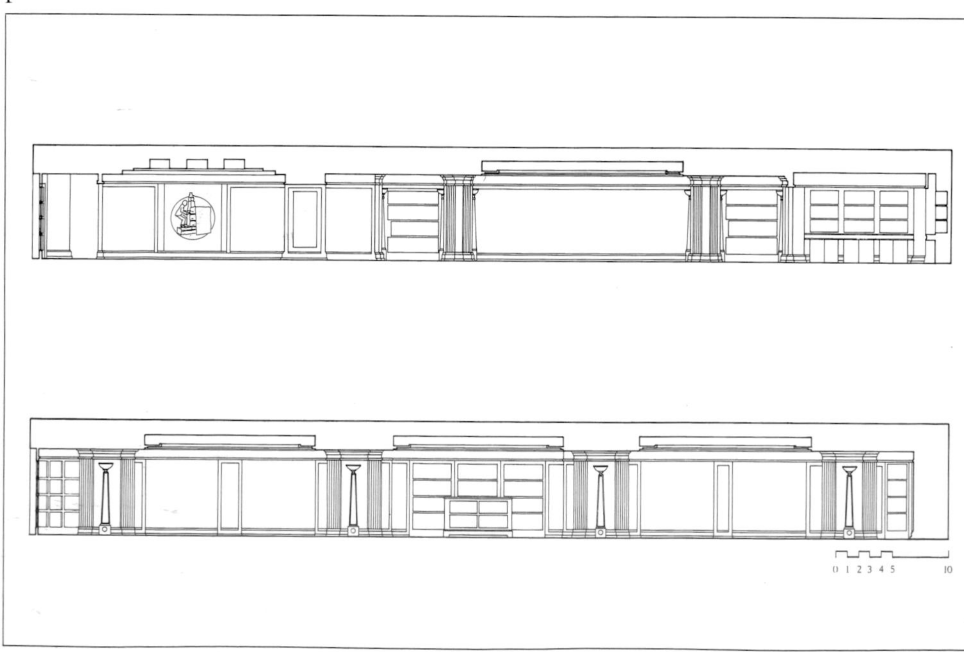

2

1.Floor plan 2.Elevations of showroom 3.Entrance 4.Detail of pier and light torchere 5.View of pier and light torchere

3

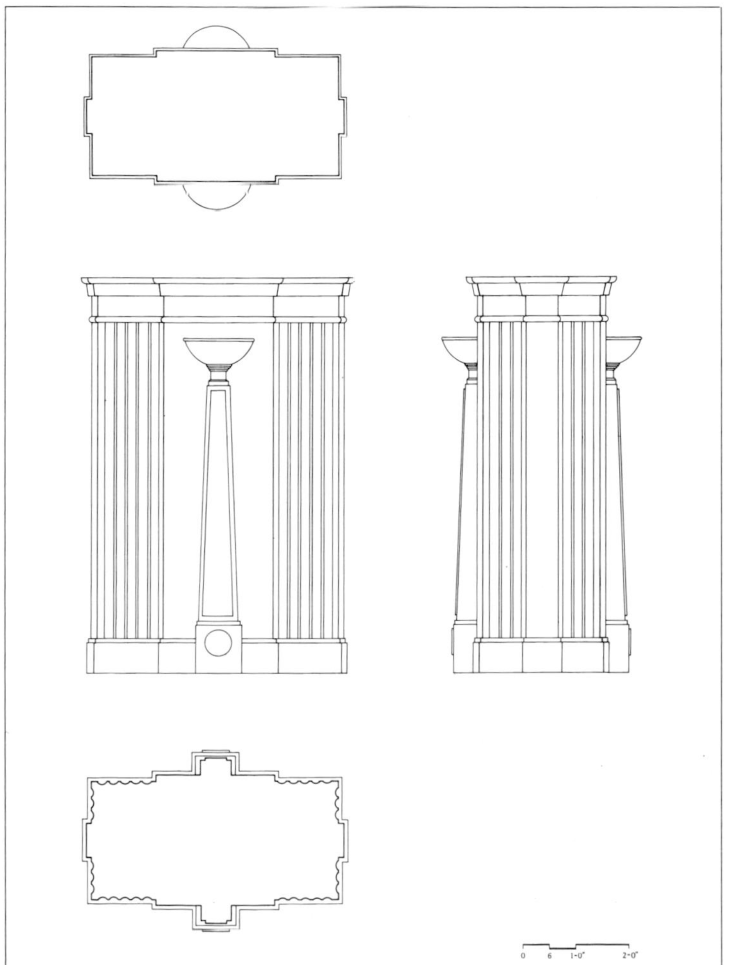

4

5

1.Reception 2.View of showroom from reception area 3.Showroom and furniture display 4.Tuscan table and fabric display area

1

2

3

4

Showroom for Shaw-Walker, Inc.
New York, New York
1982–1983

The Shaw-Walker Showroom in New York is the third in a series of contract furniture showrooms for the client. It represents a departure from the previous showrooms where small rooms and niches surround a large open space.

The New York showroom is a series of shaped rooms connected by vestibules. Each of the rooms has a regular pattern of windows in deep-set niches which offer views of the midtown skyline.

Entrance to this twenty-fourth-floor showroom is from an elevator lobby room into an oval vestibule where the receptionist is located. On axis with the entrance sequence is the conference room, which is terminated by a back-lit panel with the company name. To the right or left of the oval vestibule are the rooms displaying the product.

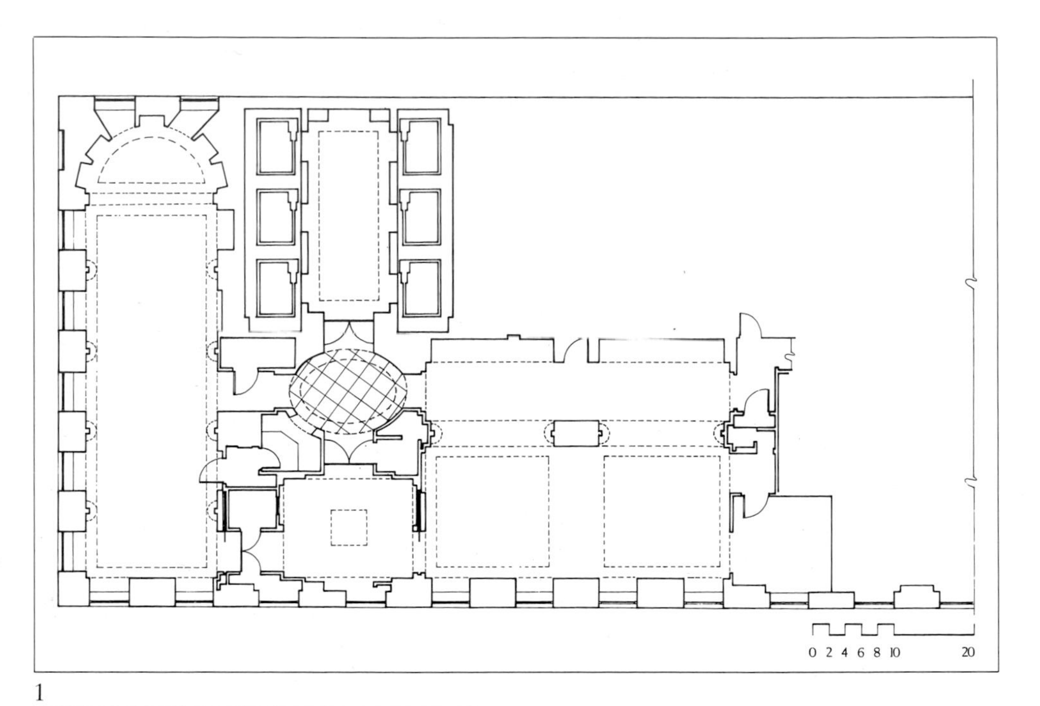

1

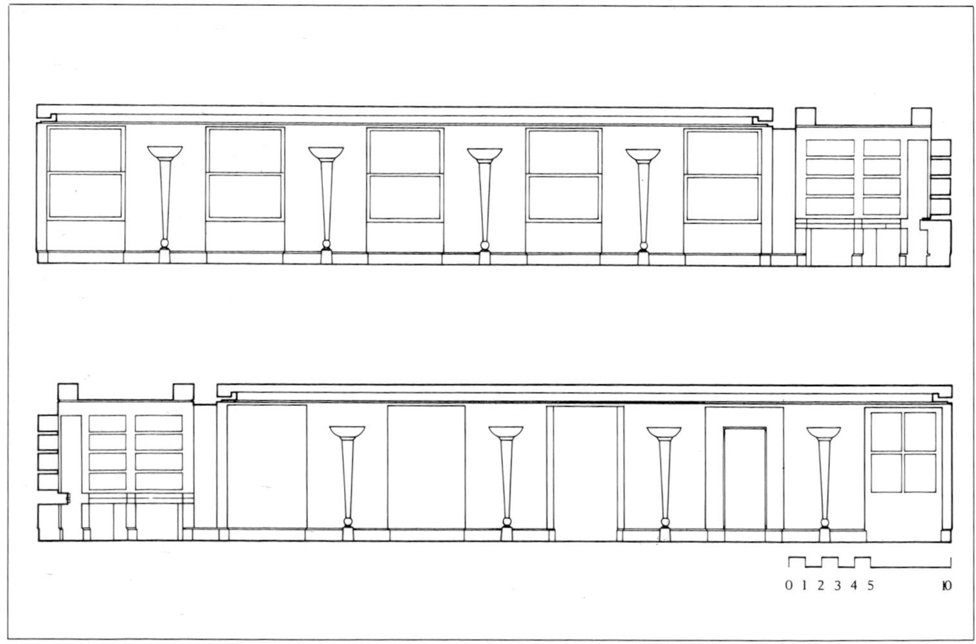

2

1. Floor plan 2. Elevations of showroom
Opposite page: Entrance foyer and conference room

SHAW WALKER

Opposite page: Partial view of entry sequence from conference room 1.Partial view of showroom and fabric display 2.Detail of light torchere 3.Partial view of entrance foyer

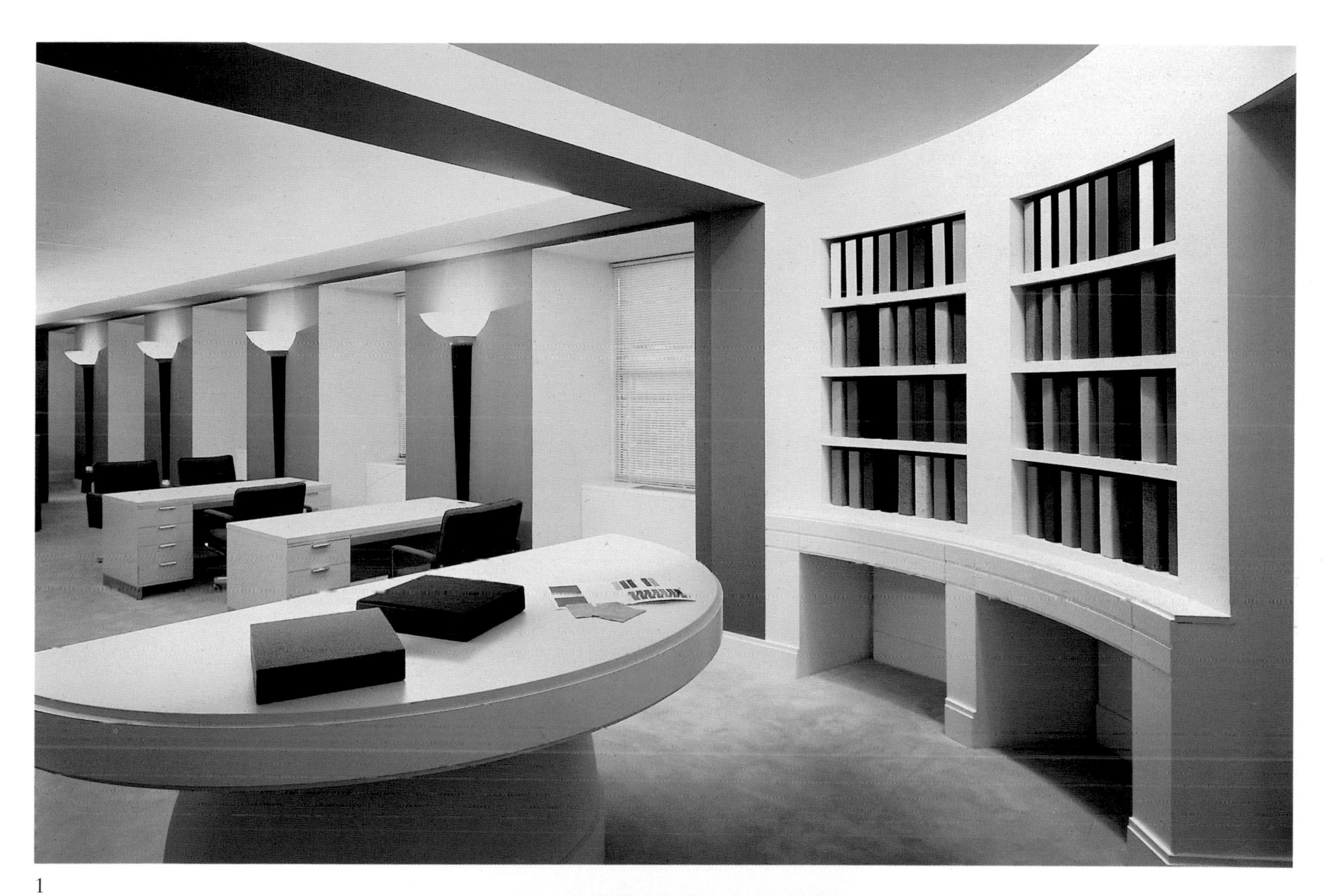

1

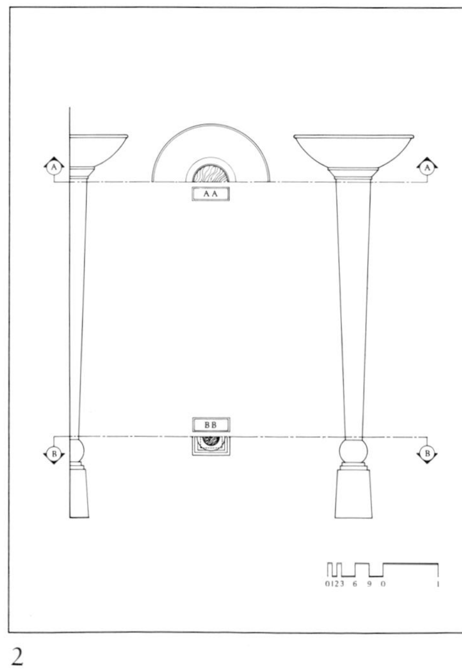

2

3

Showroom for Shaw-Walker, Inc.

Pacific Design Center
Los Angeles, California
1982

Proposed for an awkwardly configured space at a bend in a corridor, this showroom was organized as a series of Classical rooms. One passes first through an elliptical apse into an octagonal room whose convex walls of lacquered wood and frosted mirror panels provide a stopping place before continuing down through the main showroom. The axis passes through an elliptical showroom and terminates in the conference room, a mock gazebo with a latticed ceiling beneath a painted sky. The murals between the columns depict the Hollywood hills and the view out toward the city of Los Angeles, as though the walls of the Pacific Design Center had disappeared.

1.Floor plan 2.Longitudinal section 3.Entrance elevation 4.Location of showroom

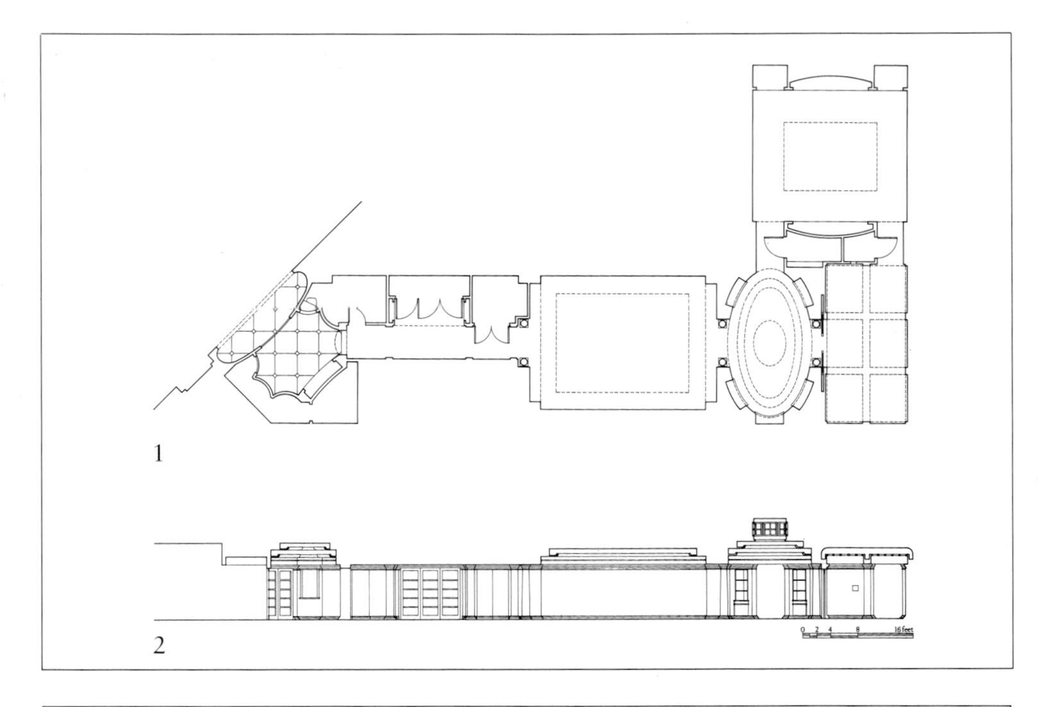

1

2

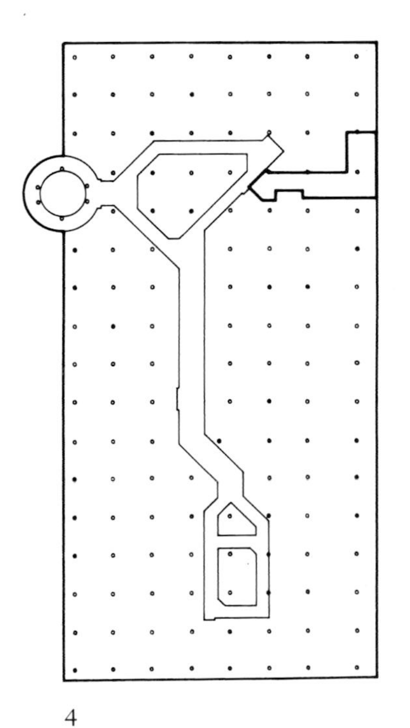

4

3

Anthony Fisher Residence
Napeague, New York
1982

1.Southeast elevation 2.Northeast elevation 3.Southwest elevation 4.Northwest elevation 5.Site plan 6.View of model 7.Attic floor plan 8.Ground floor plan 9.Second floor plan

The continuous bowed and flared roofline of this waterfront house defines a compact, iconic volume off which discreetly positioned erosions and projections are played for both picturesque and plastic effect. The configuration of the roof itself derives from local traditions of barn- and shipbuilding, and has been revived periodically in vernacular seaside cottage architecture. In this house, we have endeavored to grant the roof a greater dignity than that to which it is accustomed, by outlining it with an abstracted cornice and rake trim, supported in turn by Tuscan columns.

The house's siting on a relatively small lot with one principal view led to the use of a layered first-floor plan wherein the primary living spaces facing the water are backed by a service zone comprising servant's room, laundry, and main stair. The closed character of the street facade—in contradistinction to the generously glazed facade opposite—is relieved of its wall-like effect by the volumetric play of the subsumed entry porch against the projecting bow-windowed stair. In effect, a room in its own right, the stair is the house's major internal communicator as it leads to the two separate bedroom wings of the second floor and, ultimately, to a third-story studio.

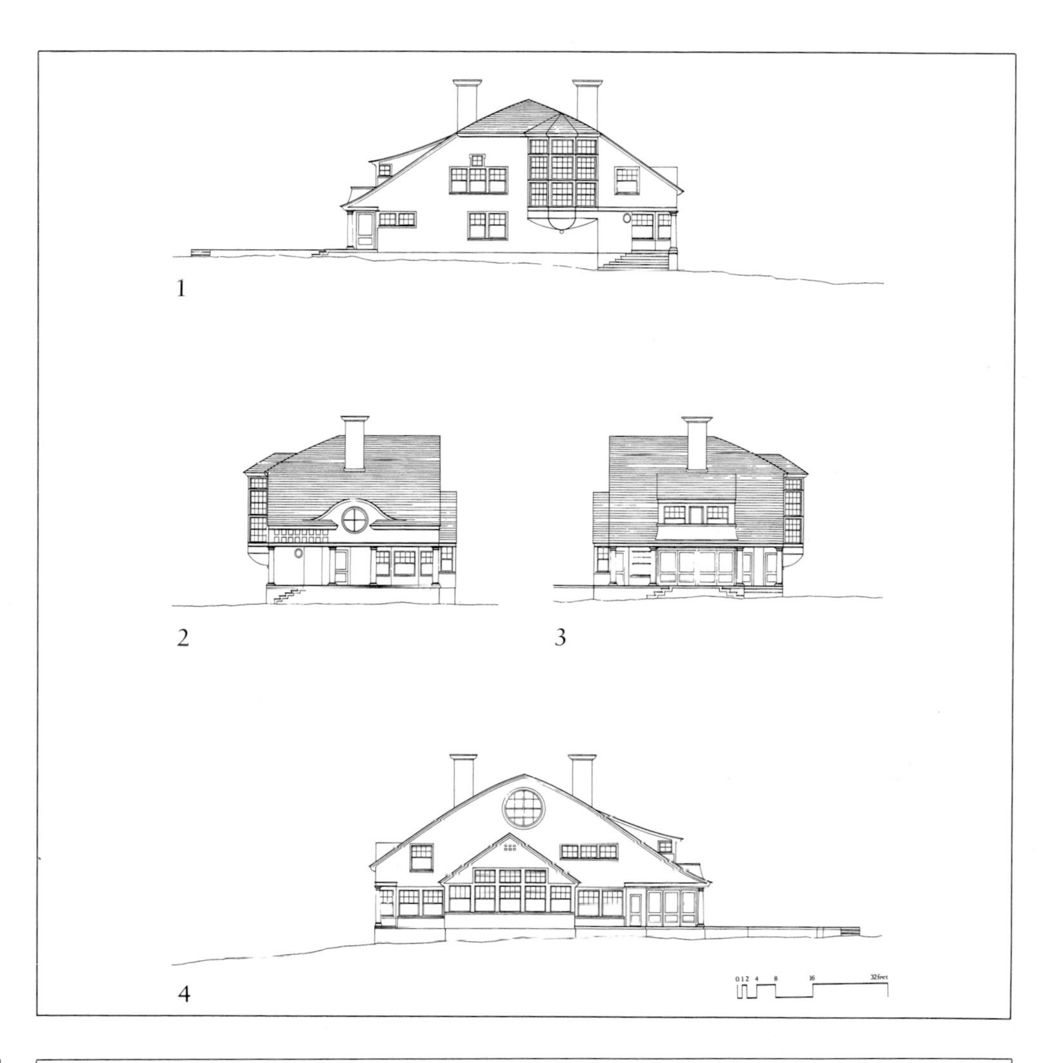

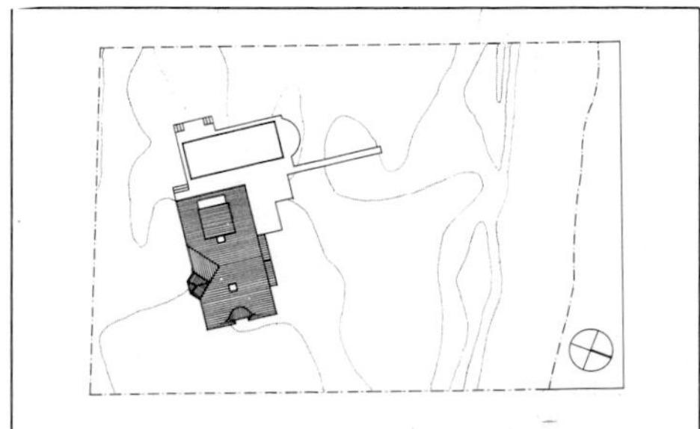

5

6

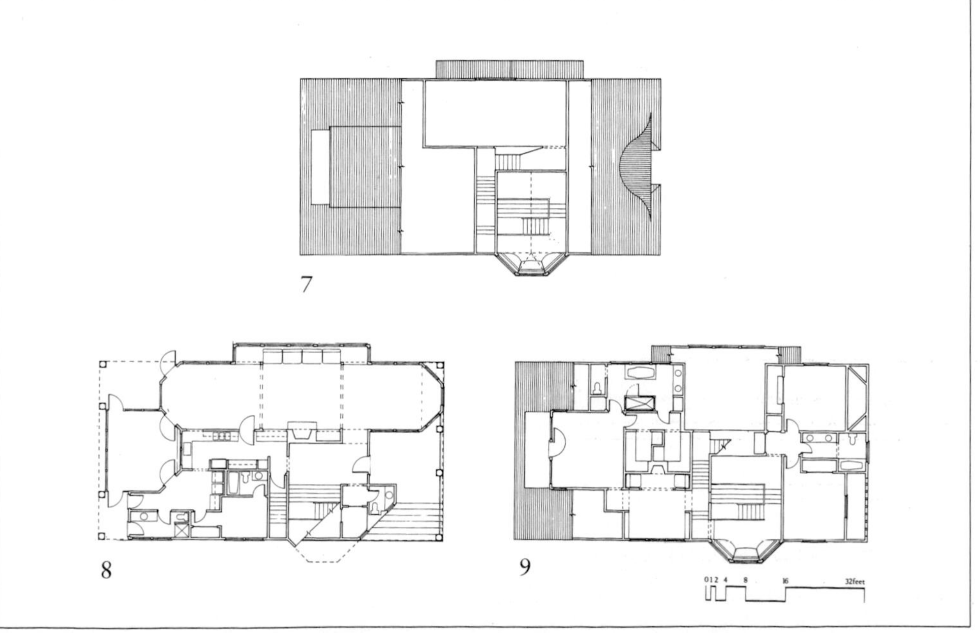

"Classical Corner"
for House and Garden Magazine
1982

One of a series of idealized rooms commissioned to feature a new line of reproduction furniture, in this case an eighteenth-century English gaming table. The abstraction of the Classical orders, multiple pilasters, overscaled wainscot, sandblasted glass, and rosy walls combine to set the tone of a modern variation on a 1930s movie set.

Tableware for Swid Powell
1982–1985

The silver candlesticks, water pitcher, and salt and pepper shakers are all based on the iconography of the column. The column of the ancient Minoan palaces, the Gothic colonnette, the Classical orders—both in their pure geometries and in their streamlined variations from the modern interpretations of the 1930s, are individually remembered in the various pieces, all of which have been interpreted to suit contemporary production techniques and the requirements of modern entertaining.

The Majestic dinner plate, ruby red in color and highlighted with gold, emphasizes, as do the silver pieces, richness of material. The plate's strap-and-buckle pattern evokes a family crest or medallion, yet remains anonymous by virtue of its abstraction.

1.Dinner plate 2.Candlesticks 3.Water pitcher 4.Salt and pepper shakers

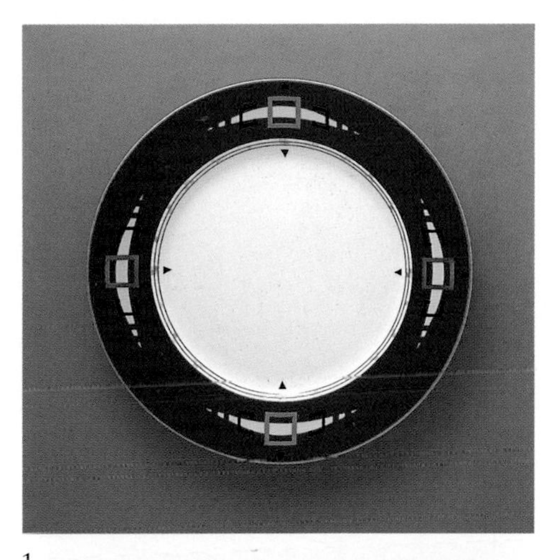

1

2

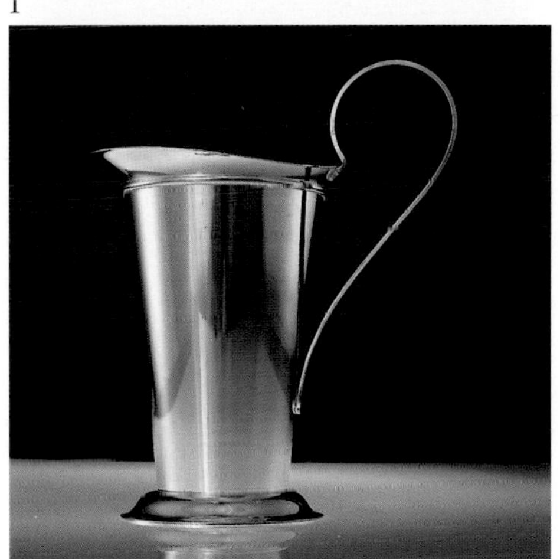

3

4

House at Seaview

Amagansett, New York
1982

Set among a jumble of vertical-siding-and-shed-roof beach houses, this renovation seeks to establish architectural order by employing simple volumetric masses linked together to suggest an assemblage of farm buildings. The principal rooms of the house are located on the second floor to take advantage of the view along the beach. The rooms open to one another to maximize the feeling of spaciousness and informality. The base of the house is sheathed in horizontal shiplapped cedar siding to suggest a rusticated base with the siding running vertically above the base.

1.North elevation 2.South elevation 3.East elevation 4.West elevation 5.Ground floor plan 6.Second floor plan 7.Site plan 8.Elevations prior to renovation: A.North B.East C.South D.West

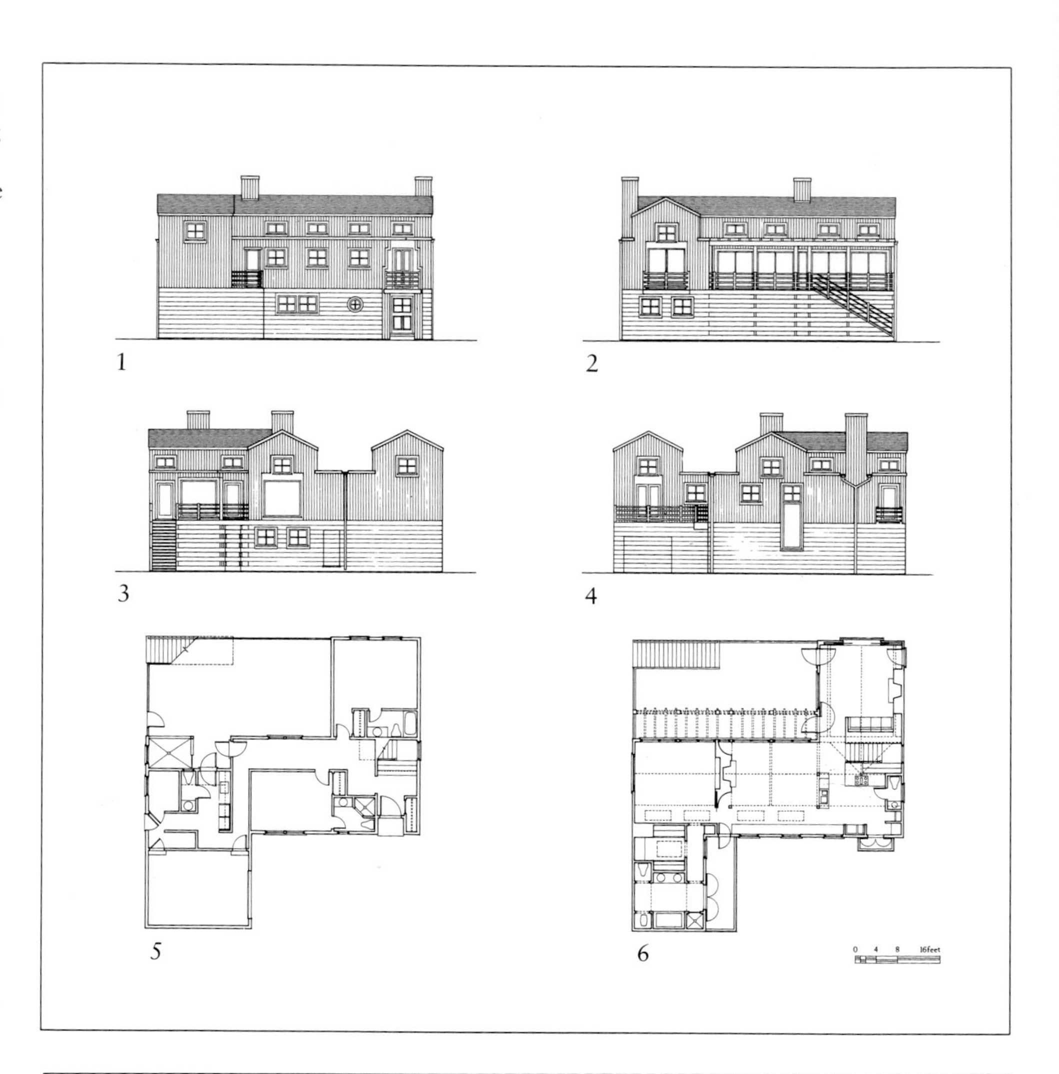

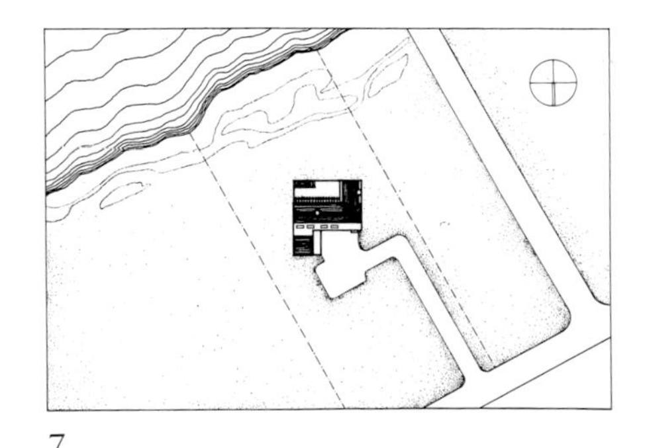

7

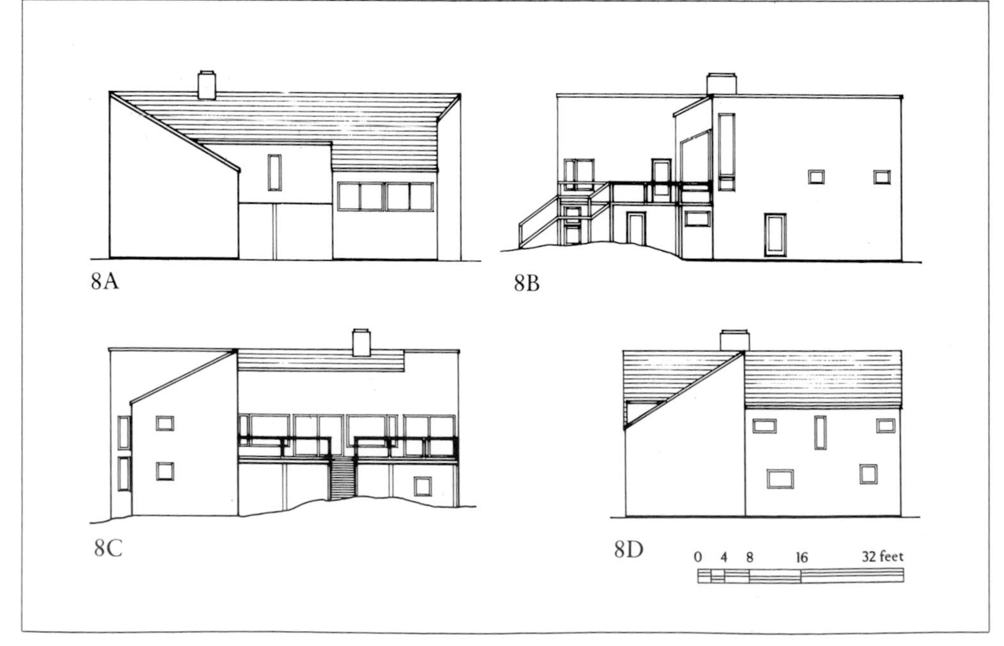

Residence
Napeague, New York
1981

1.North elevation 2.East elevation 3.West elevation 4.South elevation 5.Site plan 6.View of model 7.Ground floor plan 8.Second floor plan

Designed for an oceanfront site along an isolated stretch of highway, this summer cottage is intended as a formalized pavilion set apart from—but at the same time recognizing and accommodating—its natural surroundings. As the house straddles a sand dune, its principal living functions are raised one story to a piano nobile on the entrance side; on the south-facing ocean side, this level sits noticeably closer and more accessible to the ground. Horizontally laid wide board siding imparts a substantiality and rustication to the base story in order to enhance the comparative lightness and delicacy of the wood-shingled and glazed main floor. The base also extends out towards the east and south to define precincts for pool and terrace, and to establish a secondary, refined ground plane for the house proper.

Inside, a grand central stair ends at a landing where a more subtly suggested cross-axis leads one alternately to the private and entertainment zones of the main floor. Segmental dormers provide clerestory lighting to emphasize these axes and, in combination with the central-chimney mass, to introduce natural light to the core of the house.

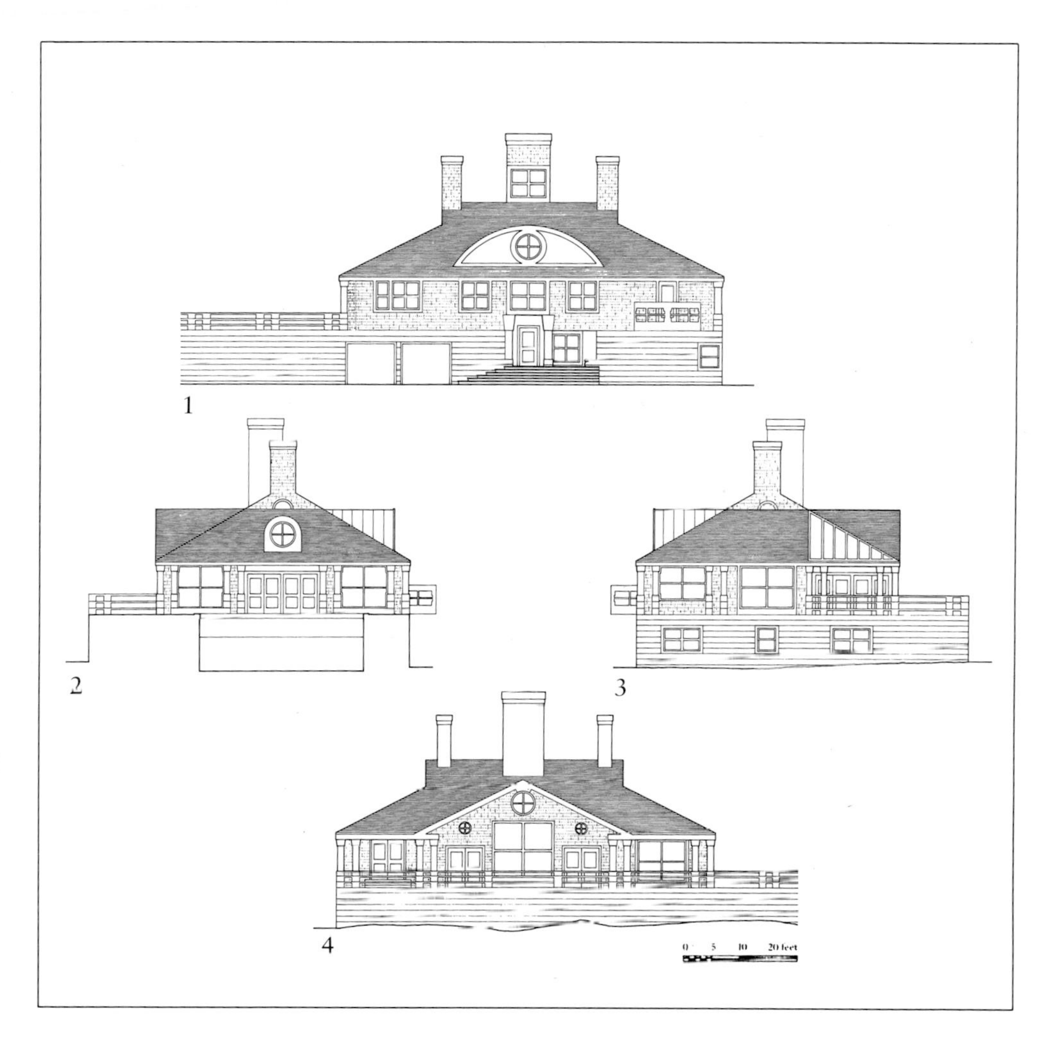

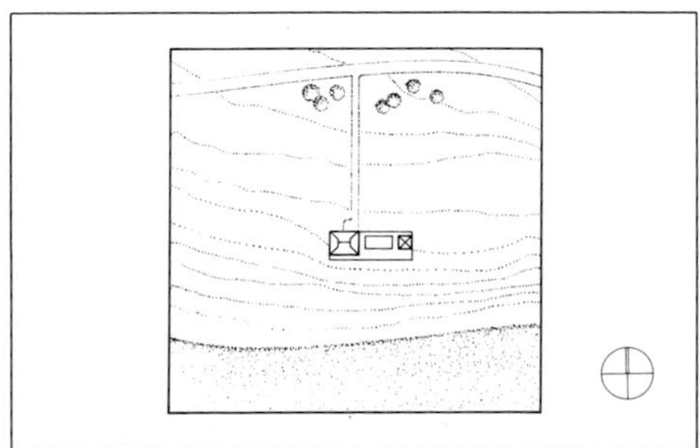

5

6

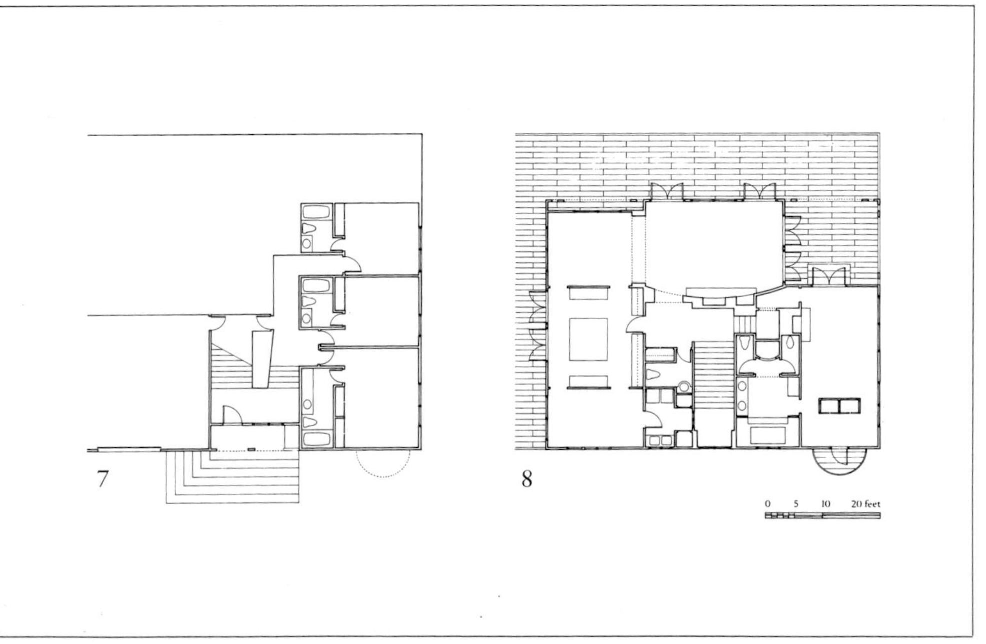

St. Andrews

Hastings-on-Hudson, New York
1982–

St. Andrews consists of 209 units of condominium housing nestled between the fairways of the nation's oldest golf course. In addition to the housing, the project includes the conversion of the former Andrew Carnegie summer cottage into a recreation center as well as an extensive overhaul of the ninety-year-old clubhouse, whose design is attributed to Stanford White.

Earmarked for an affluent clientele, the housing is designed to bring the amenities and image of a luxurious detached single-family dwelling to the more constrained spatial context of cluster row houses. Long town-house rows are avoided: most of the housing is in groups of four or six units interspersed with paired units. Composition of each individual group is carefully orchestrated to suggest large houses that have been subdivided, as opposed to individual units glued together to form a row; special end units further the sense of buildings in the round rather than continuous extrusions. The rich dark brown shingle-clad houses are enlivened with white-painted decorative moldings, latticework, and pedimented porches supported on classical columns, thereby establishing a clear visual connection to the architecture of the clubhouse and to a significant tradition in the domestic architecture of the Northeast.

1

1.Site plan 2.Muirfield: view of street elevation 3.Troon: detail of entrance 4.Muirfield: detail of Sales Center entrance

2

3

4

1.Building 22: A.Front elevation B.Garden elevation 2.Building 17: A.Front elevation B.Garden elevation 3.Building 23: A.Front elevation B.Garden elevation 4.Building 24: A.Front elevation B.Garden elevation

1A

1B

2A

2B

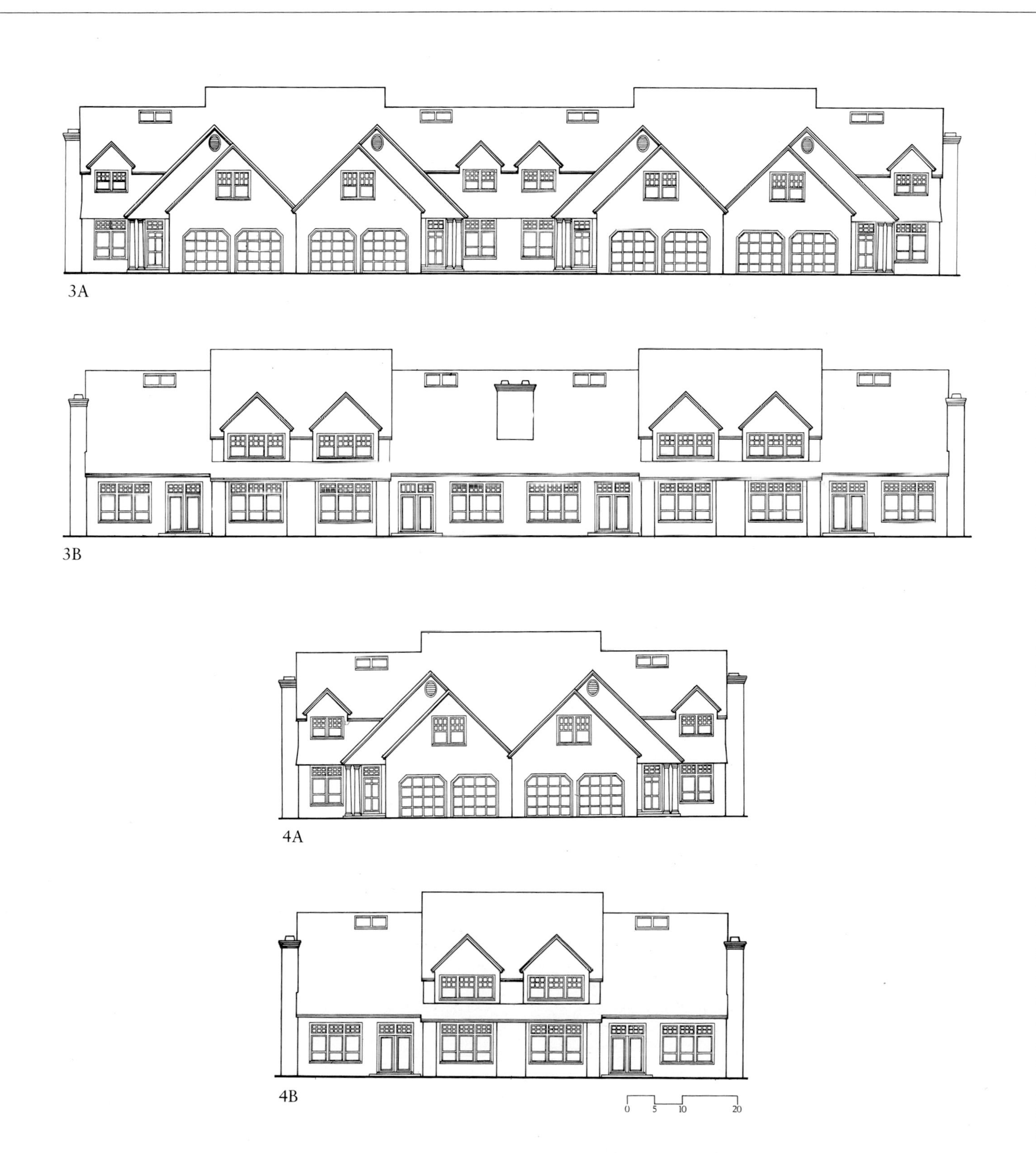
3A
3B
4A
4B
0
5
10
20

1.Carnoustie: view of end elevation
2.Sales Center showing four typical units 3.St.Andrews: Sales Center
4.Carnoustie: view of end facade

1

2

3

4

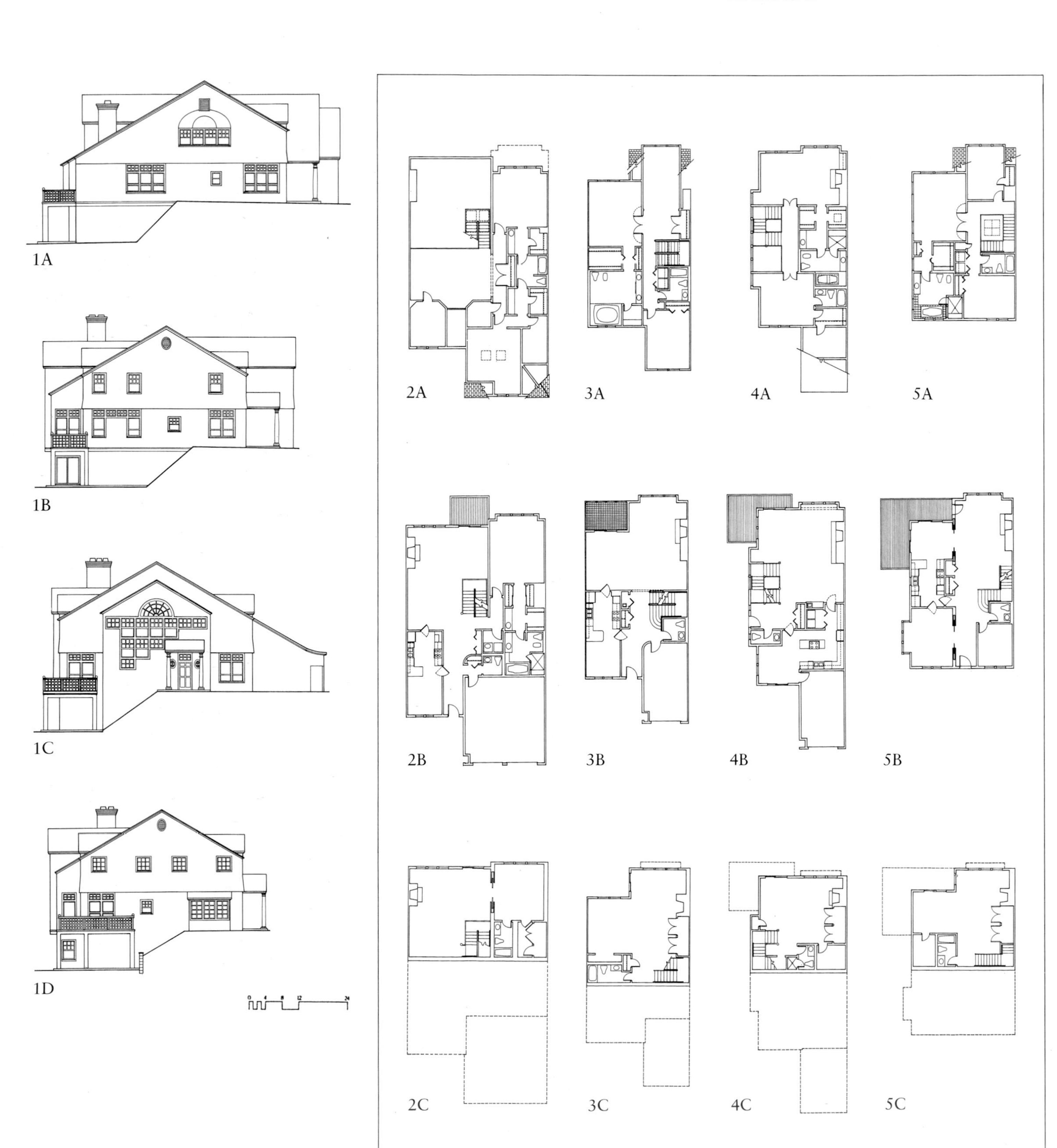

1.Residence types: A.Muirfield B.Prestwick C.Carnoustie D.Troon 2.Muirfield A.Second level B.Entry level C.Patio level 3.Prestwick: A.Second level B.Entry level C.Patio level 4.Carnoustie: A.Second level B.Entry level C.Patio level 5.Troon: A.Second level B.Entry level C.Patio level

6.Gate house A.North elevation B.South elevation C.East elevation D.West elevation 7.Irrigation pump house: A.West elevation B.East elevation C.South elevation D.North elevation 8,9.Gate house 10.Irrigation pump house

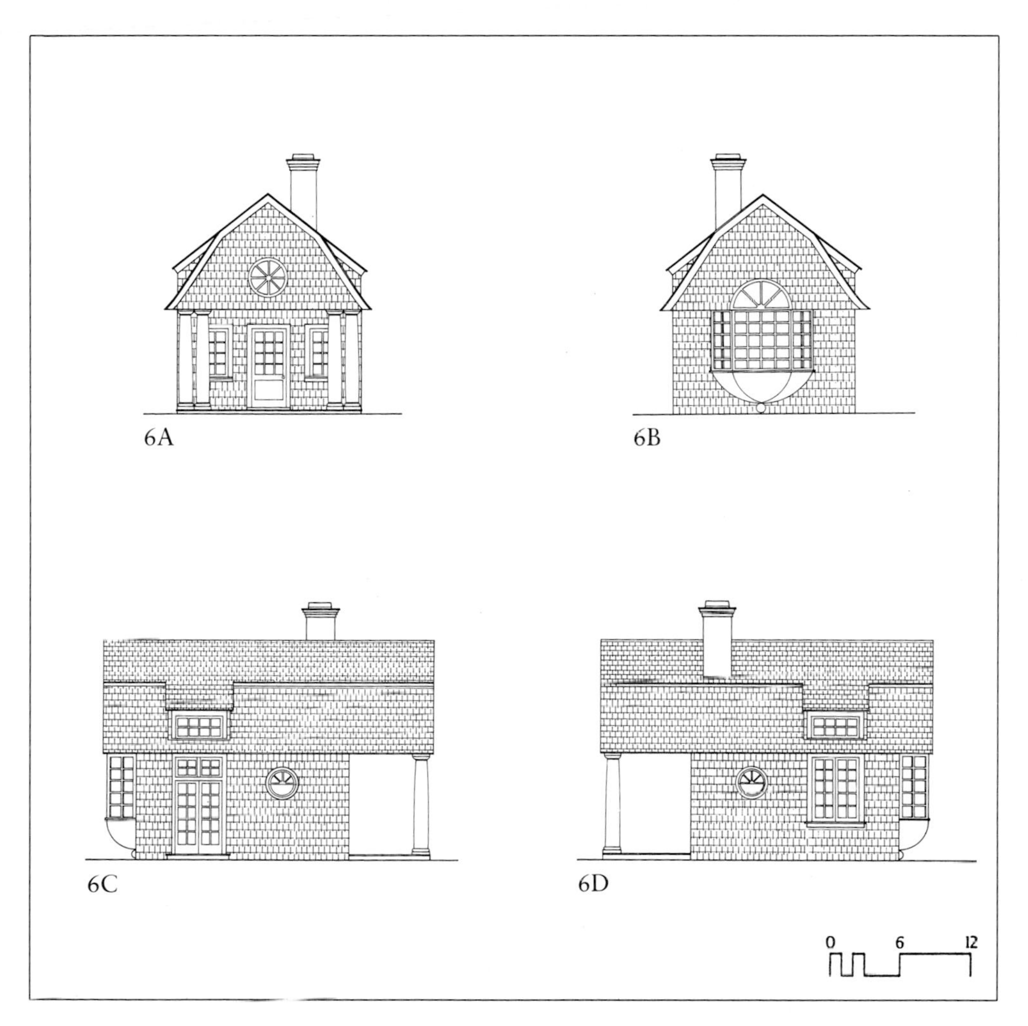

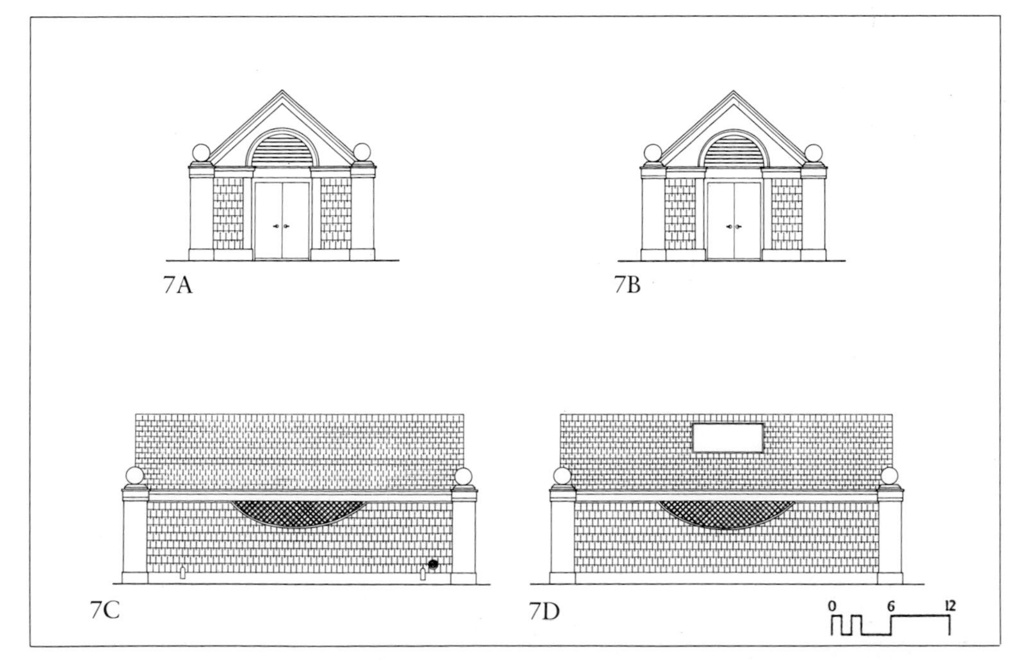

8

9

10

"Dinner at Eight" Carpet
for Furniture of the Twentieth Century
1983

The phrase "Dinner at Eight" evokes a certain genre of Hollywood film comedy that combined disingenuous innocence with metropolitan sophistication. This carpet seeks to recapture the mood of those films—their heightened sense of romance, their use of theatrical convention and of exquisitely ambiguous euphemism.

It presents a highly formalized image within a proscenium-like frame of Classical columns and theatrical drapes. The curtains are drawn, the doors about to open, and the music about to play as the comedy begins.

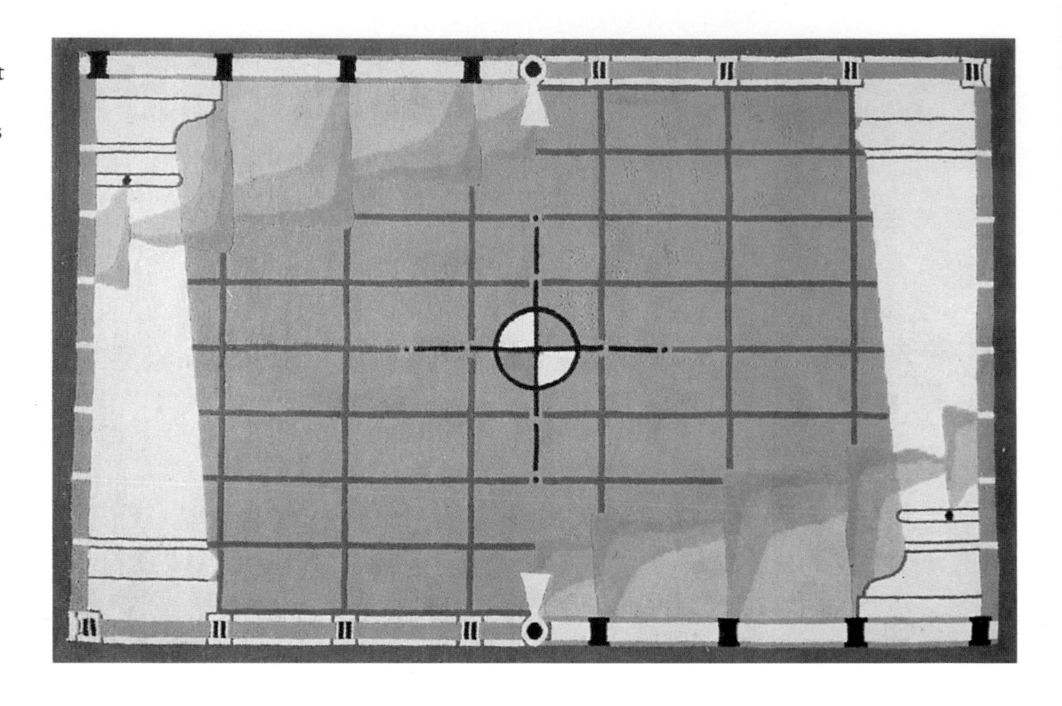

San Remo Carpet
1983

This rug was designed for a living room inside the distinctively profiled San Remo apartment building on New York's Central Park West. The medallions on each of the four sides are silhouettes of the San Remo's twin towers. They are represented in exaggerated perspective, reminiscent of jazz age graphics. The lights in the towers twinkle like the stars in the dusky, lavender Manhattan sky represented in the field. The border of the carpet is a repeated pattern taken from terra cotta plaques of another prominent New York building of the Twenties.

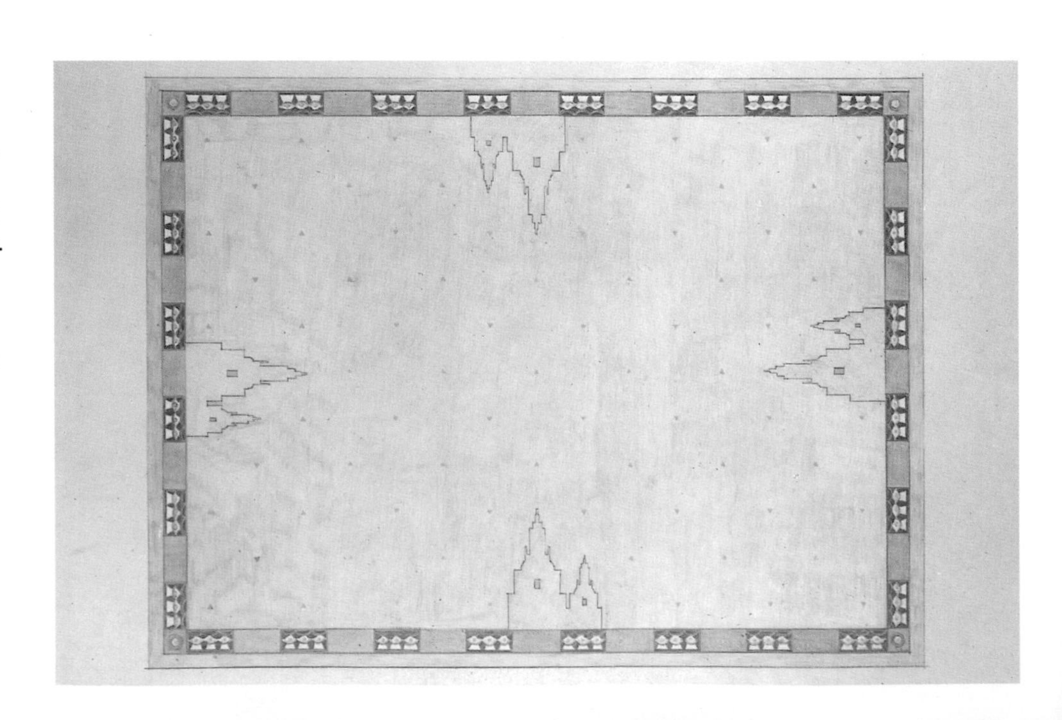

Faulkner House Apartments

University of Virginia
Charlottesville, Virginia
1982

This entry to a state-sponsored design/build competition seeks to recapture the Jeffersonian traditions of planning and massing which set the architectural tone of the University of Virginia from its inception to the advent of post-World War II modernism. Within the confines of a rather sharply pitched site and a stringent budget, this scheme establishes a geometrically ordered residential precinct amidst the relative chaos of the university's new campus by actively employing Jefferson's Great Lawn as its principal formal model. Towards that end, the programmatic mix of one-, two-, and three-bedroom student apartment units encouraged the organization of the project into nine brick pavilions, linked to each other by garden walls and oriented longitudinally about a visual axis closed at its higher elevation by the colonnaded pediment of the Neo-Georgian main house, and open to the view at the end opposite. The main pedestrian entry at this latter point is flanked by identical verandaed lodges, housing student counselors; the smaller size and simple, hipped form of these twin structures magnify the scalar reading of the buildings beyond and form an architectural frame to the vistas in either direction along the main axis.

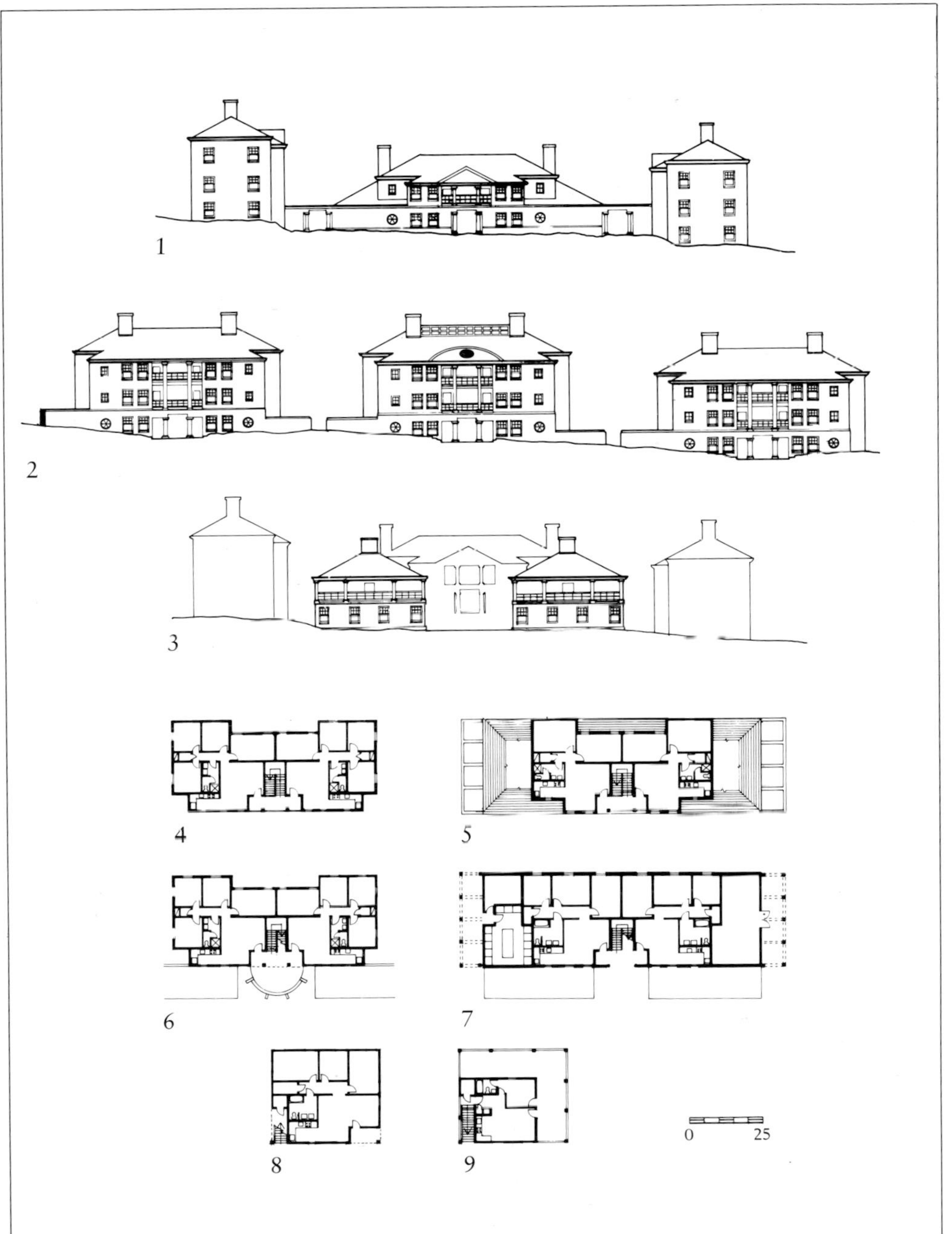

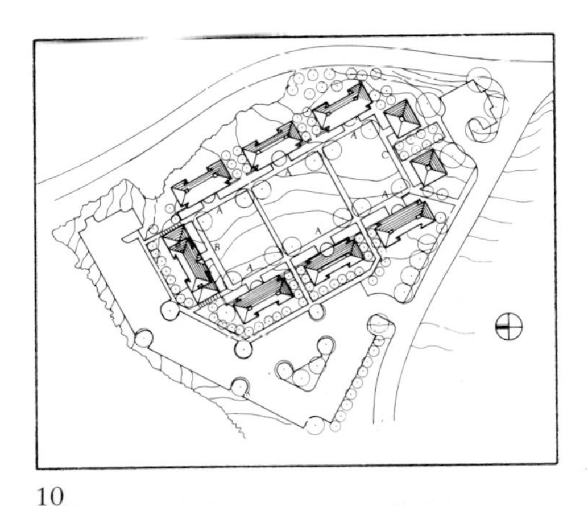

10

11

1.North court elevation 2.East court elevation 3.Entry elevation 4.Buildings A, ground and second floor plans 5.Buildings A, basement floor plan 6.Building B, ground floor plan 7.Building B, basement floor plan 8.Building C, ground floor plan 9.Building C, second floor plan 10.Site plan 11.Overhead view of model

Observatory Hill Dining Hall

University of Virginia
Charlottesville, Virginia
1982–1984

The additions to the Observatory Hill Dining Hall are metaphoric porches intended to camouflage the existing facility and to ameliorate the disjunction between that building and the university's Jeffersonian architectural tradition. In the most basic terms, the additions provide the building with a clearly defined base, middle, and top, which until now it has lacked and without which it bears no real relation to the traditional architecture of the campus. The four-bay massing of each porch addition consciously departs from the dining hall's monolithic character and imparts to it the more intimate scale of Jefferson's Lawn. Inside and out, the use of specific elements such as hipped roofs, arches, molded brick, Classical columns, and wood trim reinforces the scale and character suggested by the overall massing.

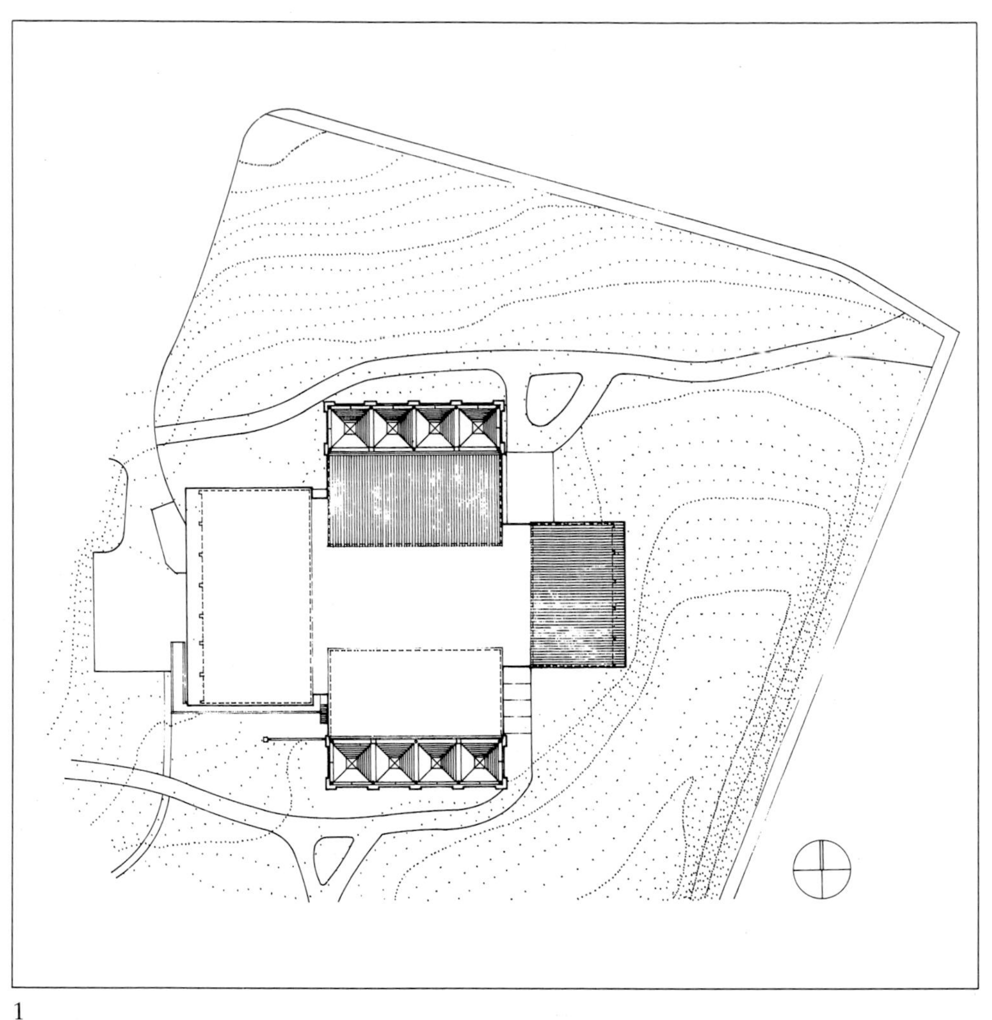

1

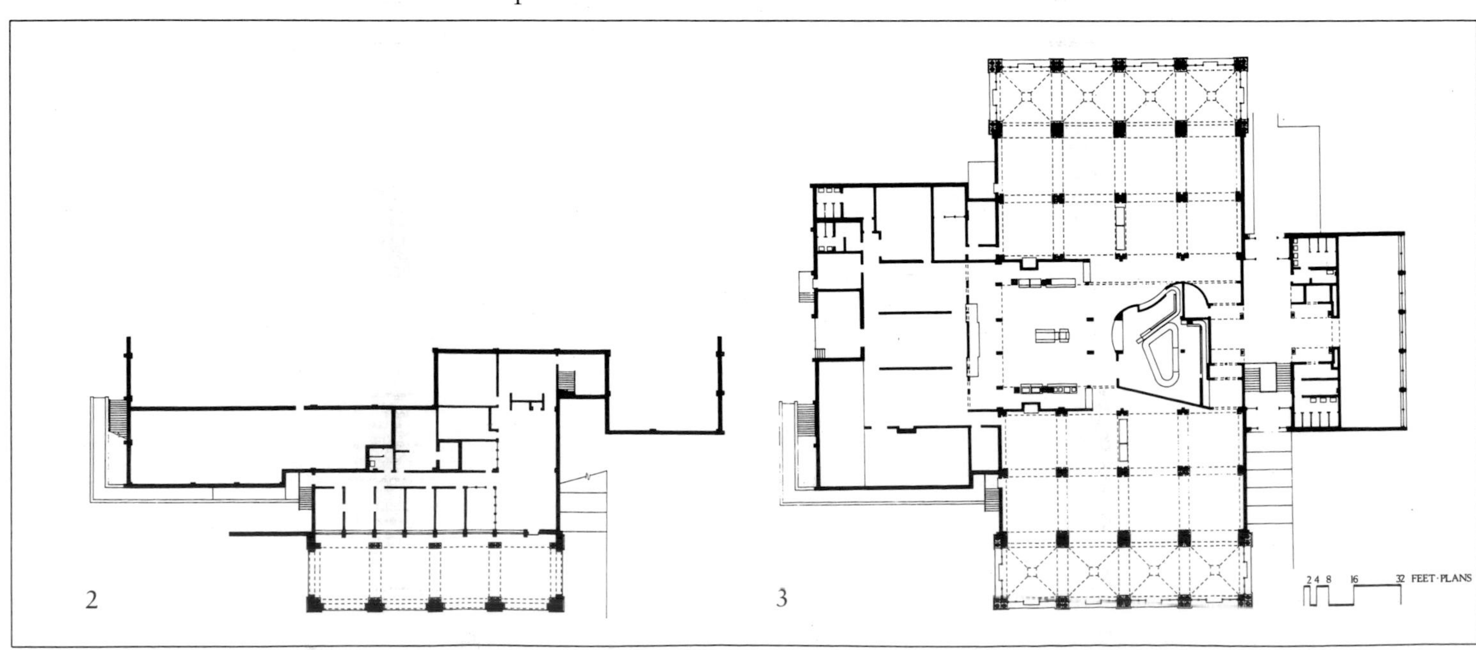

2

3

1.Site plan 2.Loggia floor plan 3.Ground floor plan 4.North elevation 5.East elevation 6.South elevation 7.West elevation

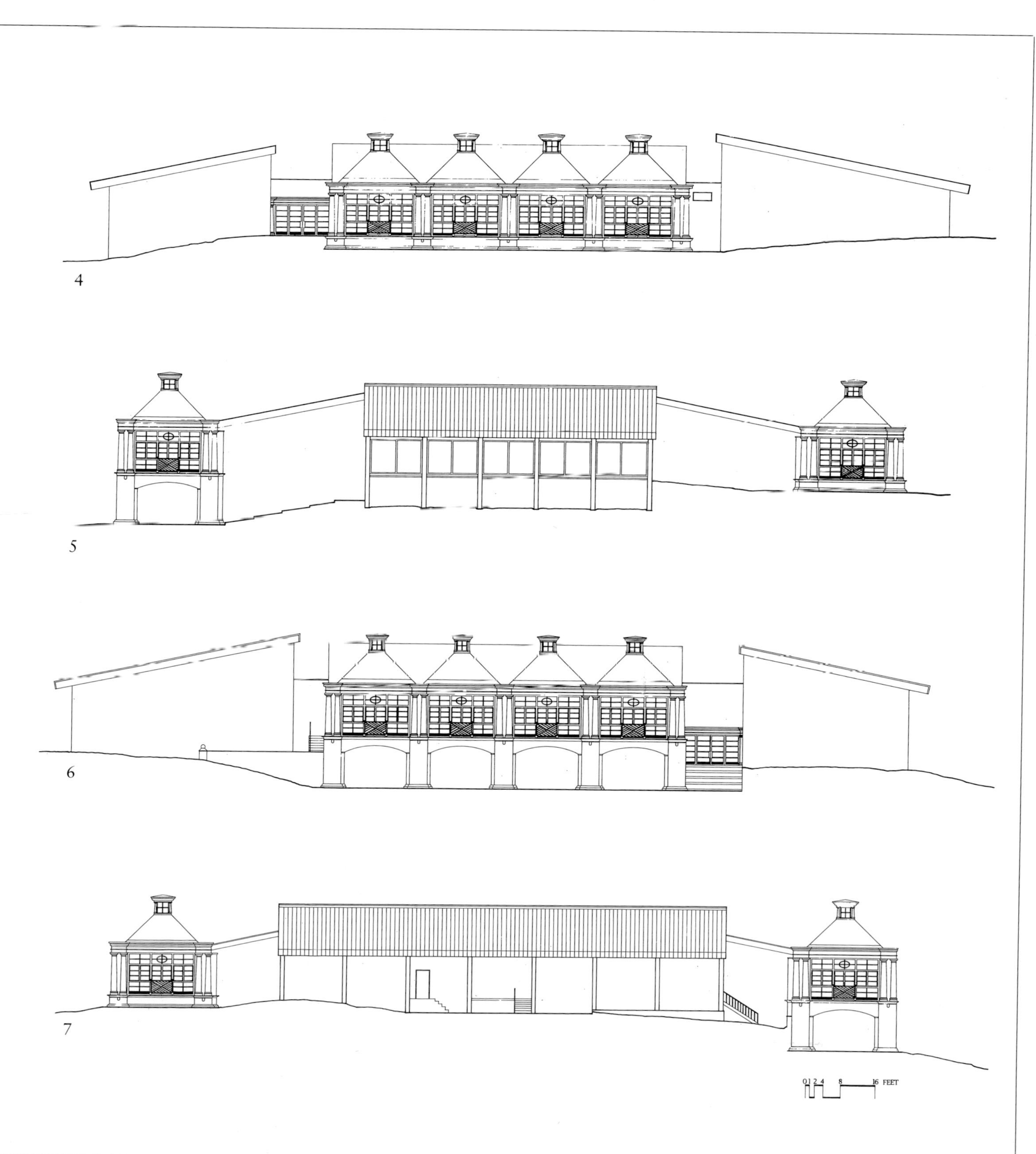

Sprigg Lane Dormitories
University of Virginia
Charlottesville, Virginia
1982–1984

The Sprigg Lane Dormitories at the University of Virginia, won in a state-sponsored, design/build competition, house 100 students in two red brick buildings. The site was bounded by a group of Georgian dormitories built in the late 1950s, by an historic nineteenth century landmark, Morea House, and by an exceptionally mature linden tree. The decision to form a courtyard defined by the buildings was made in order to reduce the bulk inherent in the program and to provide a private outdoor space, to foster in the residents a sense of community. The Georgian vocabulary used at Sprigg Lane reflects the character of the adjacent buildings and of Thomas Jefferson's campus. The bare-bones interiors were demanded by the program and state funding, but the quality of everyday life was enhanced by introducing a variety of room types and carefully shaping the common spaces, such as the living rooms and kitchens.

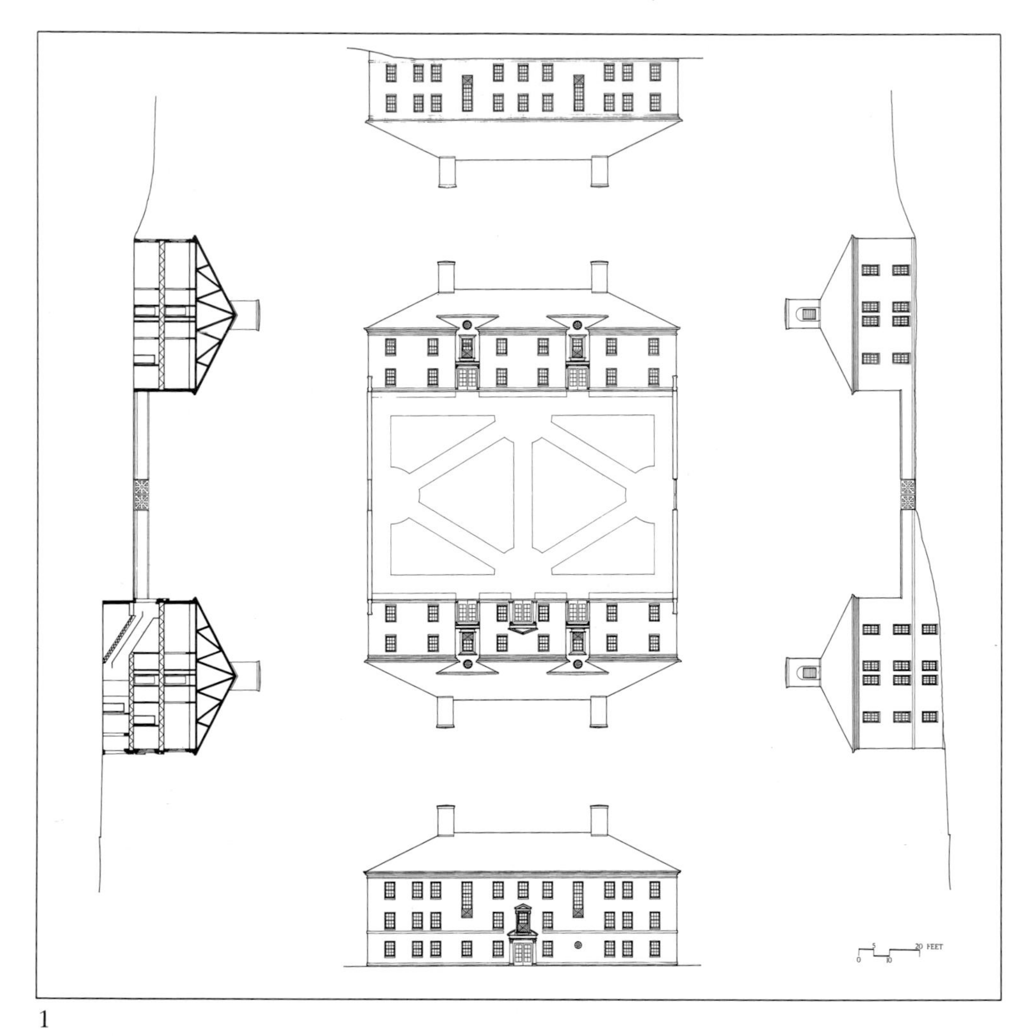

1

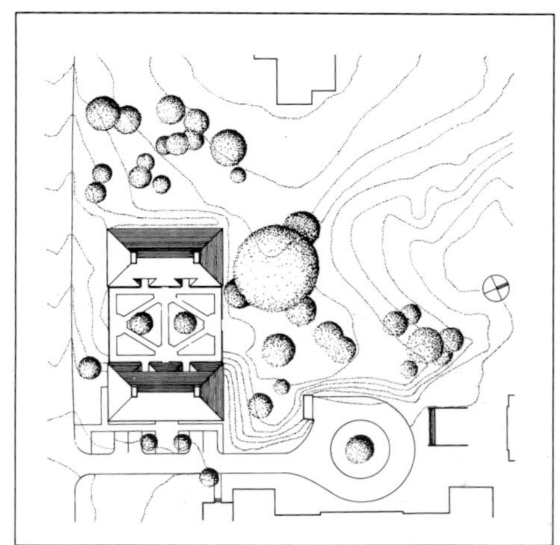

2

3

1.Elevations and section 2.Site plan 3.East facade 4.West dormitory, ground floor plan 5.East and west dormitories, second floor plan 6.East Building, basement floor plan 7.East Building, ground floor plan 8.East Building, partial elevation of entry facade 9.East Building, partial elevation of interior courtyard 10.Profile of entablature

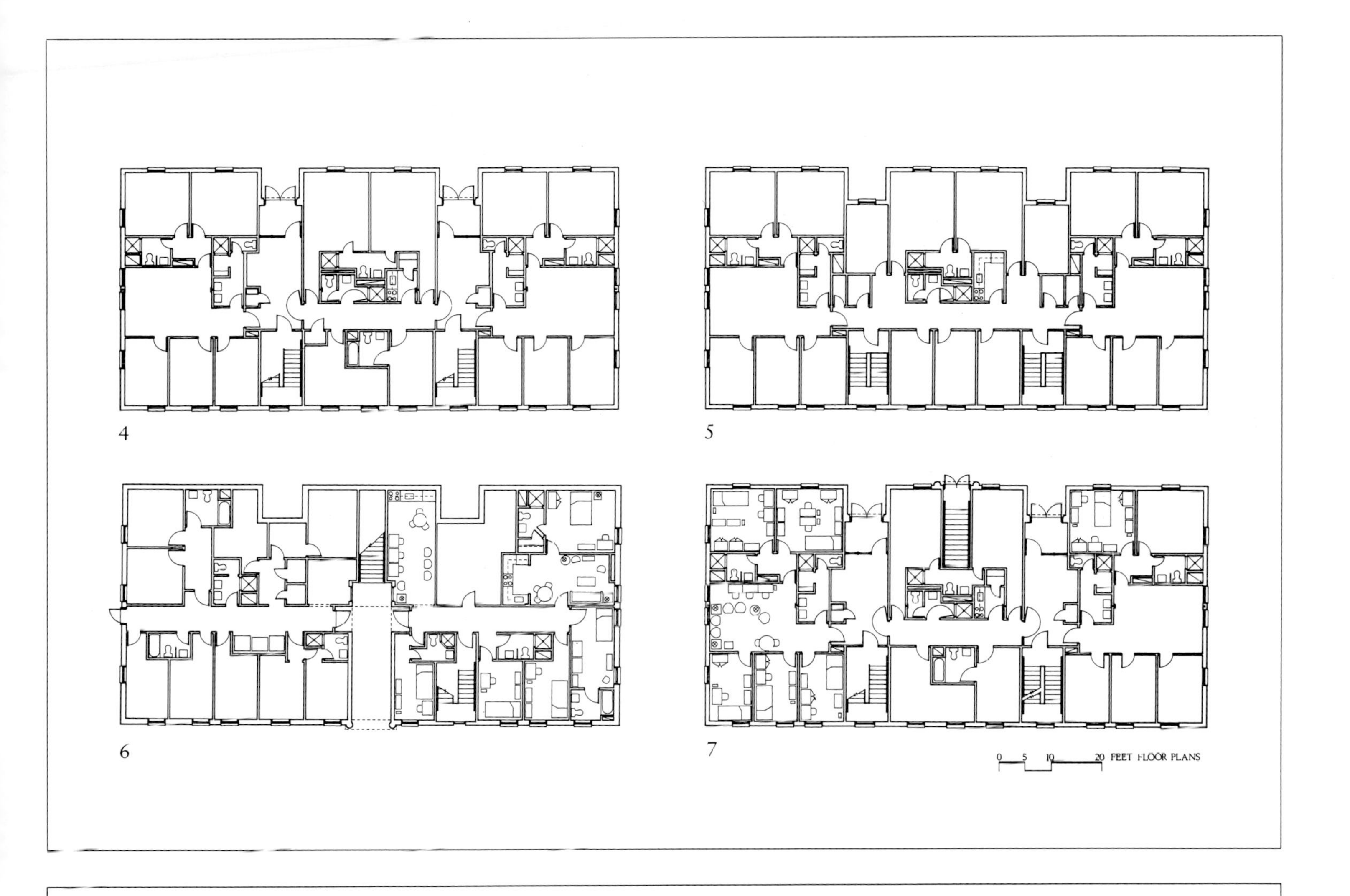

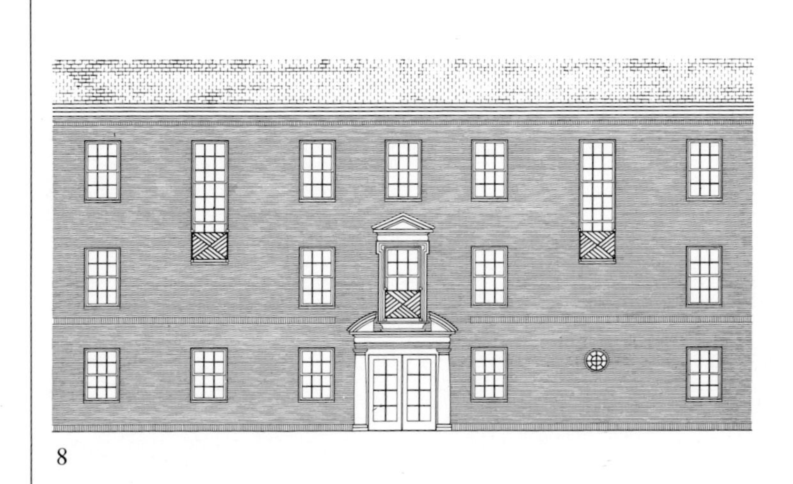

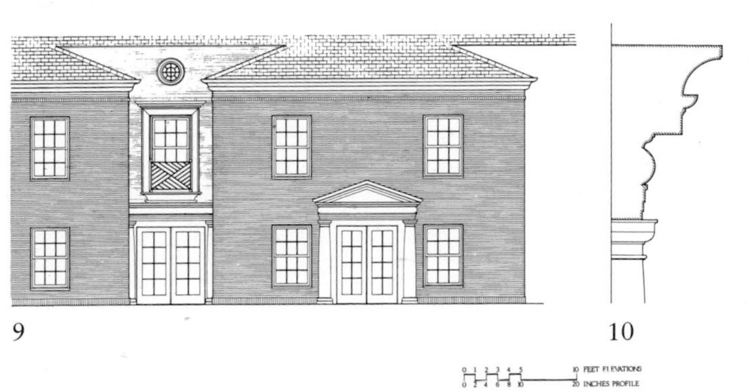

Classical Duplex Apartment
New York, New York
1980–1982

Located in a landmark building of the 1920s, this apartment represents a reconsideration of themes first established in an earlier duplex apartment of 1973–1974, whose raw space was comparable. Elements of the earlier design, such as the monumentally scaled stair, are here restudied in a richer vocabulary, one enhanced by the use of Classical language and a somewhat unorthodox palette of materials that includes a variety of marbles as well as glass block.

The entrance from the elevator leads directly into a vaulted vestibule, from which a view of the living room can be glimpsed across the stair landing. With the permission of the Landmarks Commission, the windows in the living room have been lowered and iron balconies projected out beyond the building's edge, at once enriching its facade and establishing a dialogue between the apartment, the park below and the city skyline beyond.

1

1. Entrance vestibule 2. Eleventh floor plan
3. Tenth floor plan

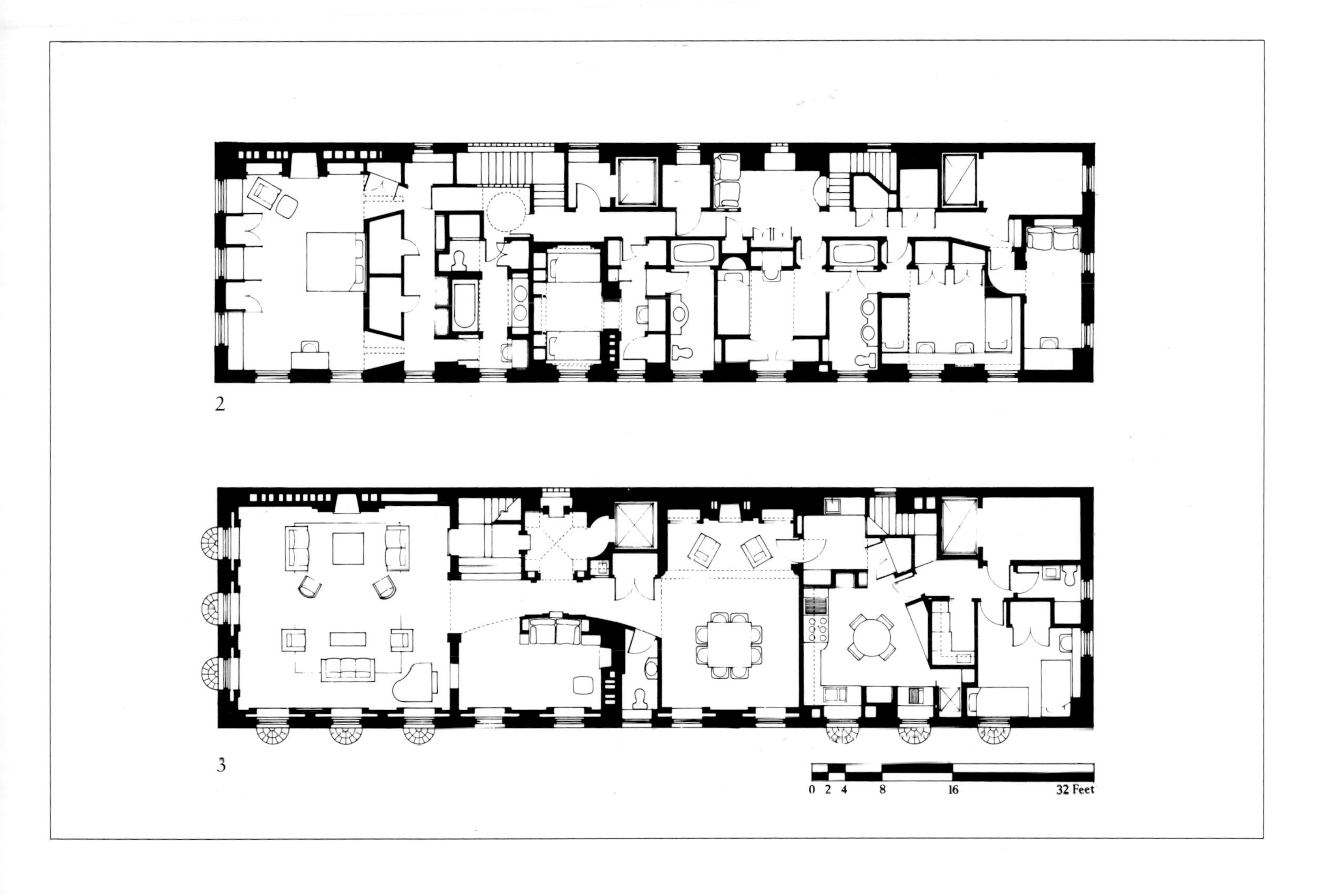

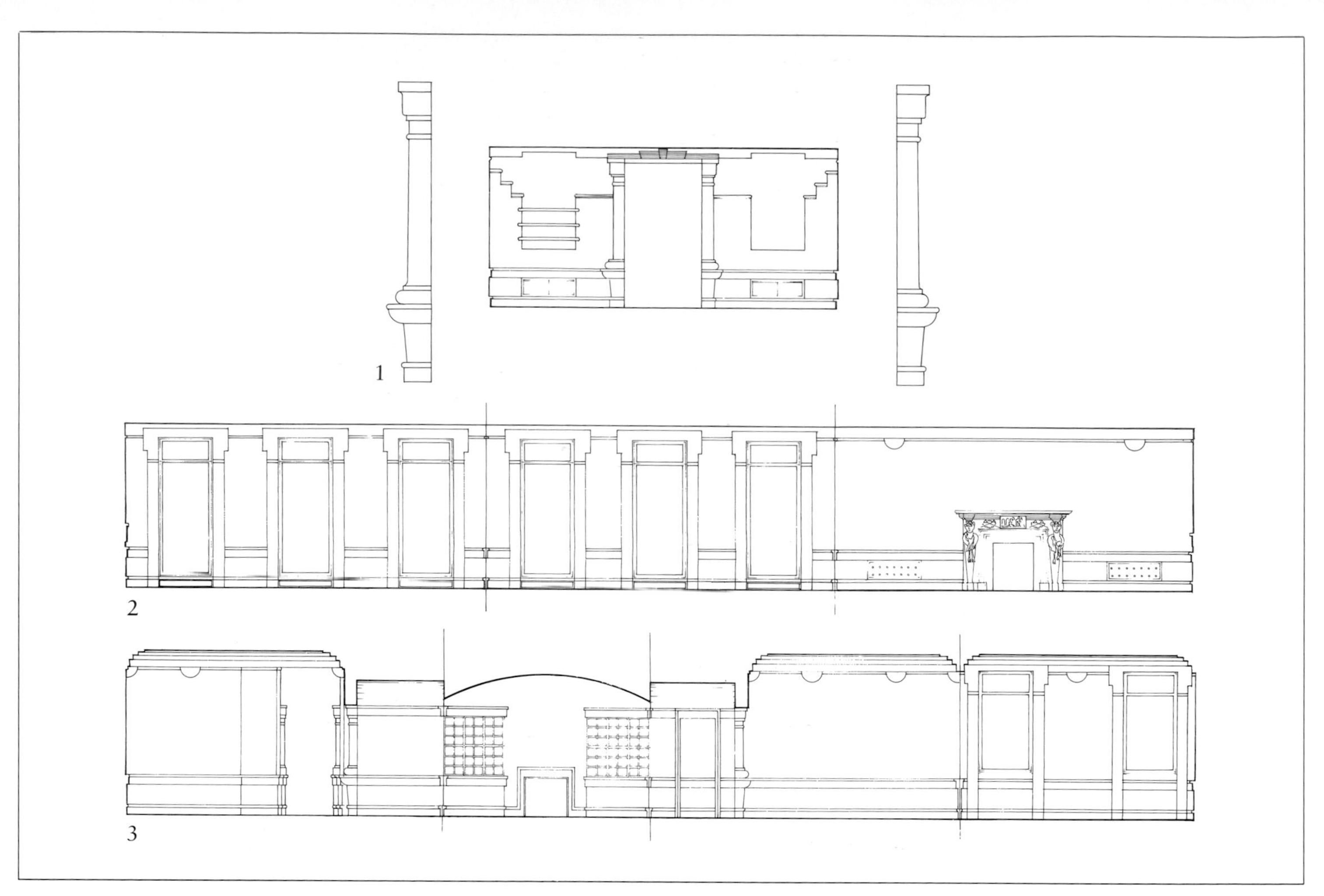
1
2
3

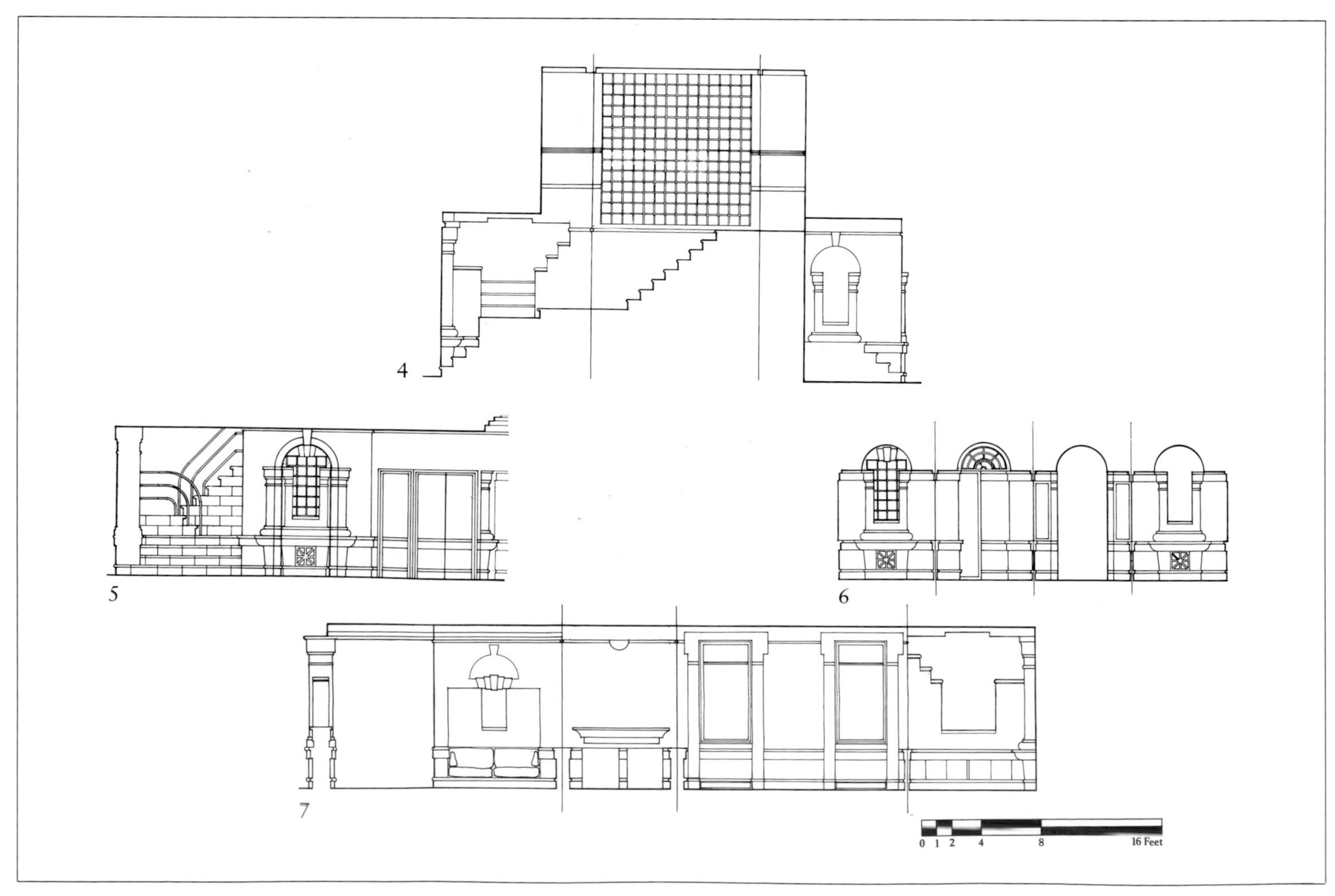
4
5
6
7
0 1 2 4 8 16 Feet

1.North elevation of living room 2.Living room elevations 3.Dining room elevations 4.Stair hall elevations 5.North elevation of hallway 6.Entrance vestibule elevations 7.Sitting room elevations 8.View of living room looking toward stair 9.View of dining room and central hallway

8

9

Residence in New Jersey
1982–1984

Facing the Atlantic Ocean, this Italianate villa takes its stylistic cue from the prevalent style of architecture produced on the Jersey Shore during its heyday in the early 1900s.

Located at the end of a cul-de-sac, the house and the landscaping form an enclosed motor court that protects the privacy of the grounds and contains the ocean view. The procession through the motor court into an oval vestibule gives way to a large room articulated with columns and a central groin vault to form three distinct bays for living and dining. A sitting room, kitchen, and pantry wrap around this main room. Upstairs the double-height groin vault separates the master bedroom suite from the children's bedrooms. All upstairs bedrooms face the view.

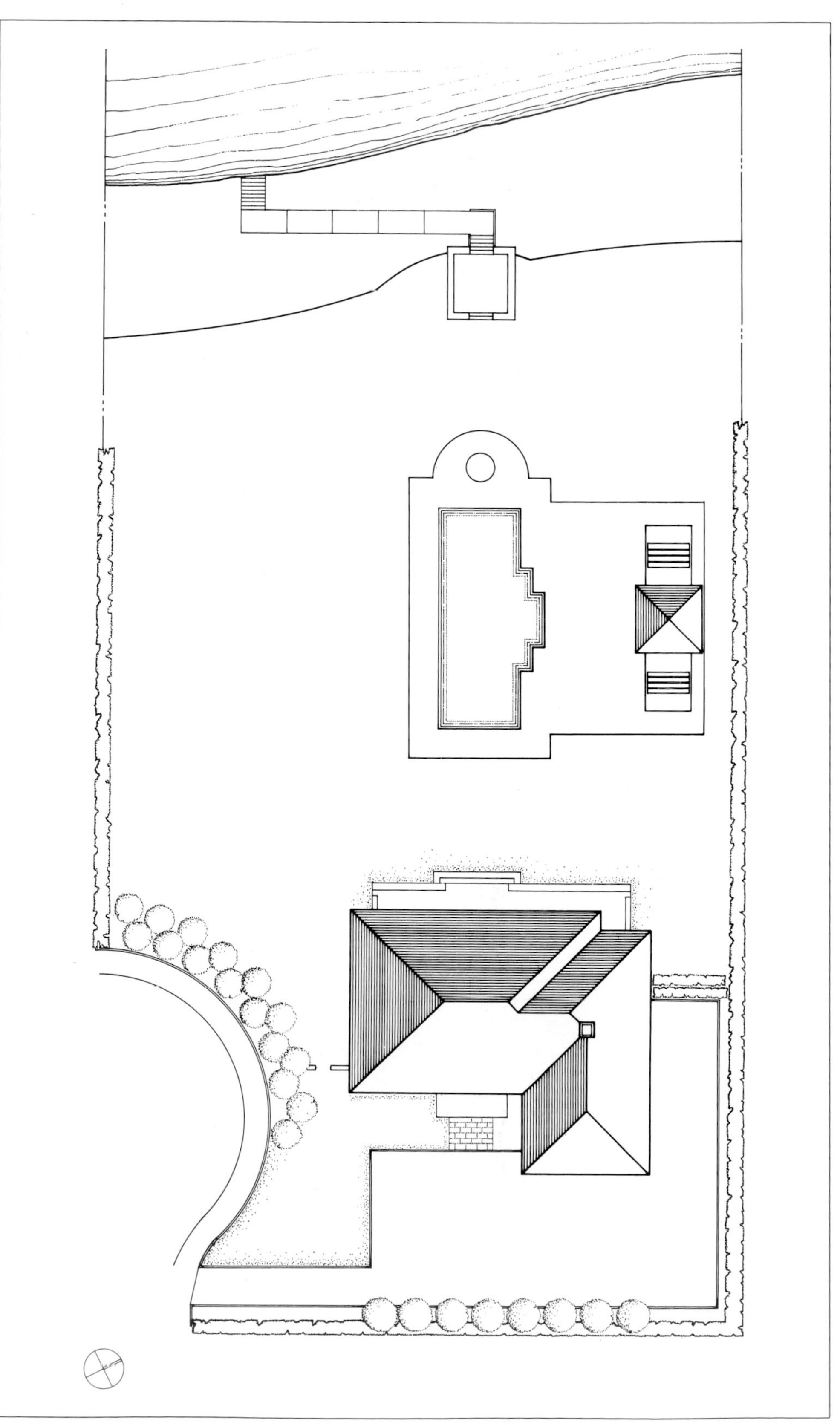

1

1.Site plan 2.West elevation 3.South elevation 4,5.Sections 6.East elevation 7.North elevation 8.Ground floor plan 9.Second floor plan

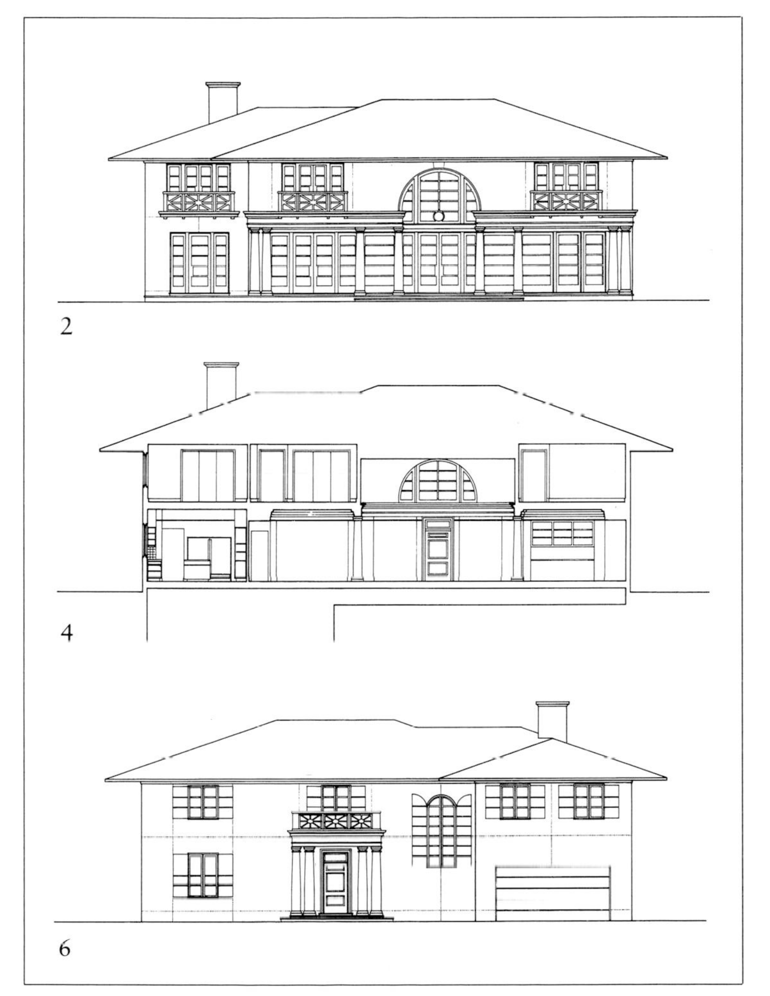

2

4

6

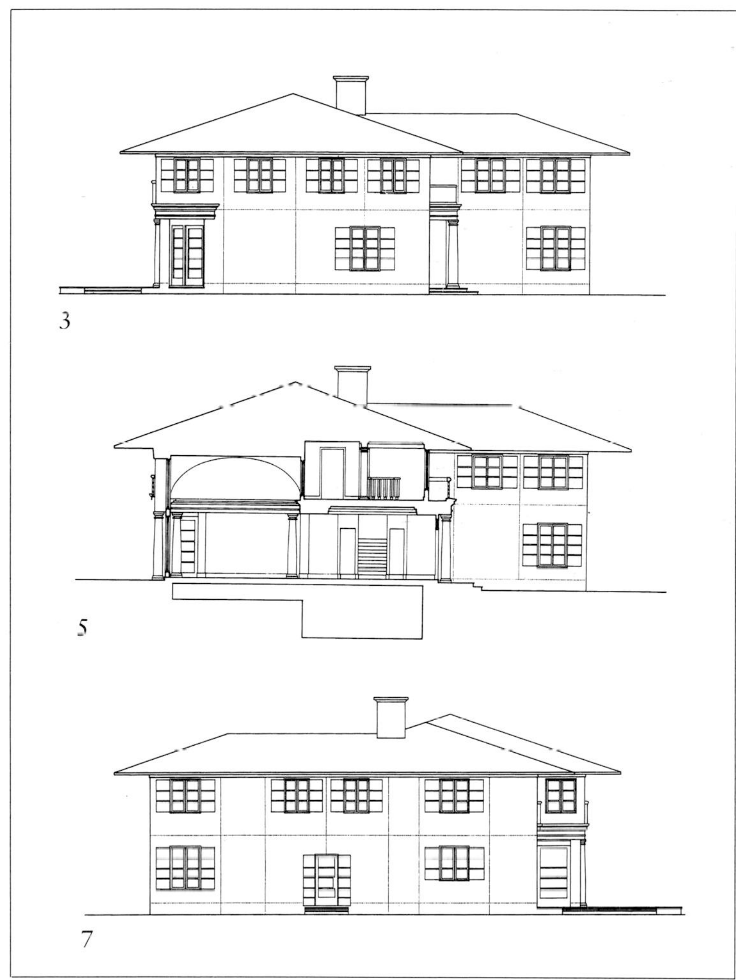

3

5

7

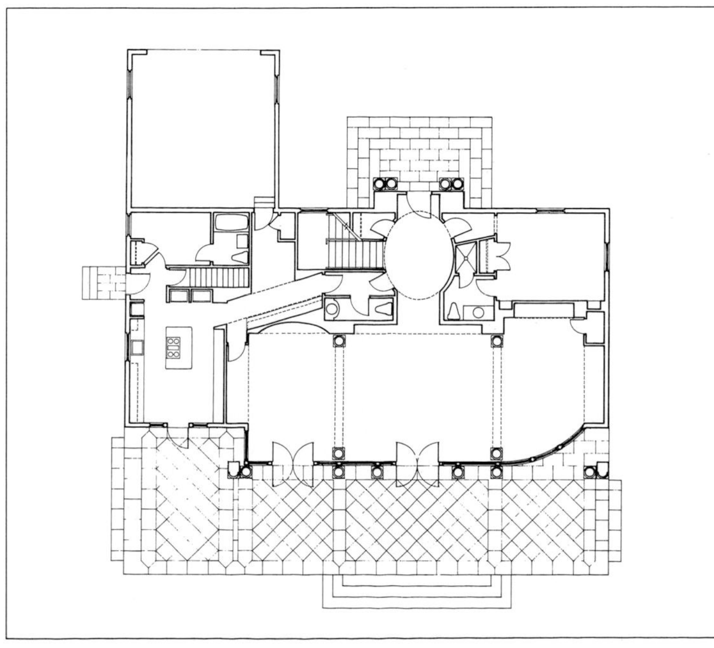

8

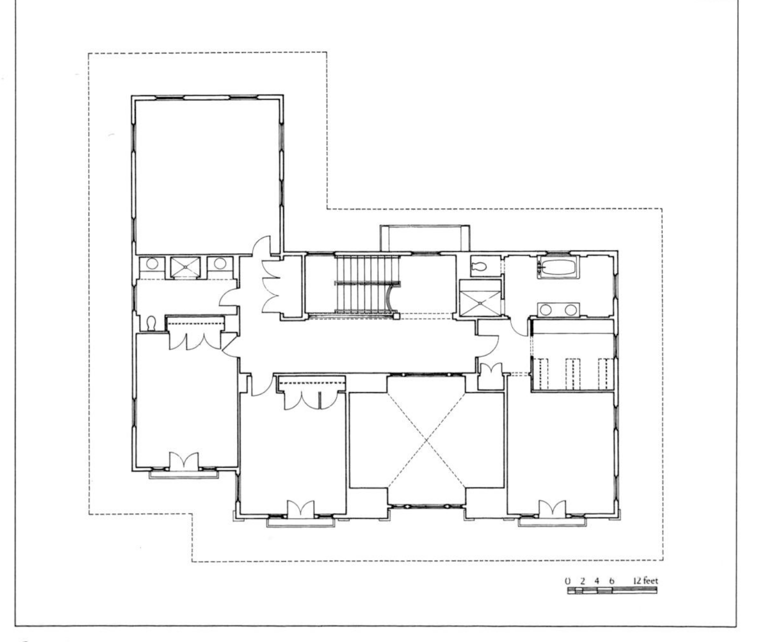

9

1.Partial view from the south 2.Front door
3.Foyer 4.Stair hall

1

2

3

4

2

1

1.Master bathroom 2.Rendering of preliminary dining and living area 3,4.View of the dining and living area 5.Living room 6.Living room west elevation

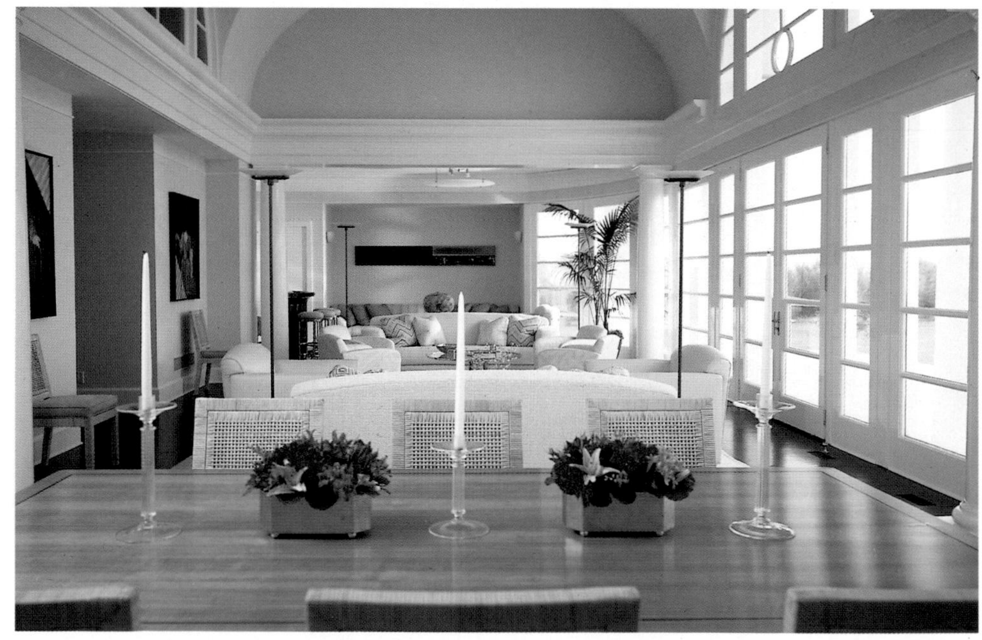

3

4

5

6

Houses for Corbel Properties
Cove Hollow Farm, New York

These houses represent a distillation of the planning and detailing precepts of Shingle Style architecture to a formulaic yet non-repetitive vocabulary, suitable for use by the speculative developer. Like many of the "builder's cottages" that proliferated in seaside resorts at the end of the last century, these houses imbue a simple overall mass with character and interest, through the judicious yet picturesque arrangement of subsumed porches, multi-paned double-hung windows, and shed-roofed dormers. In response to a program repeated in the various houses completed by the client, internal planning encourages a maximum degree of openness among the main rooms of the house and to the outdoors, without resorting to the undifferentiated spaces endemic to so much contemporary resort architecture.

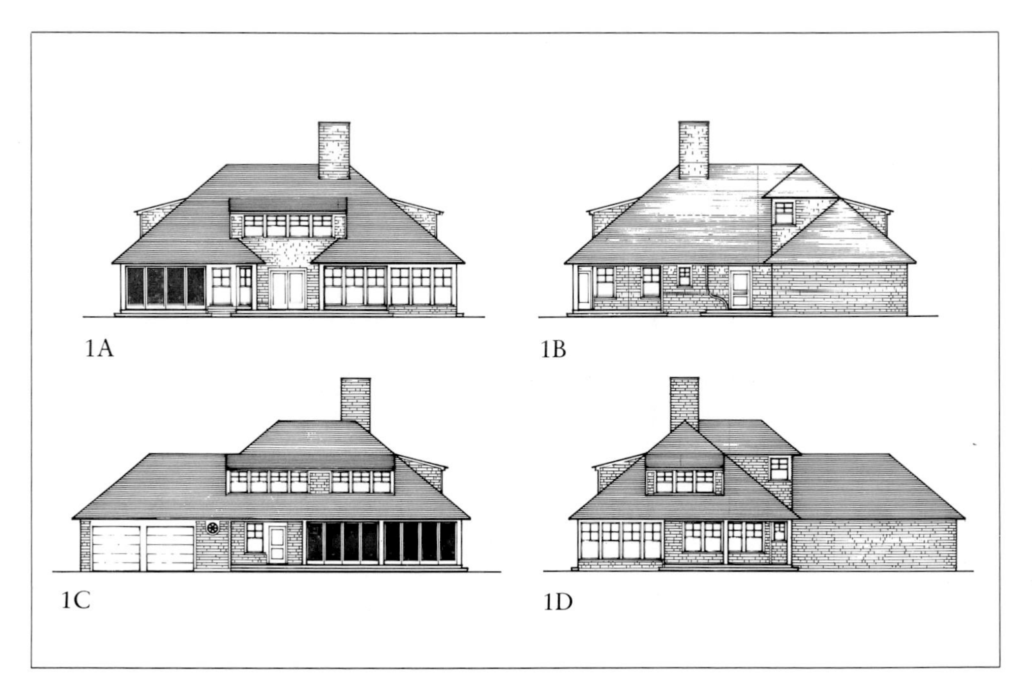

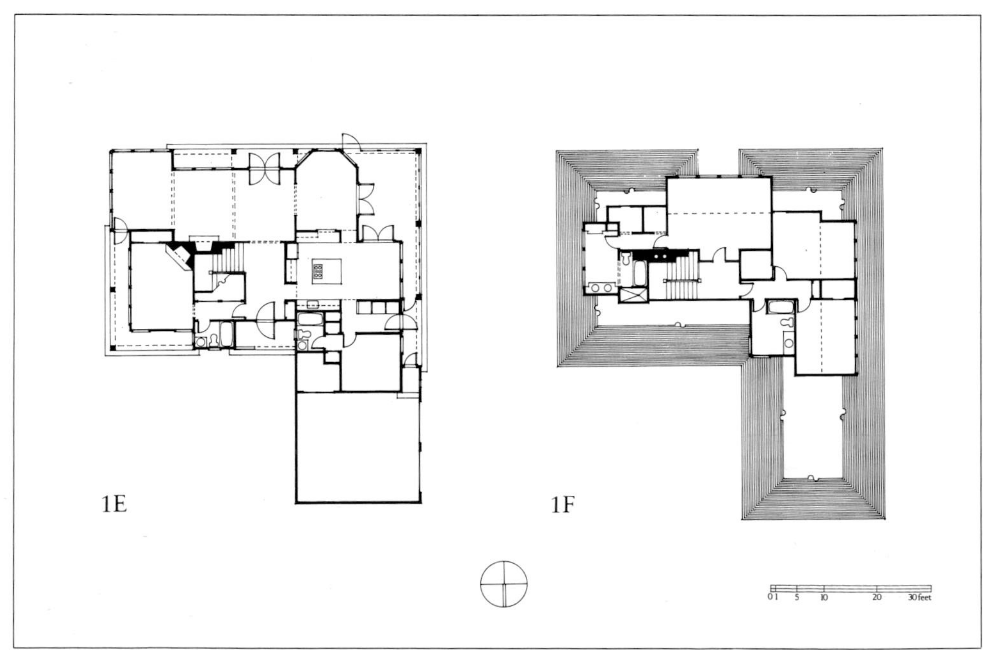

1.Lot 13, 1981–1982: A.South elevation B.North elevation C.West elevation D.East elevation E.Ground floor plan F.Second floor plan 2.Lot 14, 1983–1984: A.East elevation B.West elevation C.South elevation D.Section E.North elevation F.Second floor plan G.Ground floor plan 3.East facade

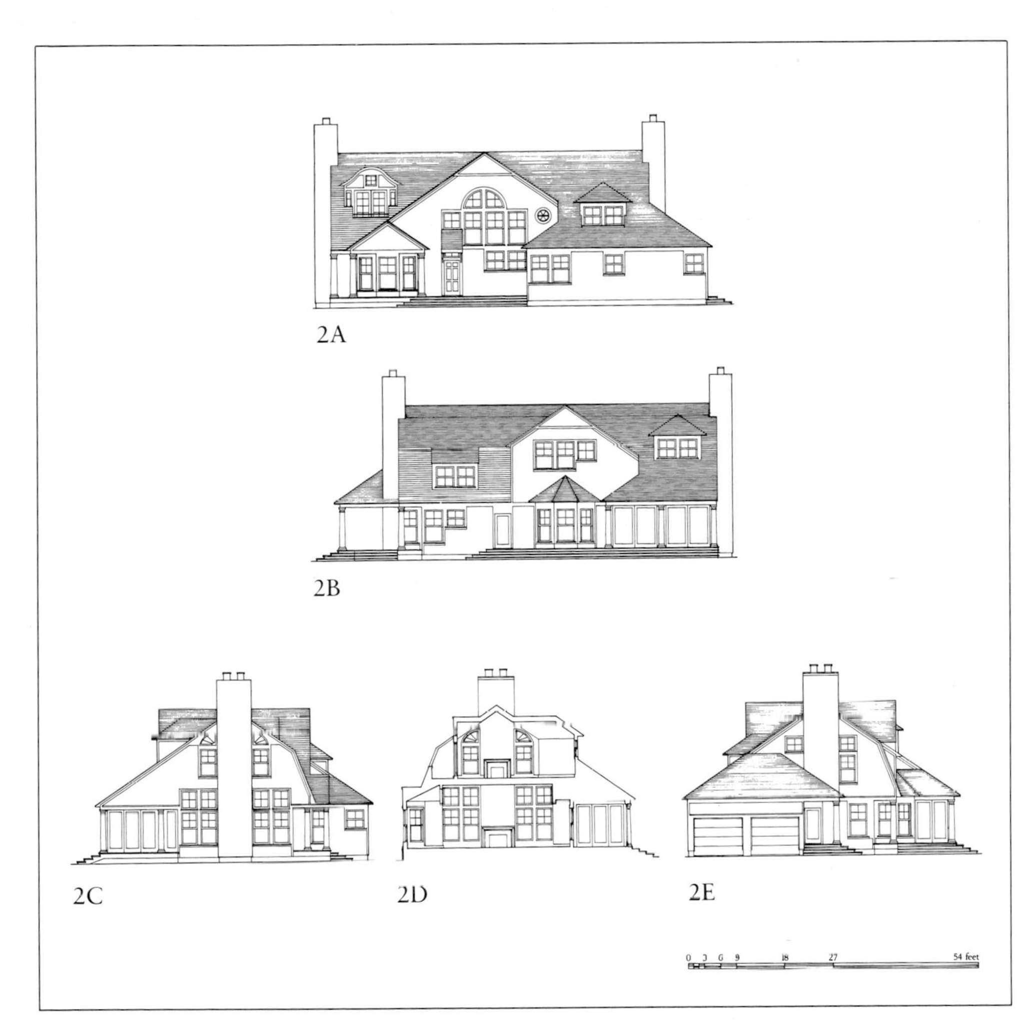

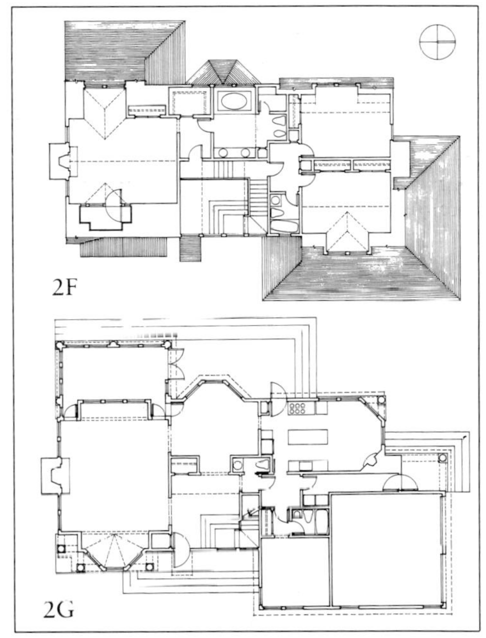

3

1.Lot 10, 1981–1983: A.South elevation B.North elevation C.West elevation D.East elevation E.Ground floor plan F.Second floor plan 2.View from the northeast 3.Living room 4.View from the southeast 5.Family room 6.Southwest corner

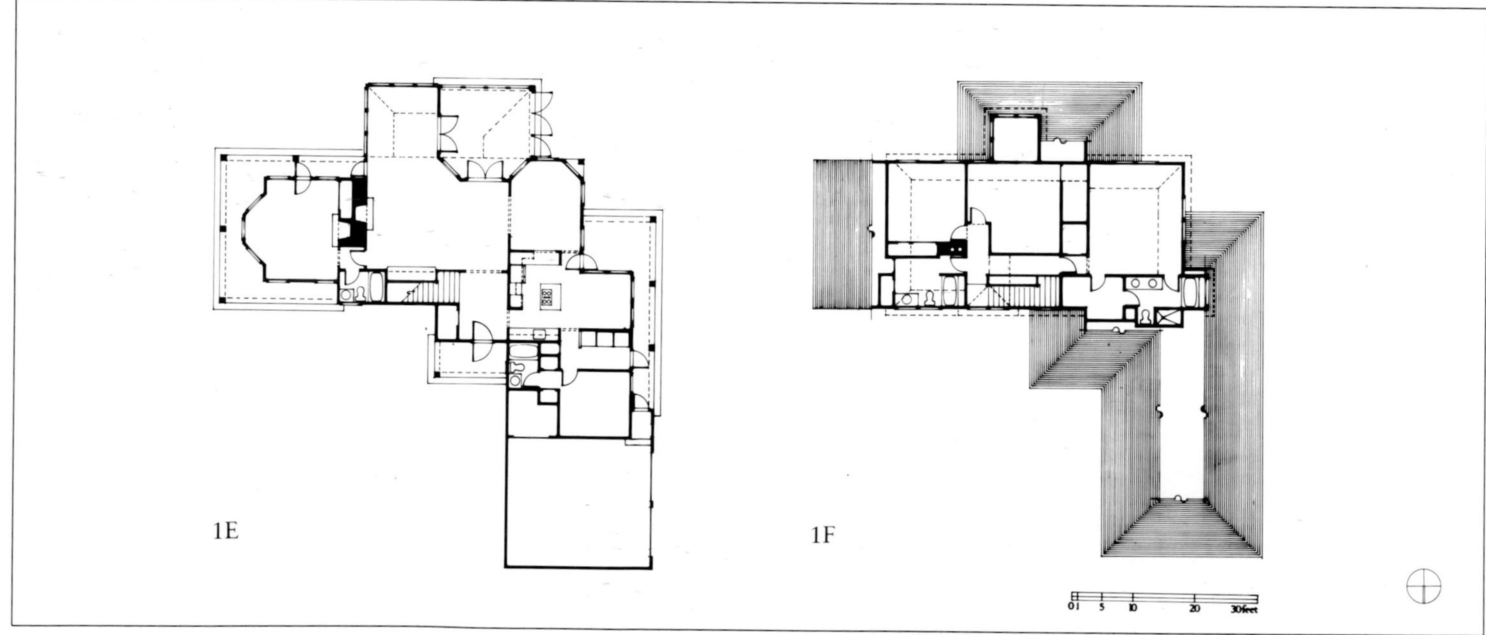

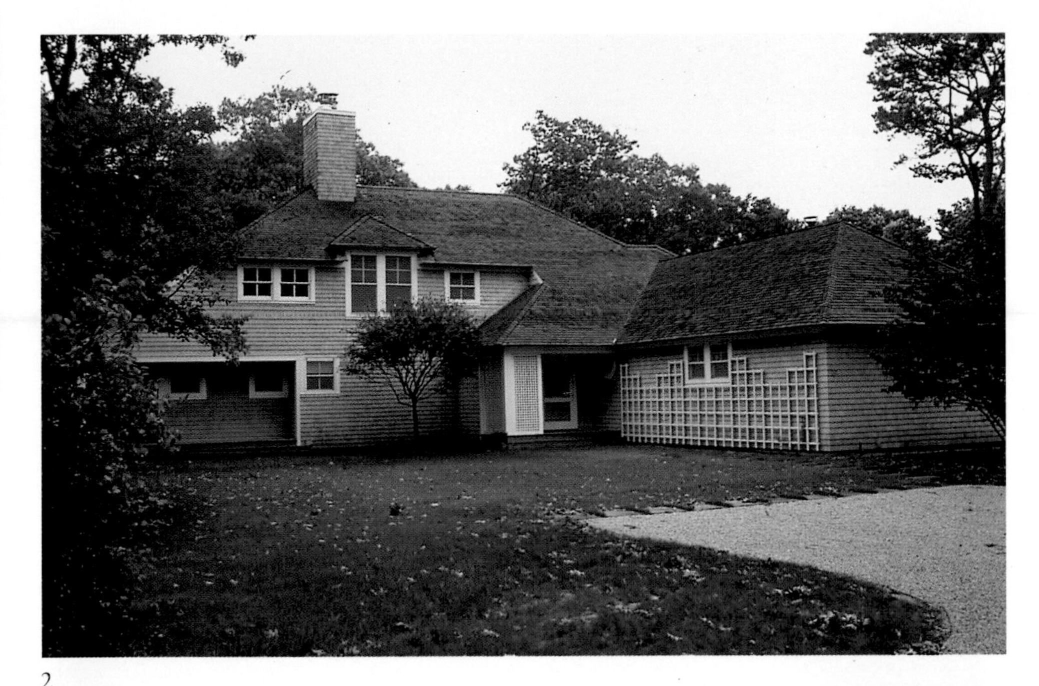

2

3

4

5

6

Schweber Apartment, The Dakota
New York, New York
1983

This apartment is located on the ground floor of the Dakota Apartments, a landmark structure by Henry J. Hardenbergh. The principal rooms of the original apartment's plan have been left unaltered, while the service and bedroom areas have been rearranged to accommodate the needs of the bachelor client. Pedestals supporting Gothic colonnettes and arches enliven a once banal hall connecting the foyer to the other end of the apartment. The kitchen has been relocated to the street side of the apartment while the bedrooms and baths are relocated to the quieter interior court side of the building.

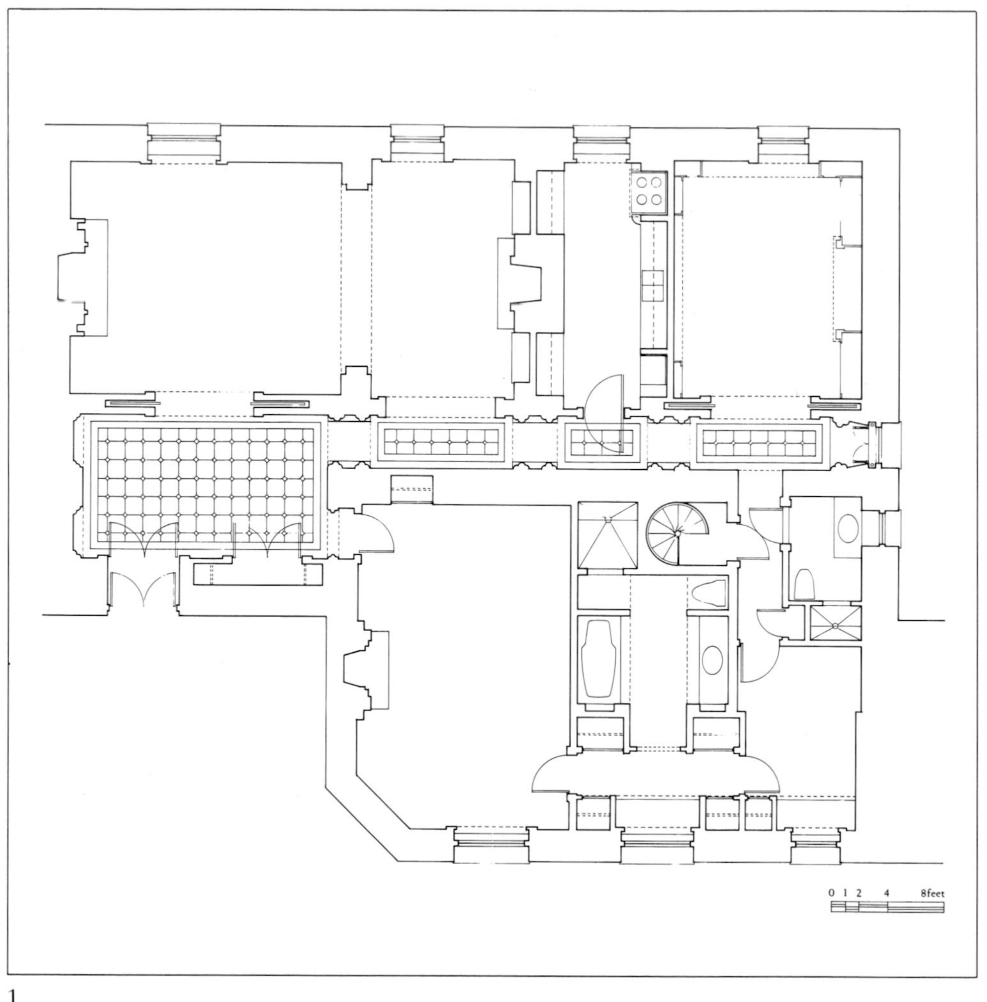

1

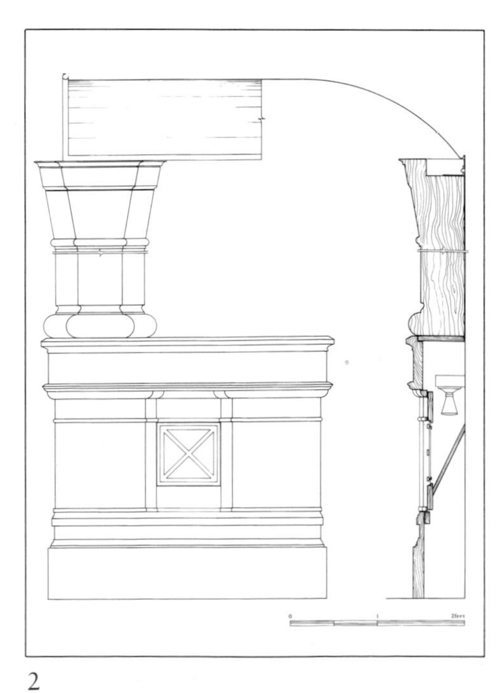
2

3

4

1.Floor plan 2.Detail of columns in gallery 3.View into dining room 4.View into media room 5.Foyer and gallery floor plan and elevations 6.Media room floor plan and elevations

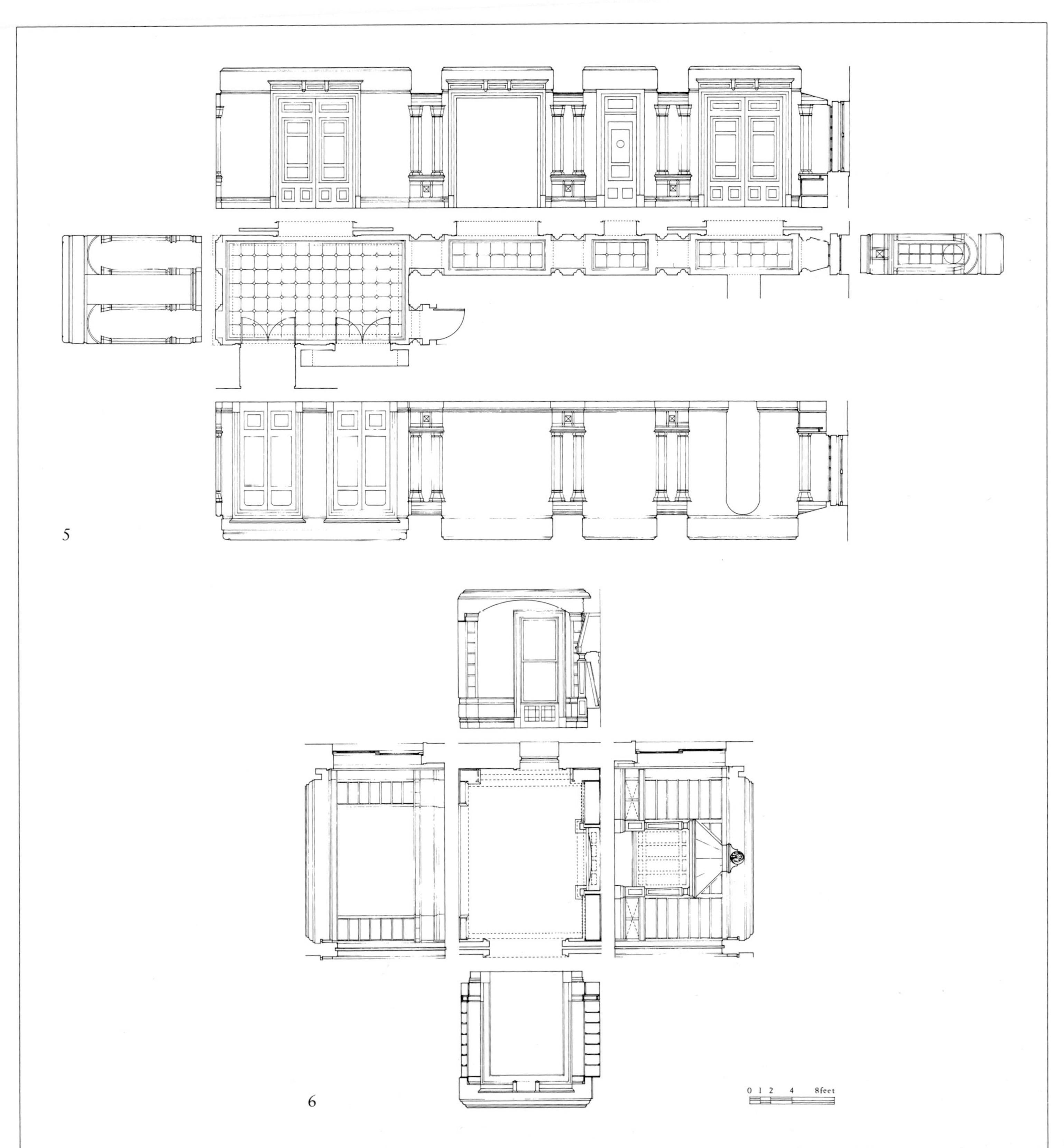

Point West Place Office Building
Framingham, Massachusetts
1983–1985

Point West Place is a 110,000-square-foot speculative office building located adjacent to the Massachusetts Turnpike on the site of a former truck depot. This five-story structure enters into a dialogue between Classicism and technological innovation. Up-to-date materials and technology are employed both to ensure practicality and efficiency and to reinterpret the forms of Classical architecture within a contemporary sensibility. The glass box of modern office buildings has been transformed through a judicious application of color and ornament to lend it a sense of confidence and dignity appropriate to its purpose. The building's clear geometrical form provides for flexible office space and gives it the large scale necessary to make a visual impact on motorists passing on the highway. The polychromatic striping of the glass curtain wall establishes a more human scale and suggests the pattern of traditional stone coursing. The colors chosen for the glass—rose and gray—establish a relationship with the pink granite balcony and entrance portico. The balcony overlooks the highway and serves as a symbol of habitation. The portico is part of a lavish entrance sequence which begins with a tree-lined court of honor that frames the building and gives it the atmosphere of a pavilion in the formal garden of a grand chateau. The temple front is an icon deeply rooted in the public imagination, suggesting permanence and dignity. Behind the portico, the curved shape of the monumental entrance hall is meant to draw the visitor inward. The lobby rises three stories through the building. Frankly theatrical, it transforms the act of entering the building into an event.

1.Site plan 2.West facade from the turnpike
3.East facade

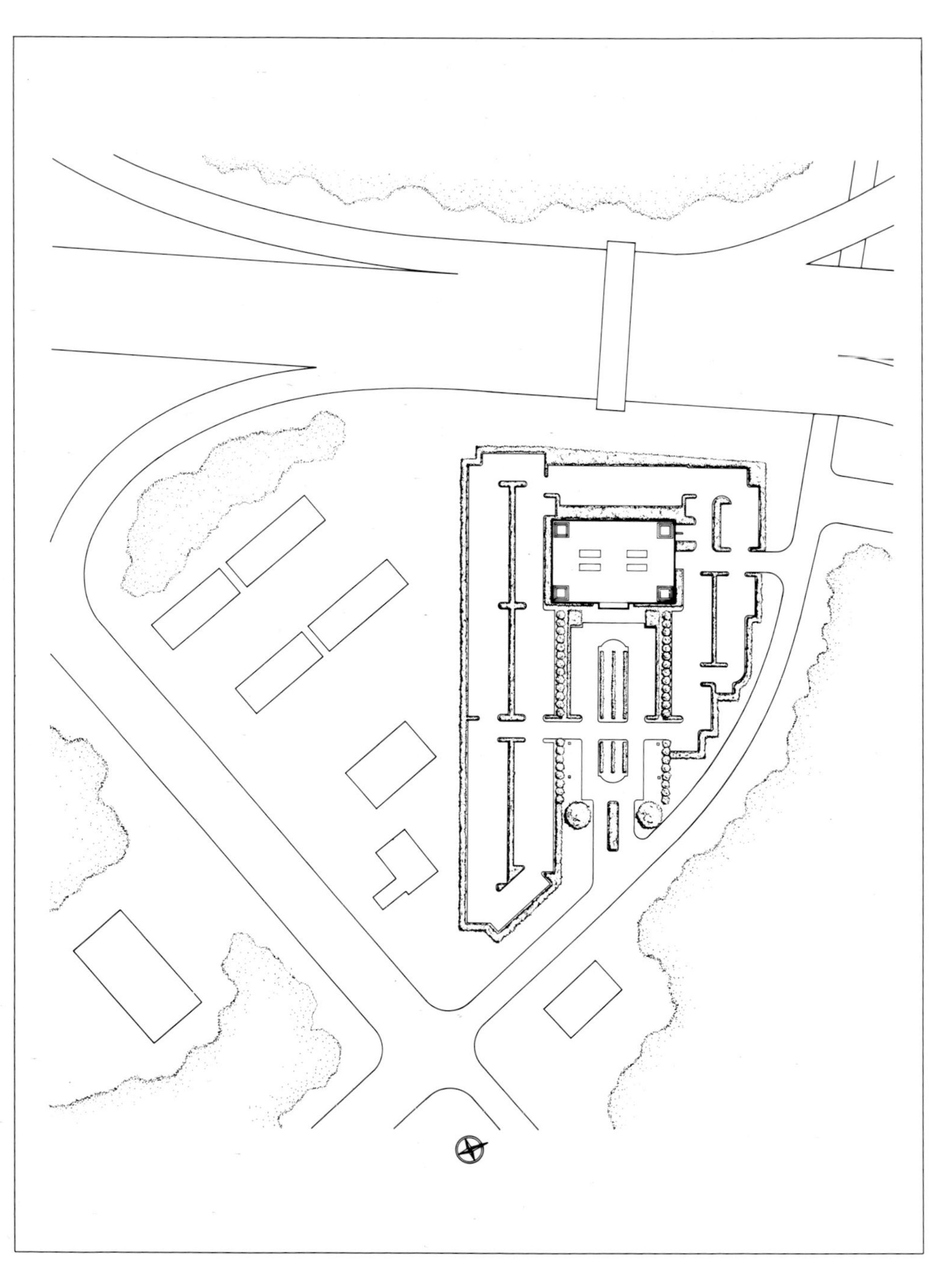

1

2

3

1.Fourth floor plan 2.Ground floor plan 3.West elevation 4.Section 5.East elevation 6.Study models of preliminary schemes 7.Oblique view of east elevation 8.Detail of northwest corner

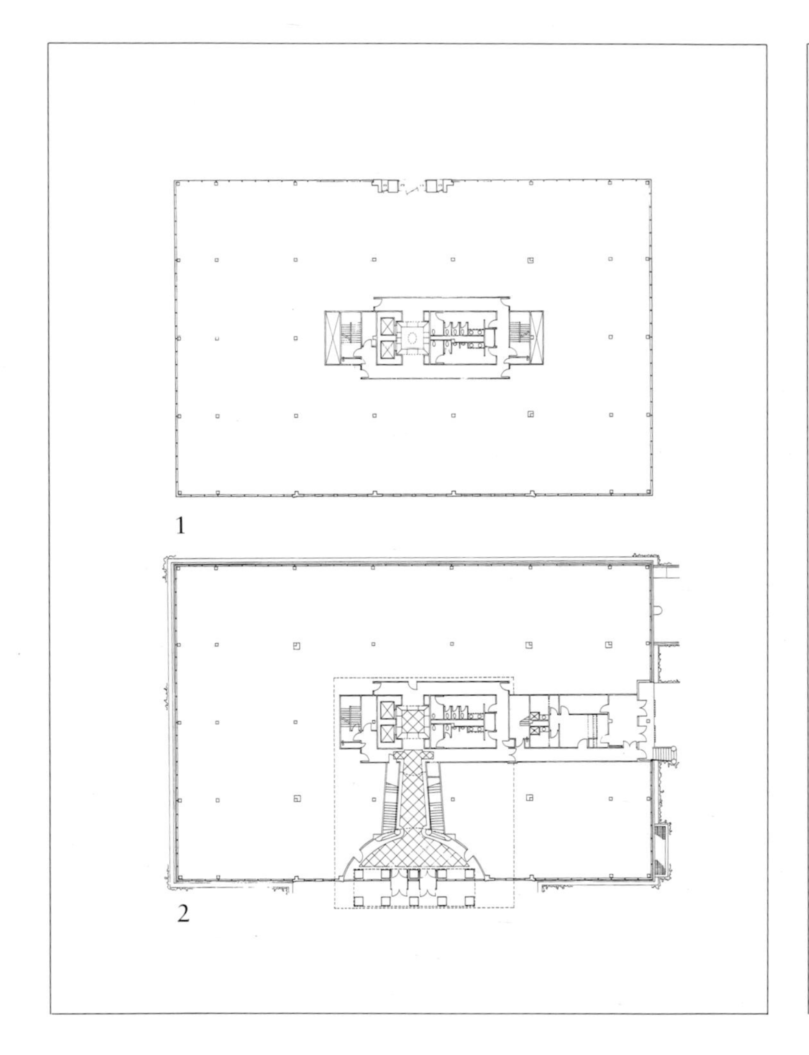

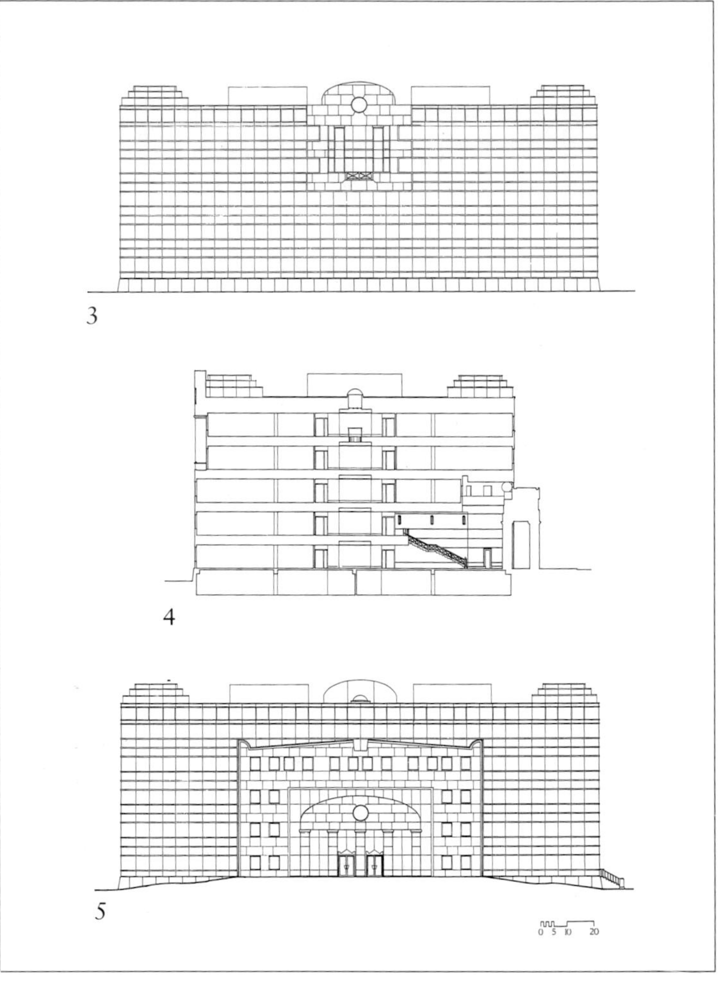

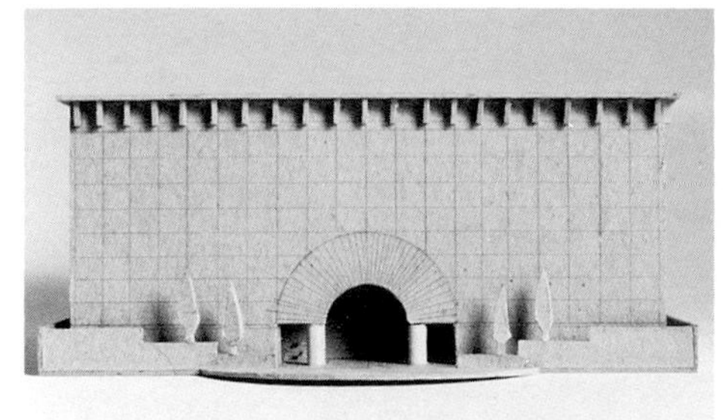

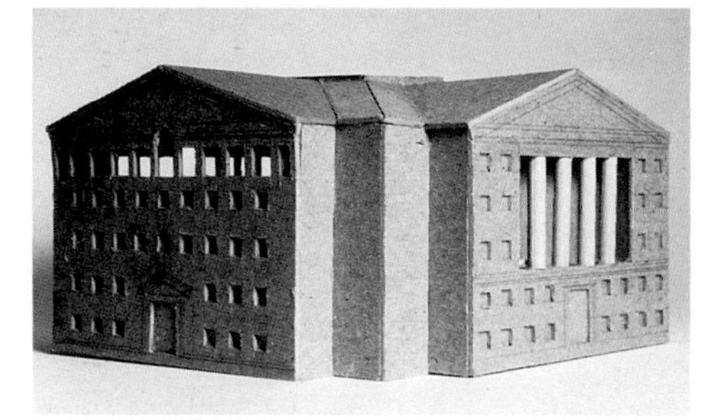

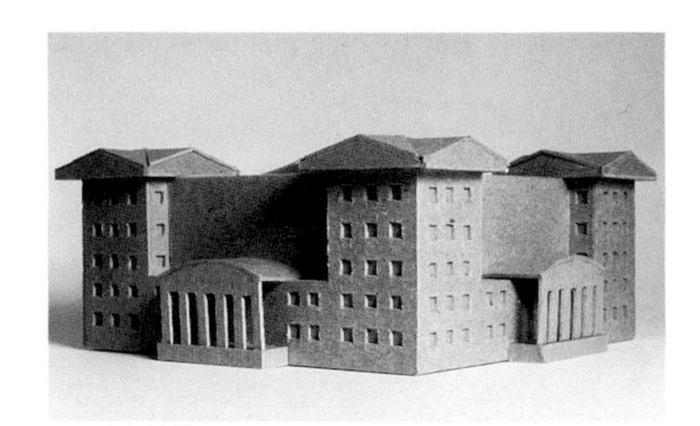

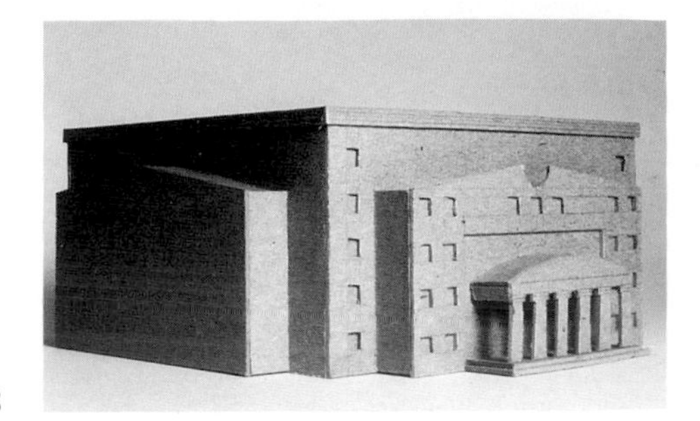

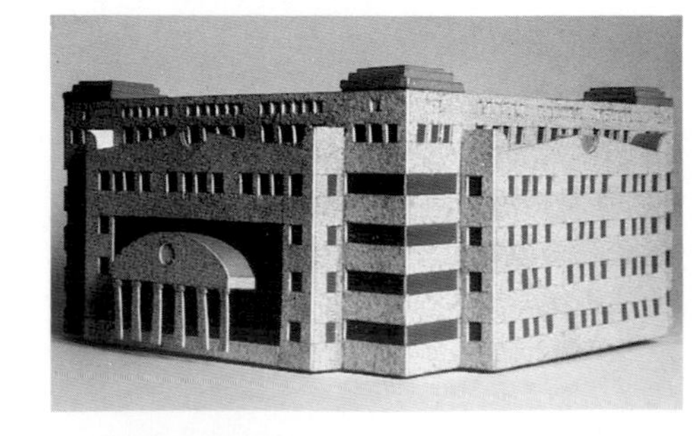

6

7

8

1. View of stair and elevator lobby
Opposite page: Partial view of lobby

1

1

1.Detail of entrance portico   2,3.The lobby

2

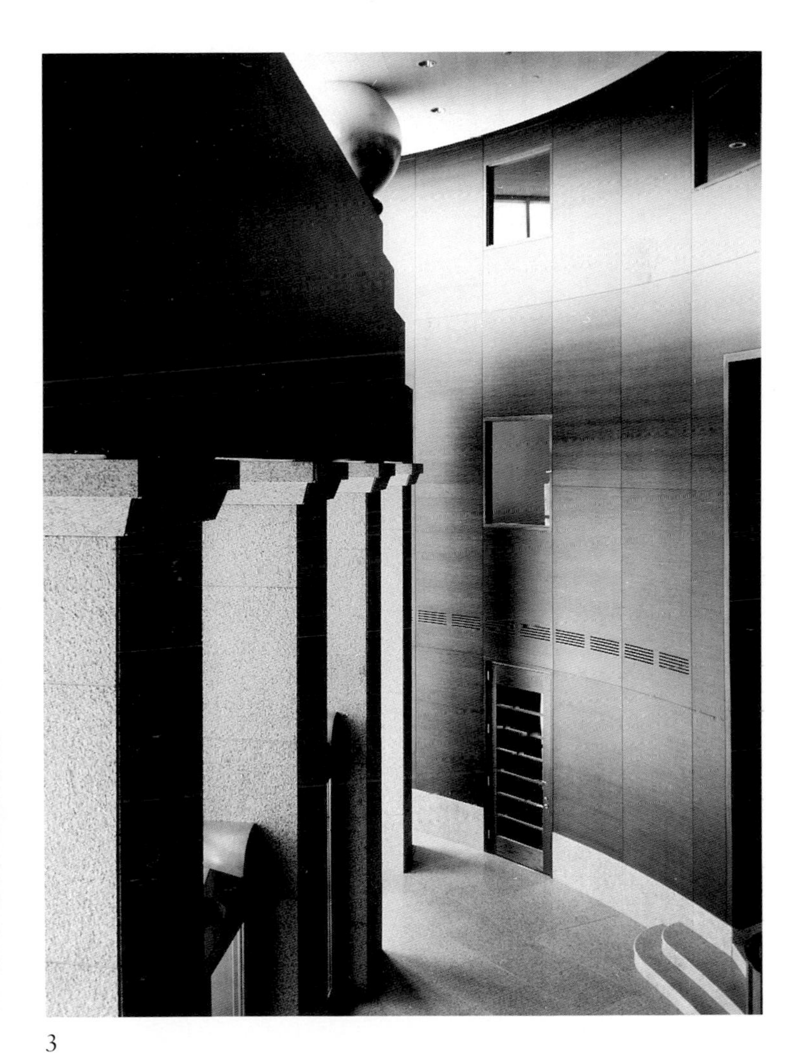

3

1

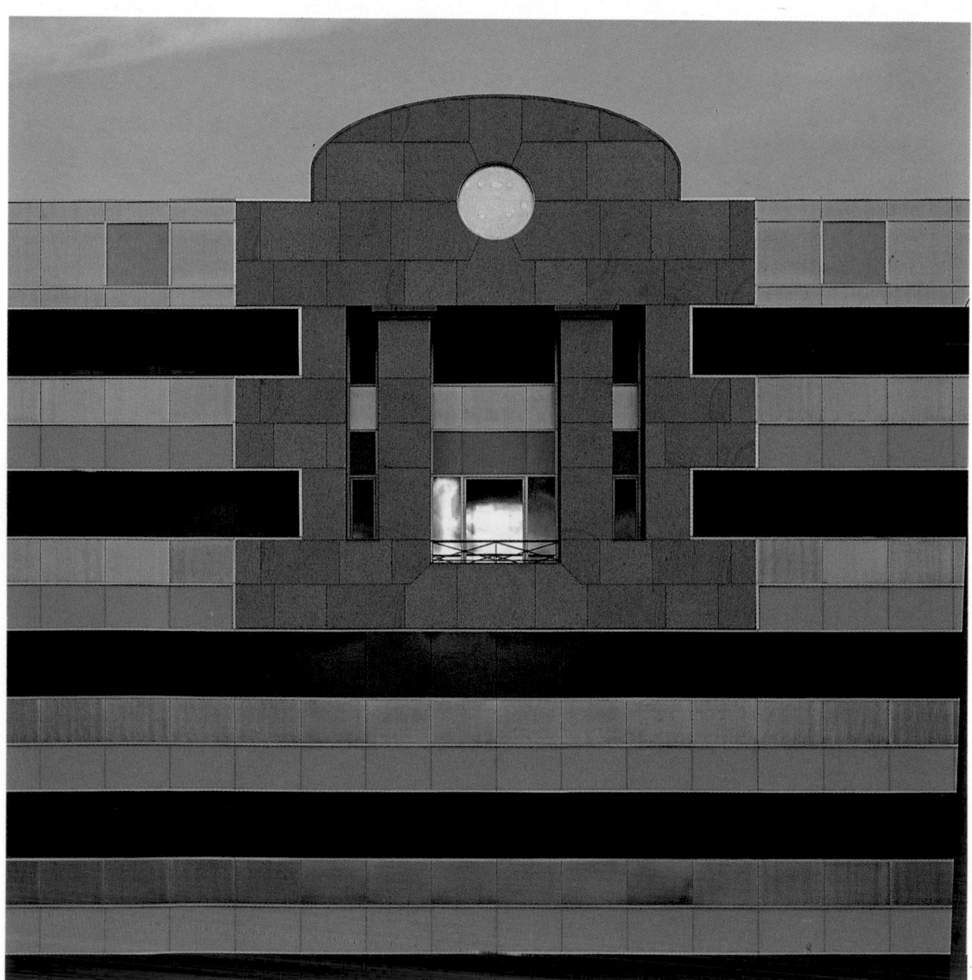

2

1. Entrance portico 2. Balcony on west facade 3. View from the east

3

Residence at West Tisbury

Martha's Vineyard, Massachusetts
1983

A small lot with strict height restrictions dictated the shape of this house. In response to the height restriction, the house is partially set into a hill. The "U" shape allows maximum square footage on the small lot while providing all the rooms with plenty of natural light. The house faces the preferred view to the north along the shore. The garage pavilion together with the house define a space to the south which is shaded from cold northern winds and thus provides a longer growing season for the flower garden.

Shingles and white trim recall the Martha's Vineyard Shingle Style vernacular. Asymmetrical towers and pavilions lend an informal additive quality to the sides and back of the house. The formal elevation composed of two symmetrical splayed wings with Serlian motifs dominates the expansive north yard and faces the preferred ocean view. The slanted dormer between the wings recalls the lines of local lighthouses.

Inside, a grand stair hall occupies the center of the house and connects all of the major downstairs rooms. A two-story octagonal library holds the southeast corner of the house, while a two-story kitchen gives the gourmet owner a grand, brightly lit space for cooking.

Large dormers allow for maximum use of the low second story. The master bedroom suite occupies the west wing and has views to the water on three sides. Due to the slope of the land, the master bedroom has access to ground level. Guest bedrooms are situated in the east wing. The upstairs corridor is relieved by balconies that overlook the double-height spaces below.

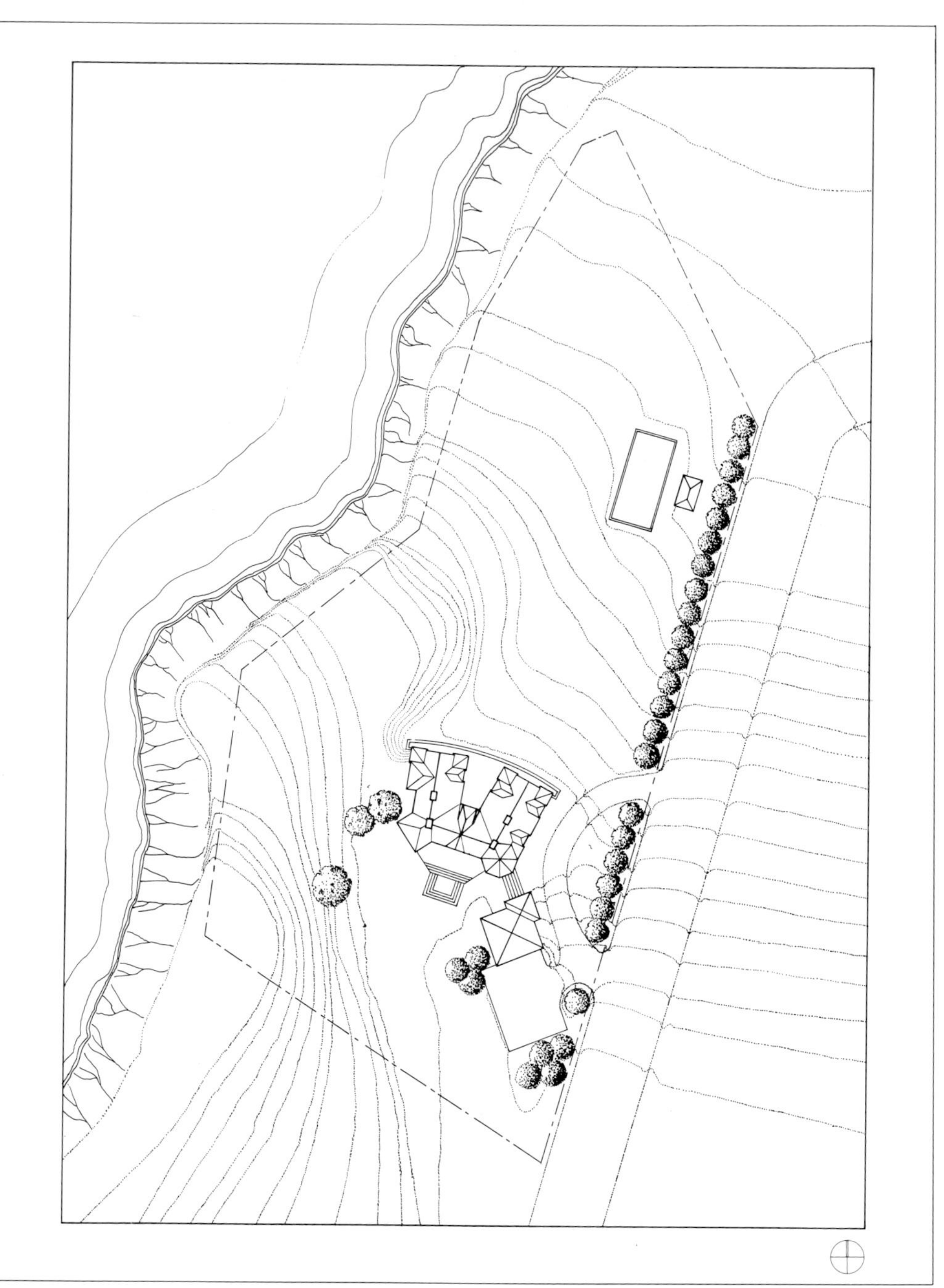

1

2

1.Site plan 2.Perspective view from the northeast 3.Aerial view of the model from the northeast 4.North elevation 5.East elevation 6.South elevation 7.West elevation 8.Second floor plan 9.Ground floor plan

3

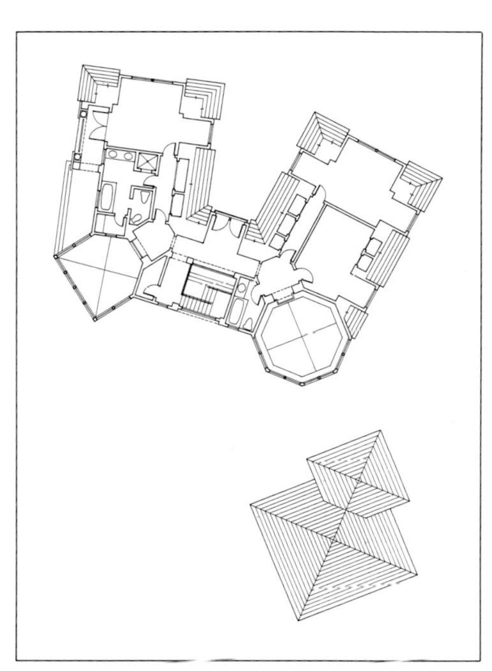

8

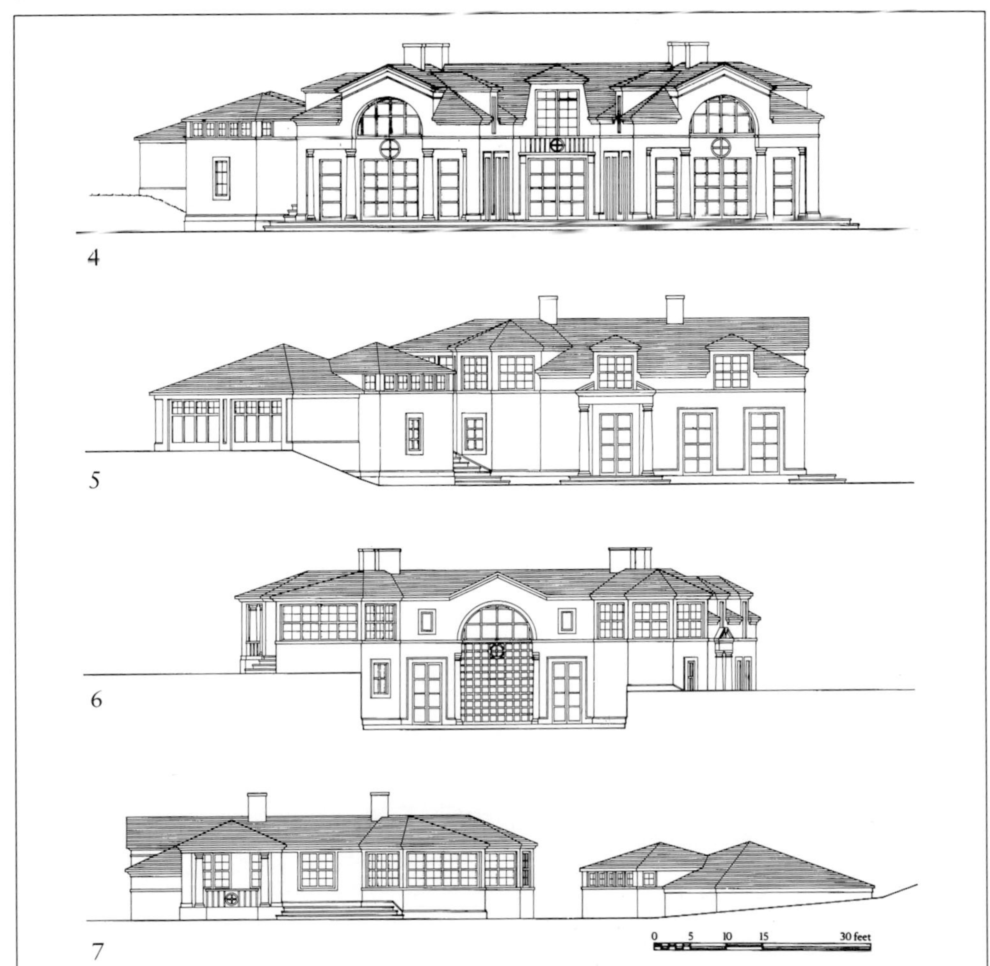

4

5

6

7

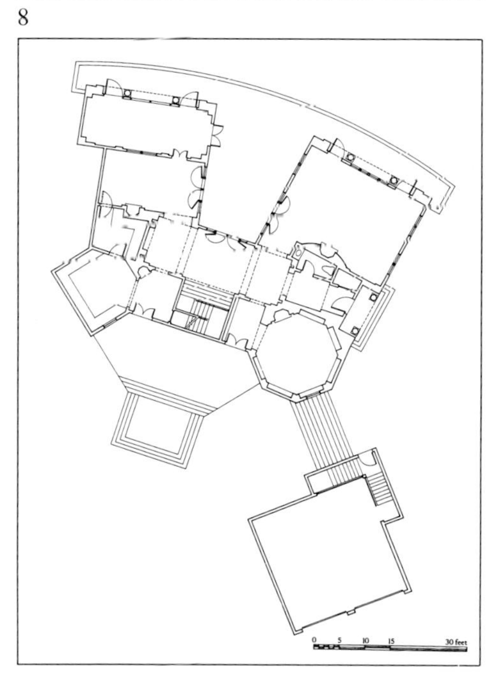

9

Residence at Hardscrabble
East Hampton, New York
1983–1985

Sited just below the crest of eastern Long Island's highest ridge, this house is approached along a winding drive that terminates in a clearly defined forecourt carved out of the woods. Upon arrival, one immediately confronts the broad, sweeping gable roof of the north facade. From this side, there is no indication of the impressive panorama beyond to the south, and only upon entering the main living areas is the view revealed. Accordingly, the planar aspect of the north elevation is juxtaposed with the more articulated veranda and screened porch along the south facade. This layering of the house from north to south is developed in the plan by locating service areas along the entrance facade, allowing the principal living spaces to open to the light and view.

In section, the house steps with the steep slope of the grade. Entry is to the middle floor, where the more public areas are located. From here, one descends to the lower floor, where guest and children's bedrooms are carved into the hill, or ascends to the master suite tucked under the expansive roof.

The dark green painted trim and the weathered red cedar shingles of the walls and roof allow the house to blend into the landscape. Granite at the exterior walls establishes the lower floor as a stable base, anchoring the building firmly to the ground while reducing the apparent size of this three-story house, allowing it to appear as a simple rustic cottage set on a base of rough stone.

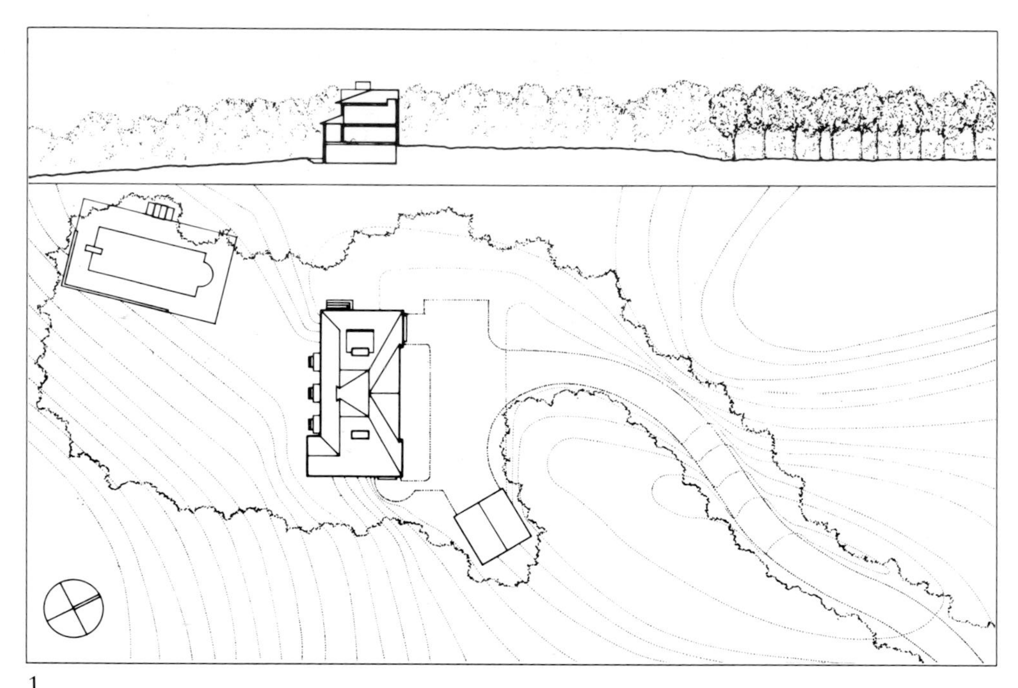

1

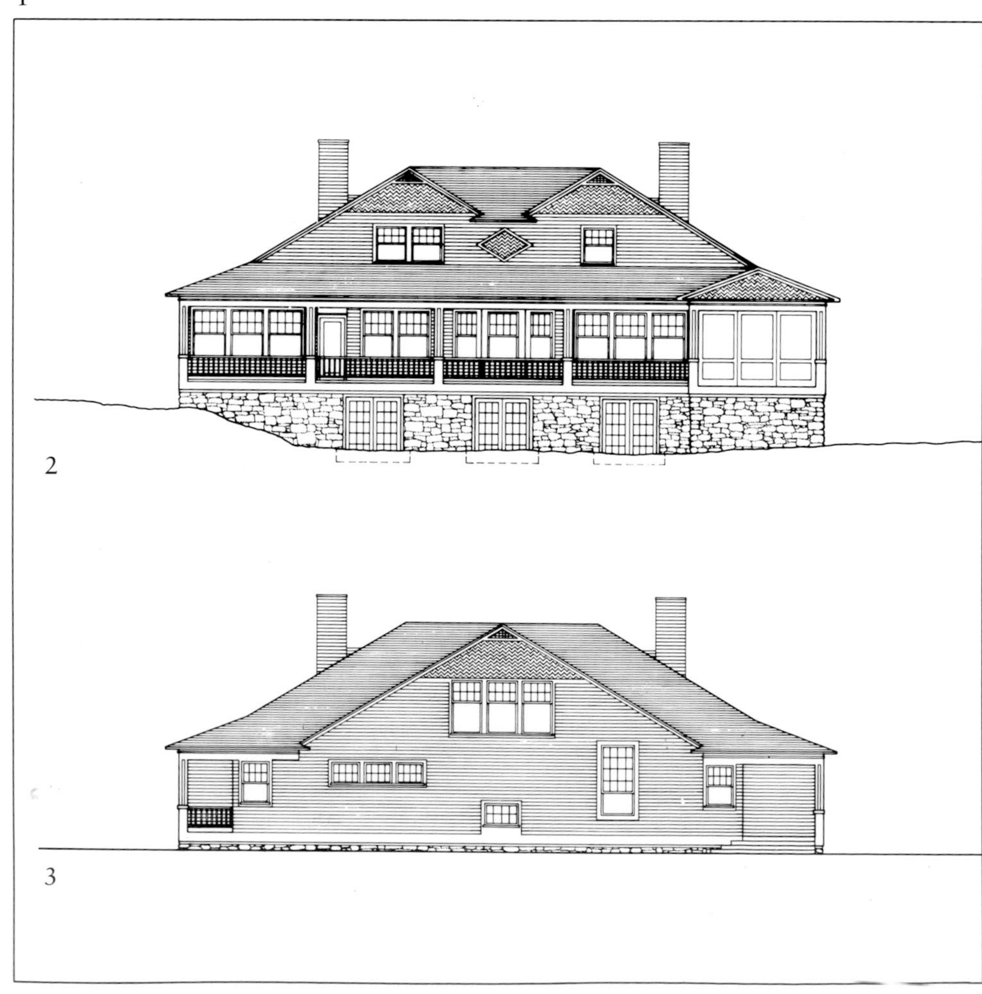

2

3

1.Site plan 2.South elevation 3.North elevation 4.View from the south 5.Ground floor plan 6.Second floor plan 7.Third floor plan

4

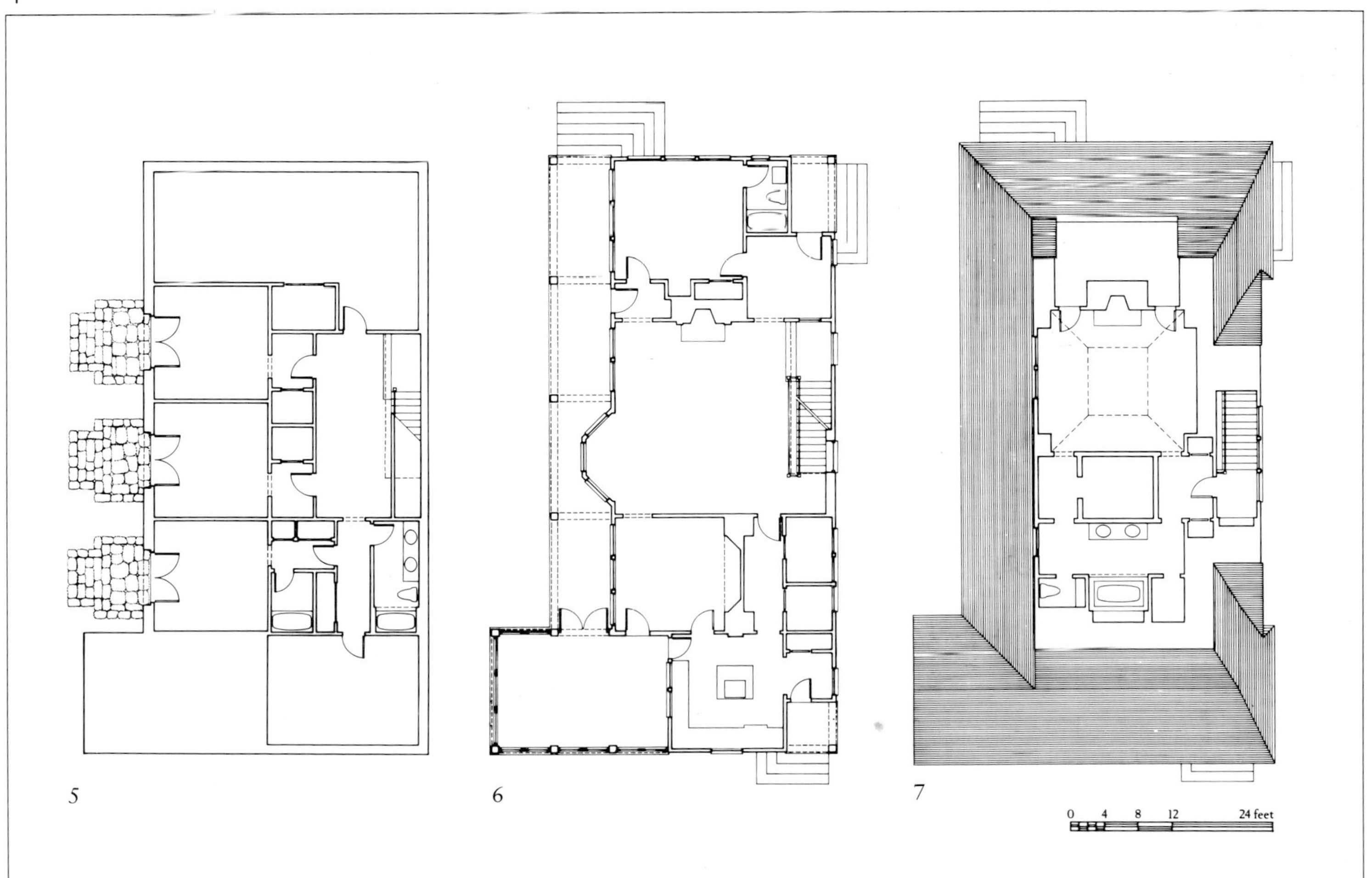

Prospect Point Office Building

La Jolla, California
1983–1985

This three-story office building occupies what is perhaps La Jolla's most prominent commercial site—the "T" shaped gateway to La Jolla village. In order to reduce the building's apparent bulk, the continuous curve of its facade is both horizontally and vertically stratified. A street-level arcade is complemented by pergolas shading terraces at the third floor setbacks: the deep puncture of the boldly scaled archway leading to the courtyard is balanced by the projection of the principal pavilion, supporting a flattened semi-dome which recalls the dome at the nearby La Valencia Hotel.

Light and air reach the center of the building through a courtyard which, while creating a private garden at the building's heart, simultaneously provides a sense of community for the various office suites that occupy the second and third floors. The courtyard is entered off-center and unfolds gradually before the visitor, exploiting an element of surprise to make it an event along the path from street to elevator.

In both its colors and its use of materials, the building responds to the Spanish Colonial architectural traditions of the La Jolla region. Exterior walls are of cream colored stucco while pitched roofs are of local clay tile. On the second floor, generously sized wood-framed French doors open onto narrow, wrought-iron balconies.

1.Site plan 2.Perspective view from Prospect Street 3.Principal elevation 4.Roof plan 5.Second floor plan 6.Third floor plan 7.Ground floor plan 8.Axonometric of courtyard entryway 9.Overhead view of model 10.Aerial view of model from the southeast

1

2

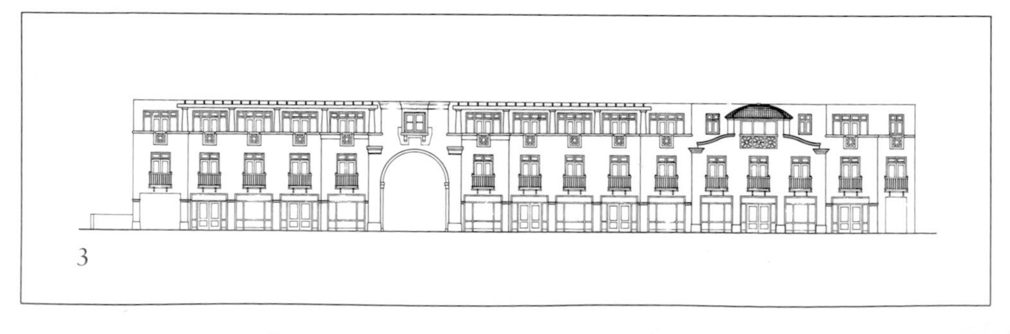

3

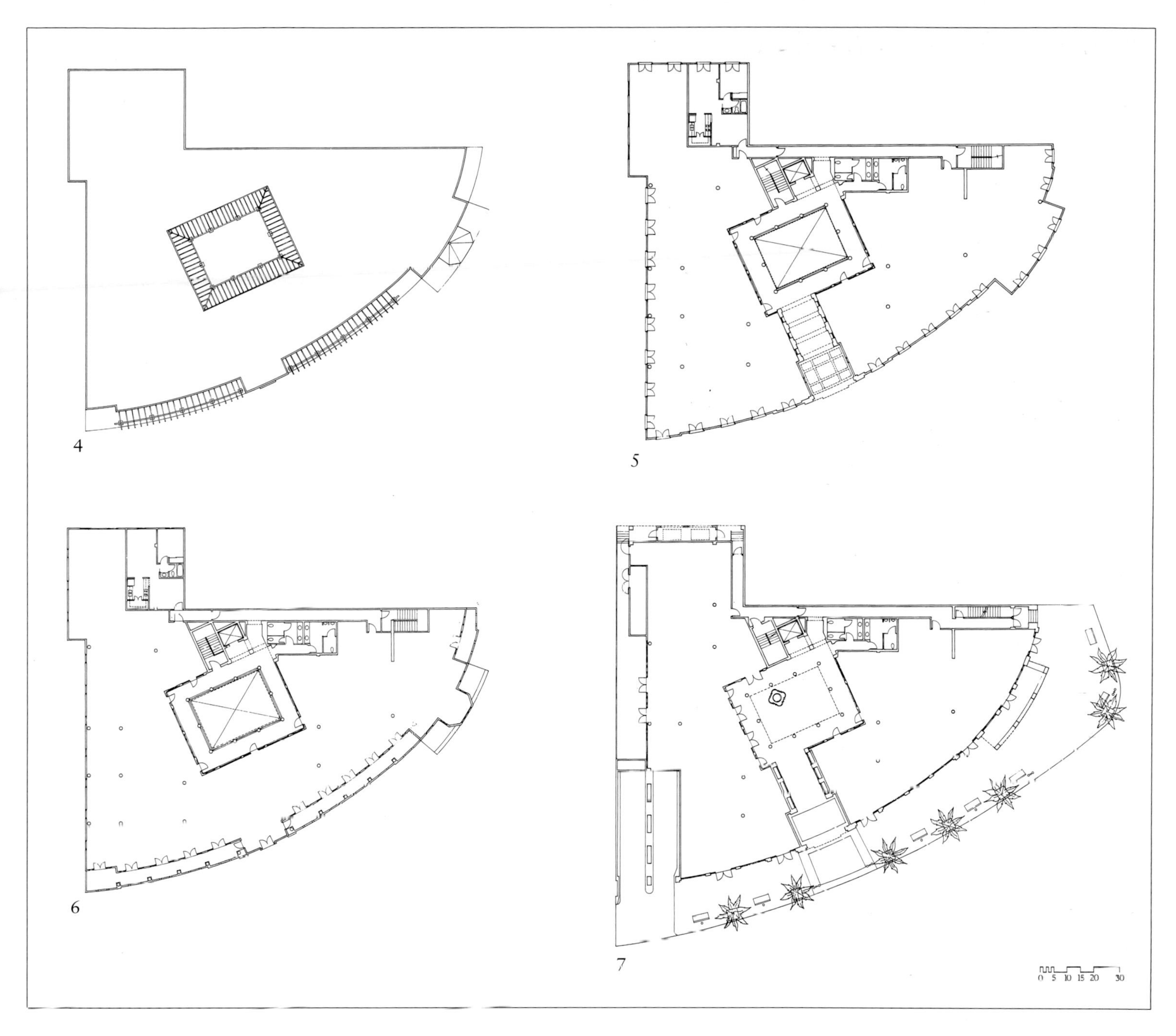

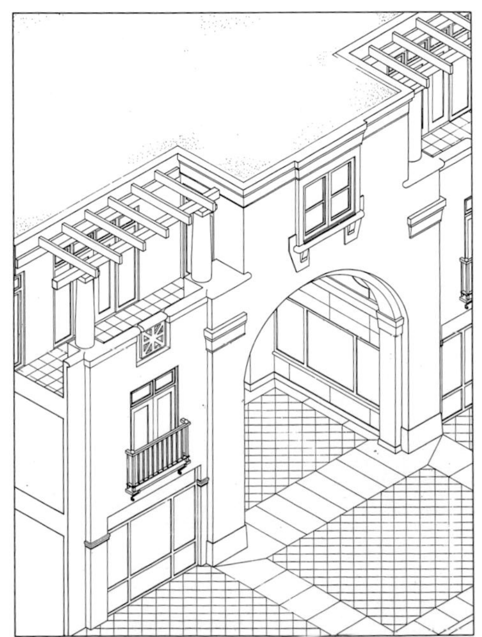

8

9

10

1

2

1. View from intersection of Prospect Street and Cave Street 2. Balconies and pergola on 2nd and 3rd floor 3. Entrance archway as seen from Cave Street 4. View of gallery leading to courtyard 5. View of the courtyard

3

4

5

1.Section through entrance gallery and courtyard 2.Axonometric of courtyard 3.Detail of entryway lamp and courtyard handrail

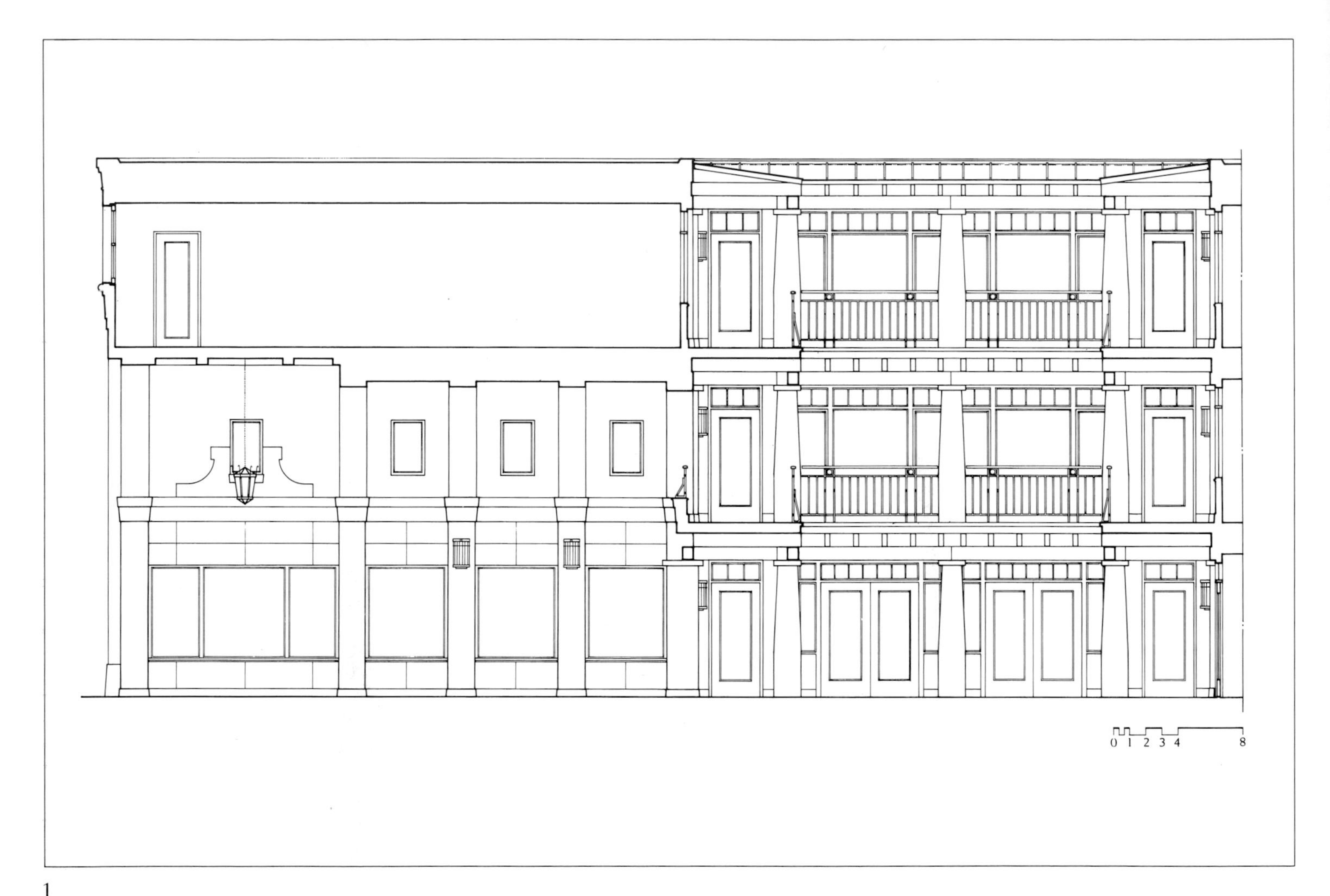

1

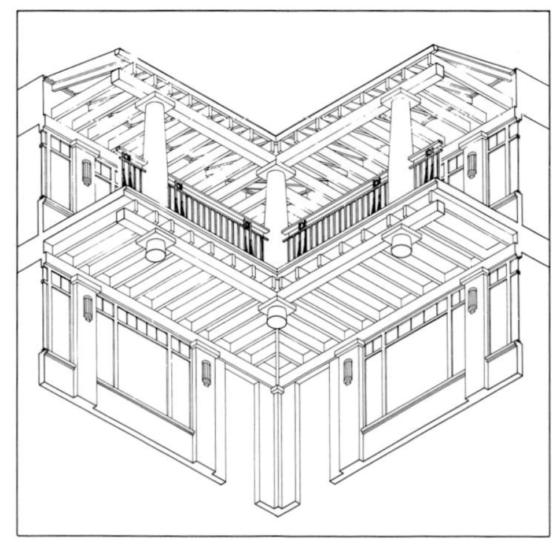

2

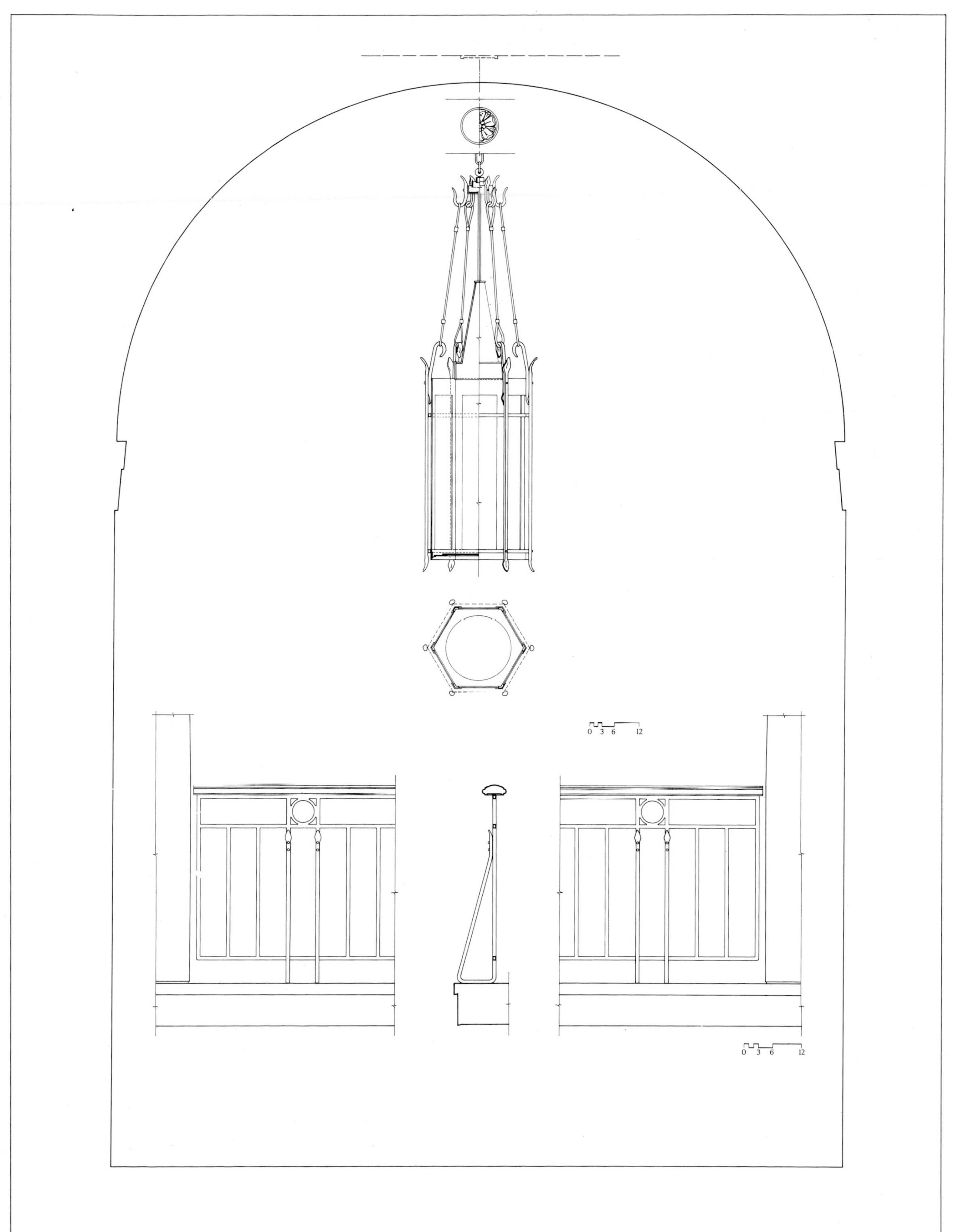

3

Additions to the New Orleans Museum of Art
New Orleans, Louisiana
1983

In response to a program that more than doubled the size of the original museum, a turn-of-the-century Neo-Grec design that had been unimaginatively added on to in the 1950s, our proposal calls for a grandly Classical composition of atria and stairs that lead to a sculpture terrace facing out across the lake.

1.Site plan 2.West elevation 3.East elevation 4.Fourth floor gallery 5.View from the west 6.Second floor plan 7.Fourth floor plan 8.Ground floor plan 9.Third floor plan

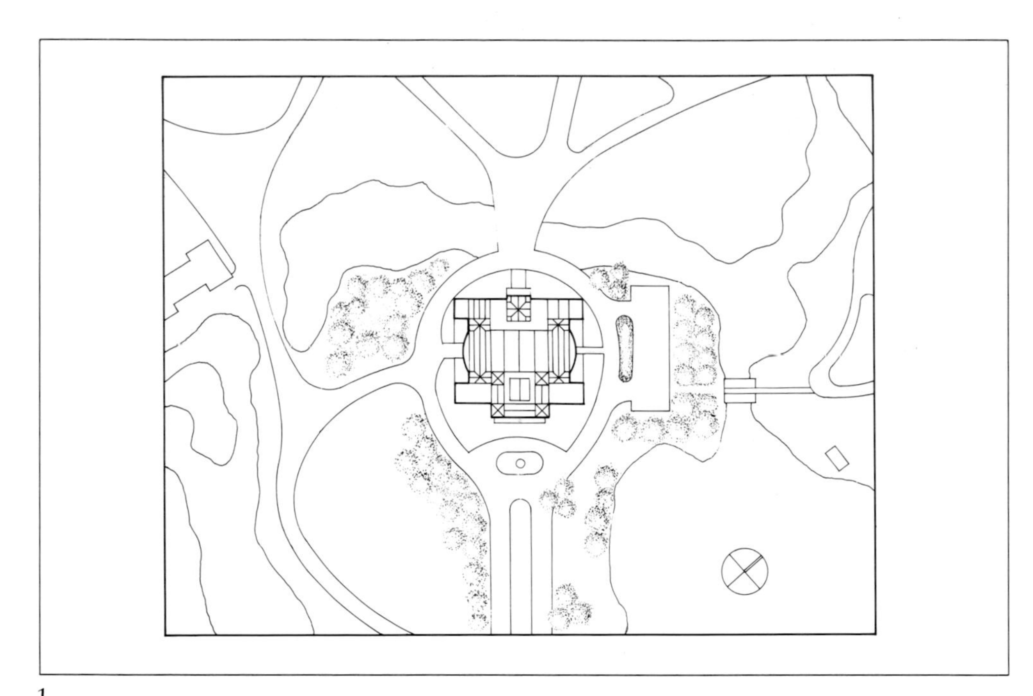

1

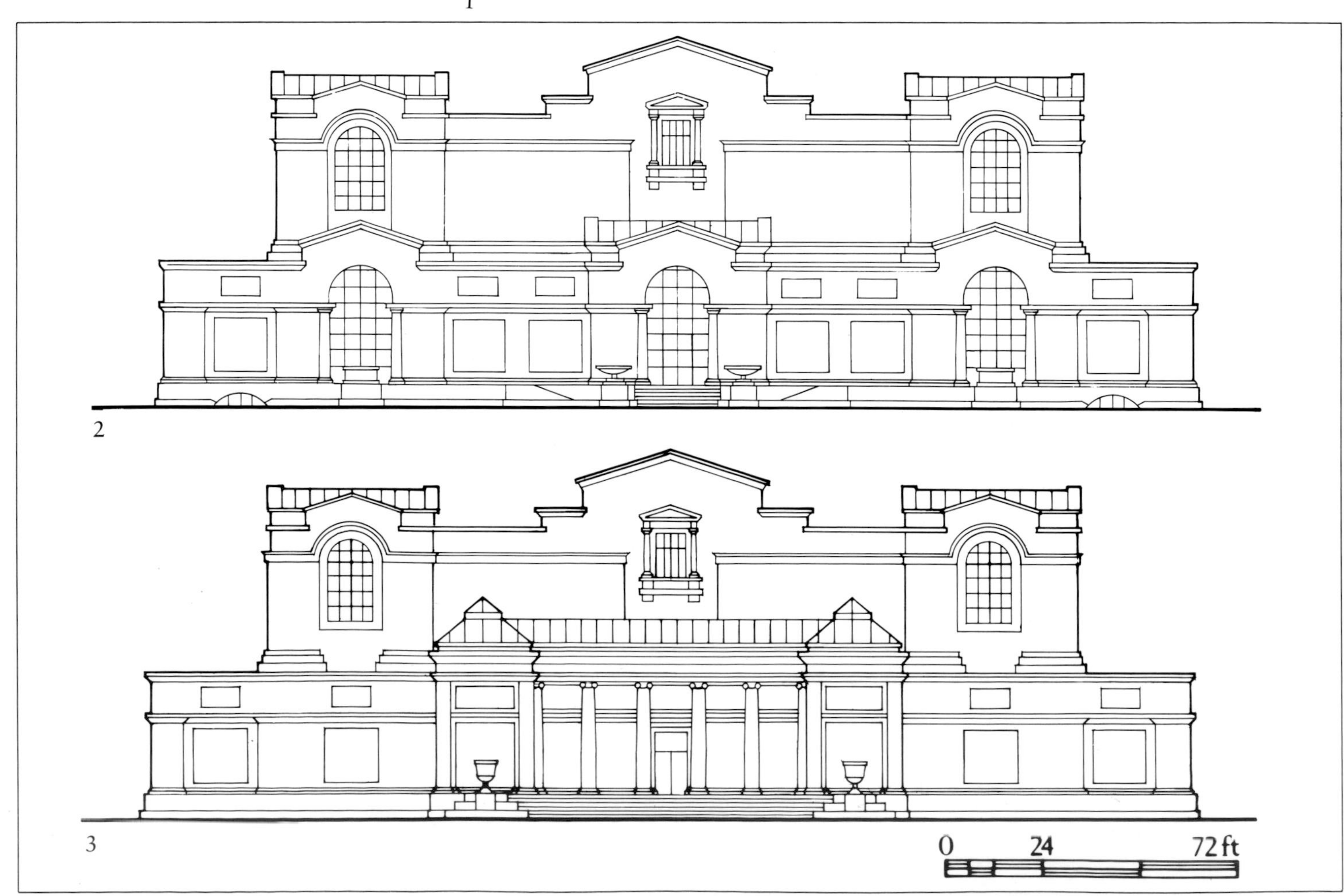

4

5

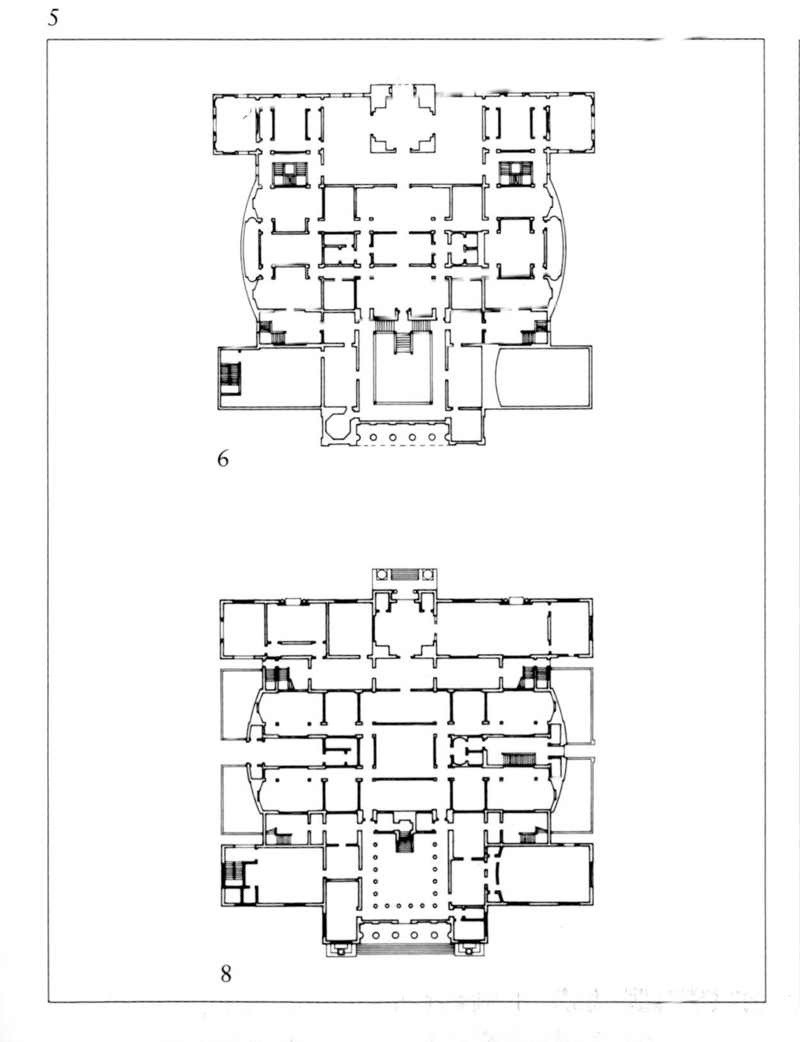
6

8

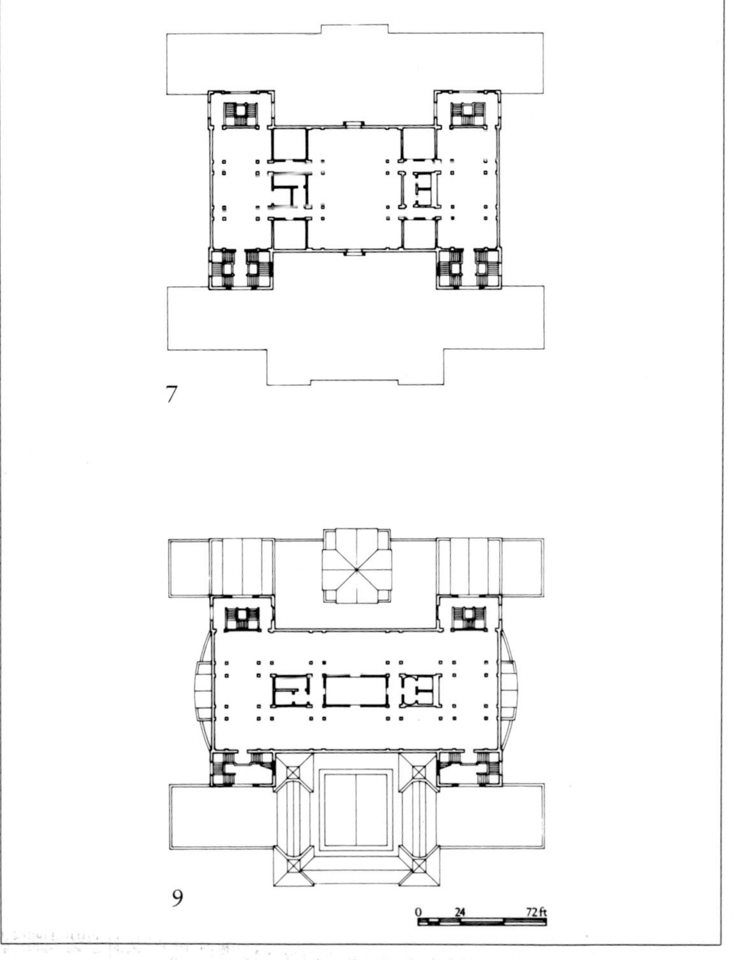
7

9

Residence
Pound Ridge, New York
1983

The house is sited on a ridge overlooking a pond. The approach to the house is along a curving drive which winds its way through the woods and to the top of the ridge. The curving entry facade greets the visitor on his final approach to the house. The exterior walls are stucco with pieces of tile randomly placed within it. The high-pitched roofs are covered with shingles which gradate in size to accentuate the slope of the roof. The major rooms enjoy expansive views through the large, elliptical bay windows which have the added benefit of introducing light into the principal spaces.

Inside, one enters the skylit stair hall. To one's left are the major rooms: the dining room raised in relation to the living room and open to it, the family room beyond the dining room, and the library at the opposite end of the living room in a tower-like wing. Though large in scale, the rooms are informal due to their open relation to each other and the crafted rusticity of the natural wood moldings, beams, and stained-glass lanterns. To the southwest corner of the house, beyond the kitchen, is the screened porch to be used by the family for much of its summer activity. In plan and elevation, it balances the southeast corner of the house containing the family room: the center of winter family activities. Upstairs, each of the generous bedrooms has its own bath and dressing area. The master bedroom and bathroom have large bay windows to afford the same view of the pond offered downstairs.

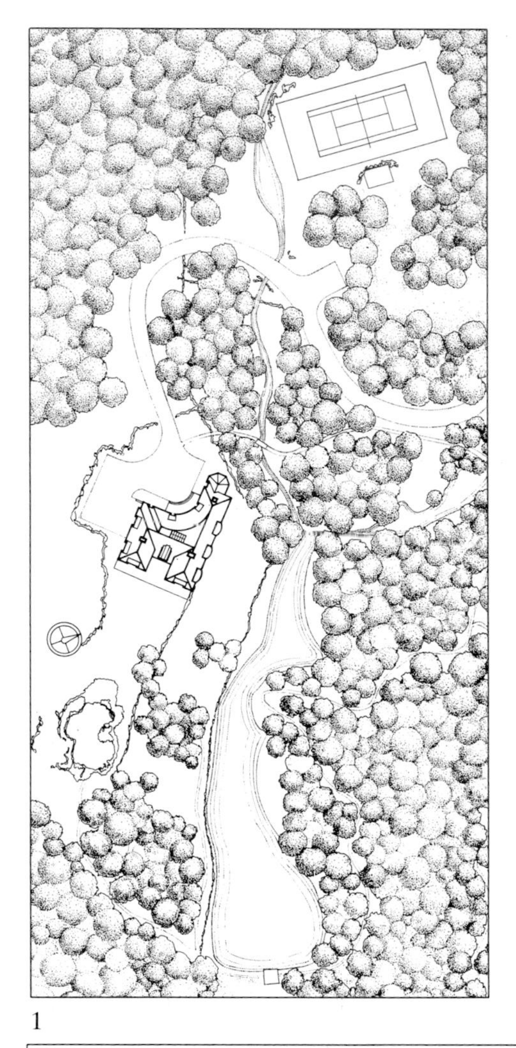

1

2

3

4

5

6

1. Site plan 2. View of model from the northeast 3. Perspective view from the northeast 4. Longitudinal section 5,6. Transverse sections 7. Northwest elevation 8. South elevation 9. East elevation 10. West elevation 11. Second floor plan 12. Ground floor plan

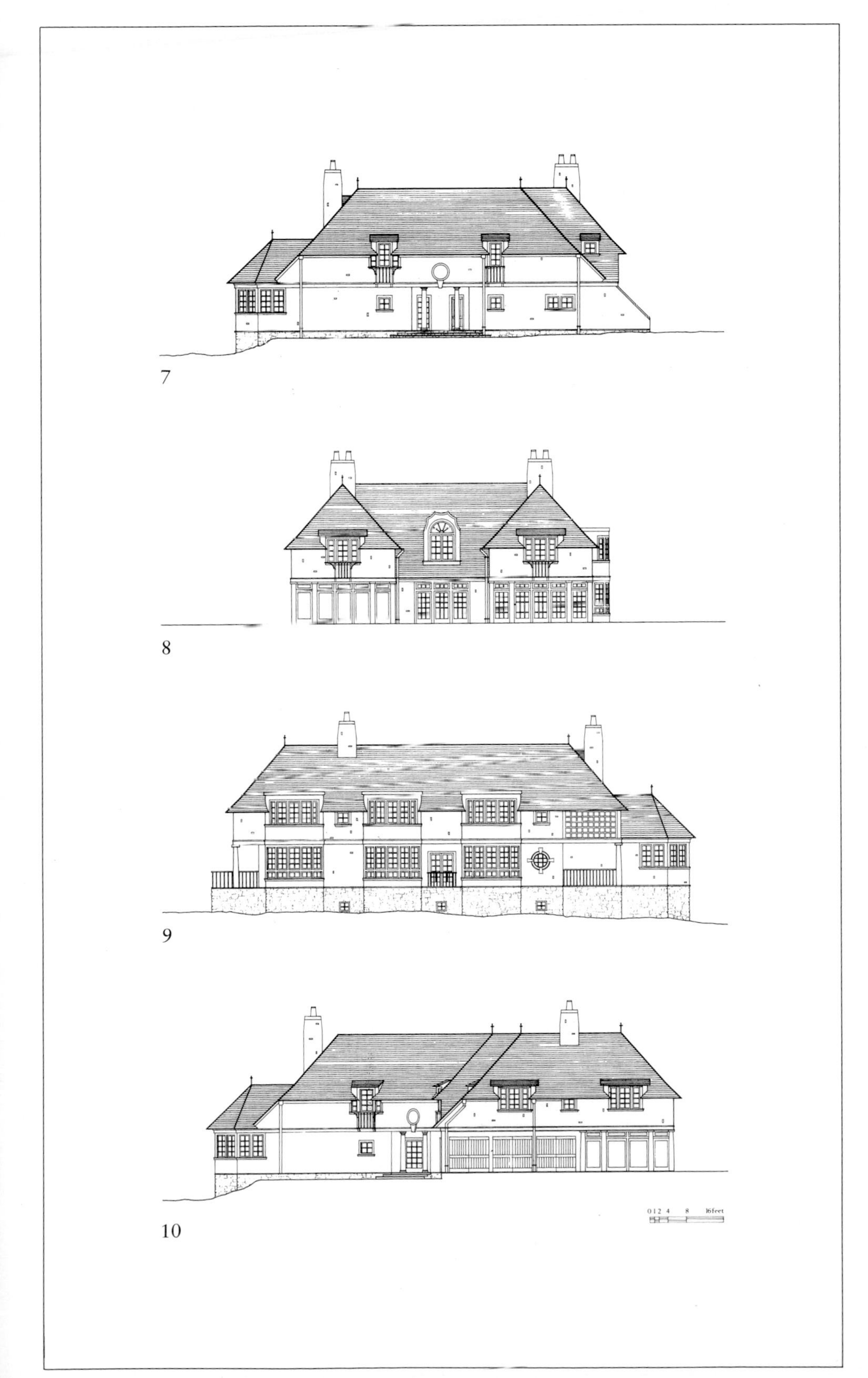

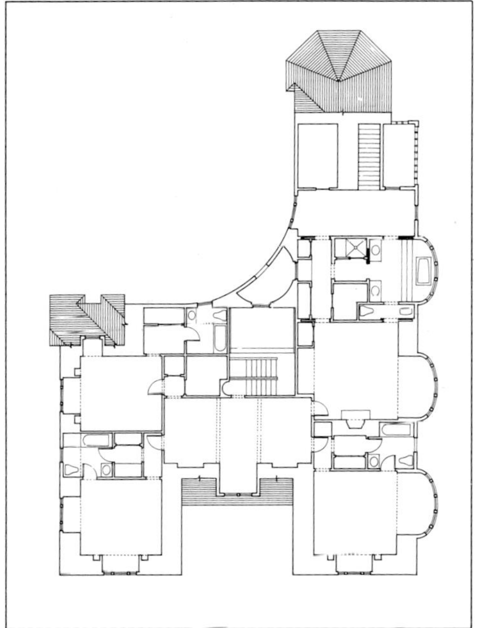

11

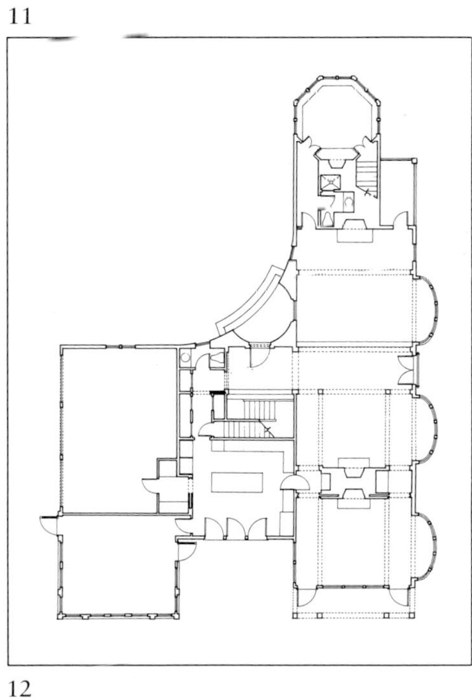

12

Villa in New Jersey
1983–

In a neighborhood where turn-of-the-century Italian villas abound, this design combines stucco walls trimmed in brick, and a gradated tile roof with an elaborate landscape that includes a sunken court and extensive flower gardens to create an integrated composition of house and garden. The layered play of the main floor groups services on the north separated from the principal enfilade on the south by a continuous axis of circulation that connects the owner's home office in the east with the family room in the west. Lounge, dining, and card rooms open to the garden across a terrace shaded by a planted pergola.

Below, an enclosed swimming pool opens to the sunken court which forms a forced perspective as it rises to the south.

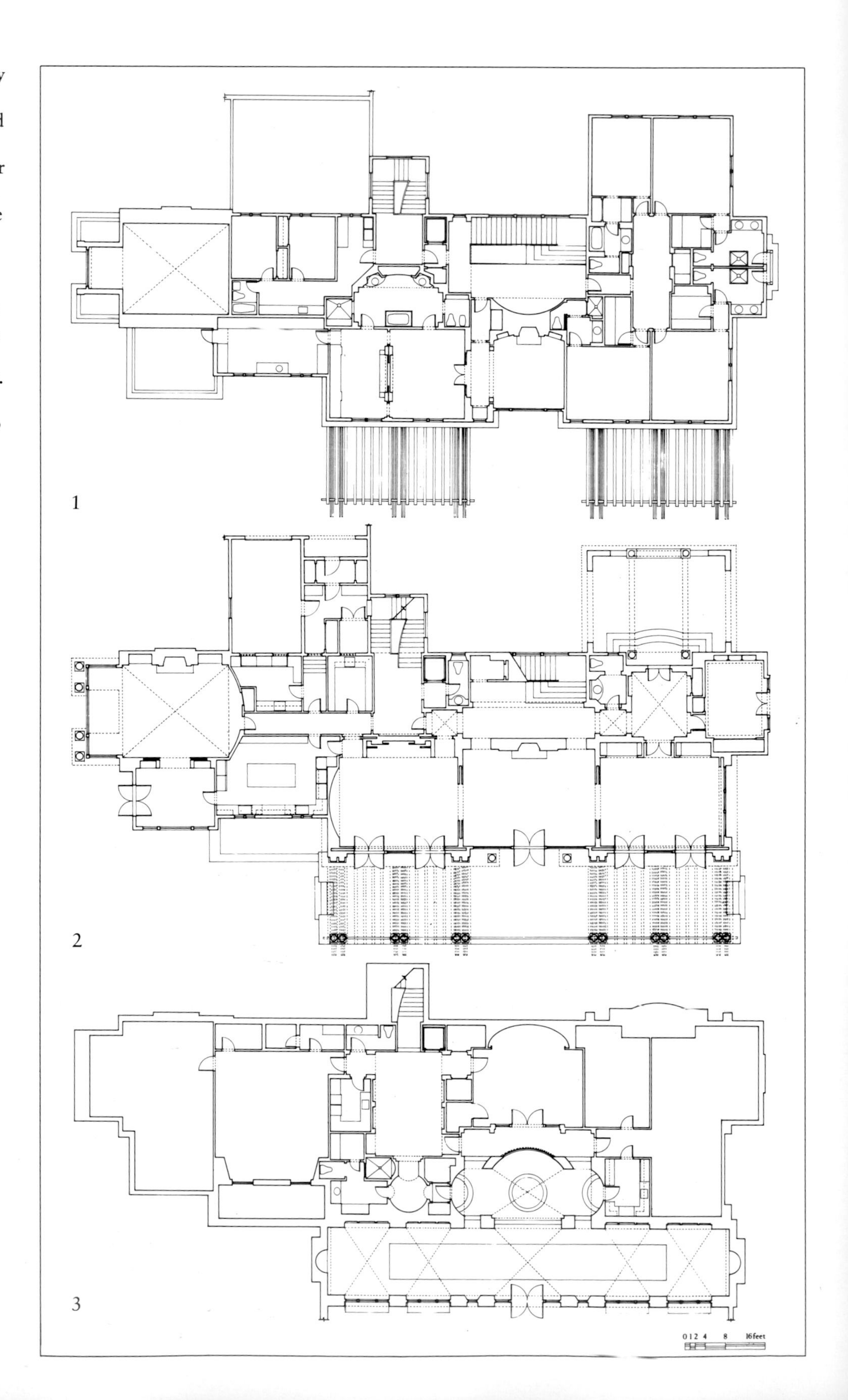

1.Third floor plan 2.Second floor plan
3.Ground floor plan 4.South elevation
5.Interior color studies: A.Living room
B.Family room C.Master suite sitting room
6.View of model from the south

4

5A

5B

5C

6

1. Site axonometric   2. Transverse section
3. Views of house under construction

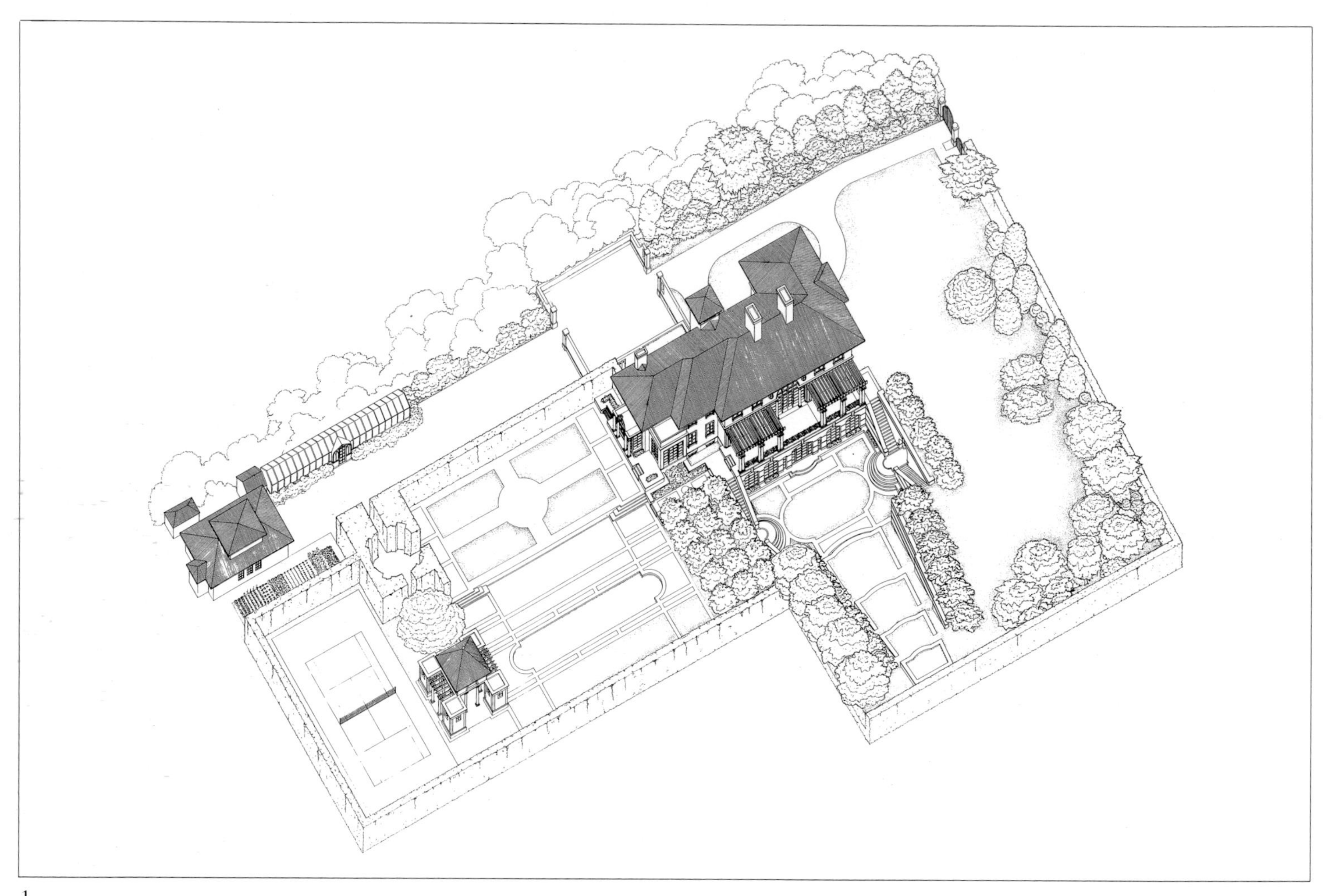

1

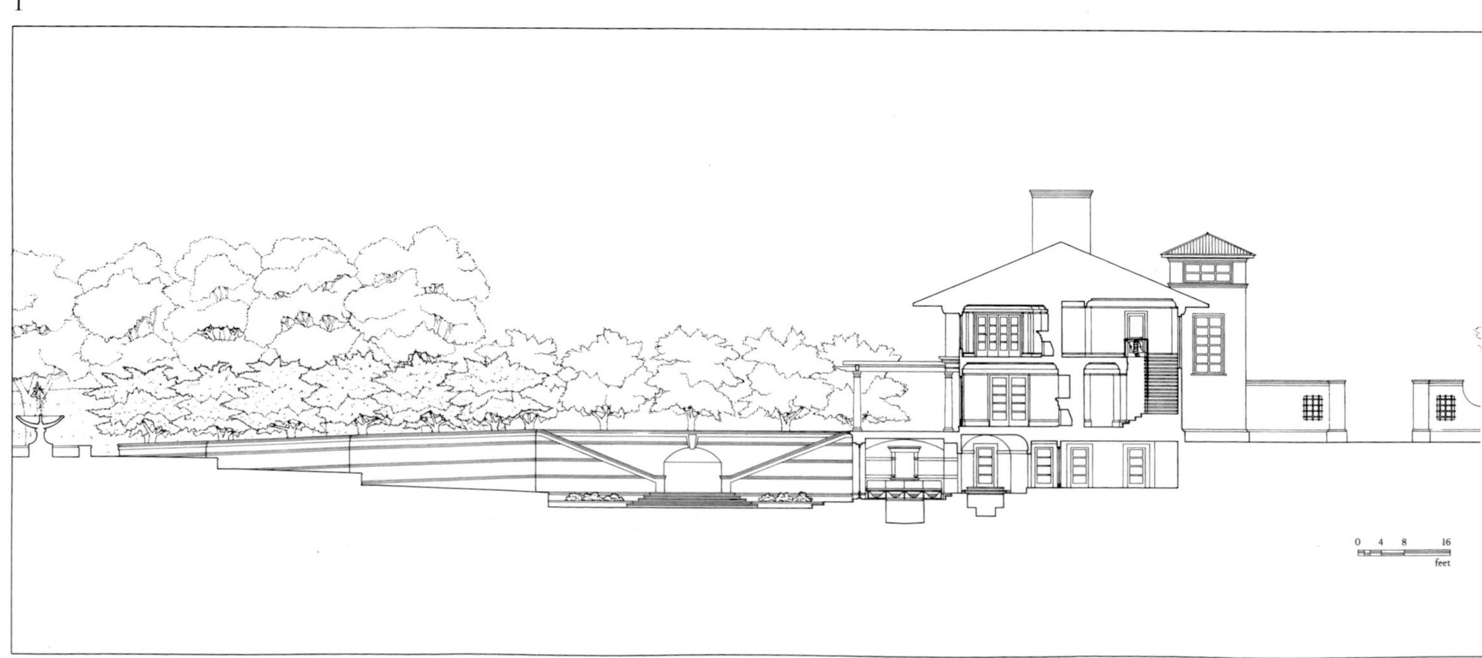

2

3

Reading Room
International House
New York, New York
1983

Situated in a dimly lit basement, this group of study rooms provides students at International House in New York with an appealing centralized study area that respects the Classical architecture of the building.

The walls of the largest room are organized by a system of piers which create niches incorporating windows, doors, and dictionary storage space. The piers give the room the sense of grandness that one might expect if the reading room had been a part of the building when it was built in the 1920s. Cove lighting provides plenty of reading light while giving the basement space an unexpected outdoor feeling. Light gray paint accentuates the open feeling of the main room, while dark green paint establishes a more intimate ambience in the surrounding smaller rooms.

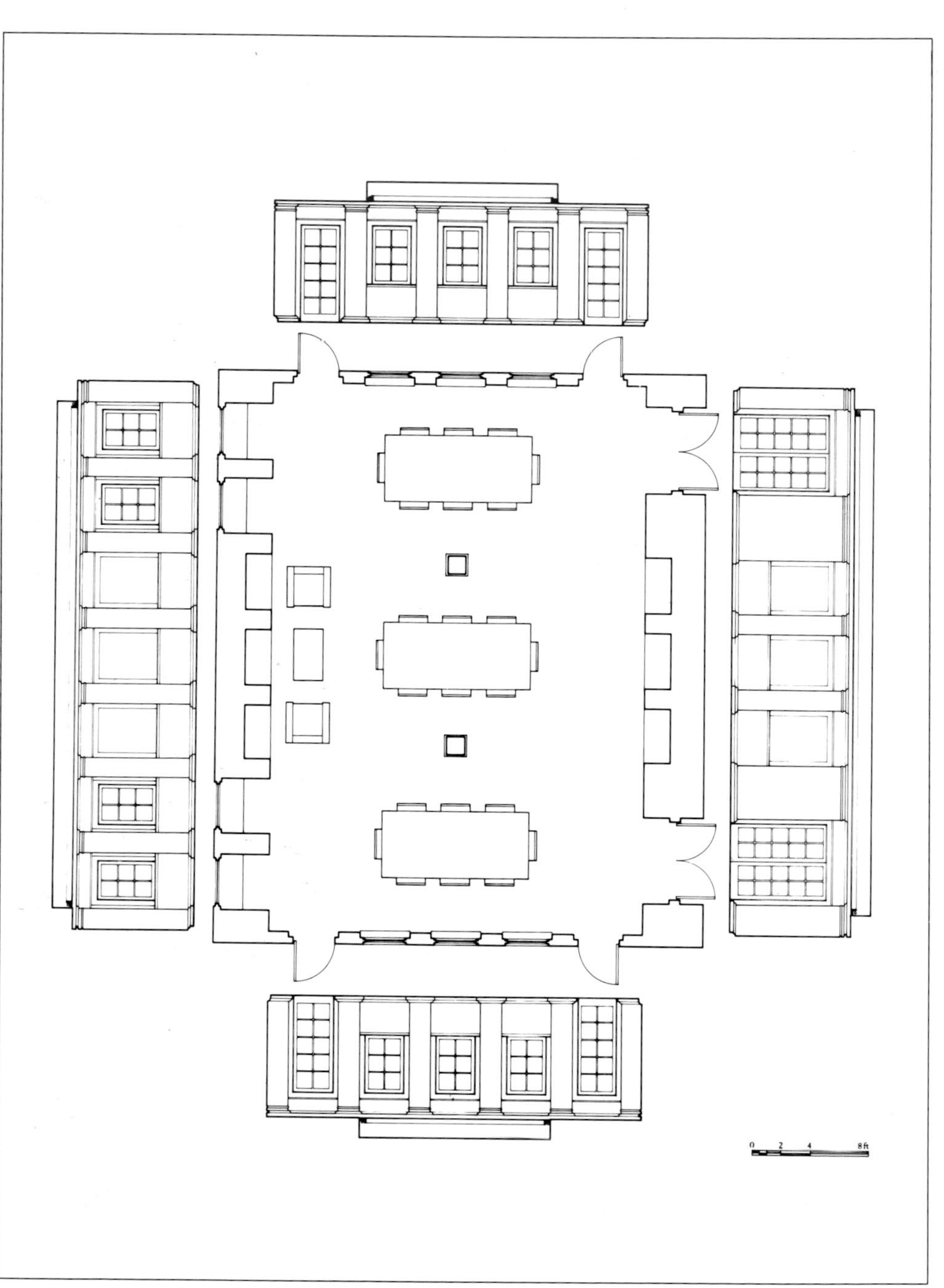

1

1.Plan and elevations 2,3,4.The reading room

2

3

4

Colfax at Beden's Brook

Skillman, New Jersey
1983–

This suburban development is located on gently sloping farmland approximately ten miles northwest of Princeton, New Jersey. When completed, Colfax will include twenty-three houses which will ring a common parkland or be accessible to it by pedestrian paths lined with dogwoods. Our involvement in the project included the preparation of design guidelines for the entire development and the design of the inner ring of houses facing the park. The guidelines emphasize the use of local stone, brick, and shingle, and encourage designs native to central New Jersey and the Delaware Valley.

Four houses facing the park have been designed and three built to date. These houses, mostly built for resale, emphasize simple, symmetrical planning with light, open stairways, and doors and brick terraces looking down the valley. We have emphasized gambrels and hipped roofs, with exterior facing materials including local brick, shingle, and stucco.

Gardens have been created for each house. Using fences, walls, and belts of trees, such features as gazebos and tennis courts nestle into the hillside. Sight lines as dictated by both the houses and their grounds use the park and the far hills as borrowed scenery.

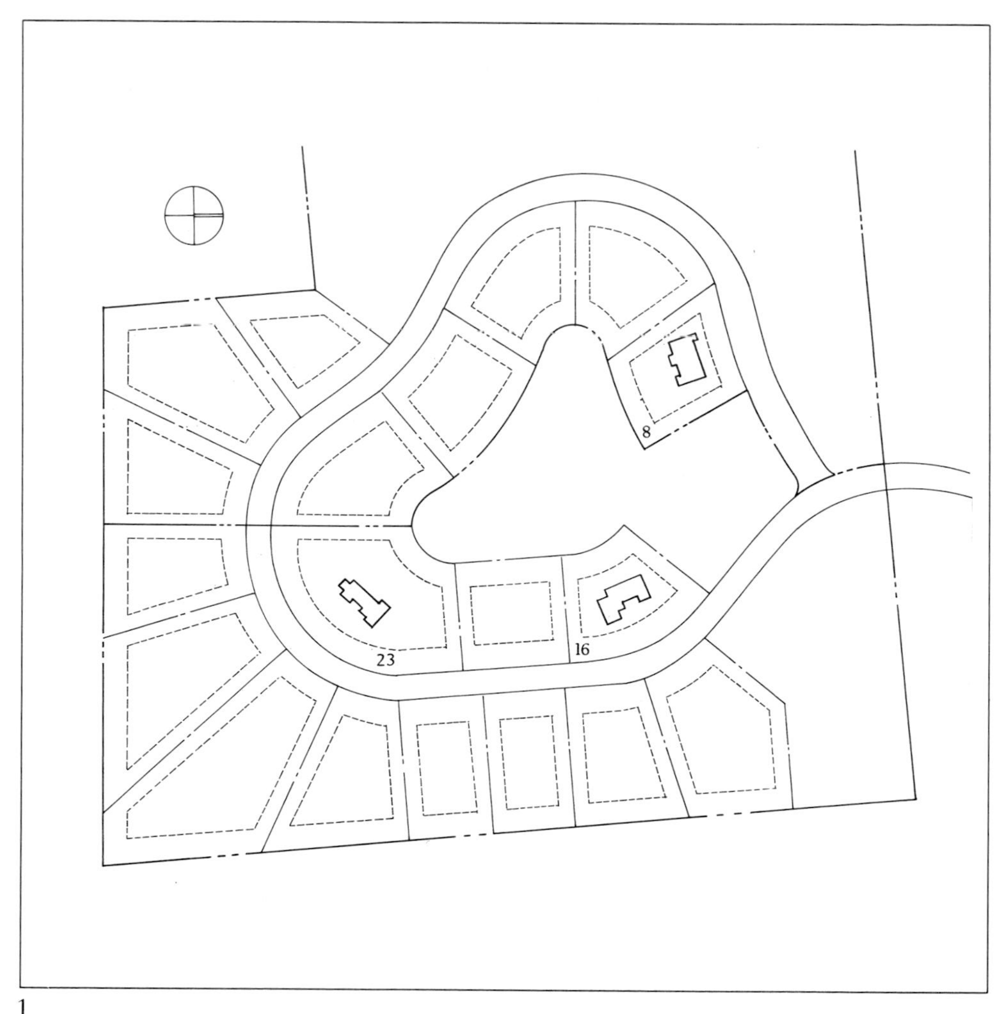

1

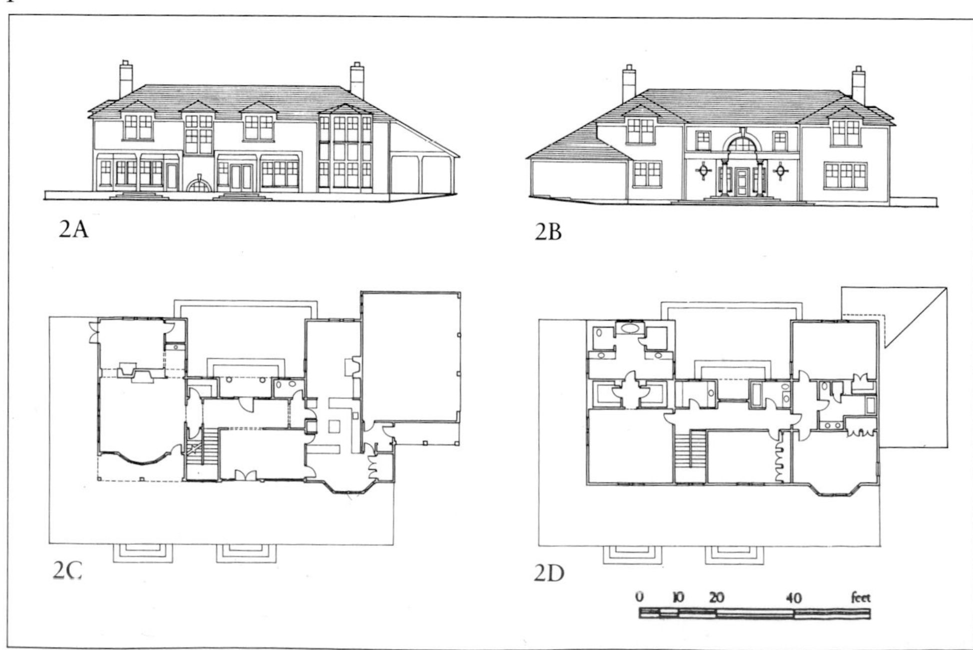

2A 2B 2C 2D

1.Site plan 2.Lot 16: A.West elevation B.East elevation C.Ground floor plan D.Second floor plan 3.Lot 8: A.North elevation B.South elevation C.Second floor plan D.Ground floor plan 4.Lot 23: A.Northwest elevation B.Southeast elevation C.Second floor plan D.Ground floor plan 5,6.Views of model

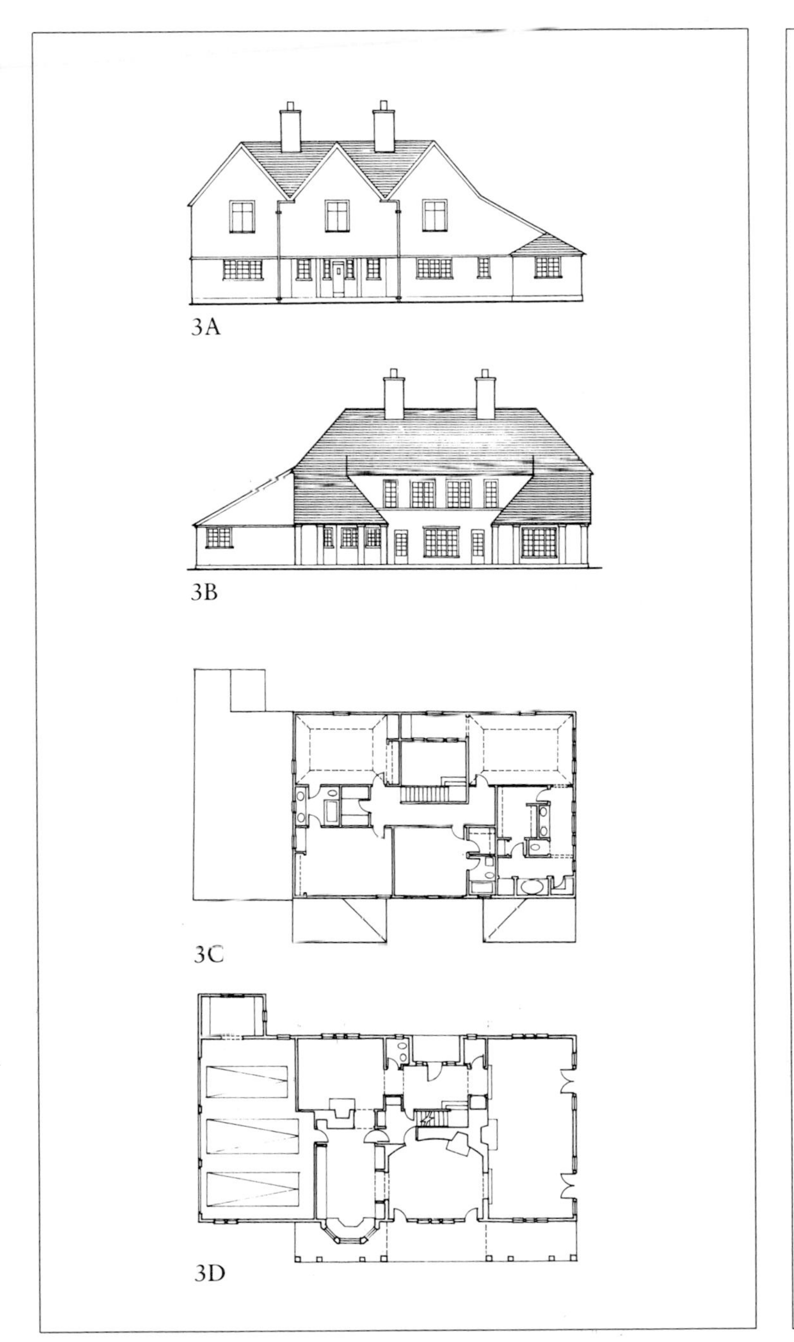

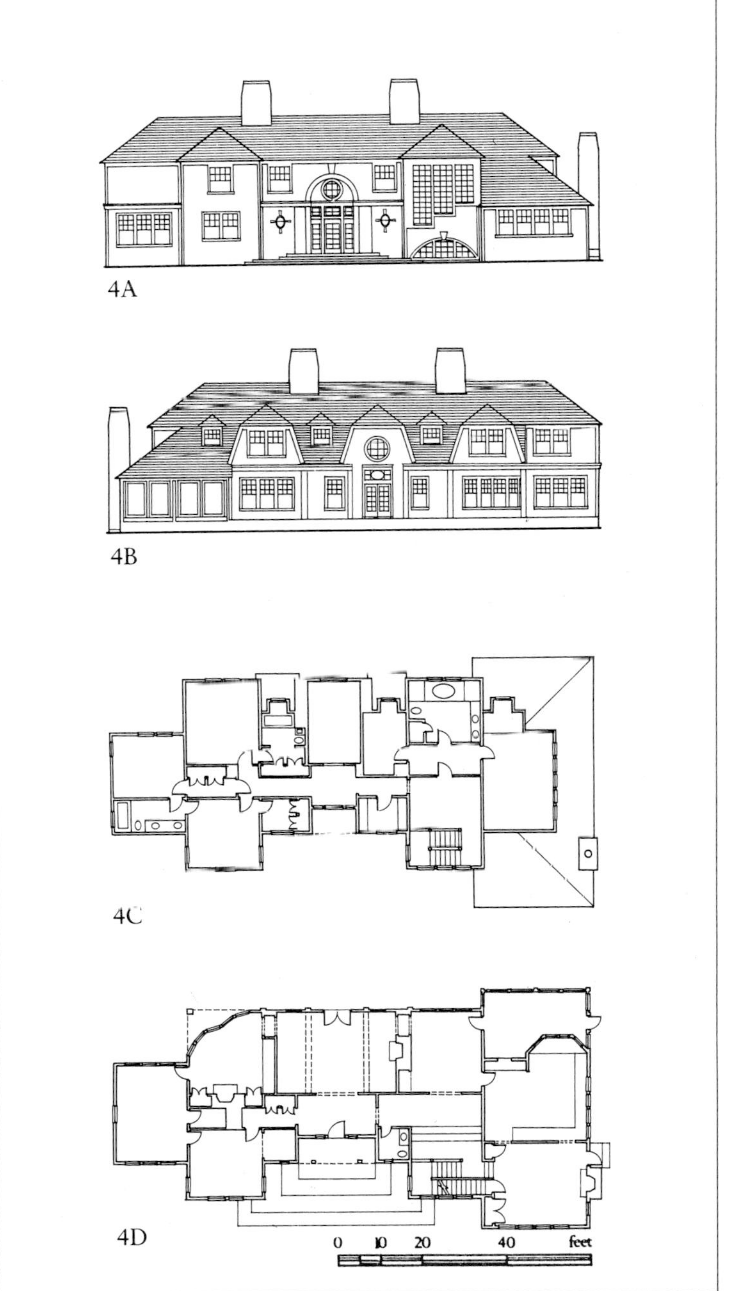

5

6

1.Lot 16: A.East facade B.West facade
2.Lot 23: A.Northwest facade
B.Southeast facade

1A

1B

2A

2B

Treadway House
Southampton, New York
1983–1985

This Shingle Style house sits on fallow farmland in Southampton; its horizontal lines, low brick plinth, and gently raked roof tie the house to a relentlessly flat landscape. Only the large gable on the north elevation breaks through the roof line at the first floor. It provides a large-scale element announcing the entrance (in a recessed porch), and the stepped arrangement of its windows follows the path of the staircase inside. On the south side, the roof is interrupted by the bedroom dormers and the two-story bay of the living room, whose elliptical window looks towards the sea like a giant eye.

The first-floor plan provides an informal connection between the primary rooms; like a traditional Shingle Style hall, the living room connects the study, dining room, and second floor. The covered porch that surrounds these rooms becomes a screened room at the southwest corner. Upstairs, a generous landing connects the master bedroom suite and the children's rooms. From the landing, a second staircase leads to the third floor studio, which offers panoramic views of the distant fields and the ocean.

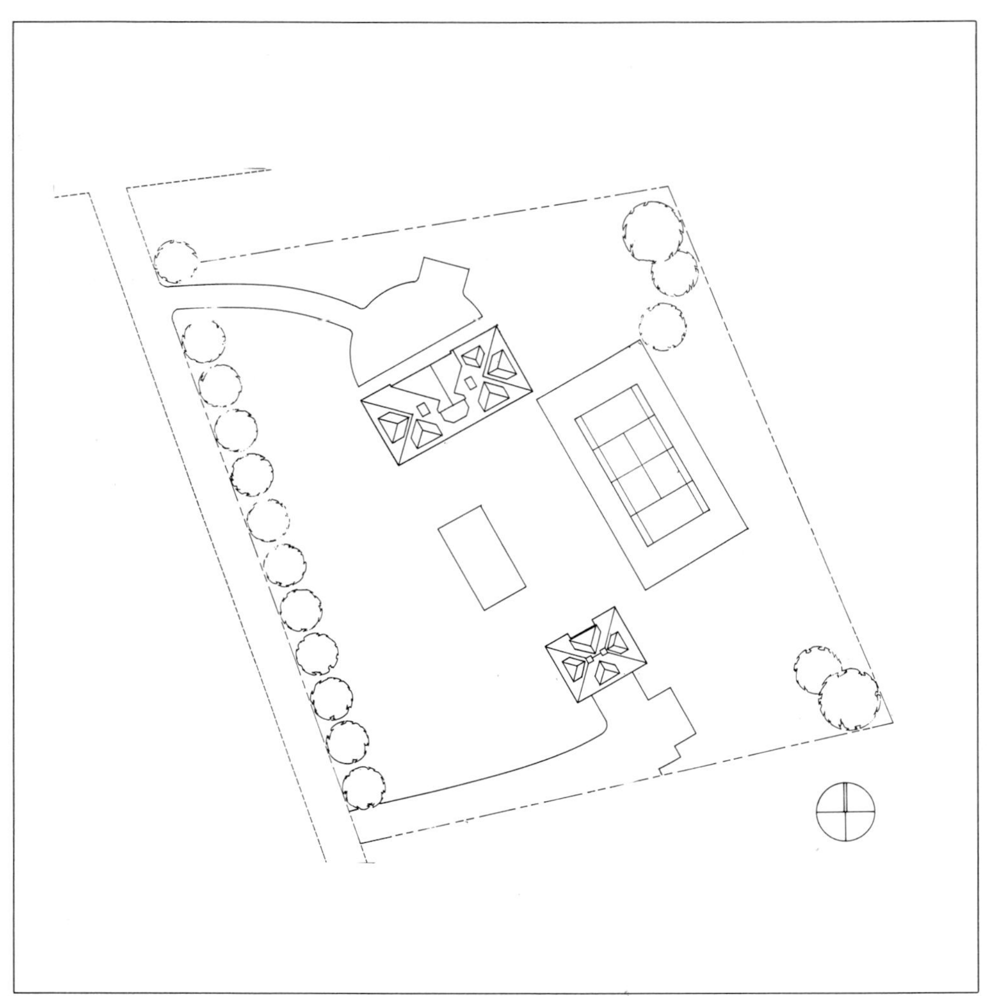

1

1.Site plan 2.Longitundinal section
3.Attic floor plan 4.Second floor plan
5.Ground floor plan 6.South elevation
7.East elevation 8.West elevation
9.North elevation

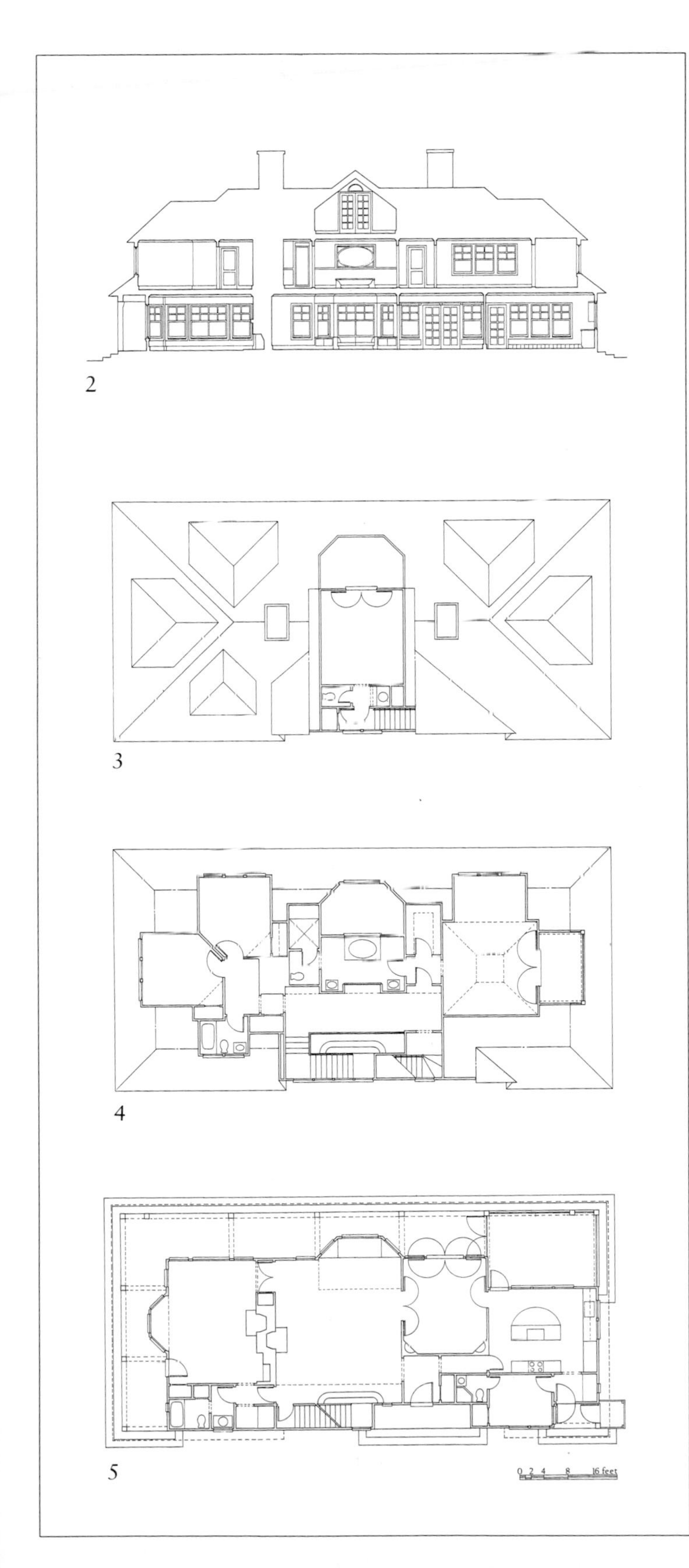

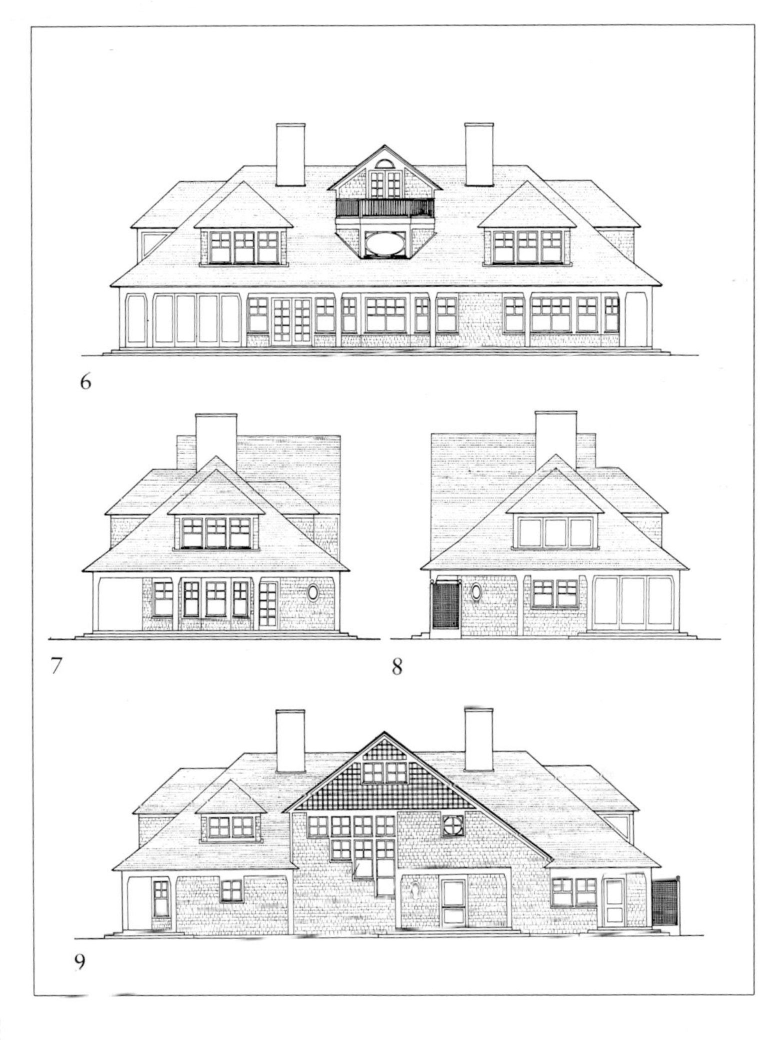

1.North facade 2.South facade

1

2

Residence in Massachusetts
1983–

This two-story shingled house of Classical proportions and details occupies a heavily wooded coastal site. Raised on expansive brick and grass terraces, the house is strategically positioned to halt the advance of trees down to the water's edge, and to command sweeping water views.

Fenestration and massing facing the wooded entrance precinct are relatively restrained in contradistinction to the more open and active composition that takes advantage of views, sunlight, and prevailing breezes on the water side. A series of longitudinal and lateral axes organize the plan into clear processions of primary and secondary rooms, and are acknowledged in the elevations by the repetitive yet variously treated employment of Serlian motifs. Within and without, detailing is of the Tuscan order reinterpreted to Doric proportions; while this is fully developed in the more formal zones of the house, the scheme adheres to its turn-of-the-century precedents by favoring abstraction from the Classical ideal in the service and private areas.

1.Southeast elevation 2.Southwest elevation 3.Northeast elevation 4.Northwest elevation 5.Aerial view of model from the southeast 6.Second floor plan 7.Ground floor plan 8.Aerial view of model from the north 9.Site plan

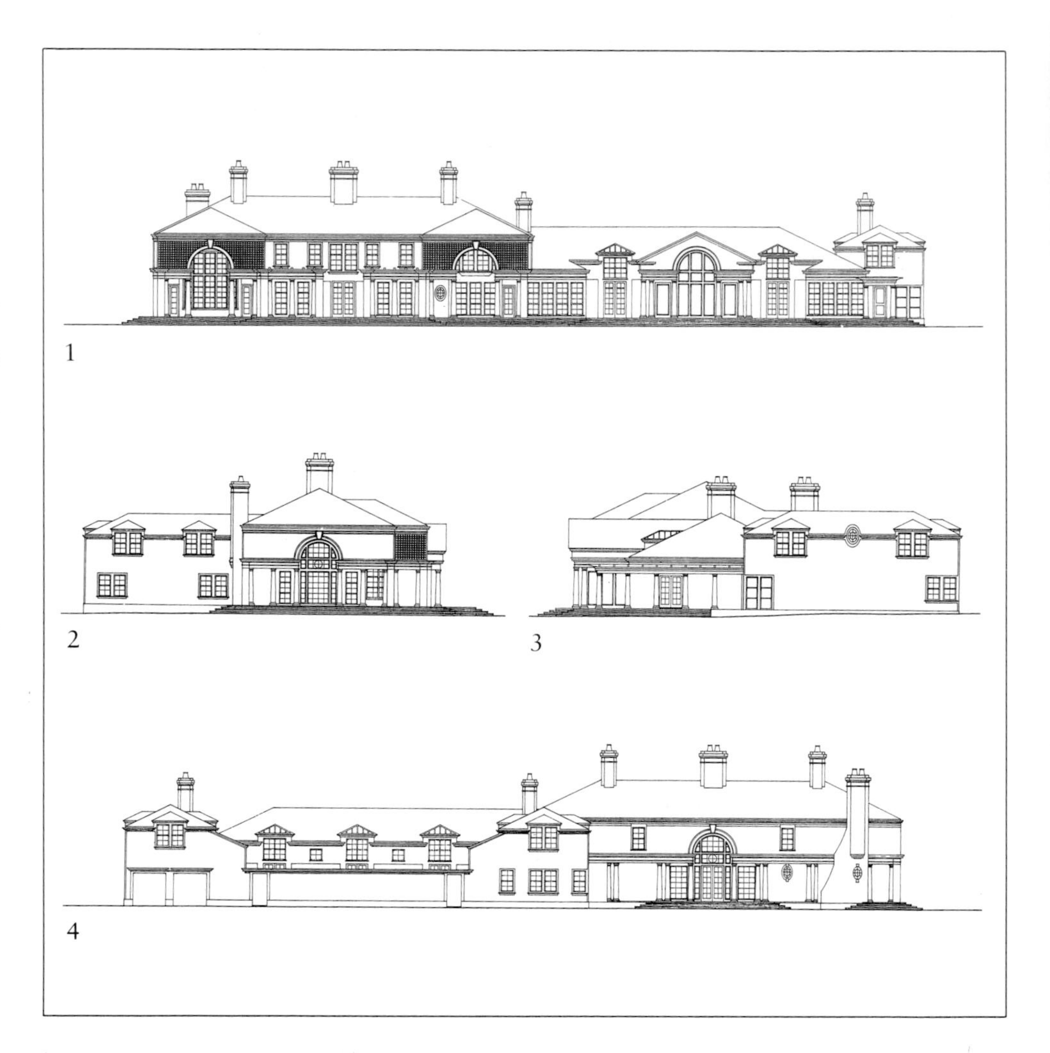

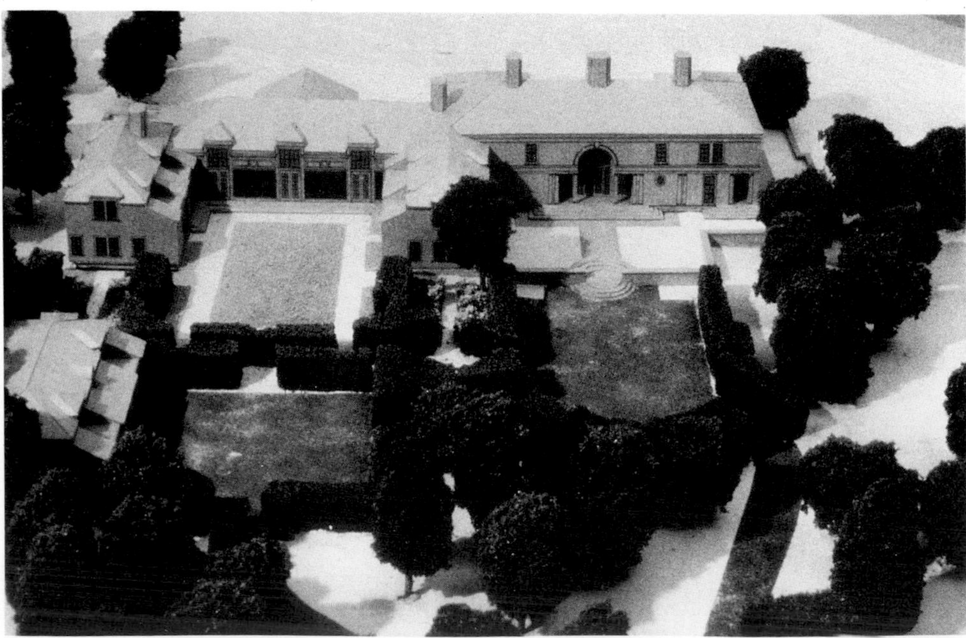

5

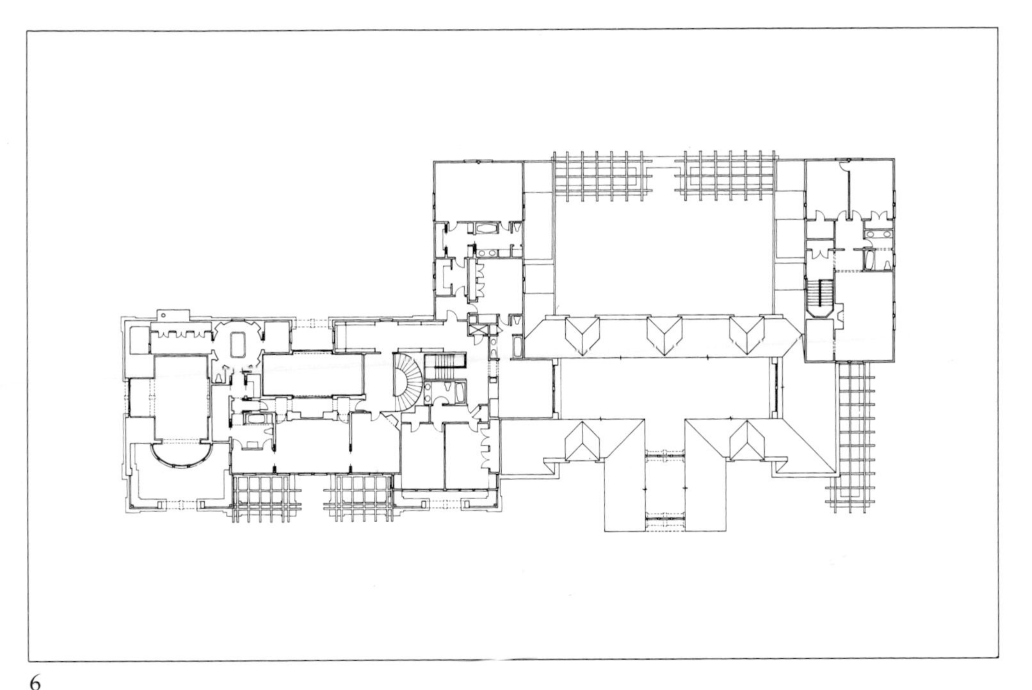

6

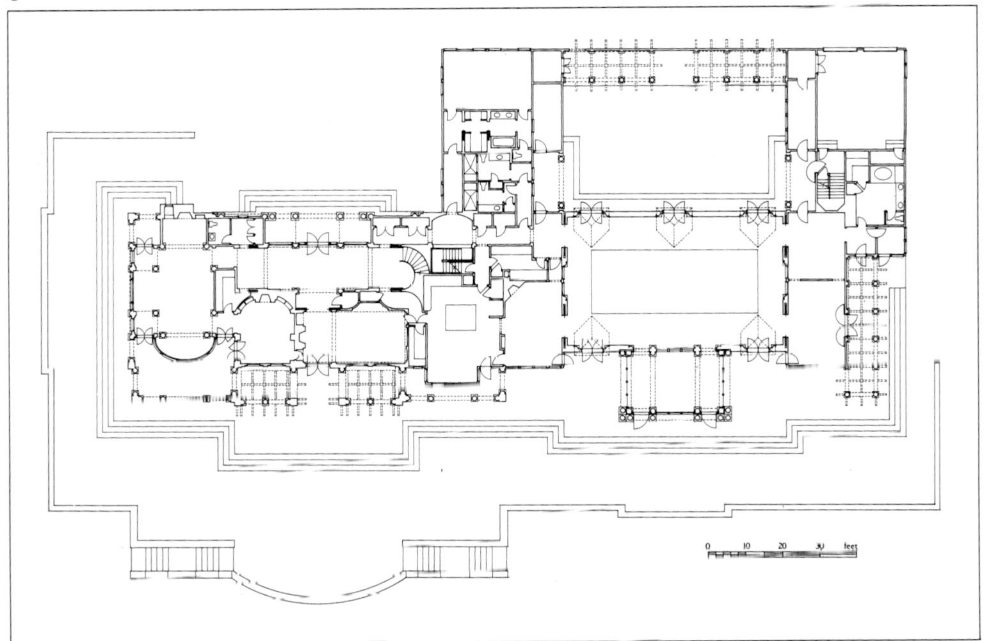

7

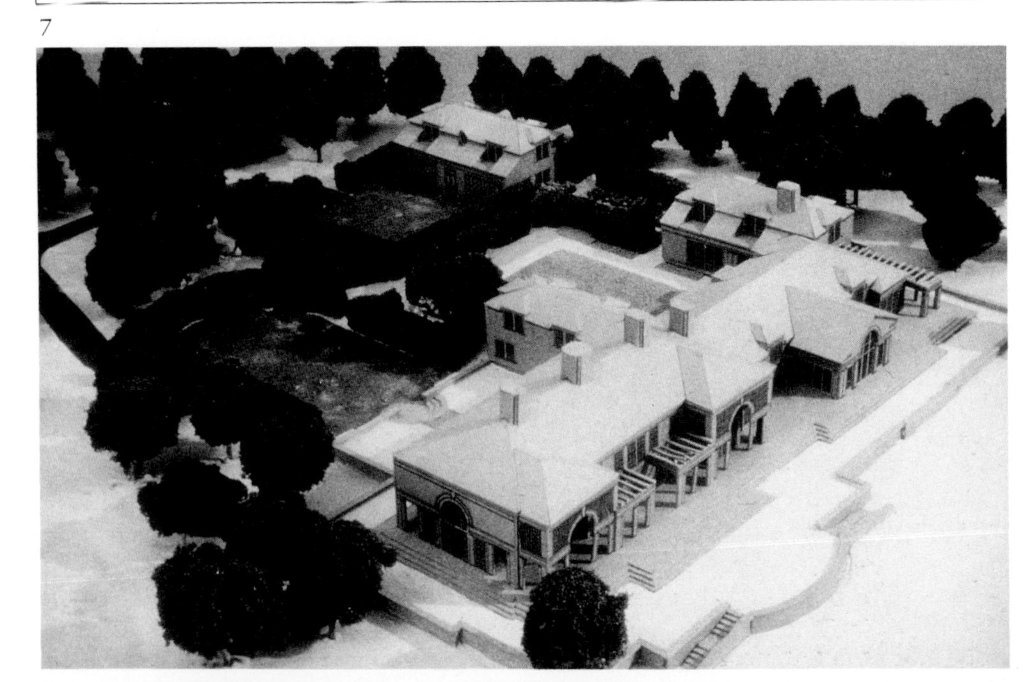

8

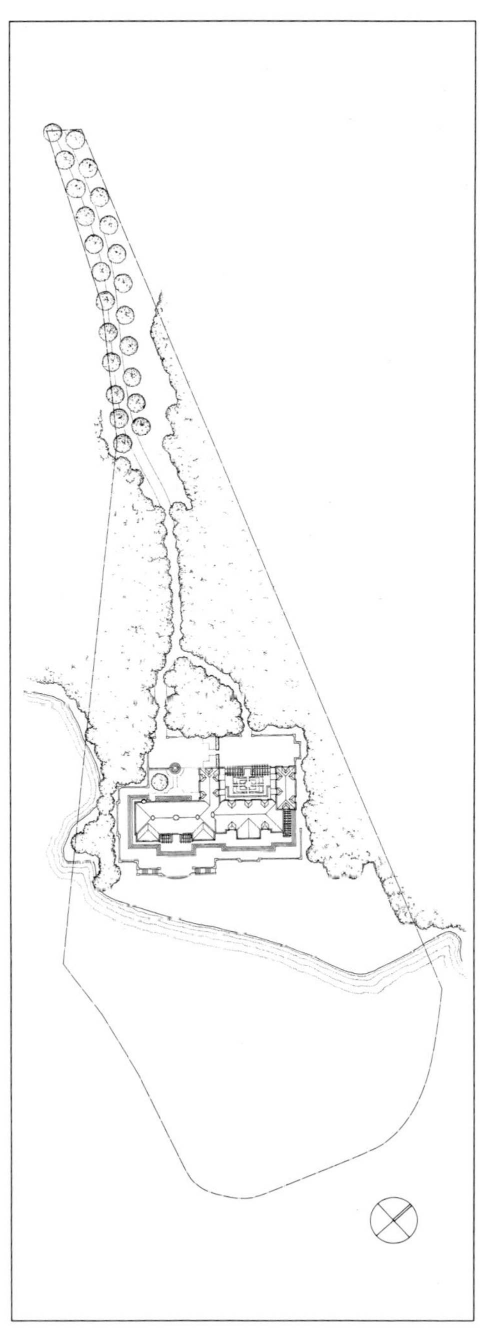

9

Cherry Creek Housing Development
Denver, Colorado
1983

This development consists of 300 apartment units in four buildings covering an entire city block. The overall massing of the buildings is carefully broken down to its smallest elements at the street level: gates, walls, and sheltered entrance doors reinforce the existing character of the surrounding residential neighborhood and serve to buffer the impact of this project in a very sensitive area of Denver presently characterized by small-scale, single-family houses.

The four complexly massed buildings are grouped around a raised landscaped courtyard which also serves to conceal a 450-car parking garage. Lower-level units open directly onto private courtyards which form the perimeter of the larger public open space. The highly developed roofscape of green tile serves to harmonize the massing of the buildings. Most of the upper-floor units have large open terraces which further break down the massing of the buildings while also offering views to the Rocky Mountains.

1.Corner of Alameda Avenue and Jackson Avenue 2.Courtyard 3.View along Alameda Avenue 4.View of model

1

2

3

4

1.Alameda Avenue elevation 2.Jackson Street elevation 3.Transverse section 4.Longitudinal section 5.Parking level floor plan 6.Terrace level floor plan 7.Roof plan 8.Ground floor plan 9.Typical floor plan 10.Sixth floor plan

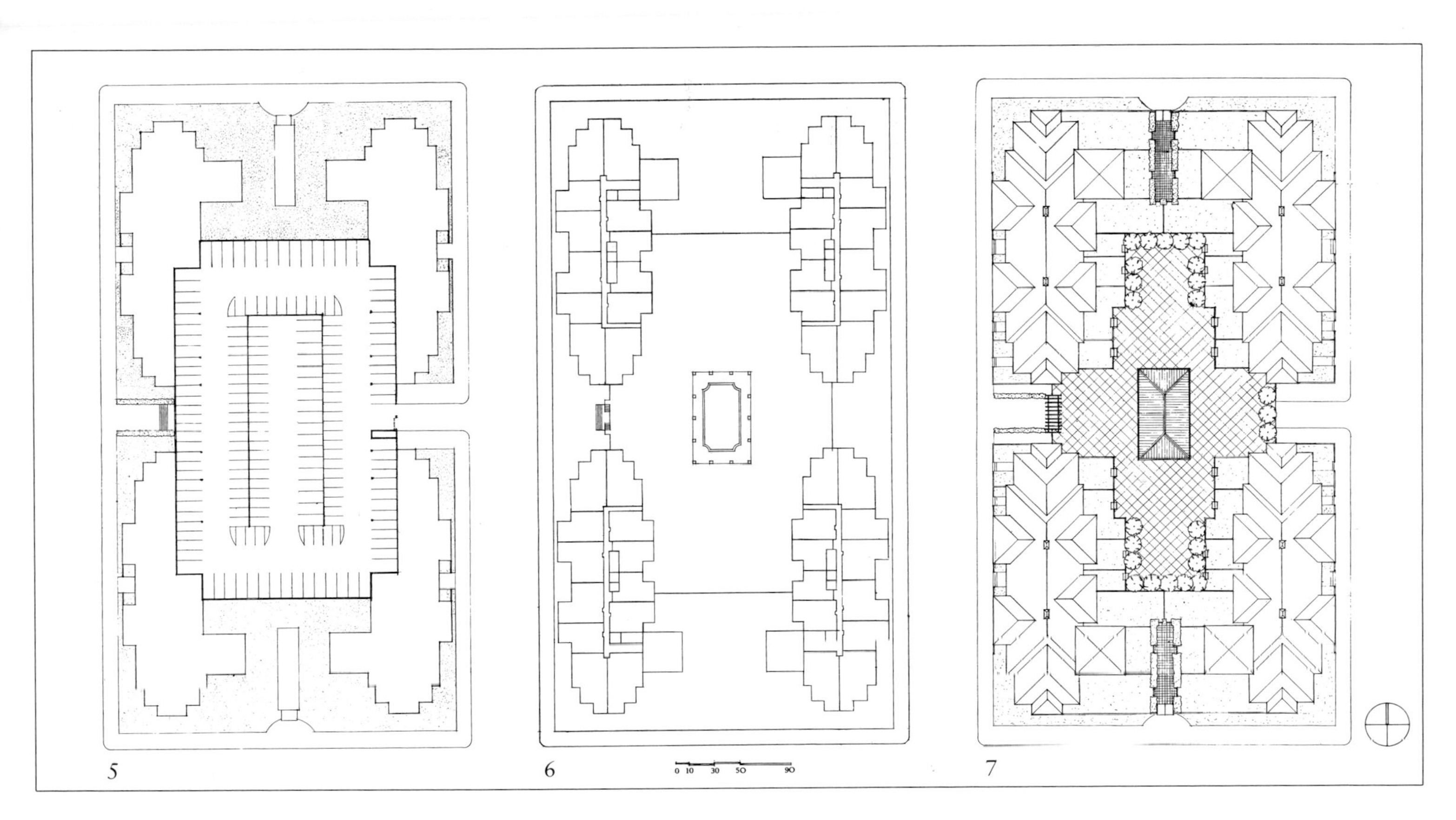
5
6
0 10 30 50 90
7

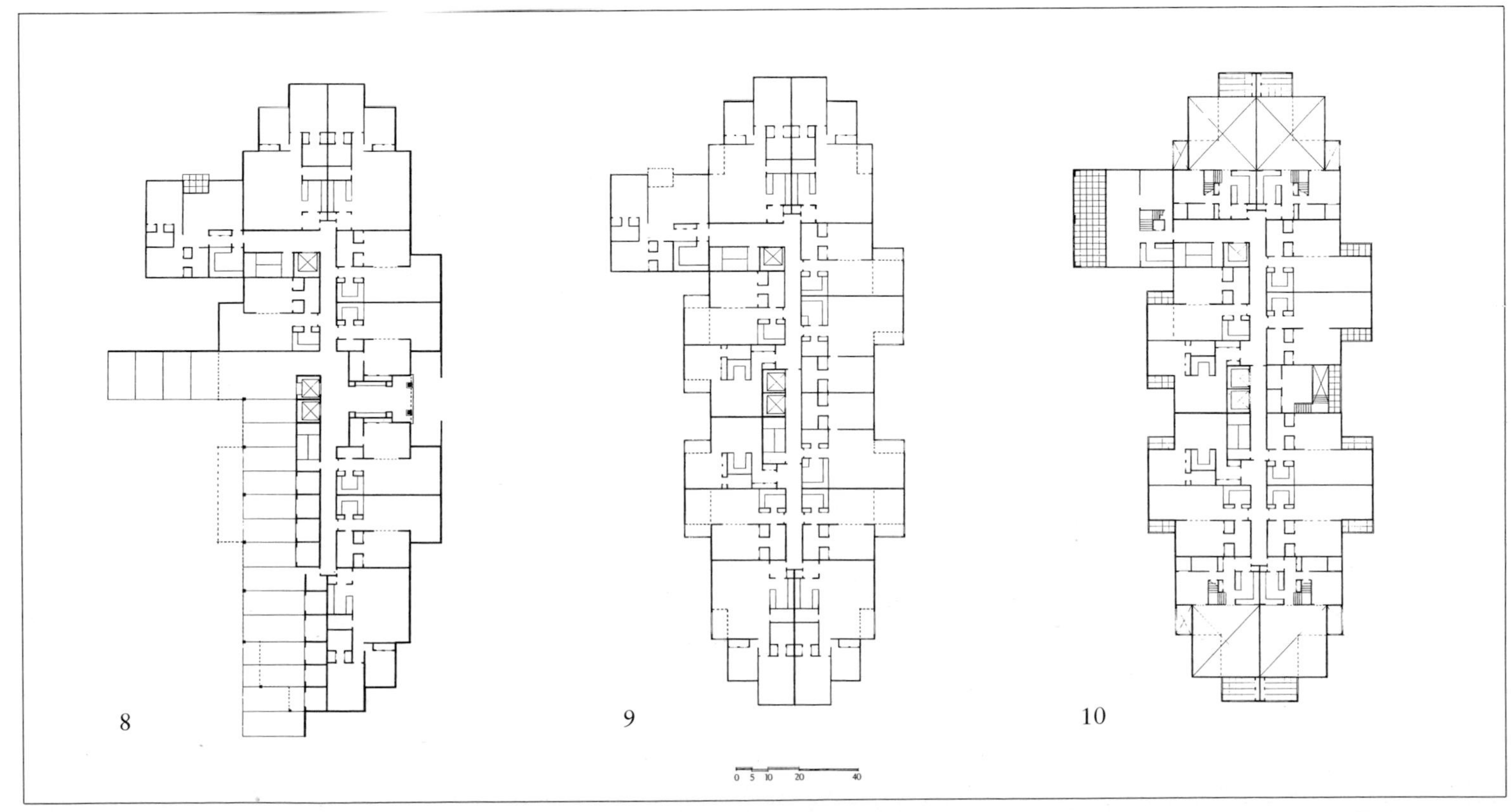
8
9
10
0 5 10 20 40

Fox Hollow Run
Chappaqua, New York
1983

Intended for a large, topographically challenging suburban site, this project takes advantage of the local Greek Revival vernacular to propose modest house groupings that maximize privacy and view. Simple, gabled shapes are juxtaposed to break down the scale of even the smallest units.

1

1.Site plan 2.House 3: A.Principal elevation B.Floor plan 3.House 4: A.Principal elevation B.Side elevation C.Ground floor plan D.Second floor plan

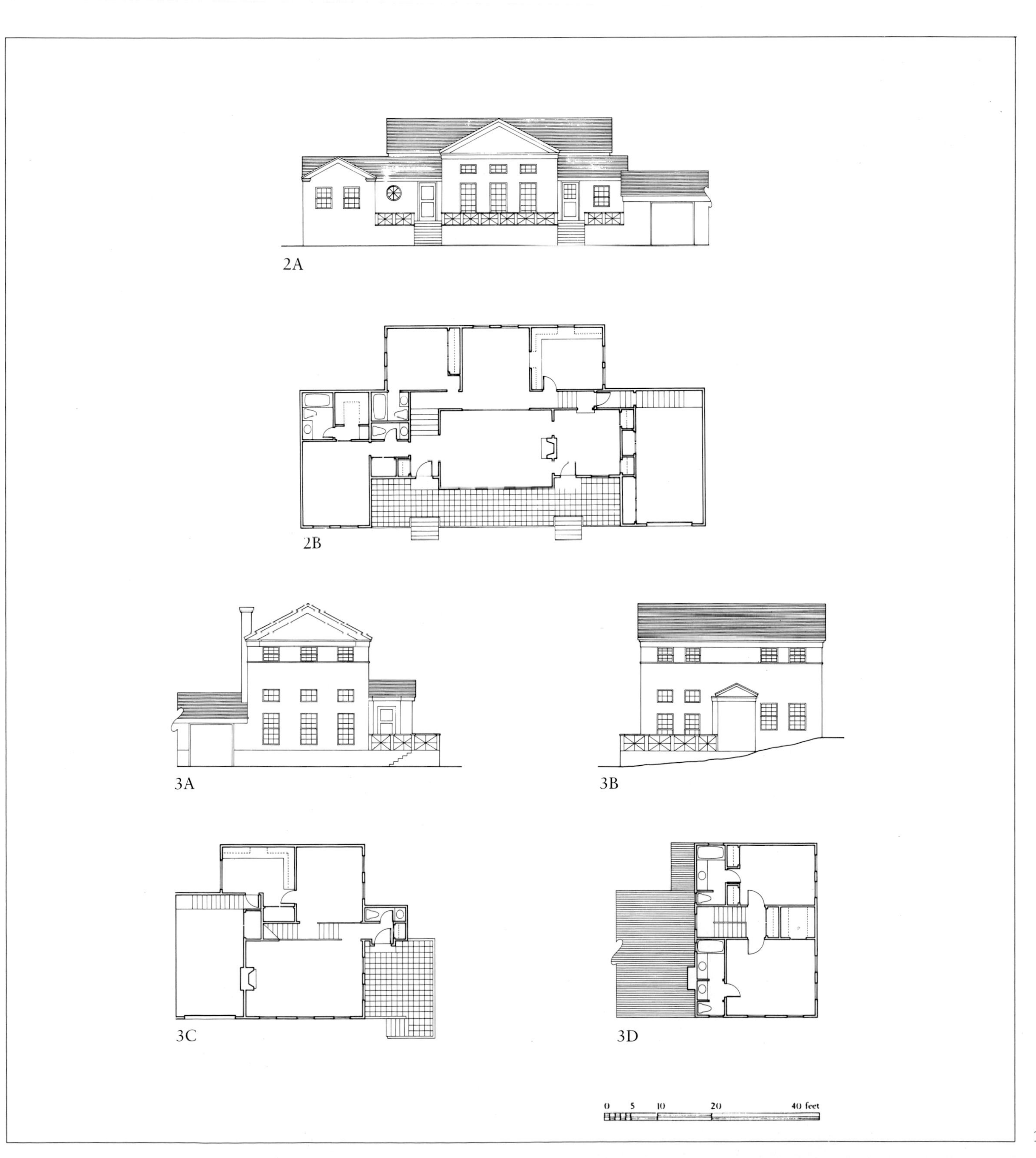

1.House 5: A.Principal elevation B.Side elevation C.Ground floor plan D.Second floor plan 2.House 6: A.Principal elevation B.Side elevation C.Ground floor plan D.Second floor plan

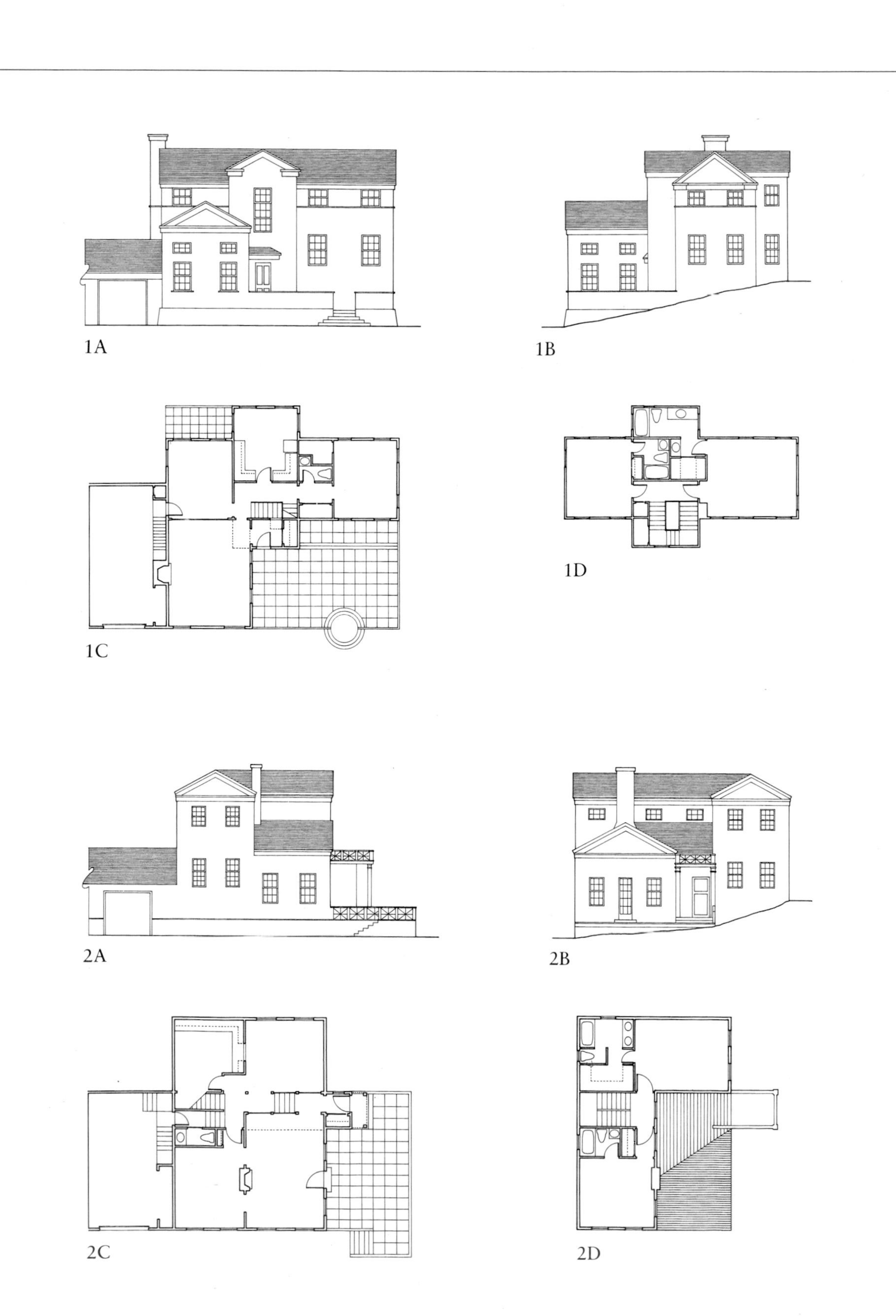

3.House 7: A.Principal elevation B.Side elevation C.Ground floor plan D.Second floor plan 4.House 8: A.Principal elevation B.Side elevation C.Ground floor plan D.Second floor plan

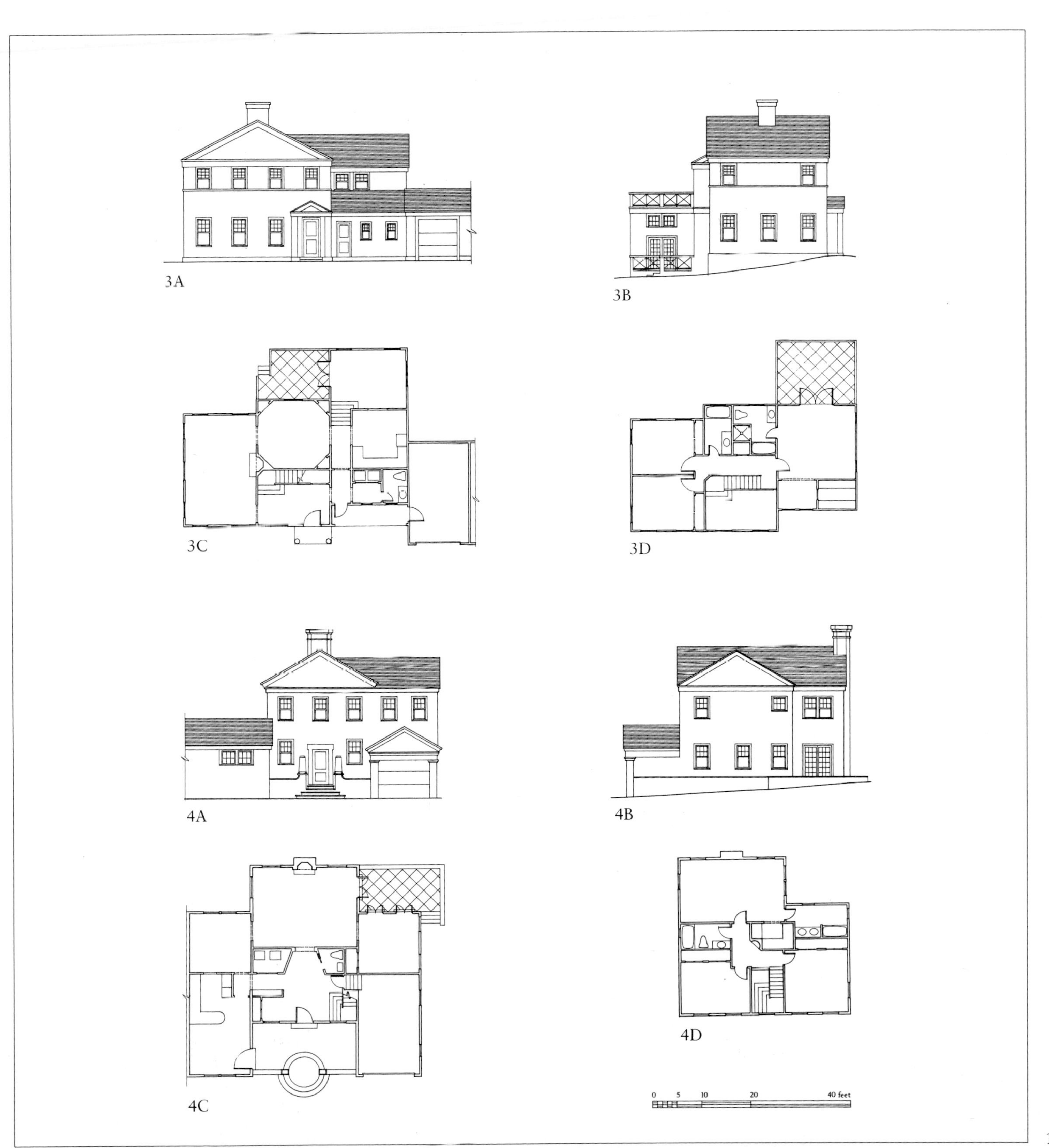

Copperflagg Corporation Residential Development

Staten Island, New York
1983–

The goal of this project is twofold: on the one hand, it is an attempt to invest a speculative suburban development with architectural coherence and dignity; on the other, to work sensitively within the delicate context of a designated landmark district. The site is part of the former estate of Ernest Flagg—the great Beaux-Arts trained architect best known for designing the Singer Tower in New York, the Corcoran Library in Washington, D.C., and the United States Naval Academy at Annapolis. Flagg erected his own Dutch Colonial style mansion on the highest point of Staten Island and surrounded it with a lavish array of outbuildings and small suburban houses, which he intended as exemplars of a standardized system of construction that would become a model for future developers, and which he published in his 1922 book *Small Houses: Their Economical Design and Construction.*

There are two phases to the development. Along the approach to the mansion, where the issues of contextualism are especially critical, a number of existing French Norman outbuildings are interwoven with new houses that echo Flagg's designs. This group of houses creates a semi-formal forecourt to Flagg's own house (now occupied by a religious order), while the formal garden at its center provides a communal focus for the new development. On the remainder of the site, prospective owners may choose from a wider variety of styles including Georgian, Arts and Crafts, and Dutch Colonial—styles that pick up themes found in Flagg's buildings and relate to the more general context of Staten Island's history. Building footprints, materials, and details are limited by a stringent set of design guidelines, but our goal has been to produce that rich diversity within order that has always been the glory of America's suburbs.

Beyond the specific issues of contextualism, this project is an investigation of planned suburban design—a field which architects have largely abandoned to the speculative developer. The suburb at its best is not anti-urban; it is capable of rising above the limits of the freestanding house to create a sense of a specific place in an Arcadian setting where individuality, community, and the natural landscape coexist.

1A

1B

1C

1D

1.Ernest Flagg's Estate: A.Aerial view B.Ernest Flagg House C.Palm House D.Photo taken in 1950 2.Site plan showing designated landmark area 3.Detail plan of landmark area

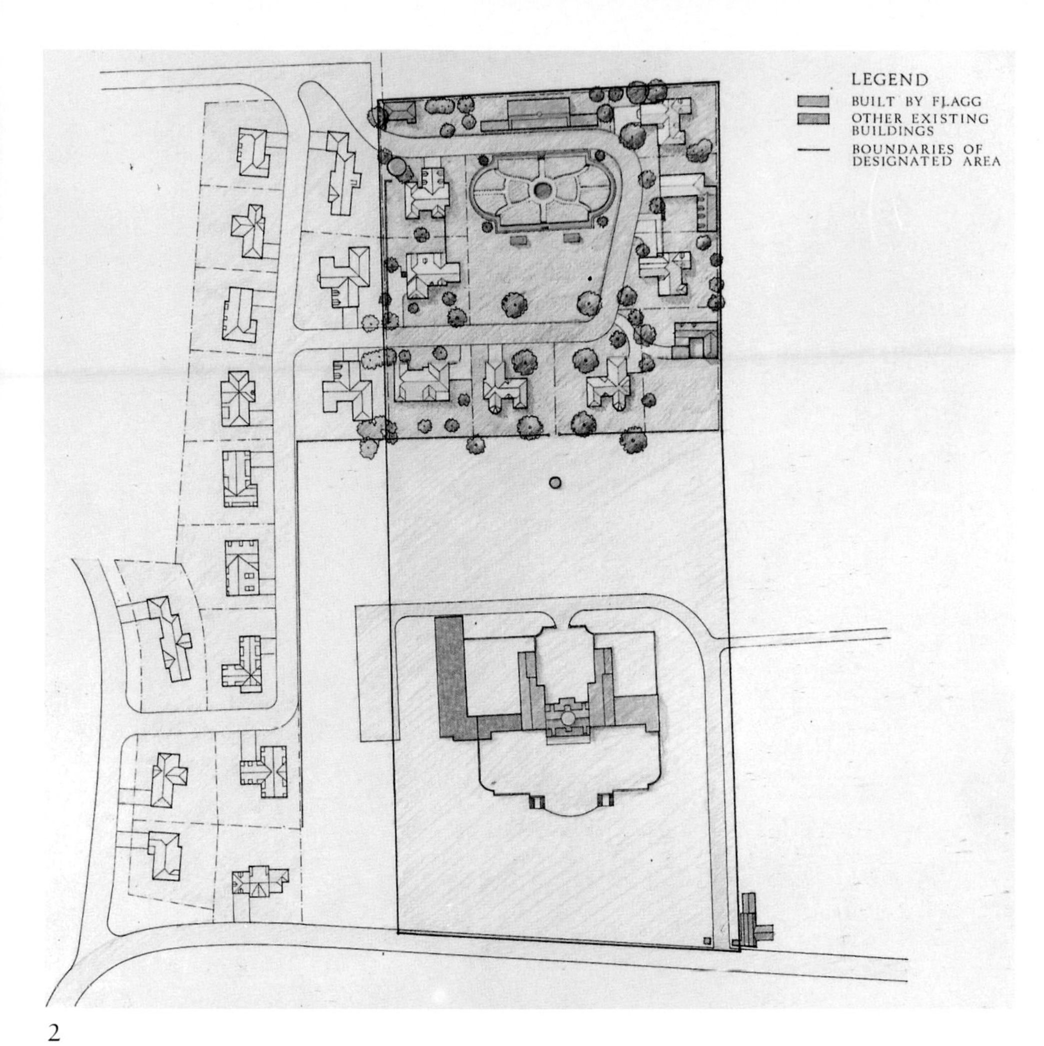

2

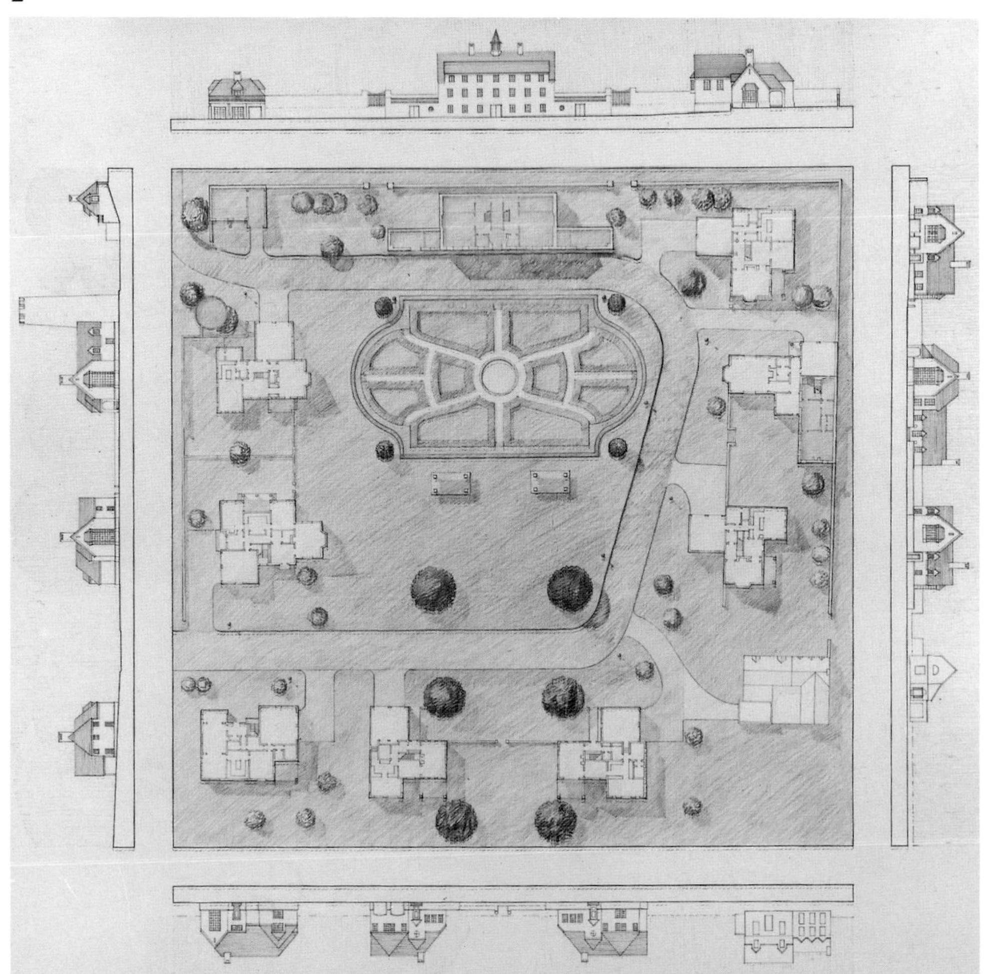

3

1

2A

2B

1.Perspective of rendering of project
2.The Stable: A.Front elevation B.Rendering of renovated Stable 3.The Garage cottage: A.Southeast elevation B.Northwest elevation C.Northeast elevation D.Second floor plan E.Ground floor plan F.Site plan G.Rendering of renovated Garage

4.The Palm House: A.Southwest elevation B.Southeast elevation C.Northwest elevation D.Ground floor plan E.Second floor plan F.Site plan

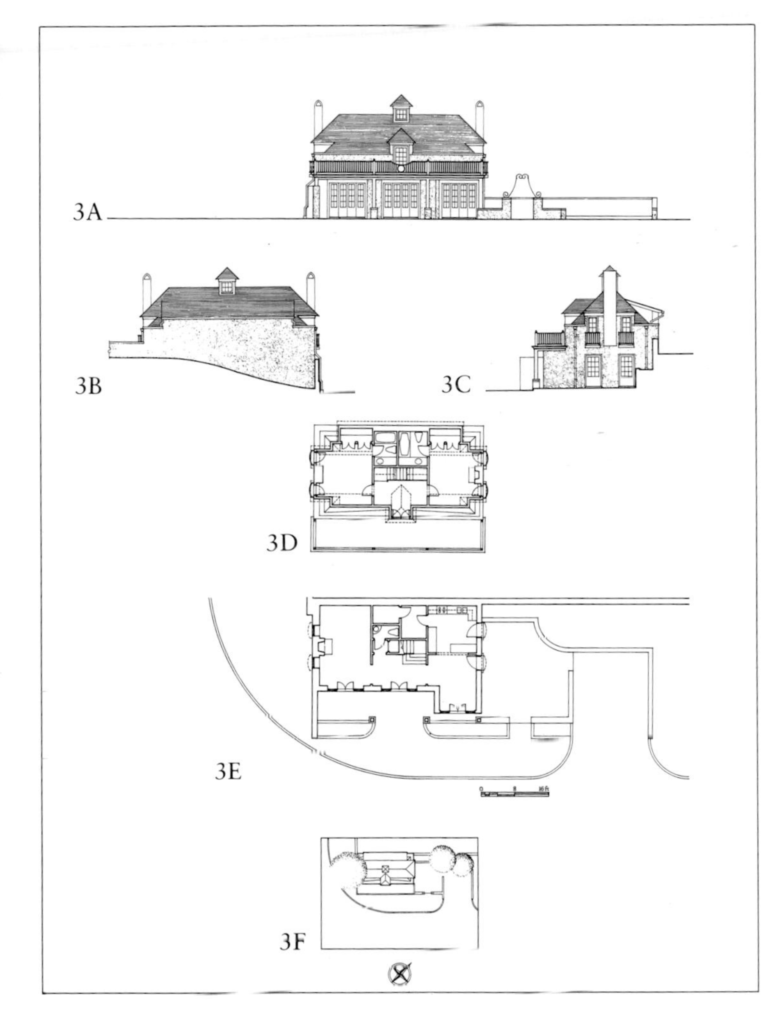

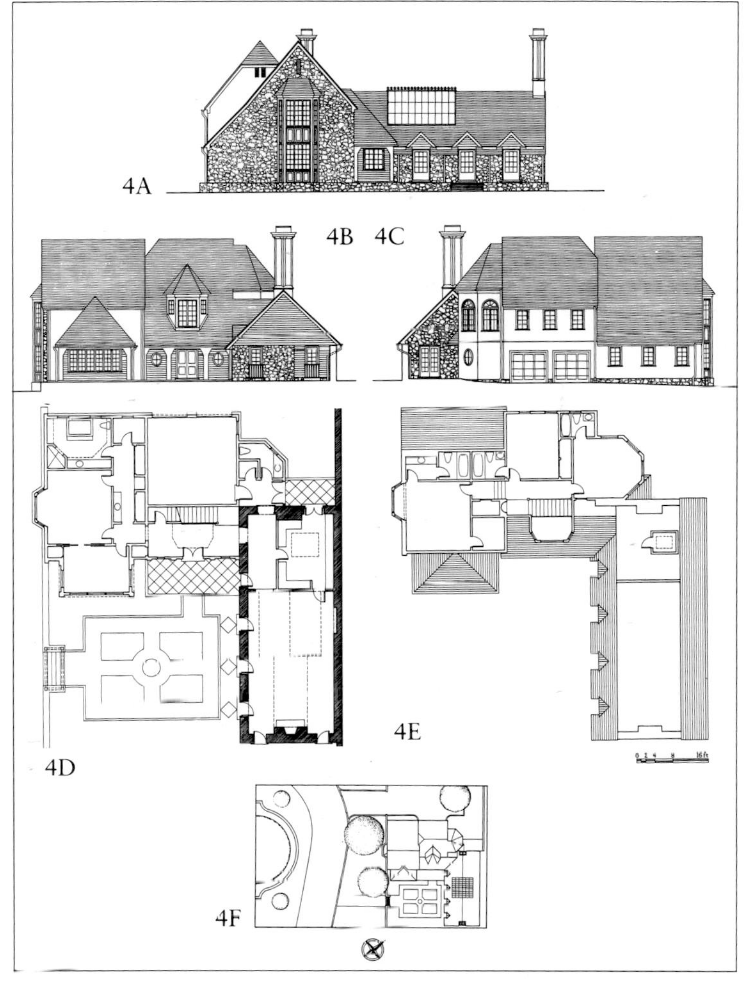

3G

1.House at 5 Flagg Court: A.West elevation B.Northeast elevation C.Southeast elevation D.Ground floor plan E.Second floor plan F.Site plan 2.House at 16 Flagg Court: A.Southeast elevation B.Ground floor plan C.Second floor plan

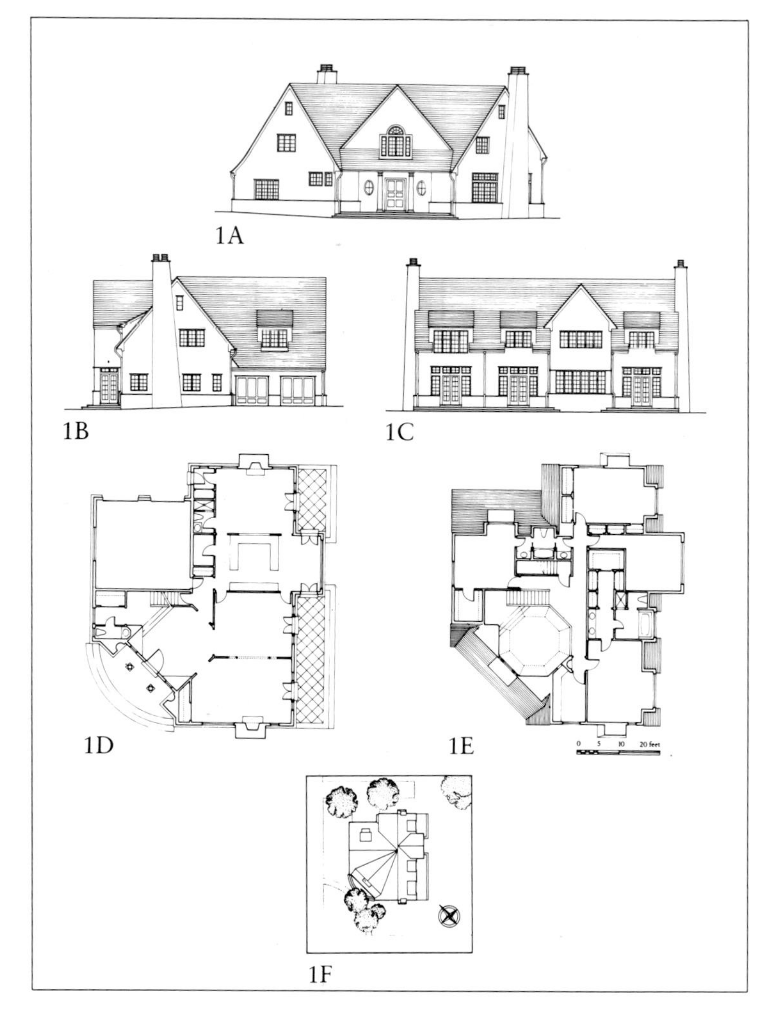

3.House at 39 Flagg Court: A.Northwest elevation B.Ground floor plan C.Second floor plan 4.View from the northeast 5.House at 81 Copperflagg Lane: A.South elevation B.Northwest elevation C.Southwest elevation D.Section E.Ground floor plan F.Second floor plan G.Site plan

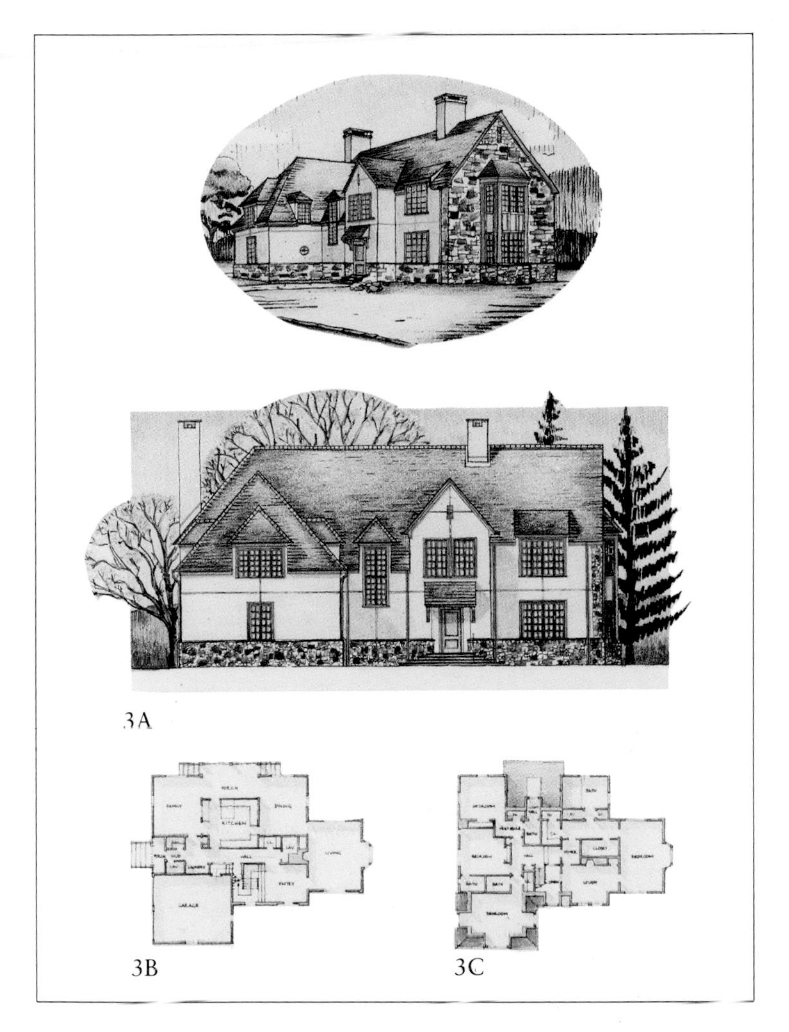

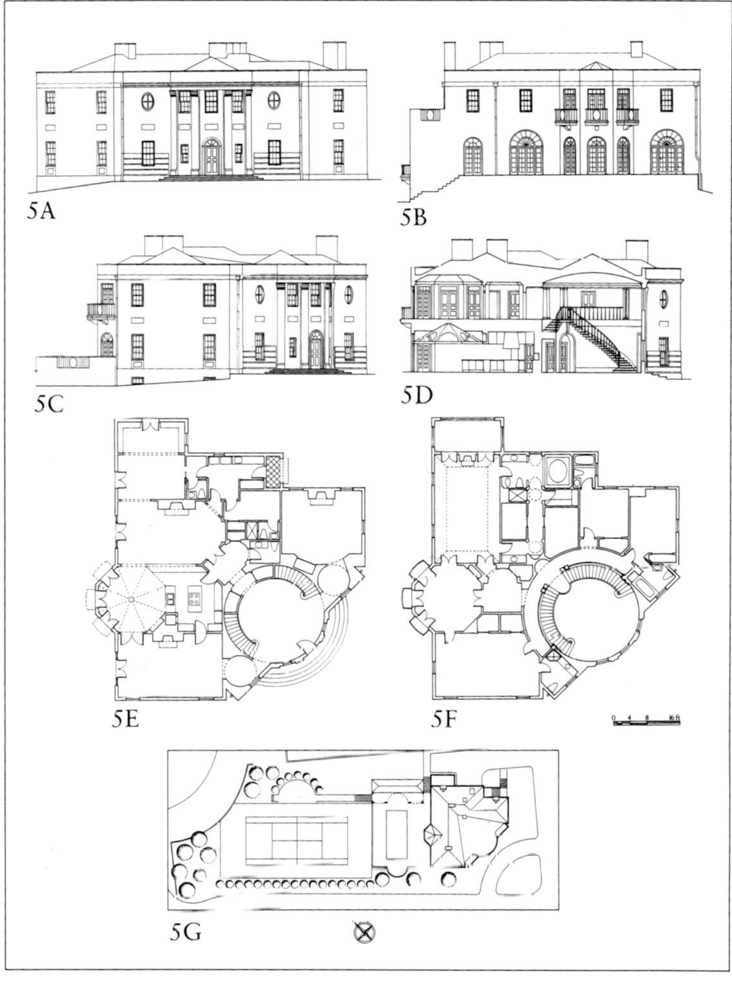

4

Pattern book house prototypes for outside landmark area

1.Montpelier: A.Principal elevation B.Ground floor plan C.Second floor plan 2.Federal: A.Principal elevation B.Ground floor plan C.Second floor plan

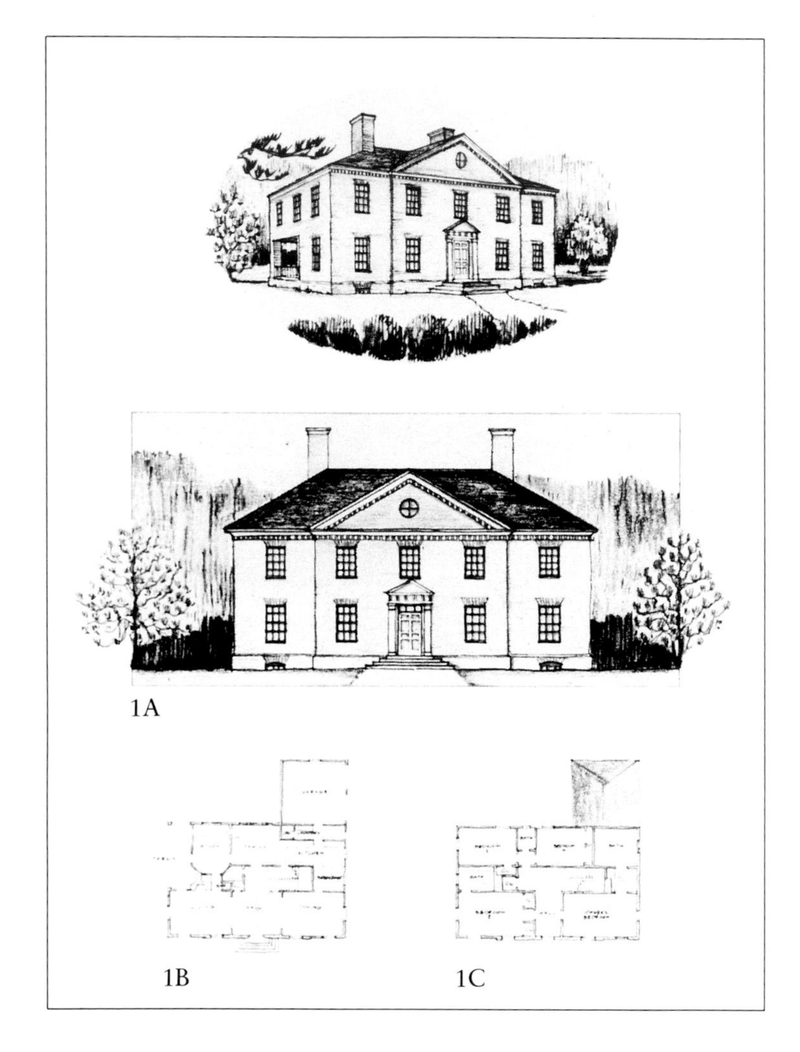

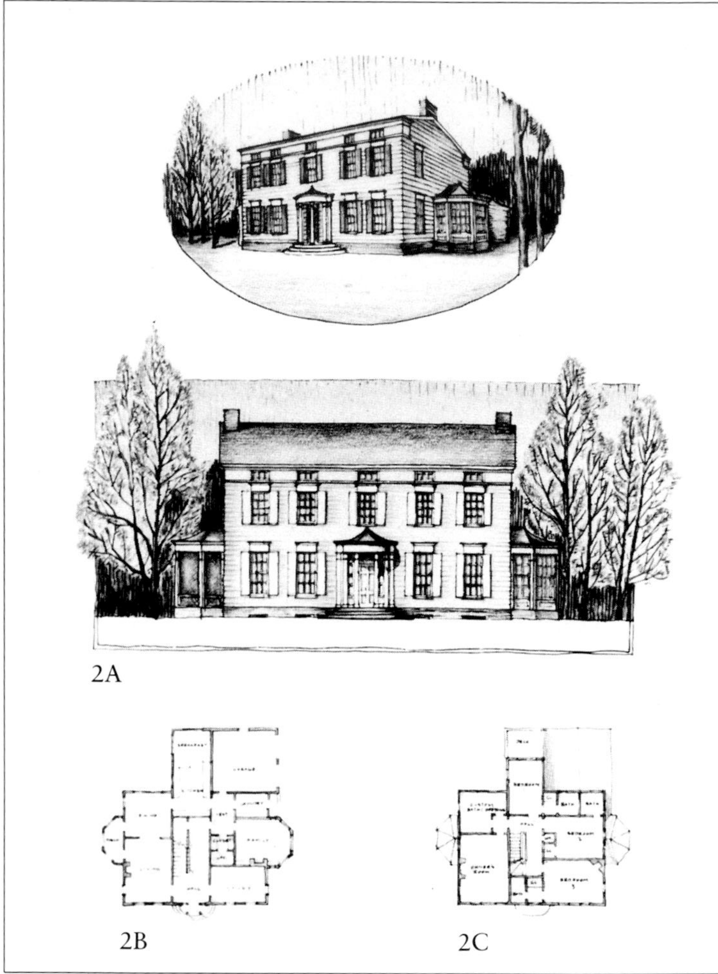

3.Mount Airy: A.Principal elevation
B.Ground floor plan C.Second floor plan
4.Tide Water: A.Principal elevation
B.Ground floor plan C.Second floor plan

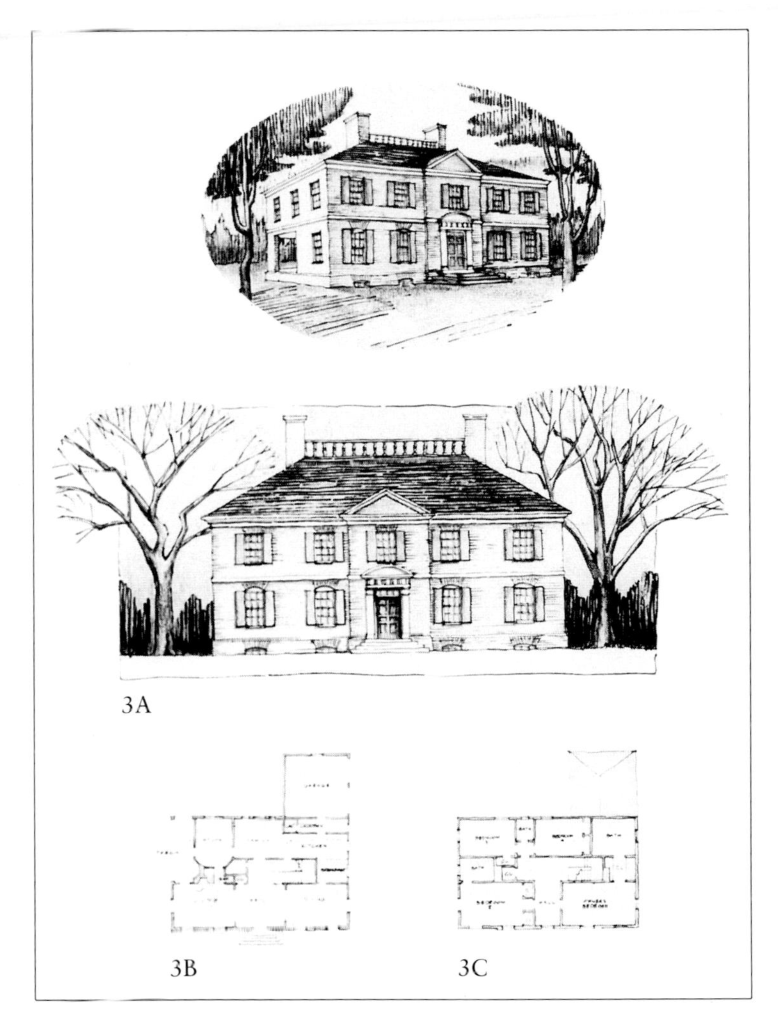

3A

3B 3C

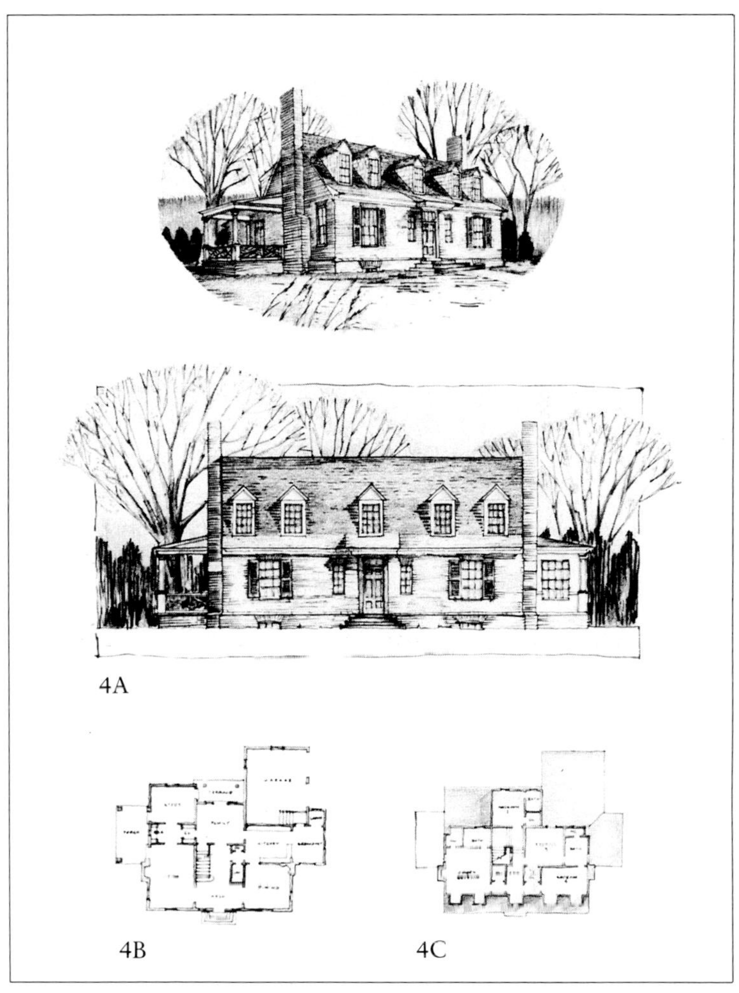

4A

4B 4C

1. Dutch Colonial: A. Principal elevation
B. Ground floor plan C. Second floor plan
2. Greek Revival: A. Principal elevation
B. Ground floor plan C. Second floor plan

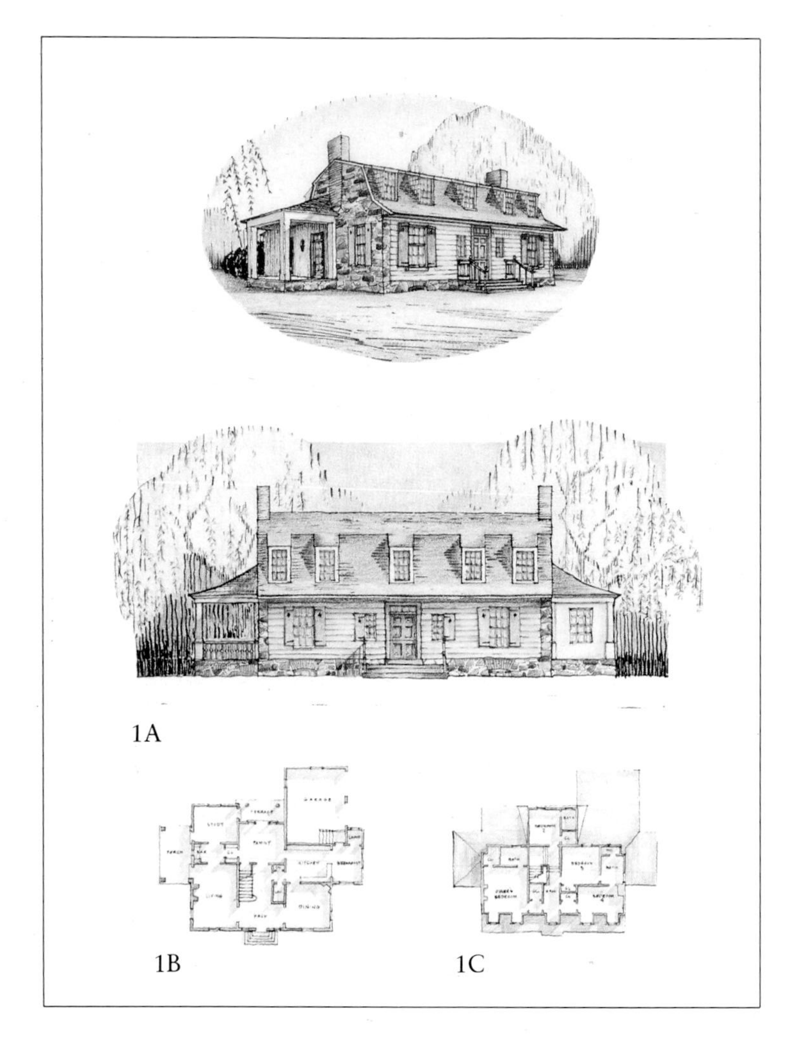

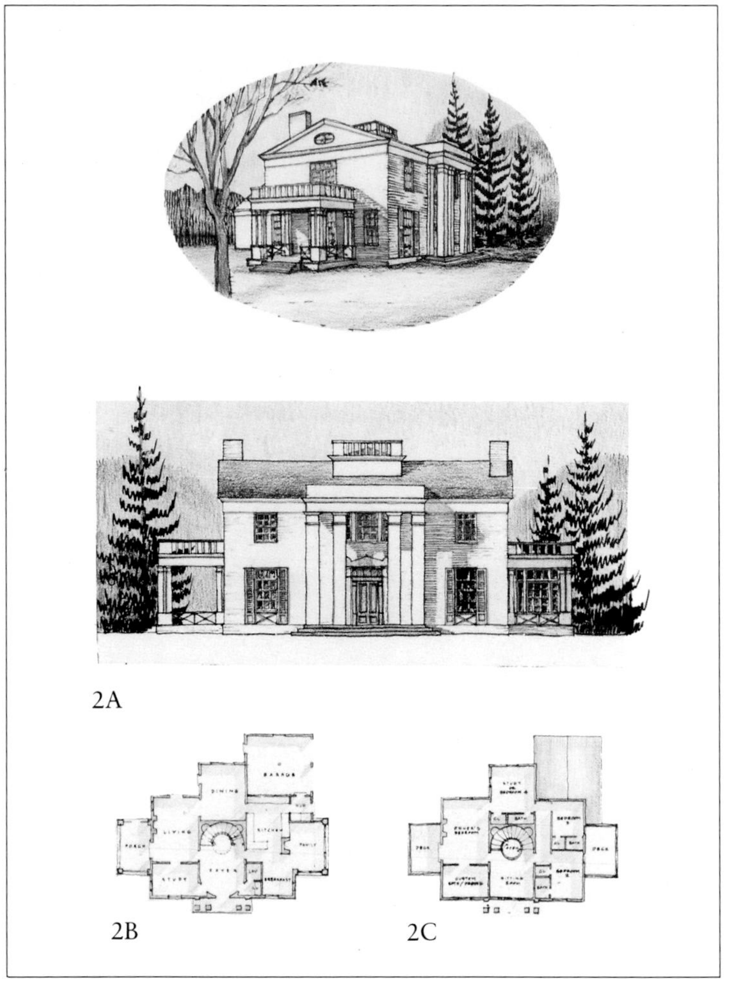

3.Regency: A.Principal elevation B.Ground floor plan C.Second floor plan 4.House at 60 Copperflagg Lane: A.Northeast elevation B.Southwest elevation C.Section D.Ground floor plan E.Second floor plan F.Site plan 5.View of model 6.Northeast facade under construction

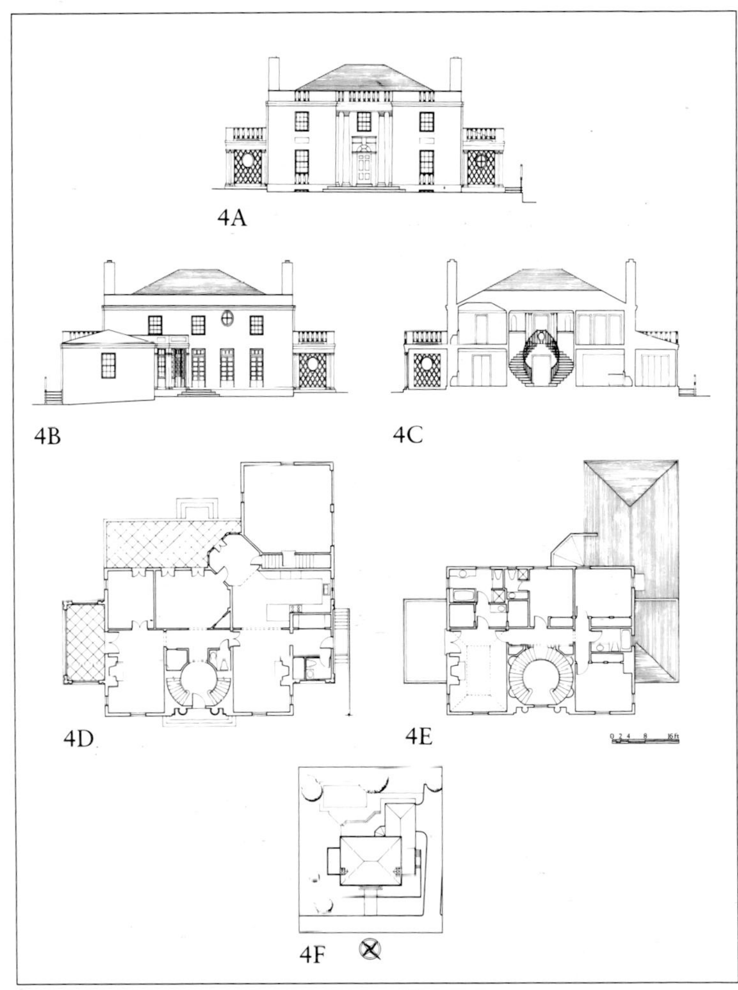

5

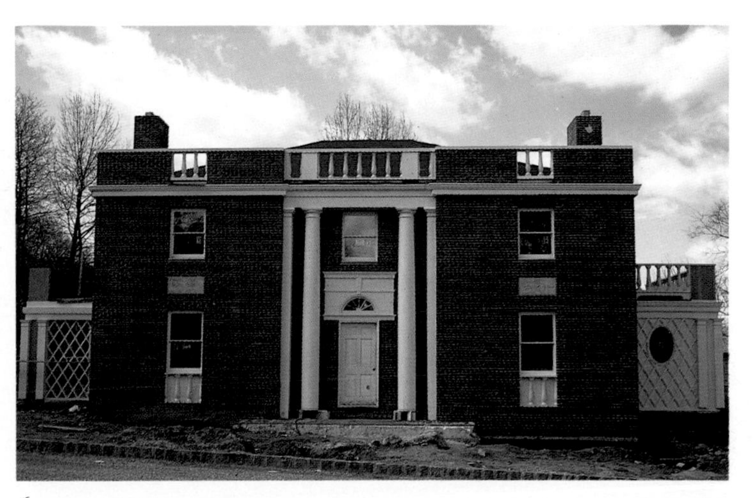

6

Performing Arts Center
Anchorage, Alaska
1983

The Anchorage Performing Arts Center is a grand yet accessible landmark, focusing community and cultural life by providing a dramatic setting for gatherings while acting as a municipal symbol to spark civic pride. The lobby of the opera house stands at one of Anchorage's busiest corners. More than just a lobby, it is an enclosed public gathering space—a great indoor piazza suitable for Anchorage's climate. The lobby, with its sweep of stairs and generous and imaginatively lit volume, is intended not only to serve the theater but also to become the city's official living room. Facing the convention center and the future F Street park, the lobby is the architectural keynote of the ensemble.

Each theater rises above the arcade and has a clearly articulated entrance marquee to preserve the cherished individuality of the separate groups.

All-weather, arcaded passageways and glazed lobbies unify the rest of the complex, providing a lively, inviting facade around almost the entire block and preventing the blank-walled, blind-eyed look typical of so many recent theater complexes. The complex would make a distinct contribution to the vitality of downtown life. Of obvious value in Anchorage's demanding climate, the enclosed loggia-like spaces connect the Alaska Performing Arts Center to the surrounding city and provide space for small shops, theatrical and municipal exhibits, restaurants and cafes. Even when the theaters are dark, the lobbies and arcades would be open to the streets; at performance times the festive air that accompanies all theater events would spill out and make the surrounding streets part of the drama.

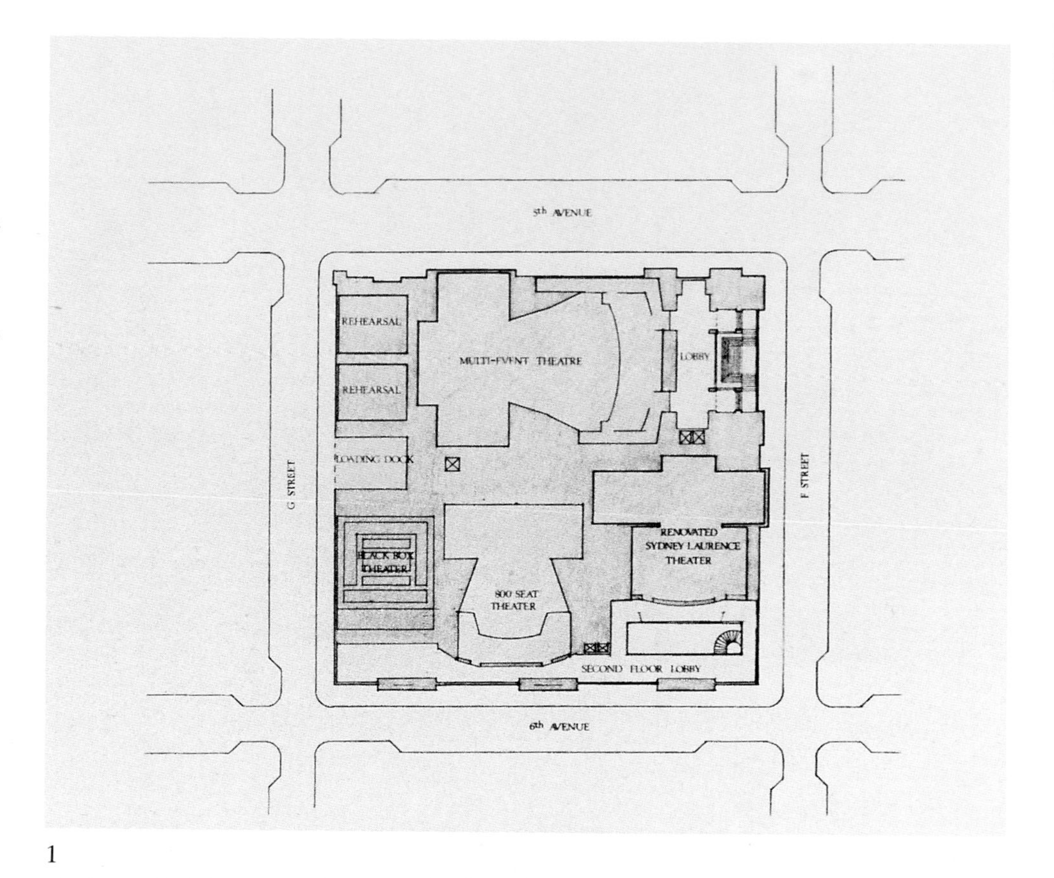

1

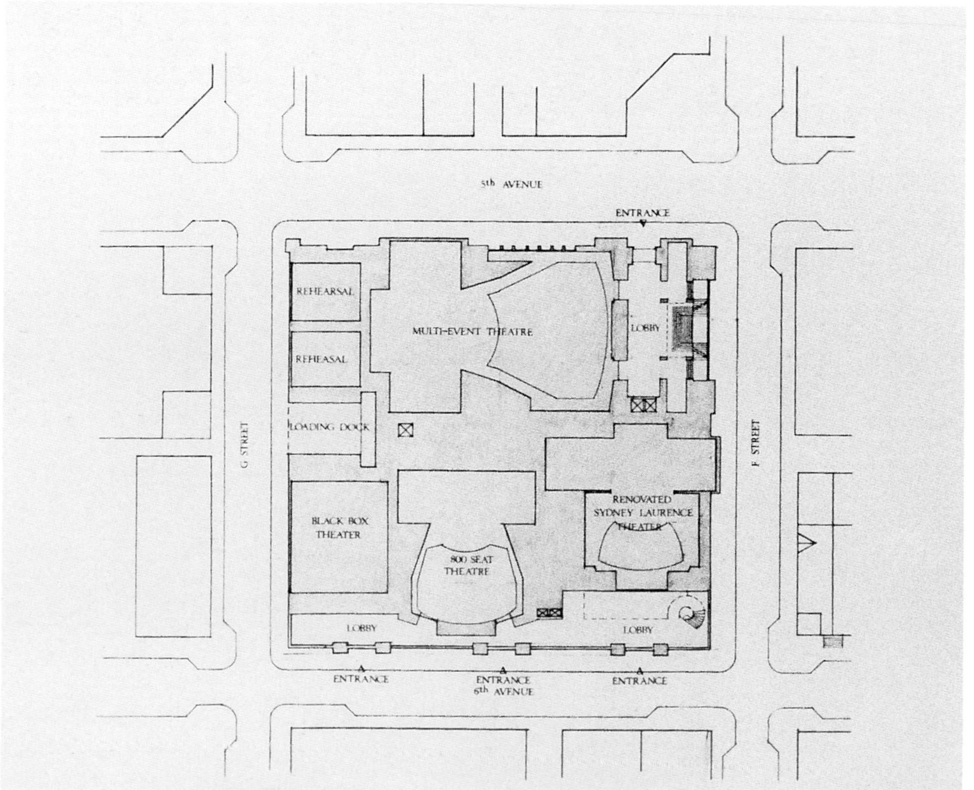

2

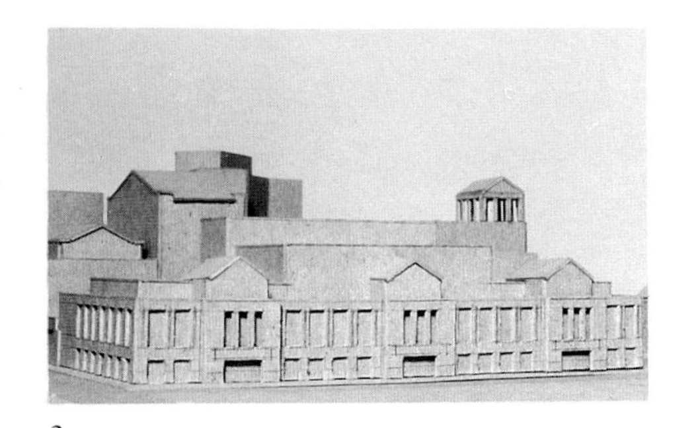

3

1.Second floor plan 2.Ground floor plan 3.View of model from the southwest 4.View from the southeast 5.View from the convention center 6.View of lobby and grand stair 7.South elevation 8.East elevation 9.North elevation 10.West elevation

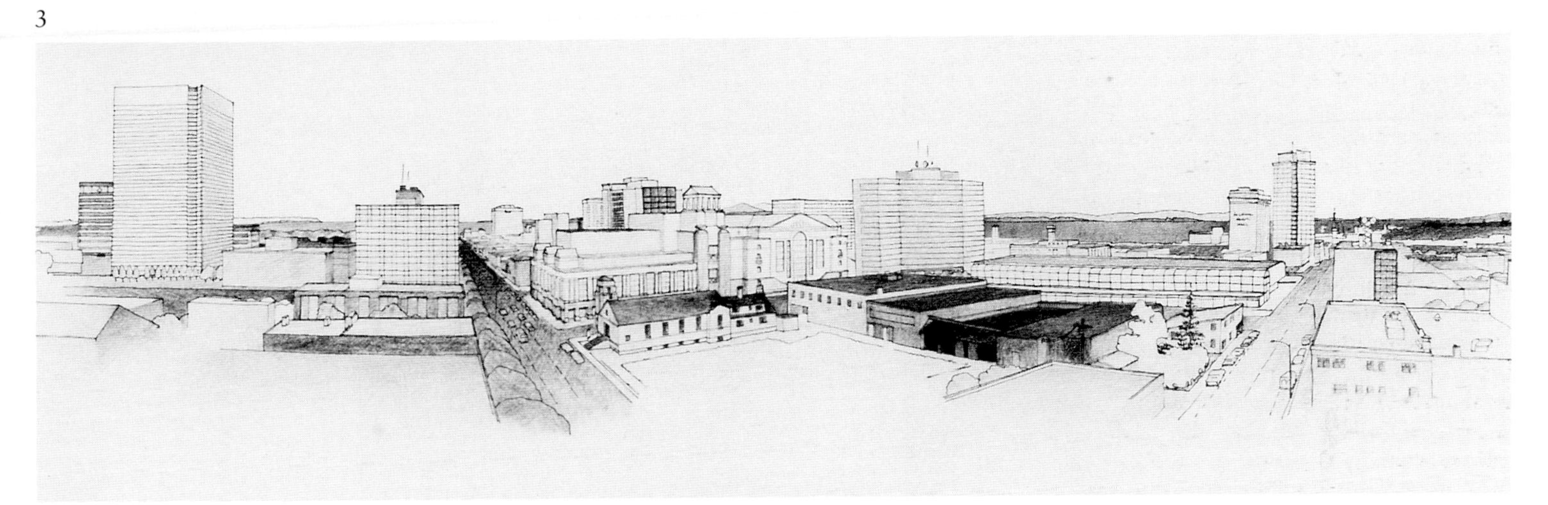

4

5

6

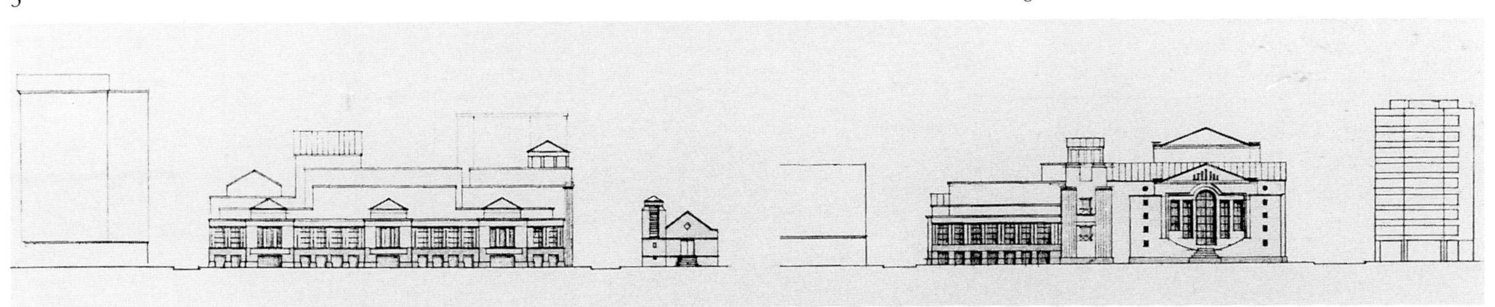

7

8

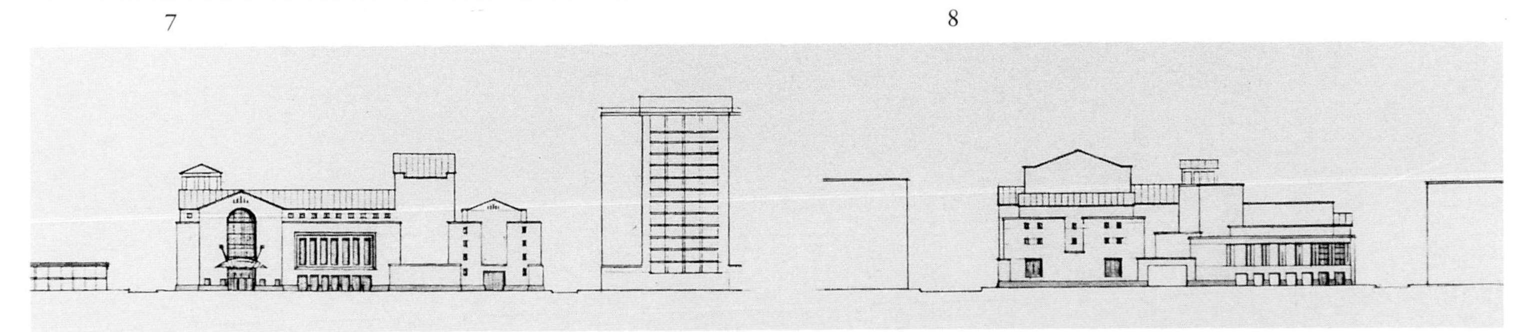

9

10

Residence on Lake Agawam

Southampton, New York
1983

This lakefront house consciously recalls the gambreled barns and farmhouses of pre-Revolutionary Long Island, as well as the Dutch Colonial style resort "cottages" of the late nineteenth and early twentieth centuries. At the entrance facade, an asymmetrical composition of turrets, gables, covered porches, and shed dormers scales down the long mass; at the water side, similar elements assume a symmetry and grandeur to respond in kind to the shingled mansions on the opposite shore. The combination of Classical and rustic details—such as the Tuscan entablatures supported by Y-bracketed posts—counters the tendency towards overbearing formality on the one hand, and towards cloying picturesqueness on the other.

The plan is organized about a modified center hall off which the principal formal rooms open. The second story, containing bedrooms, extends beyond the mass, subsuming porches and shading the extensively glazed first floor. A secret stair leads to an attic-level exercise room whose gabled projection above the west-facing elliptical bay is based on the central motif of McKim, Mead and White's James Breese house, a notable Southampton landmark.

The house is the climactic element of an elaborate landscape composition that incorporates formal and service gardens, primary and secondary driveways, and a carriage house renovated into a tennis and pool pavilion. Set at the end of its gently swerving drive, the house all but obstructs the view of the lake from the east so as to magnify its impact from inside.

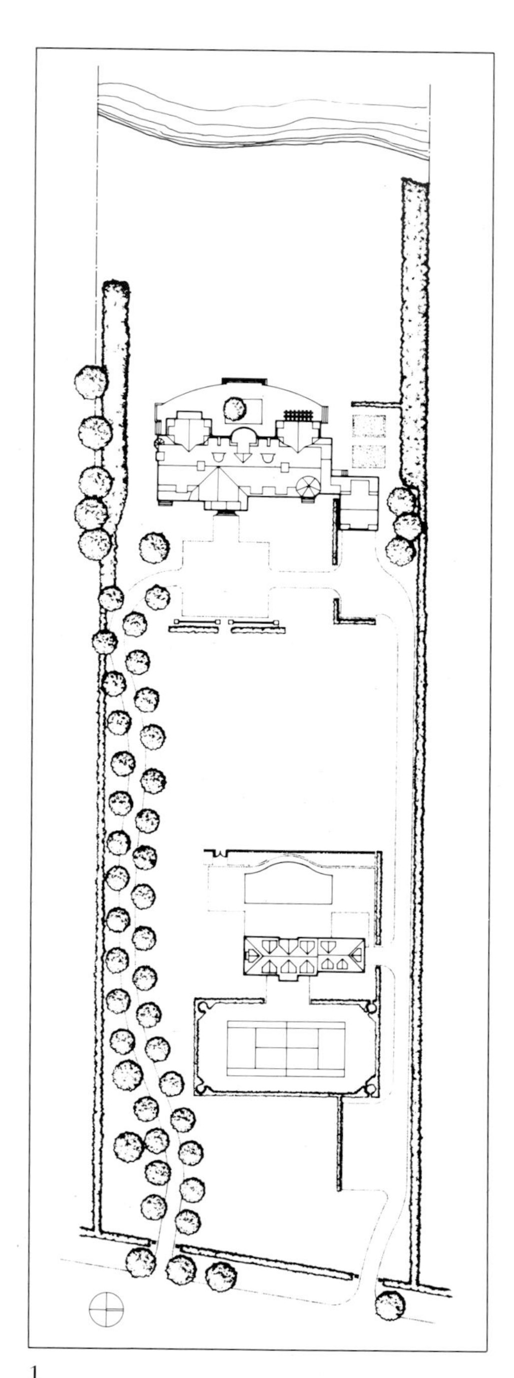

1

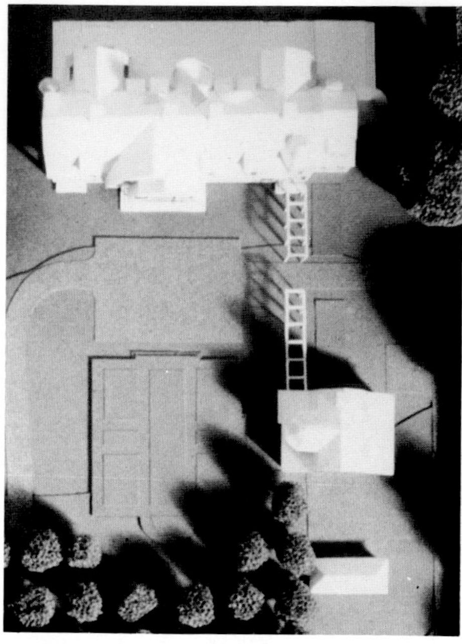

2A

2B

1.Site plan 2.Model of preliminary scheme:
A.Overhead view B.View from the west
3.East elevation 4.West elevation
5.North elevation 6.South elevation

1.Section through entry hall 2.Section through turret 3.Second floor plan 4.Ground floor plan 5.Model of final scheme: A.View from the northeast B.Overhead view

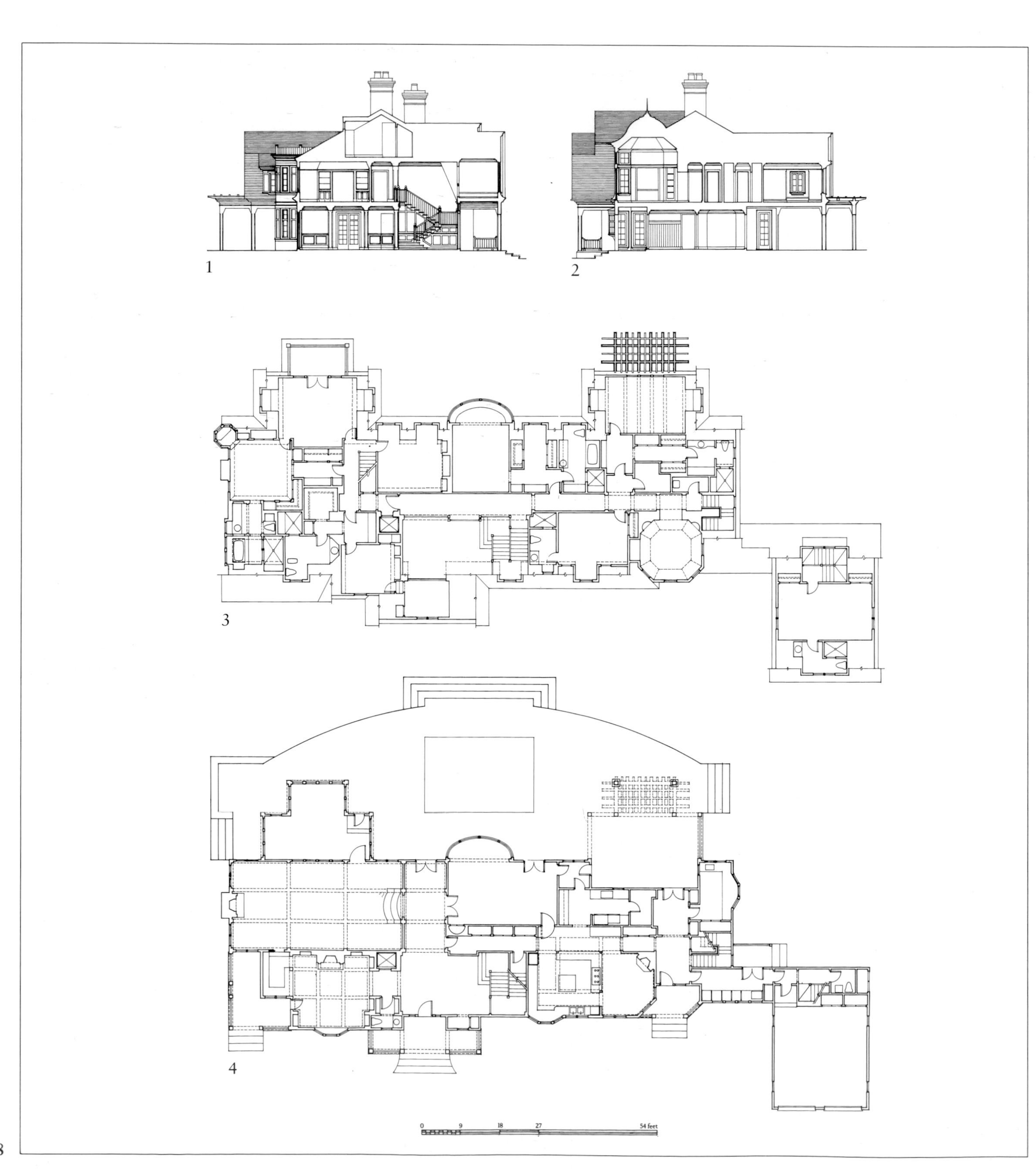

5A

5B

Residence
Hewlett Harbor, New York
1984–

This house addresses two very different contexts: the gently landscaped terrain of a golf course across the street in front, and a navigable channel that opens through the tidal marshes to Hewlett Bay in the back.

The entry court, a precisely formed exterior room, is the first in a series of spaces forming a sequence from the street to the water's edge. It is bounded by brick walls on two sides and on the third by the facade which takes cues from Sir John Soane's Pitzhanger Manor and from the Ashmolean Museum by C. R. Cockerell.

The unorthodox six-bay composition of the facade, from which the center column has been omitted, is intensified by the void frieze of the entablature above the entry-porch roof which spills out from it, and the front door below. These elements, together with the delicately scaled colonnettes supporting a porch canopy, mediate between the public scale of the colossal Ionic order and the more intimate scale of the rooms within the house.

Beyond the facade, the proportions of the Ionic order and the order itself are used to create a series of rooms where the richly developed scale and detail of Classicism are used to articulate the openness and spatial interplay of a modern house. The principal rooms open, through French doors, to a terrace which wraps around the west side of the house, creating a plinth and extending the rooms toward the water.

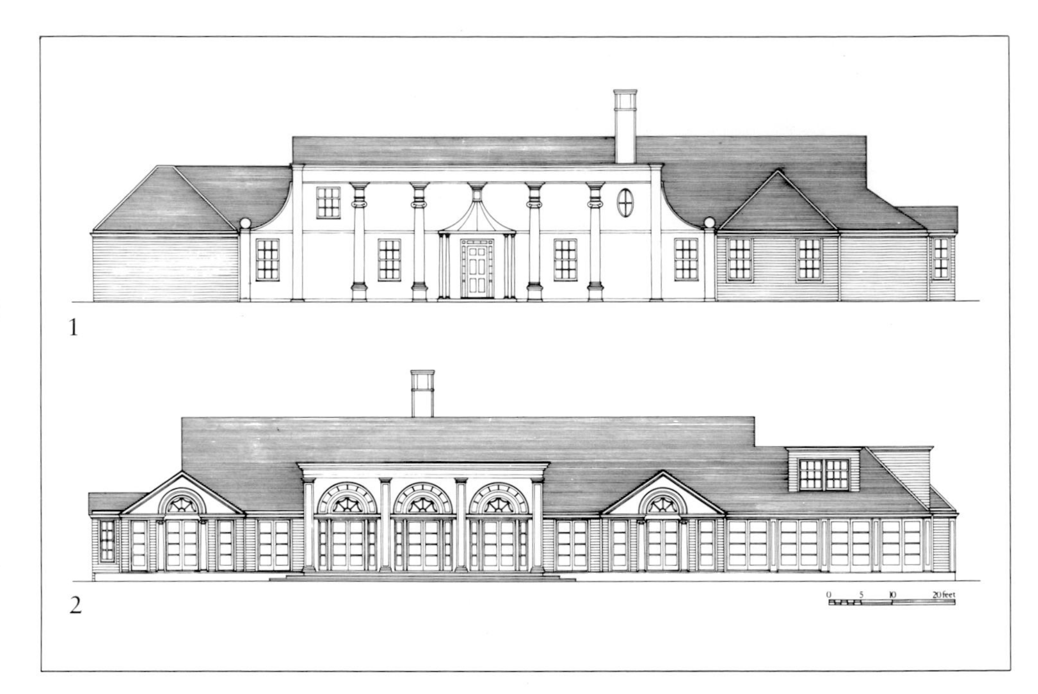

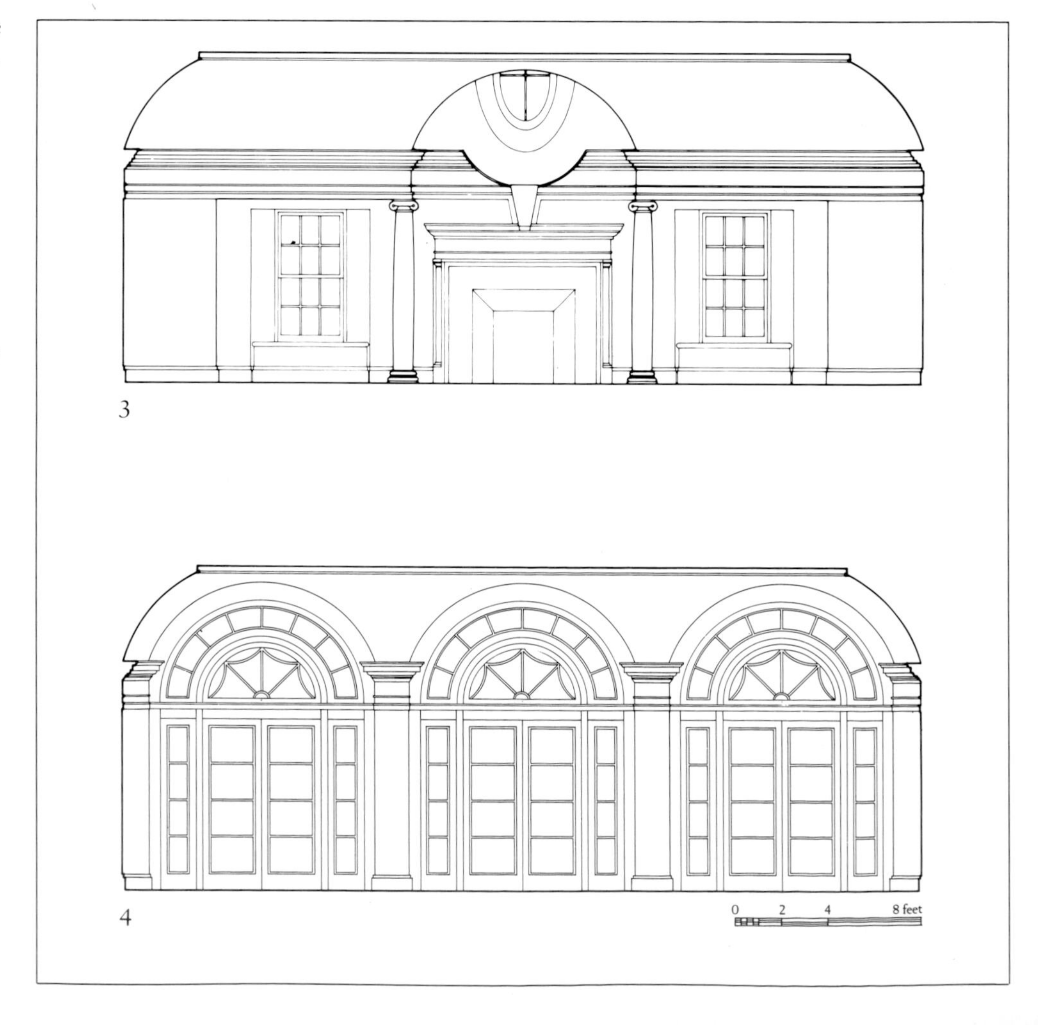

1.East elevation 2.West elevation 3.Living room east elevation 4.Living room west elevation 5.Second floor plan 6.Ground floor plan 7.Site plan 8.Existing conditions 9.Aerial view of model from the northeast 10.View of model of principal elevation 11.View of east wall of living room model

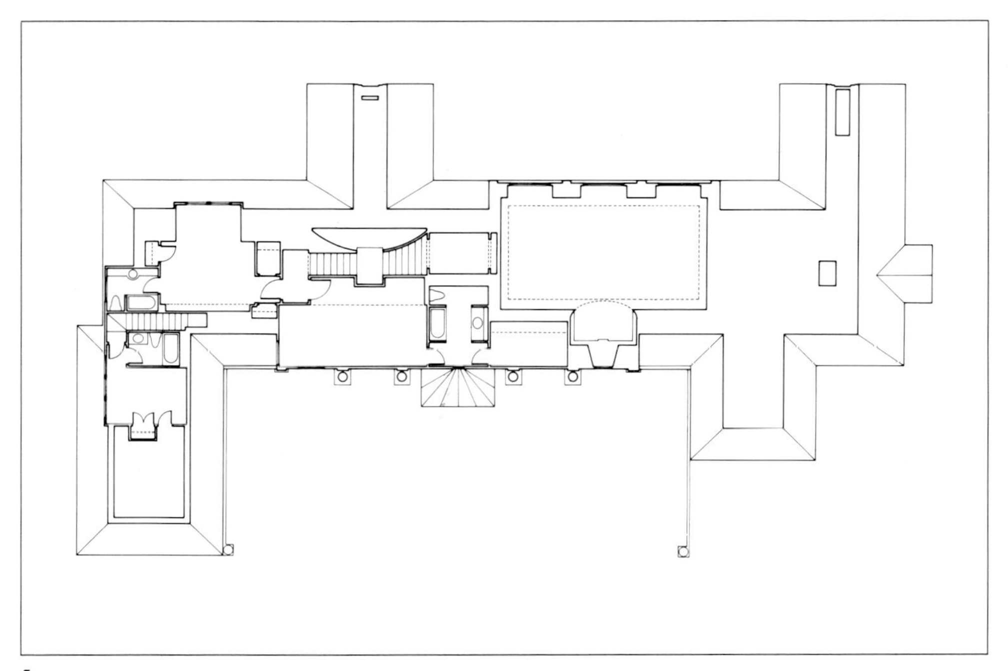

5

8

9

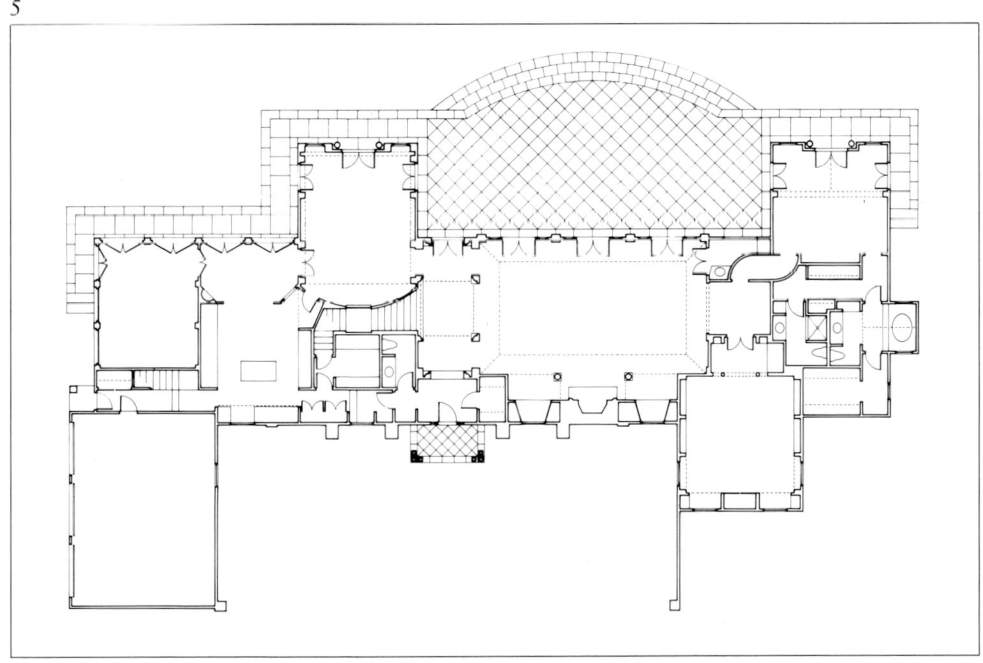

6

10

11

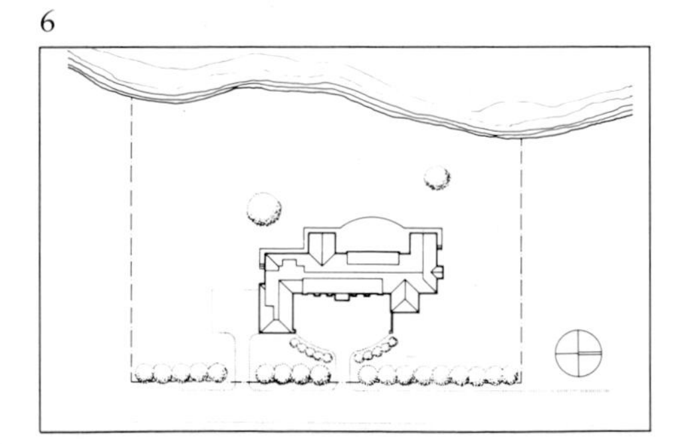

7

Residence
Brooklyn, New York
1983–

This single-family detached house occupies a narrow lot in an established neighborhood. The design attempts to refine the architectural themes that typify the neighboring houses, and to establish a unique identity through the quality and character of its detailing and the rich mixture of its materials. The basement and first floor are rusticated with alternating bands of red brick and granite, while the second floor is faced with cream-colored stucco. The walls are punctured with painted steel casement windows and capped by a green glazed tile hipped roof. The dormers serve as clerestories for the second floor bathrooms, providing additional light to the middle of the house.

Rooms are gathered about an entry hall that rises two floors through the house and culminates in a gilt dome. The constricted plan is perceptually aggrandized by generous twelve-foot ceilings and by the arrangement of the rooms along an axis that permits space to be visually borrowed from adjacent hallways and rooms.

1.Roof plan 2.Attic floor plan 3.Second floor plan 4.Ground floor plan 5.Aerial view of garden model 6.East elevation 7.Partial elevation of street

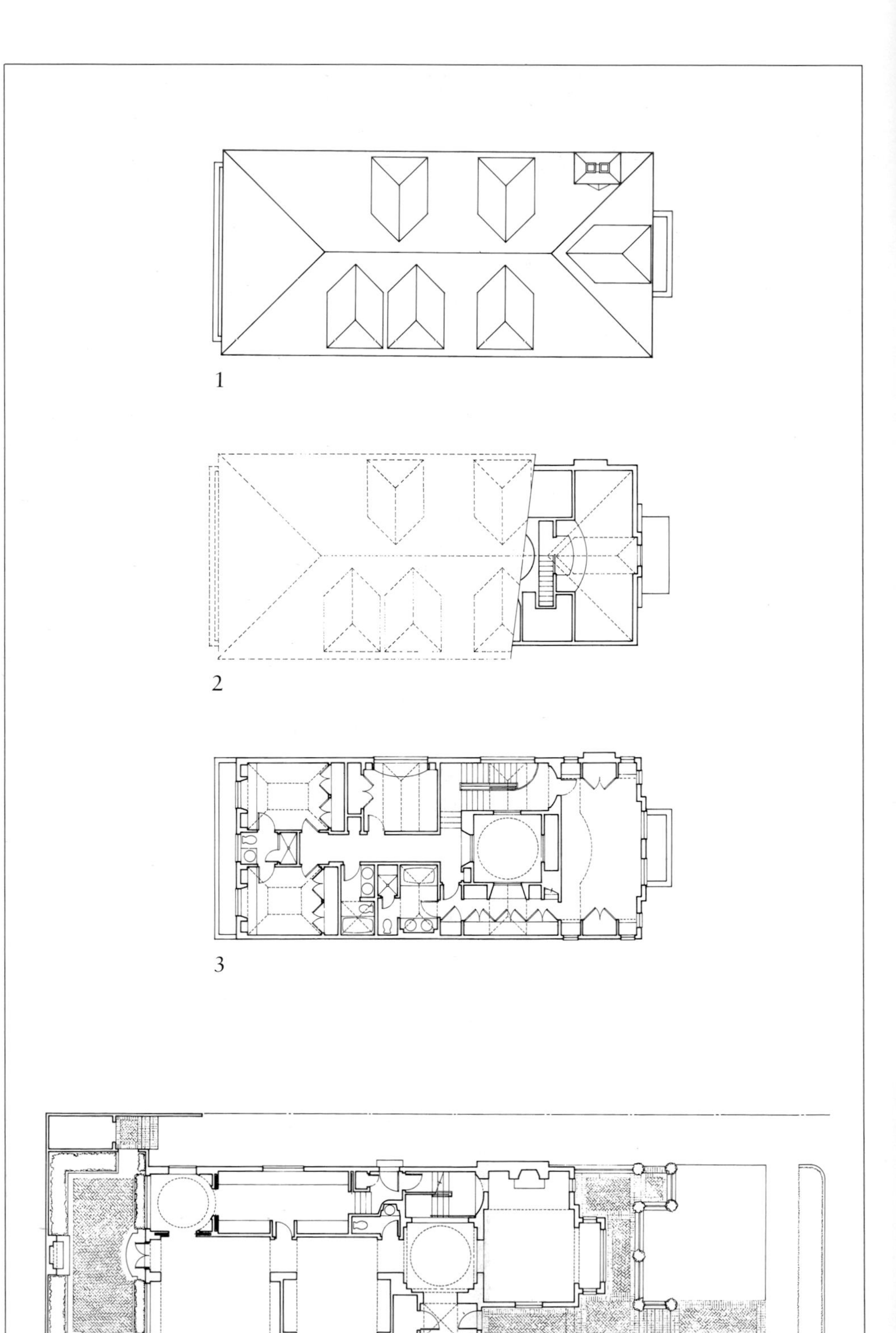

5

6

7

1.East elevation 2.Section through living room 3.Section through entry foyer 4.West elevation 5.North elevation 6.Longitudinal section 7.South elevation 8.Detail of east elevation

1

2

3

4

0 2 4 8 16 feet

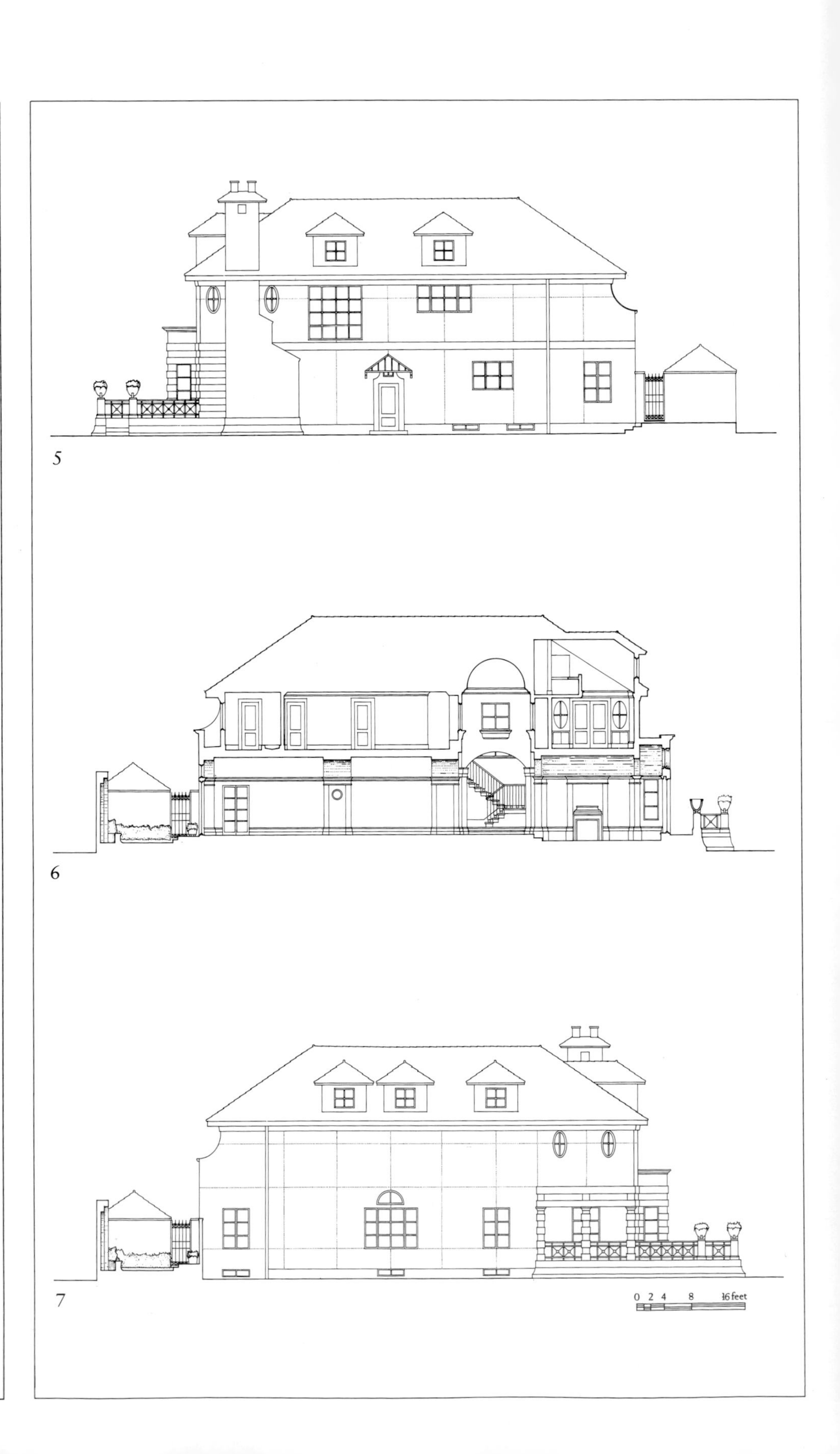

0
2
4
6
12 feet

Student Pub
International House
New York, New York
1984

Given its location in a residence hall in New York City, where unlimited varieties of nightlife are available elsewhere, the Student Pub offers students a dramatic, self-consciously theatrical environment that brings a breath of downtown sophistication to Morningside Heights.

In order to comfortably accommodate both large and intimate gatherings, the plan offers a compromise between flowing space and discrete units. At one end, a raised platform flanked by piers can serve as a stage. The freestanding bar is placed in the center of the room for maximum accessibility. It stands beneath a light metallic frame, recalling the outlines of a classical temple or an archetypal house; its transparency allows the space to function visually as one room, or as two smaller scale spaces to either side of the bar. A framework of stripped classical pilasters and beams also modulates the room. A high wainscot serves as a shelf for drinks and throws concealed lighting onto the walls. Lighting creates the sense of an artificial horizon line and the illusion of space beyond: an effect that is accentuated by the murals, whose bold strokes of black at the top fade to white below. The murals call to mind the Abstract Expressionist painters who made New York their home; suggesting some white dawn in the glowering cityscape or a host of other romantic views, they add a striking image to a city of diversions.

1.Floor plan 2.The game room 3.The dance room 4,5.The bar 6.Dance room elevations 7.Longitudinal section

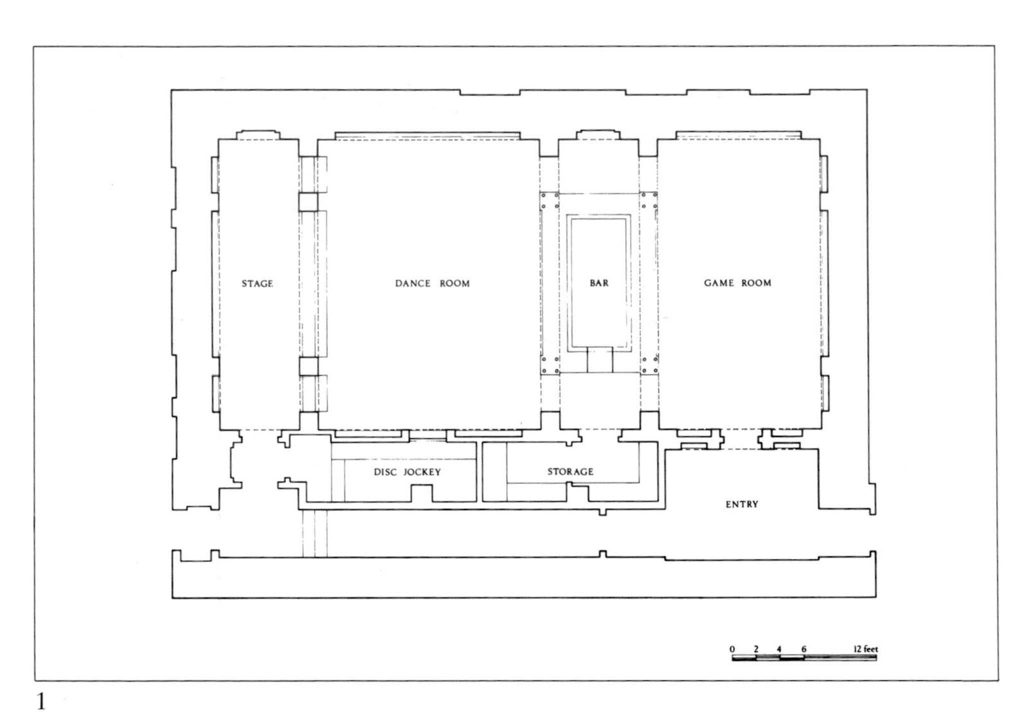

1

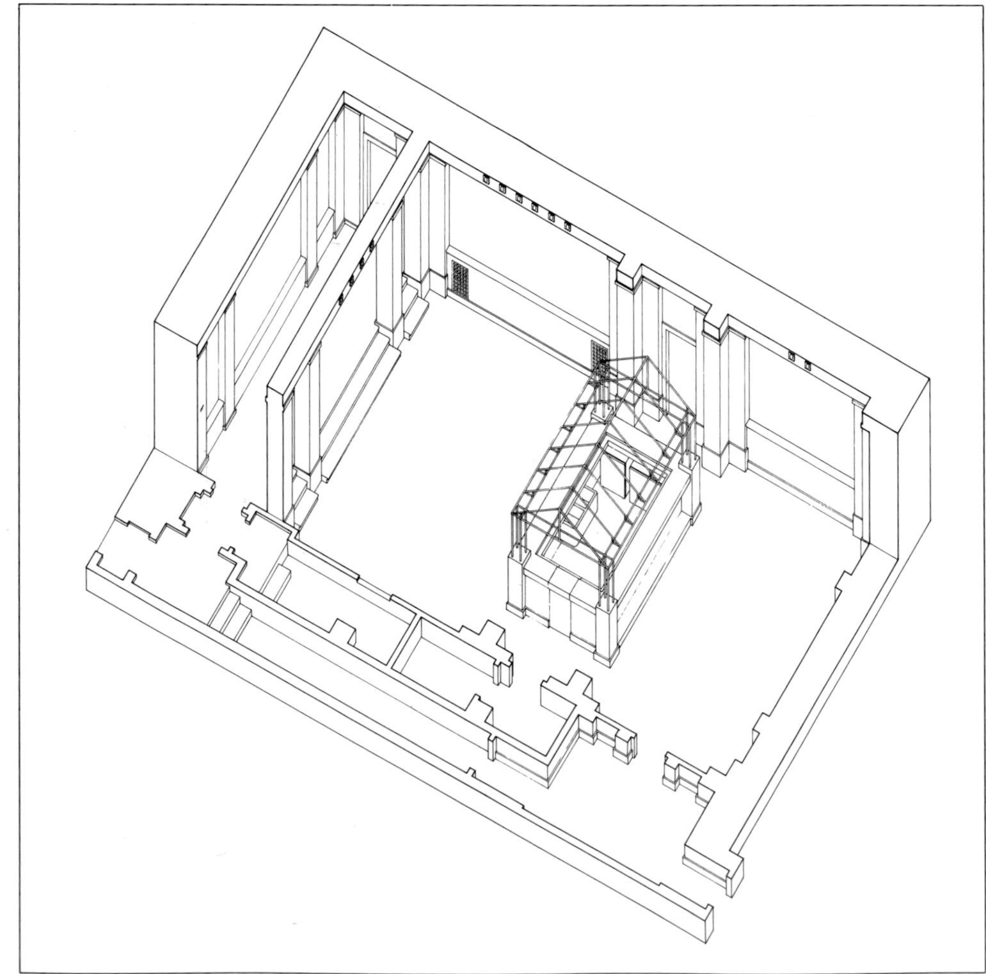

2

3

4

5

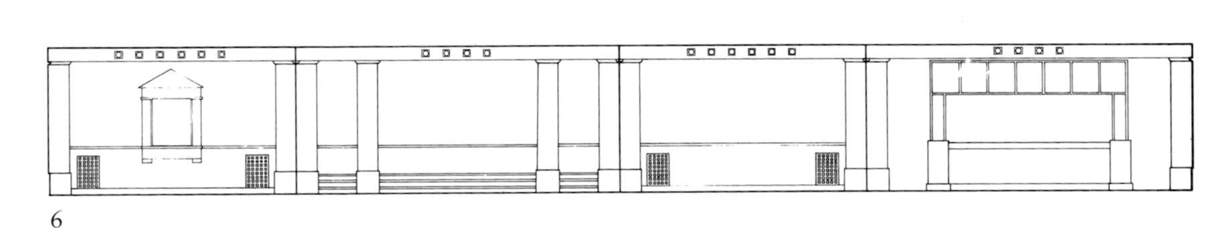
6

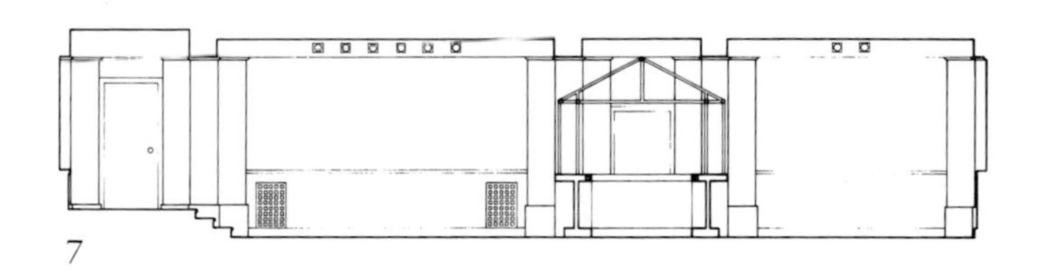

7

Residence
Quogue, New York
1984–

The two-story lighthouse-like tower at the southwest corner of the house offers a panoramic view of Shinnecock Bay from the living room and master bedroom within, as it commands the four-acre peninsula site. From the widow's walk on the roof, the owner will survey the ocean beyond the barrier sandbar. The large gambreled roof sweeps down over the verandas which encircle the house and affords the interior rooms comforting shade from the summer sun. The main roof mass is punctuated by a variety of dormer types and engages the smaller, subordinate garage and screened-porch roofs. The entry facade combines the vernacular gambrel with a classical entry portico and a Palladian stair-hall window.

Inside, the entry hall is the center of the first floor; it leads to the reception room, library, living and dining rooms, and the staircase to the second floor. Upstairs, the master bedroom suite is raised above the level of the rest of the second floor to enhance the view from these rooms and to allow for a raised faceted ceiling to the living room and library below. A tall covered porch surrounds the end of the master bedroom and serves as a lookout to the boats passing in the bay.

1.Site plan 2.Northwest elevation 3.Southwest elevation 4.Northeast elevation 5.Southeast elevation 6.Ground floor plan 7.Second floor plan 8,9,10,11.Views of model

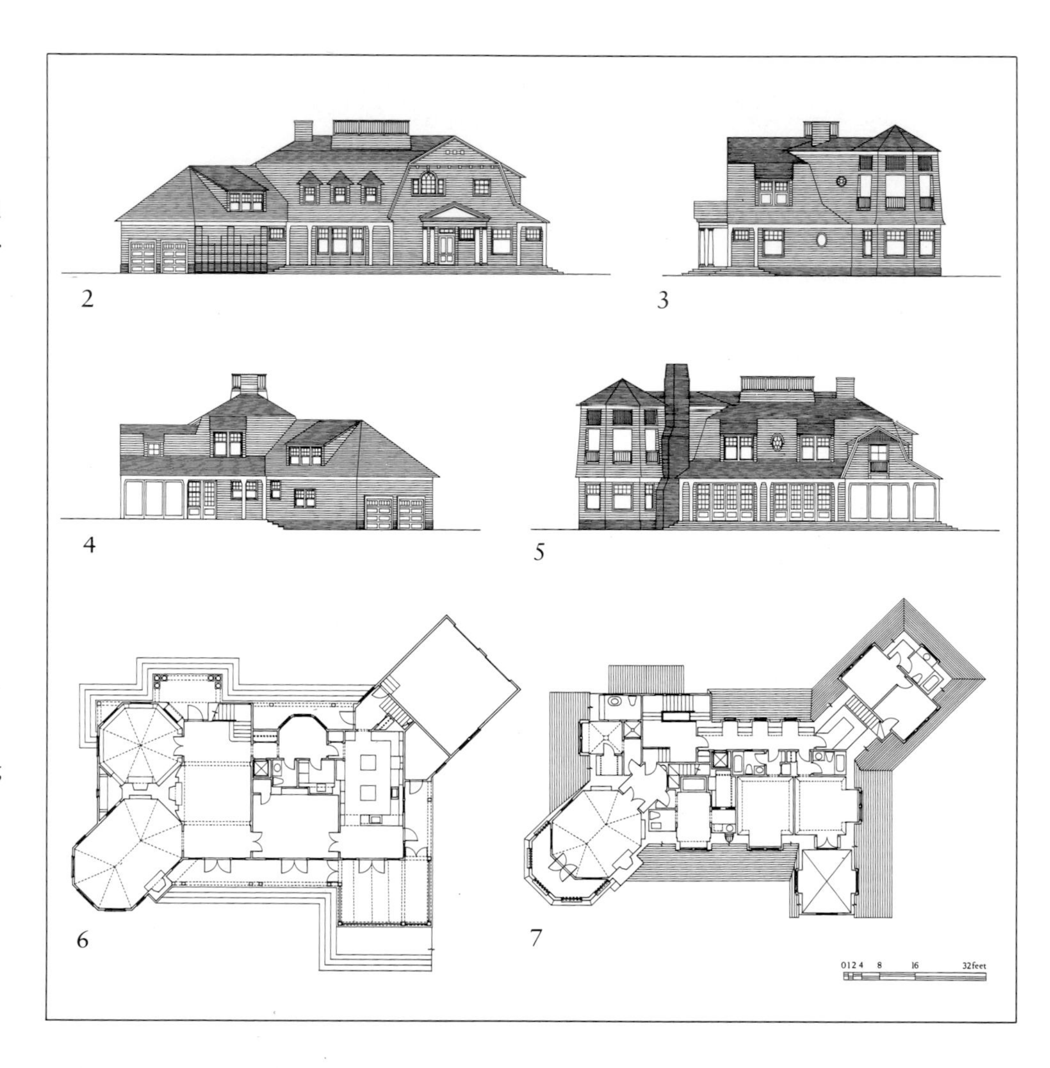

8

9

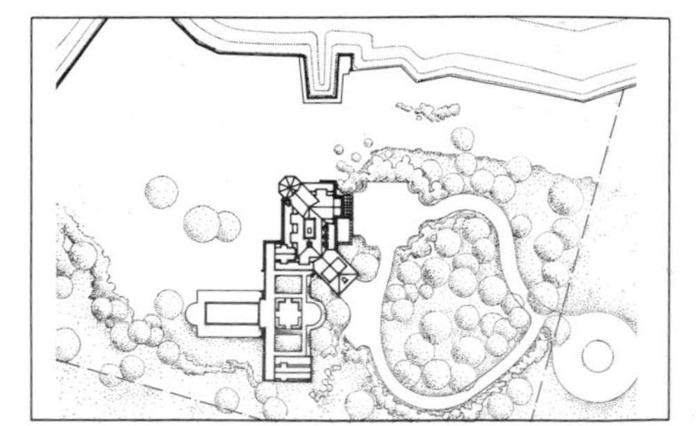
1

10

11

Urban Villa

Brooklyn, New York
1984

This single family detached house occupies a narrow lot in an established Brooklyn neighborhood. Massing of the house is determined by the strict requirements of the zoning envelope, and in this way it bears a strong relationship with other houses in the neighborhood. The house establishes its unique identity through Classical detailing and the traditional use of fine building materials which include a brick water table, light stucco walls, leaded glass windows, and a slate roof.

1.South elevation 2.East elevation 3.North elevation 4.West elevation 5.Site plan 6.Ground floor plan 7.Second floor plan 8.Third floor plan 9,10.Views of model

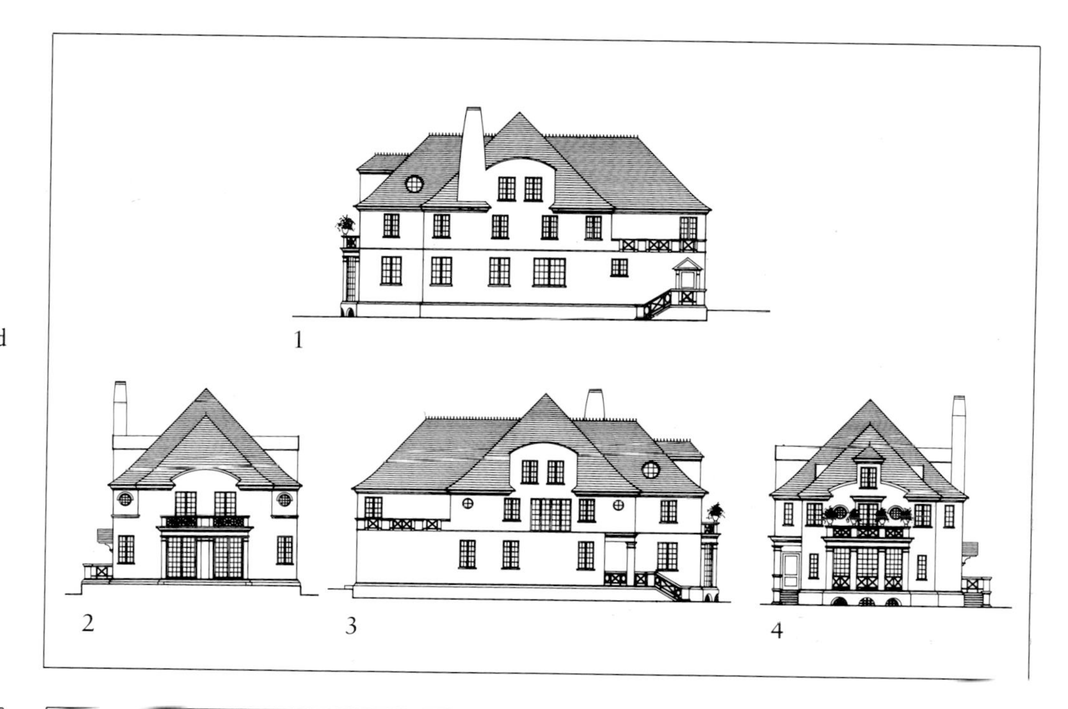

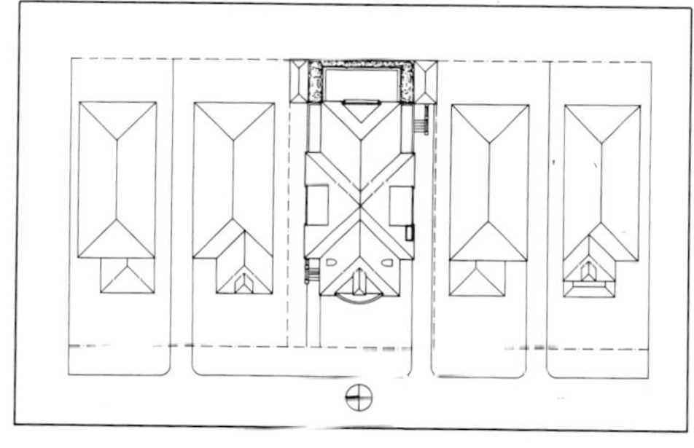

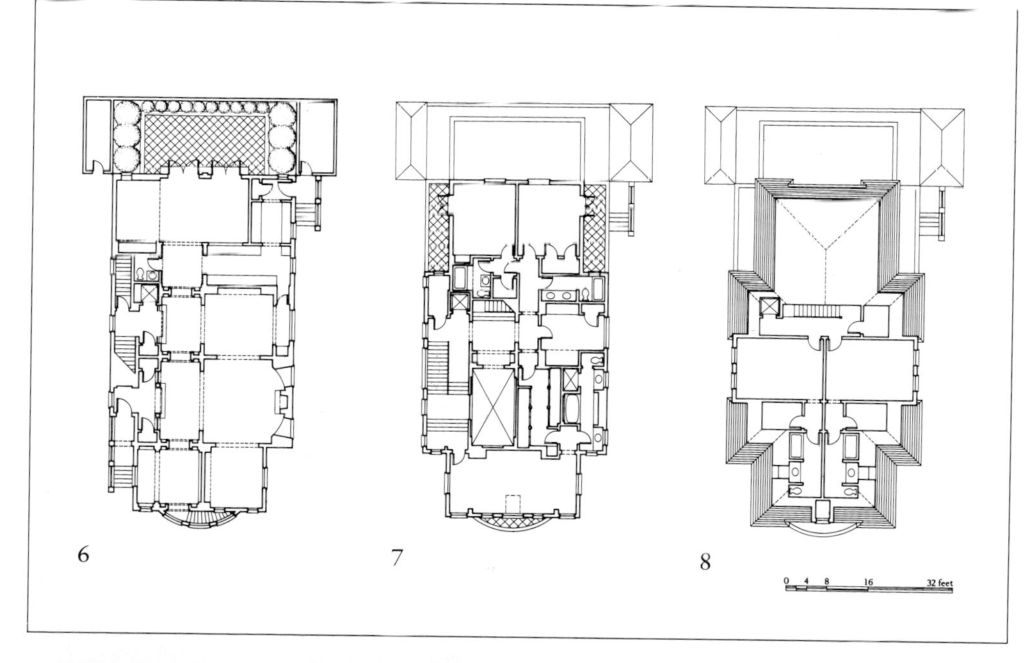

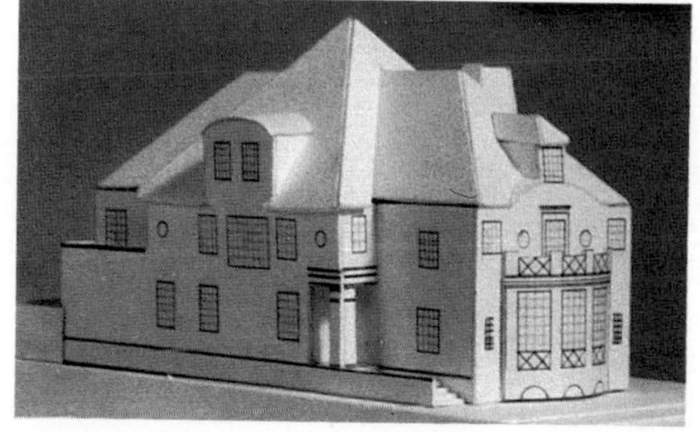
9

10

1.Second floor plan 2.Fourth floor plan
3.Ground floor plan 4.Third floor plan
5.Detail of typical bay 6.Transverse section through atrium 7.Longitudinal section through atrium

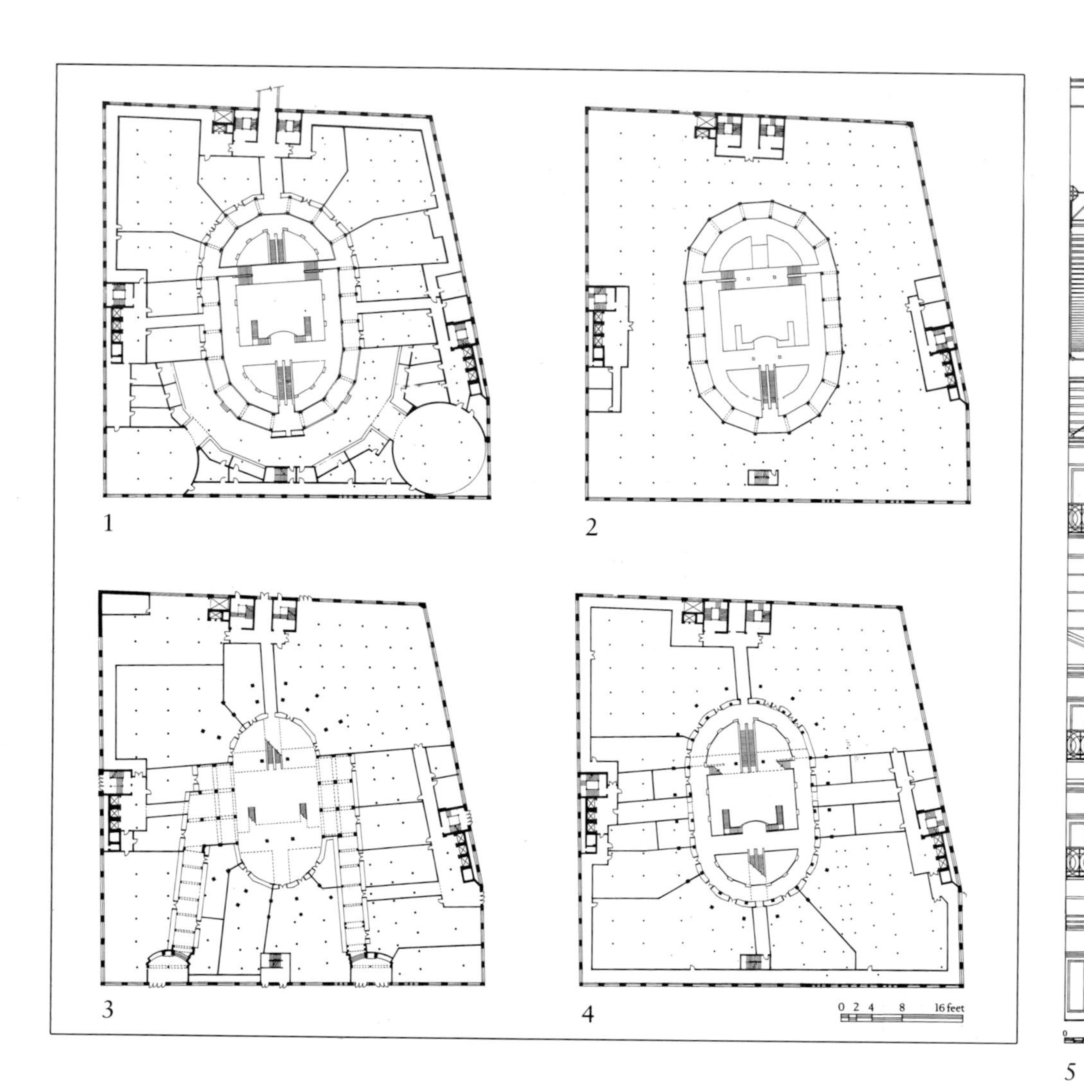

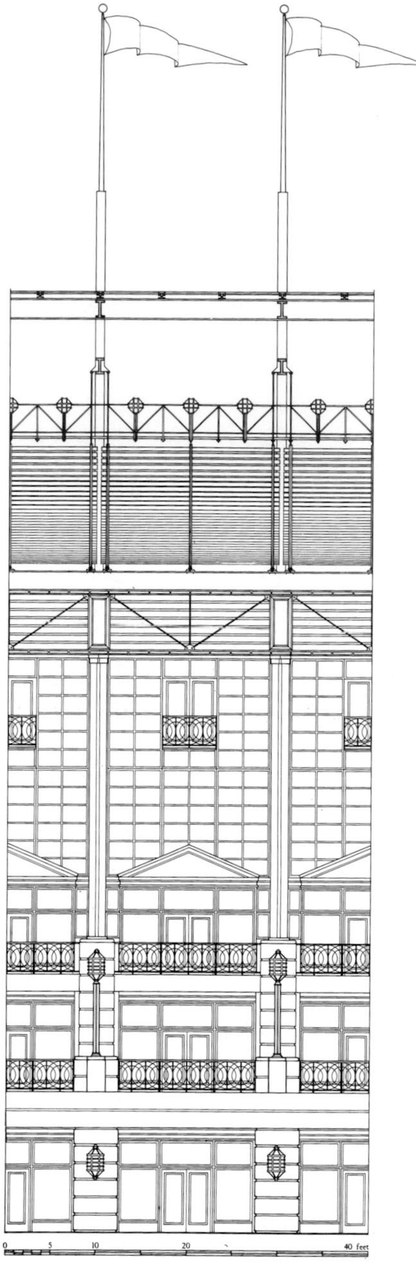

5

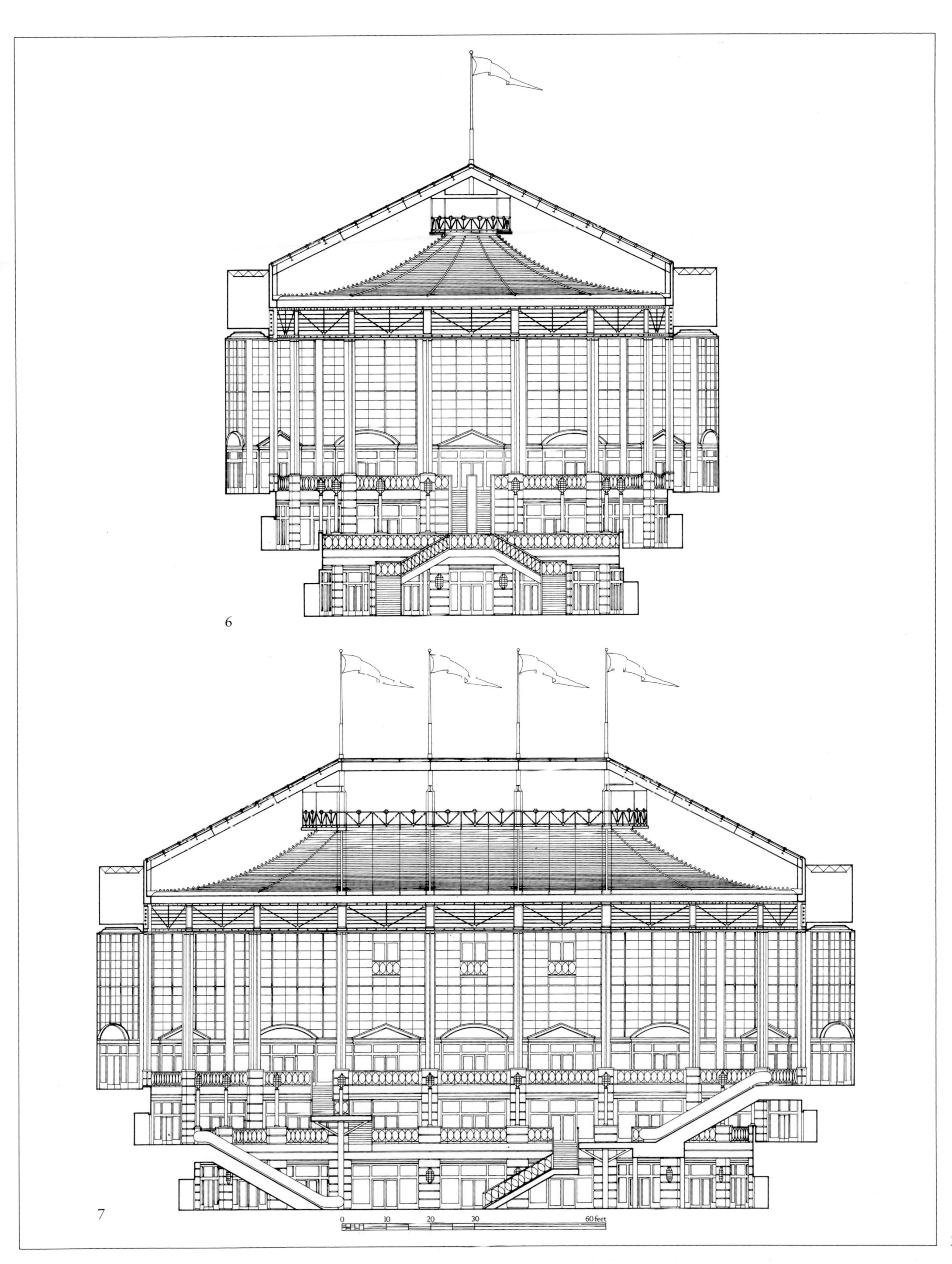
6
7
0
10
20
30
60 feet

1992 Chicago World's Fair
1984

In January of 1984, our office was invited to join six others in developing a master plan for the Chicago 1992 Universal Exposition. The plan deals with two major concerns: first, the fair must be a once-in-a-lifetime event that demands to be experienced in person rather than through the electronic media; second, it must leave lasting, beneficial residuals for the city of Chicago in the form of parks, cultural facilities, renewed urban infrastructure, and jobs. Given these often competing goals, the team of Robert A. M. Stern, Thomas Beeby, Charles Moore, Jaquelin Robertson, and Stanley Tigerman worked with Skidmore, Owings & Merrill, Chicago/William E. Brazley & Associates to produce a master plan which addresses the programmatic needs of the fair and the city and creates a powerful and varied architectural identity.

Located on the lakefront, south of the Loop, the fair site extends to the south the island created for the 1933 Century of Progress Fair. Waterways and basins between the island and the mainland serve as an organizing fabric, a means of transportation, and a series of focal points for the fair's theme districts. A newly excavated waterway running parallel to Nineteenth Street connects Lake Michigan and the fair site with the south branch of the Chicago River, providing a permanent amenity intended to stimulate redevelopment in South Chicago.

The fair's three principal entrances correspond to its primary districts. To the north, an entrance at Roosevelt Road provides access to the cultural district, where the existing planetarium, aquarium, and natural history museum are complemented by new facilities for the performing and visual arts. A central entrance at Nineteenth Street opens to the circular court of honor, from which a curved grid of pedestrian streets leads to various national pavilions. To the south, the Thirtieth Street entrance leads to the entertainment and recreation district.

1

1.Aerial view of proposed plan for the fair 2,3.The Court of Honor 4.The conservatory 5.View of the Court of Honor model

2

3

4

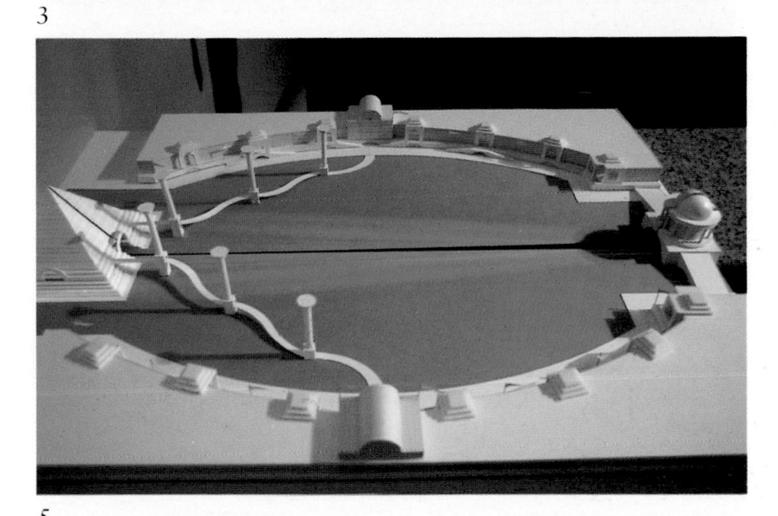

5

Preakness Hills Country Club

Wayne, New Jersey
1984

The Preakness Hills Country Club started life as an 1880s country house; four unsympathetic additions have nearly obscured the original building and marred an idyllic landscape. Our renovation is intended both to improve the functional workings of the building and to establish a visual connection with America's great turn-of-the-century country clubs.

The site plan has been revised in order to better integrate the building with the landscape. The swimming pool has been moved from the front of the clubhouse to make way for a wide greensward and a tree-lined driveway. The new pool enjoys south and west exposures, with views of the club's thirty-acre lake. The new pool pavilion also serves the existing tennis courts. Parking has been shifted to one corner of the site, where it is removed from clubhouse functions and serves as a buffer between the clubhouse and the street.

The interiors have been rearranged to enjoy panoramic views of the golf course to the east and south. The major public rooms survey the first and tenth tees and the ninth and eighteenth greens. A south-facing terrace allows for an extended period of outdoor dining. The sloping site allows the proshop, locker rooms, and cart storage to be tucked below the main floor and open directly to the first tee and the eighteenth green.

Our facades seek to break down the scale of the building; the pavilionated massing and classical vocabulary create the effect of a series of garden pavilions woven into the landscape.

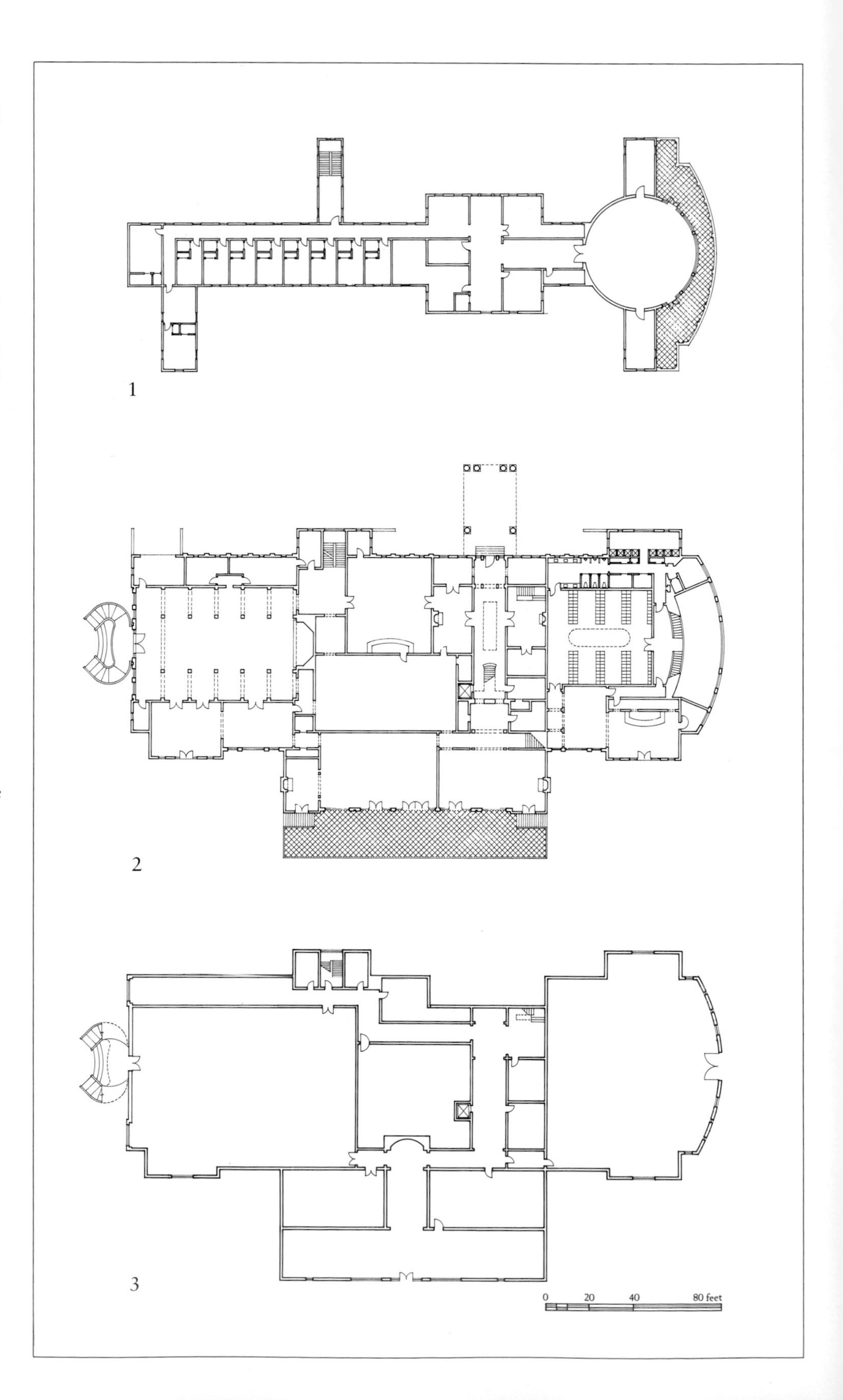

1.Second floor plan 2.Ground floor plan
3.Basement floor plan 4.West elevation
5.East elevation 6.South elevation
7.North elevation 8.Site plan

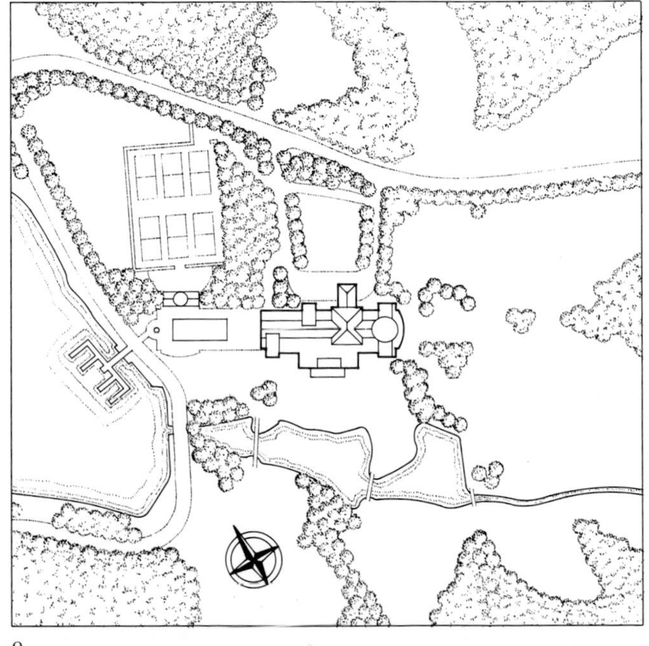

8

Private High School
Brooklyn, New York
1984

This private high school for 650 students transcends the dreary, dehumanizing imagery of the typical "factory of learning." Our school is both a temple and a house of education. Located on a corner site, the building forms a wall against a busy commercial street and creates a quiet, secure courtyard in the rear. The brick elevations establish a dialogue between the domestic scale of repetitive classroom windows and more iconographically loaded elements. The heroically scaled entrance, the pedimented temple which houses the auditorium and gym, and the apse containing the library and offices, all hint at the grandeur of public life in order to achieve a dignified and scholastic tone.

1,2.Views of model 3.East elevation
4.West elevation 5.South elevation
6.North elevation 7.Ground floor plan
8.Third floor plan 9.Basement floor plan
10.Second floor plan

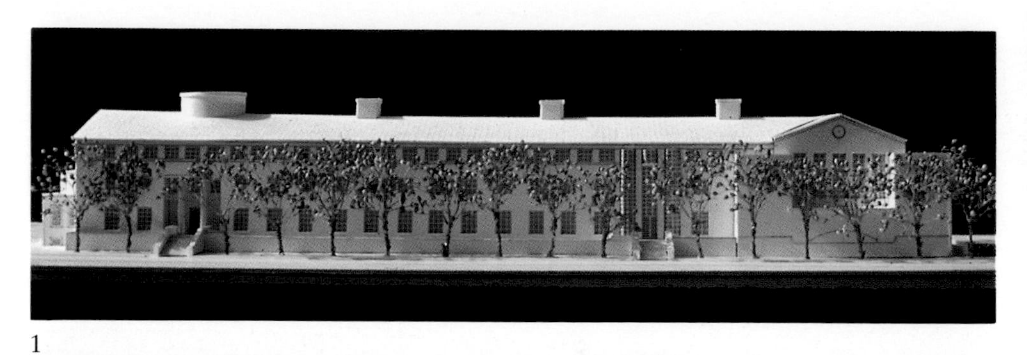

1

2

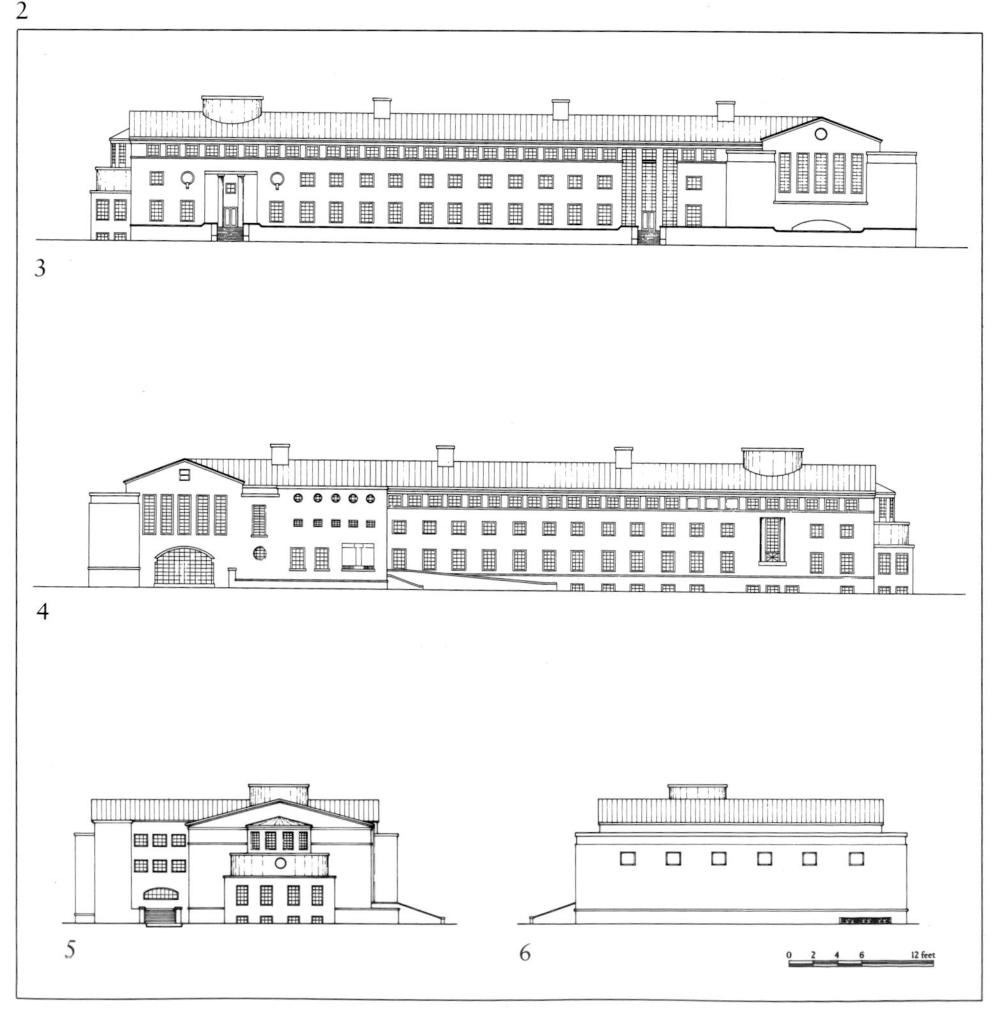

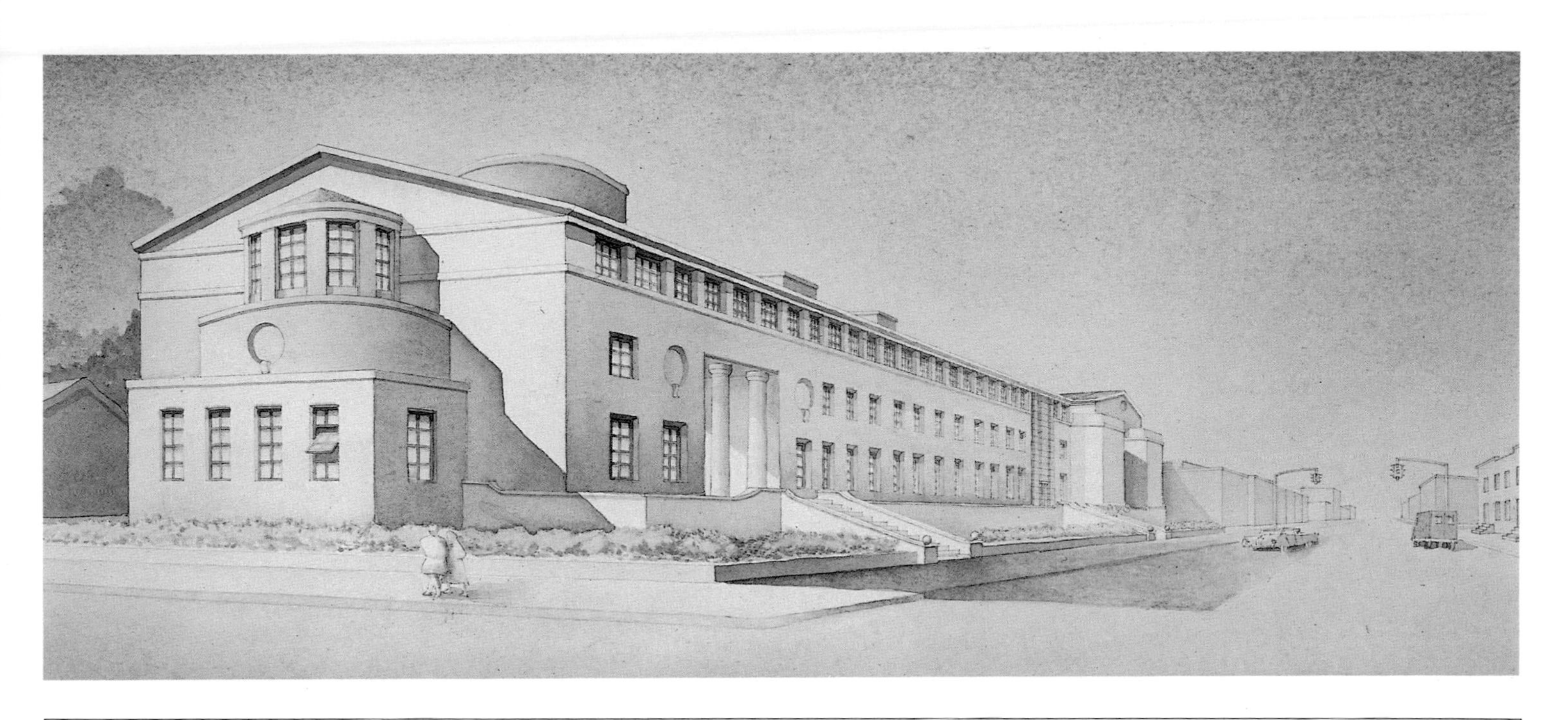

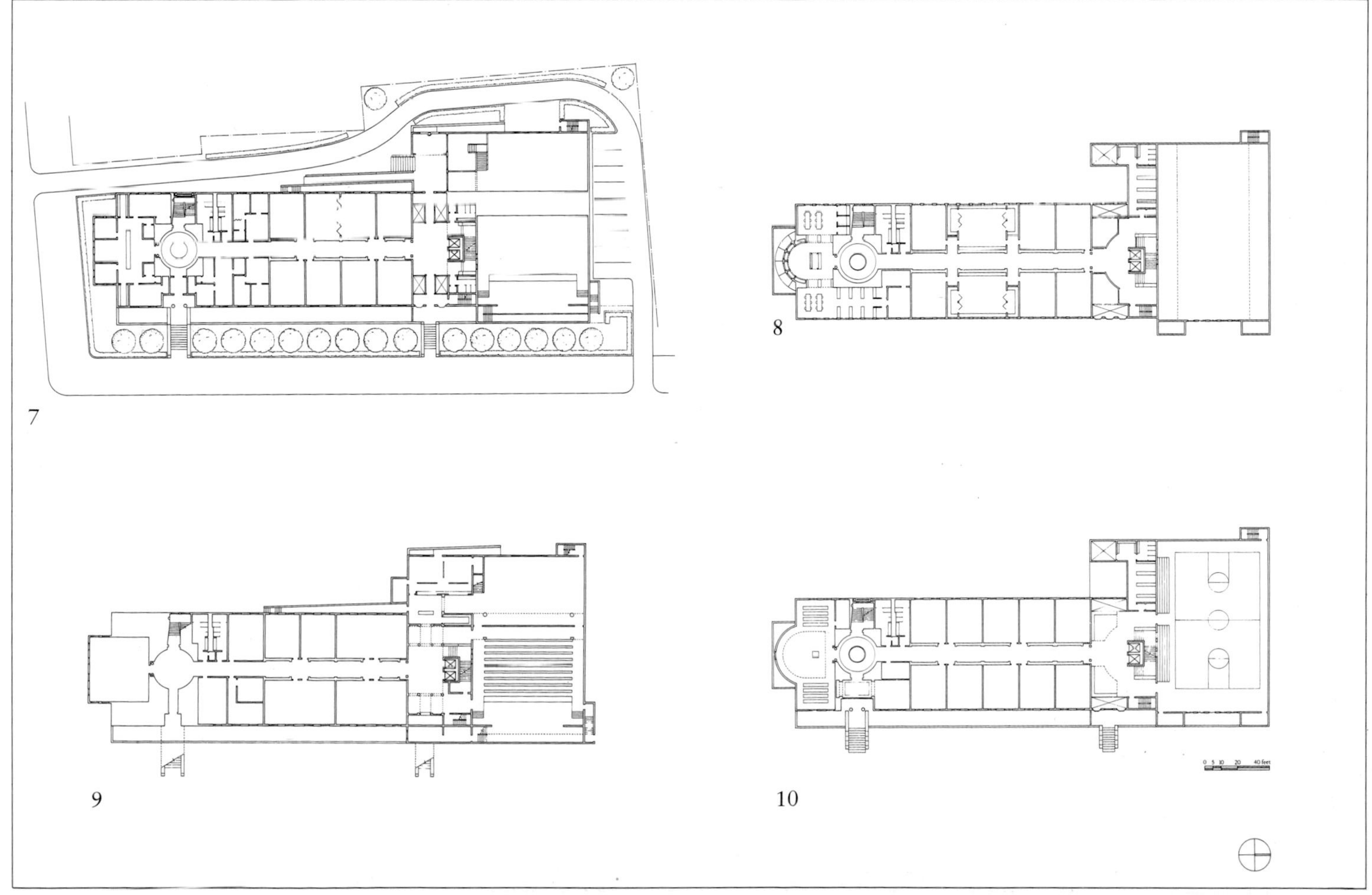
7
8
9
10
0 5 10 20 40 feet

Sephardic Study Center

Brooklyn, New York
1984

This synagogue occupies a corner site in a mixed-use area of Brooklyn. The massing of the building, largely determined by the zoning requirements of the residential neighborhood, attempts to present a more civic scale along both streets. The exterior is a rich combination of materials: stone walls, tile roof, and bronze windows that provide a sense of permanence and dignity to this symbolic building type.

The plan is that of a traditional centralized prayer room with altar and ark lit dramatically from the east-facing window.

1.Plan of sanctuary level 2.Mezzanine floor plan 3.Site plan 4.East elevation 5.South elevation 6.West elevation 7.North elevation 8.Longitudinal section 9.View of model from the northeast

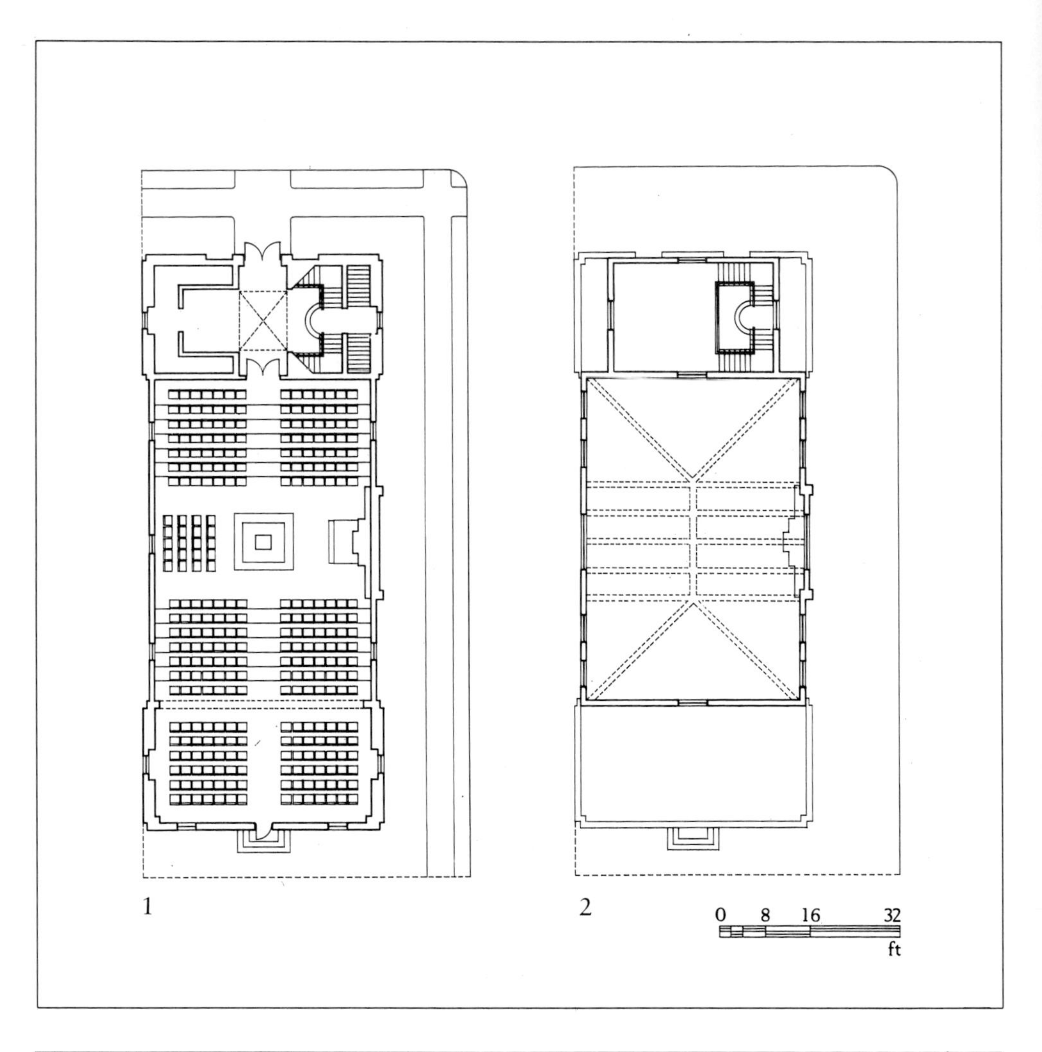

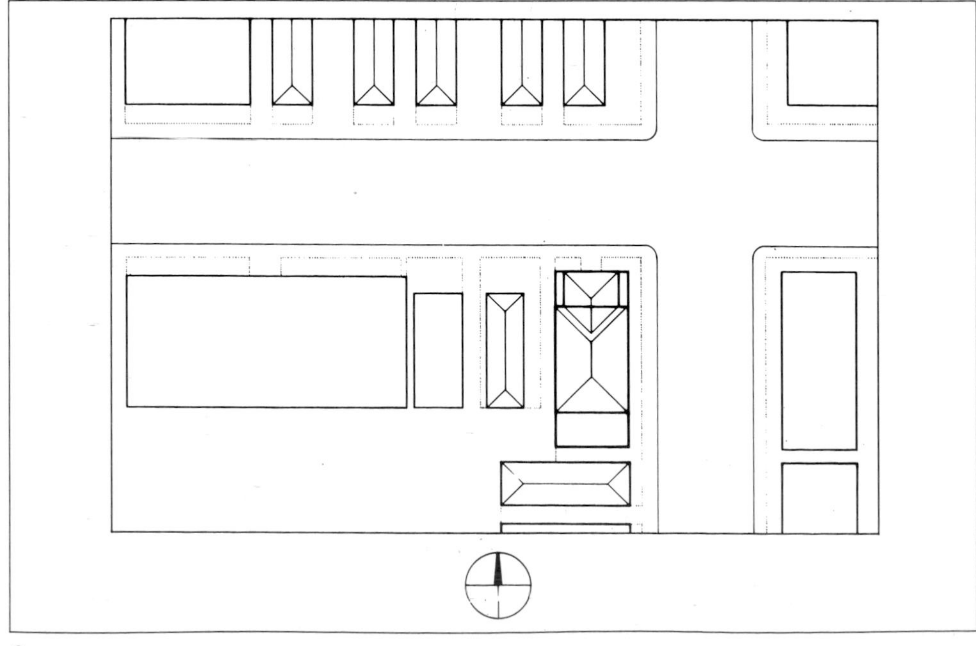

3

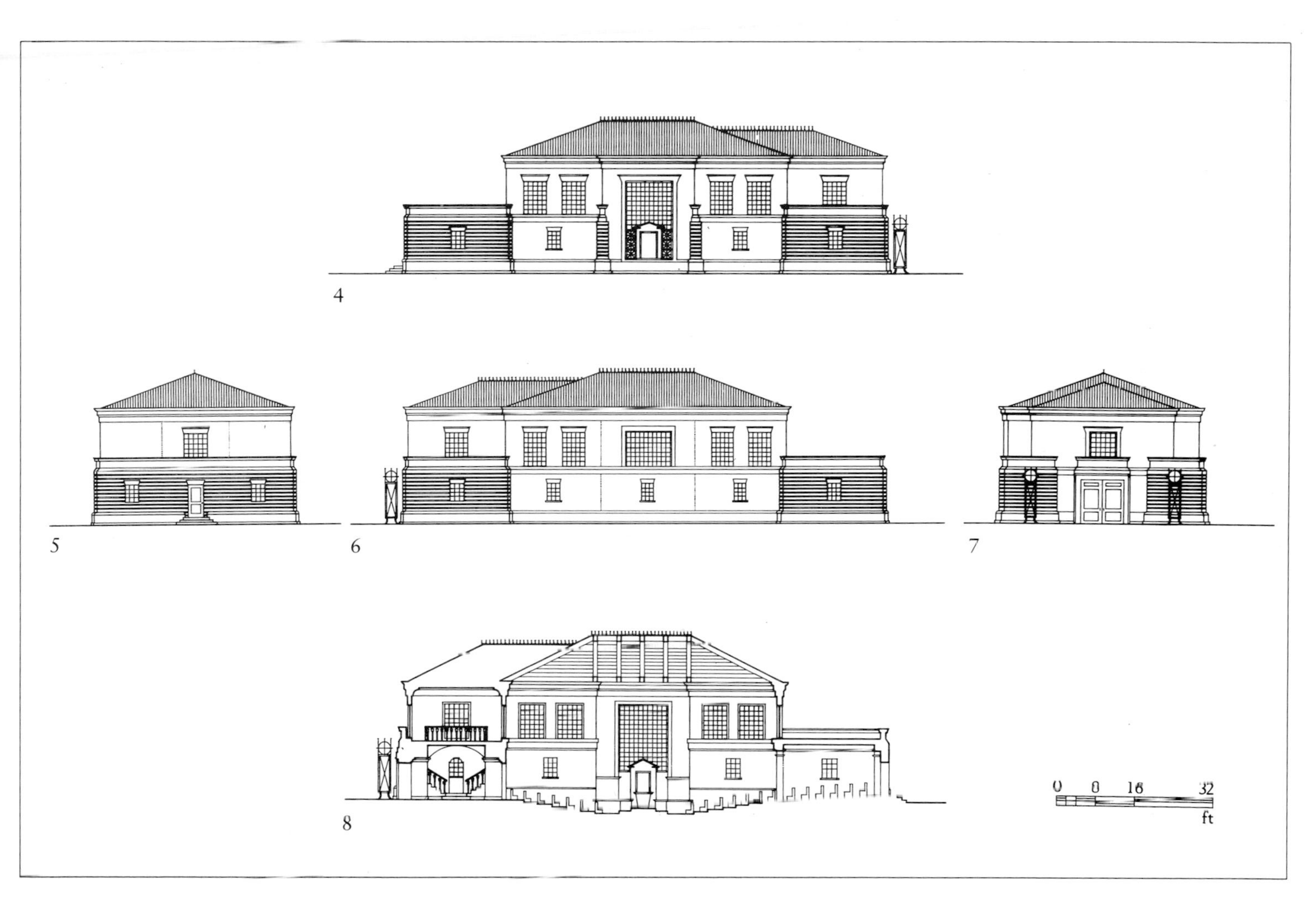

9

Two Newton Place
Newton, Massachusetts
1984–

This three-story, 110,000-square-foot brick-and-limestone office building will complement Skidmore Owings and Merrill's earlier building for the same client in the commercial center of Newton, Massachusetts. The two buildings with their curving facades, consistent parapet line, and similar detailing present a powerful urban statement. Two Newton Place departs from the strict planarity of the repetitive punched window facade of One Newton Place through the introduction of two-story-high oriel windows, layering of the brick facade, and grouping of windows to syncopate the long, gently curving facade.

Office space wraps around two skylit atria, maximizing coverage of the site. This double atrium is bisected by a passerelle separating the three-story-high atrium from the more private two-story-high atrium. Offices front directly onto these atria to maximize desirable rental space throughout the building.

Parking for 275 cars is accommodated in a below-grade garage.

1,2,3,4.Models of preliminary schemes 5.Model of final scheme 6.Principal elevation 7.View of the lobby 8.View of the site 9.Site plan

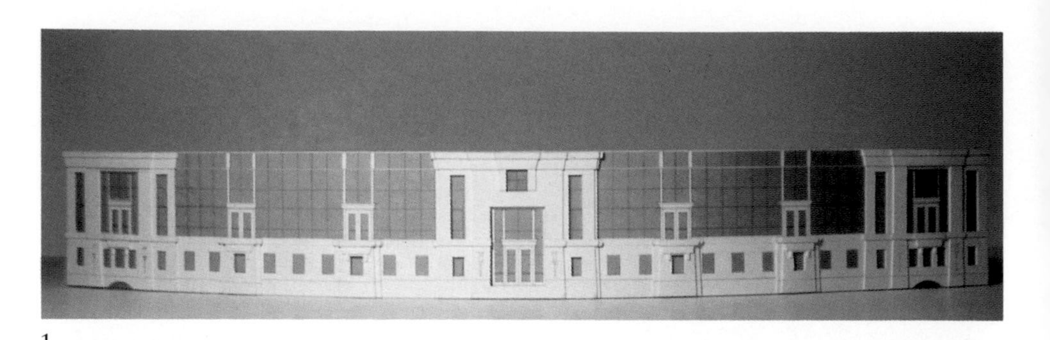

1

2

3

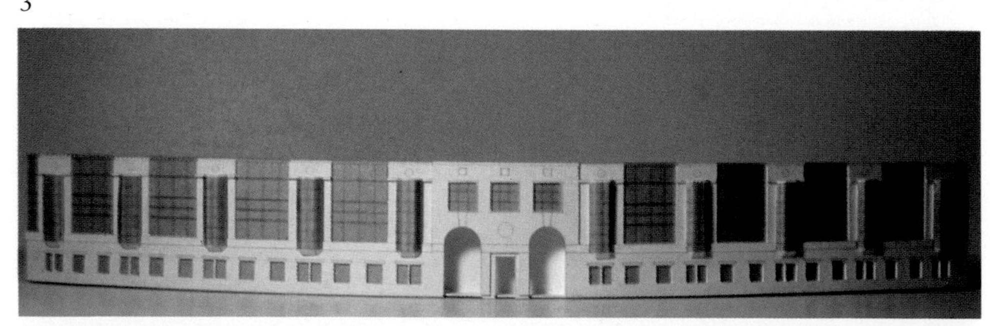

4

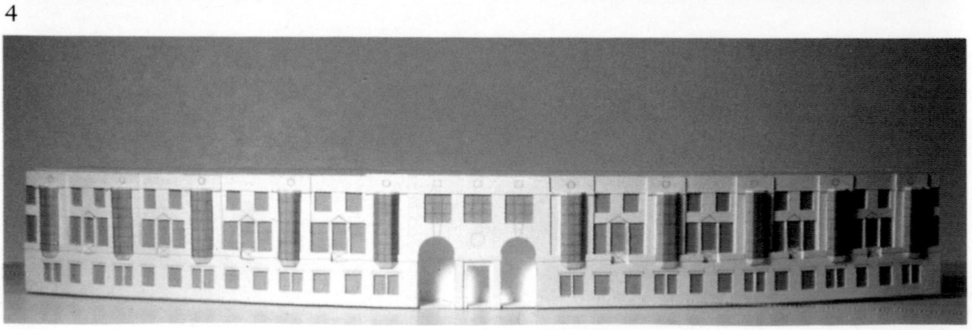

5

6

7

8

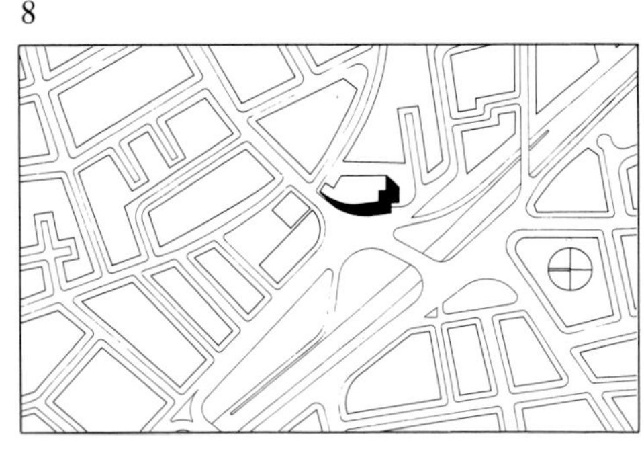

9

1.Detail of entrance 2.Lobby elevations:
A.West B.South C.North D.East
3.West elevation 4.Third floor plan
5.Second floor plan 6.Ground floor plan

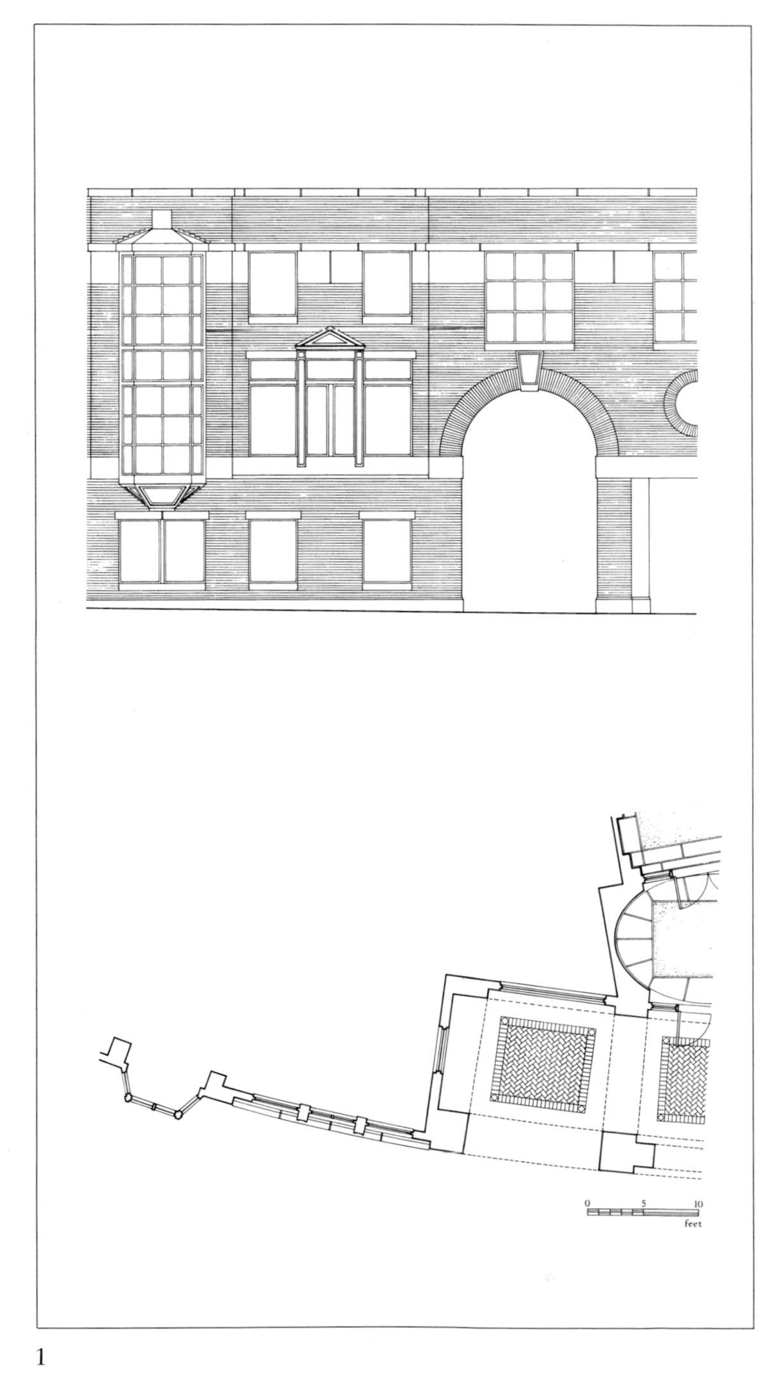

1

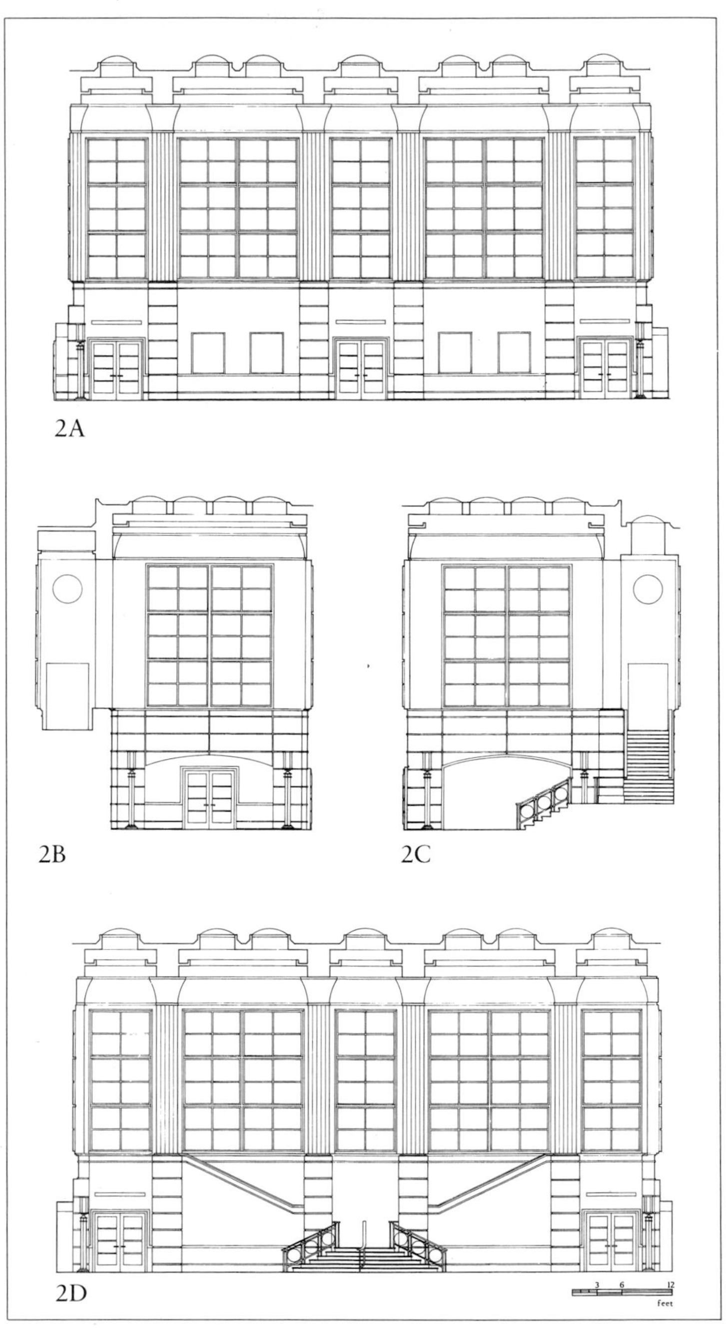

3

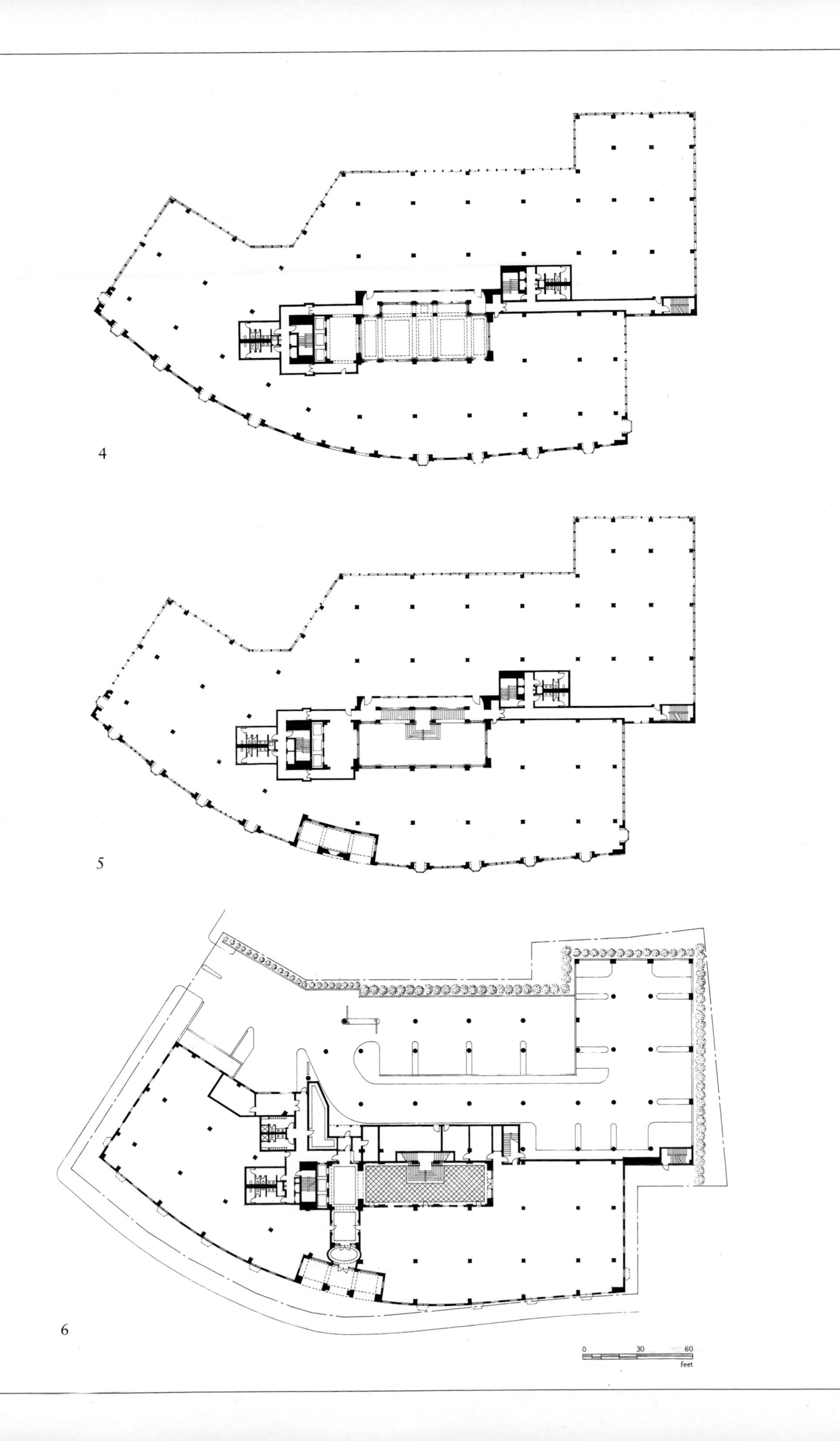
4
5
6
0
30
60
feet

Seaside Hotel
Seaside, Florida
1984

The Seaside Hotel is part of a planned resort community that consciously emulates the best qualities of nineteenth-century southern town planning. In keeping with the Victorian character of Seaside's residential architecture, the hotel's design invites guests to relax on generous verandas under broad overhanging roofs.

The main wing contains the lobby and public functions of the hotel, most of which are raised up to take advantage of the views of the coastline. A bridge spans the state highway and connects the main wing running parallel with the beach to a secondary wing housing retail space behind the covered arcade which defines the town square on the ground floor, and houses hotel rooms on the floors above. Open-air, single-loaded corridors, afford all rooms views of the ocean and access to porches.

Stained-wood siding, metal roofs, and wood balconies capture the informal quality of many of the local buildings. Festooned with canvas awnings and colorful pennants, the hotel celebrates life by the sea.

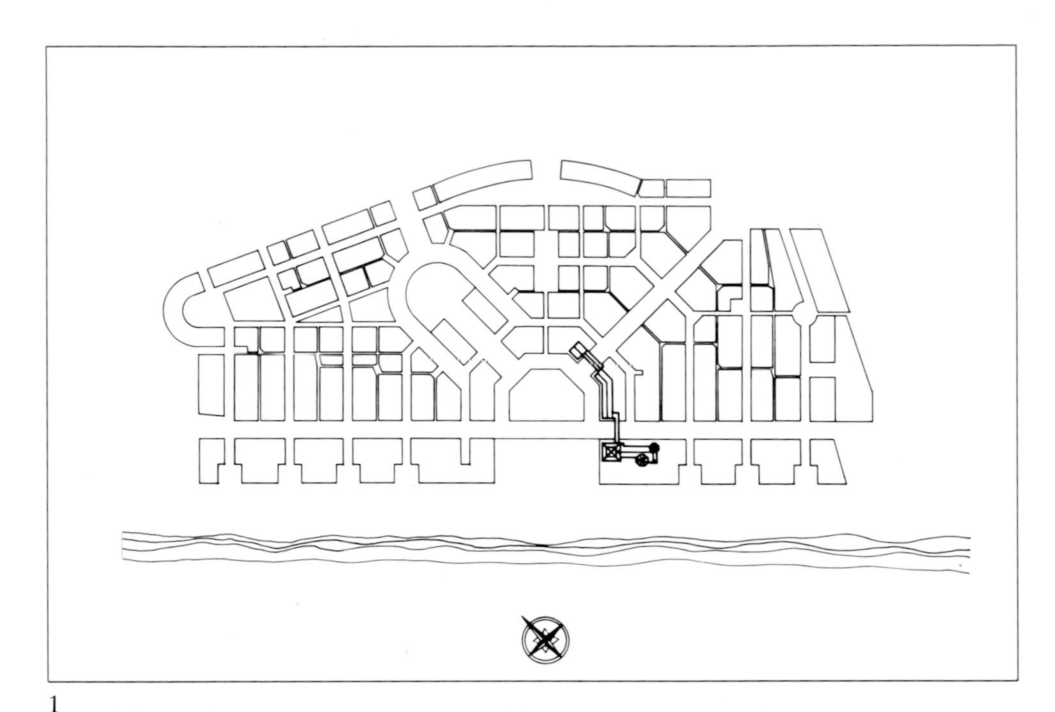

1

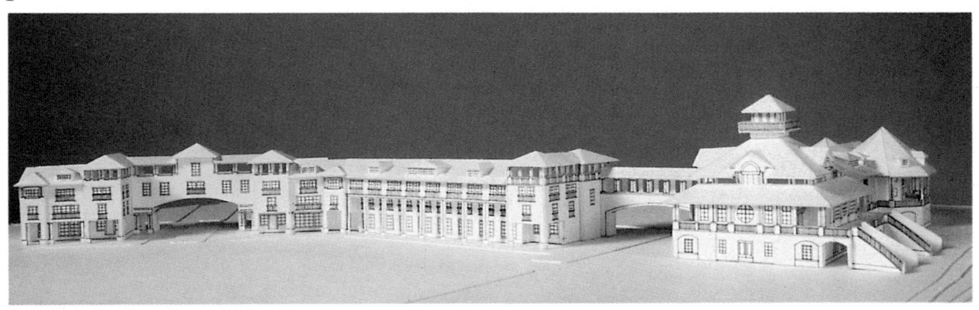

2

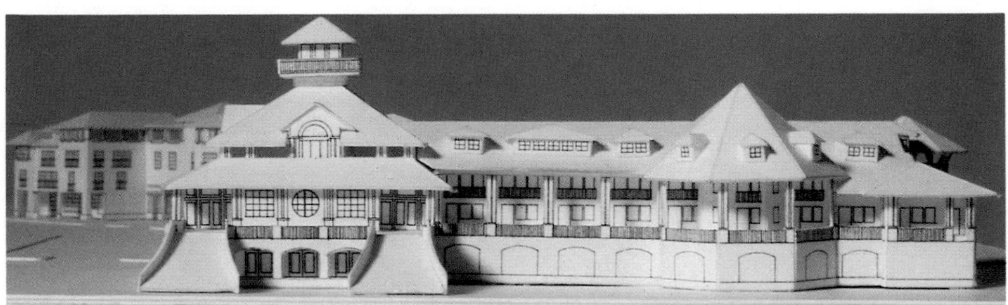

3

1.Site plan 2,3.Views of model 4.West elevation 5.North elevation 6.South elevation 7.Second floor plan 8.Fourth floor plan 9.Ground floor plan 10.Third floor plan

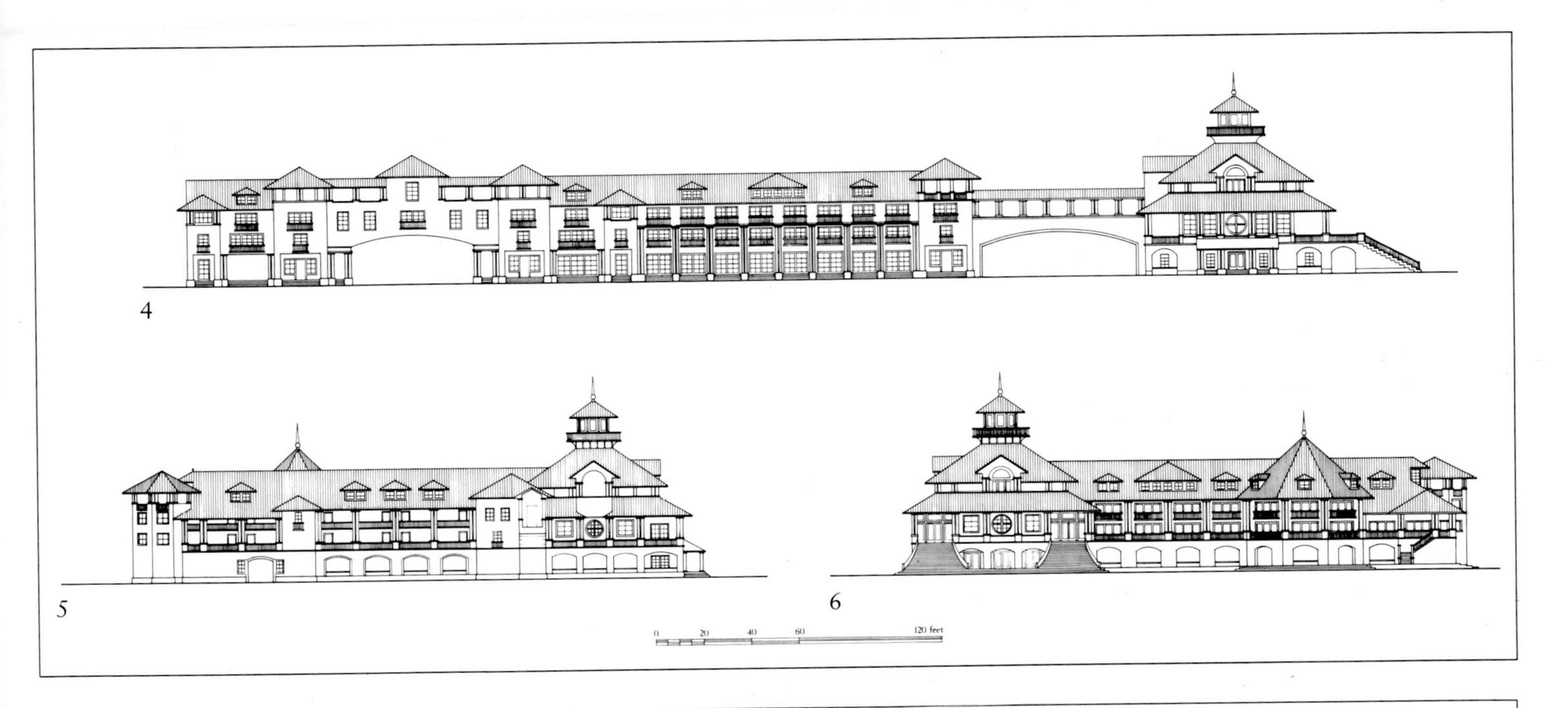
4
5
6
0
20
40
60
120 feet

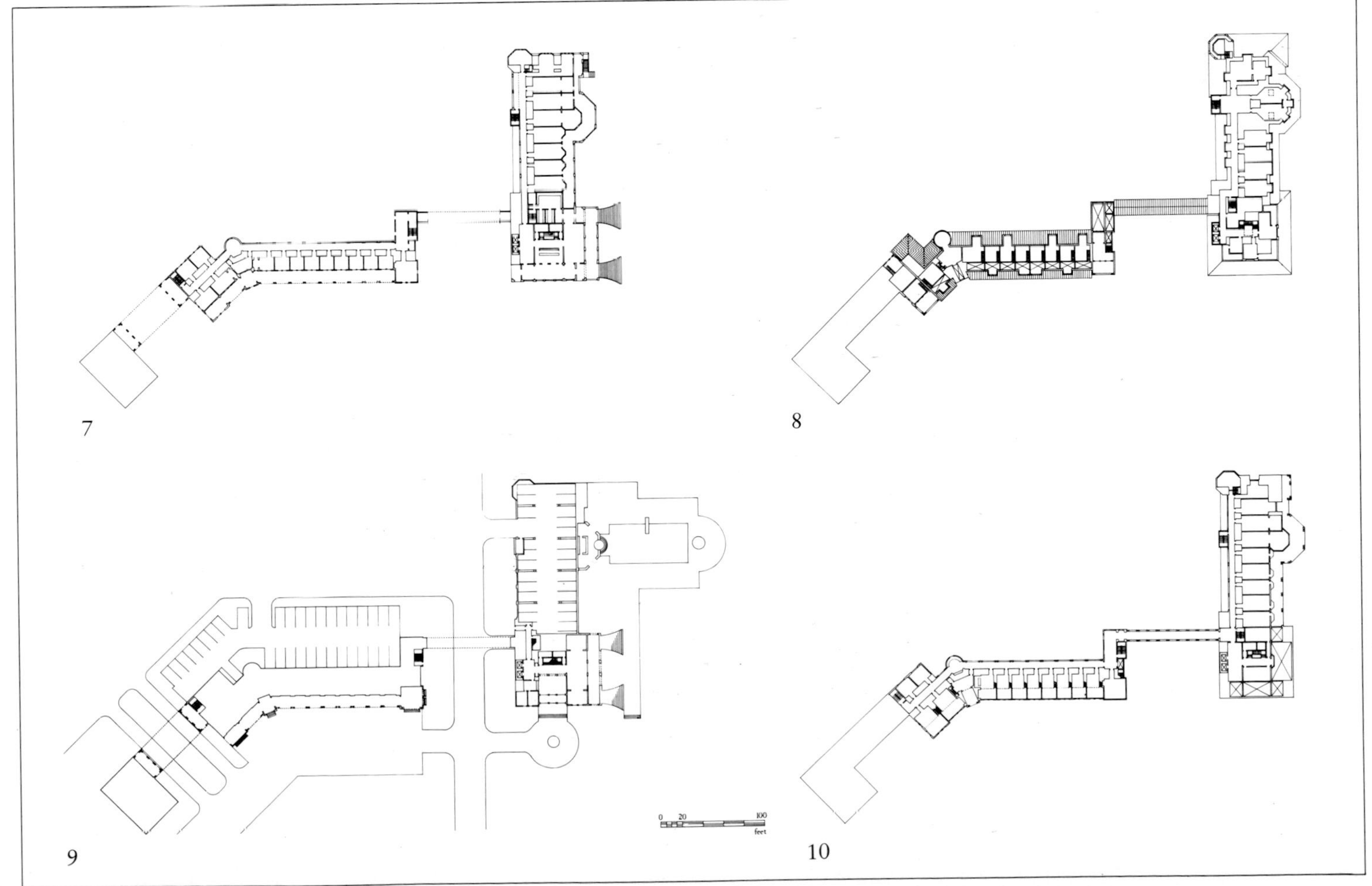
7
8
9
10
0
20
100
feet

Newport News Cultural Arts Pavilion

Newport News, Virginia
1984

A theater is an opportunity to combine the drama of players and playwrights with the drama of public occasion. An arts pavilion can achieve more than the mere accommodation of the mechanics of theatergoing and theater production; it can give permanent symbolic expression to the idea of theater itself, and to the community's commitment to a better way of life.

Our proposal deliberately contrasts with the standard image of recent art complexes—impersonal blank boxes set on isolated plazas—which draw back from the life of the city and the theatricality of the occasion to evoke suburban shopping malls. Our scheme fills the site to reinforce the sense of the town. It creates an open-air public theater at the project's literal and symbolic heart, where the social axis of the community intersects an axis linking the two theaters of the pavilion.

Twin stage towers flank the open-air theater to transform the pavilion into a symbolic temple of the arts, an image whose traditional dignity is realized in the most modern way with an open-work frame that expresses the building's basic structural system and creates a canopy for the rehearsed and unrehearsed dramas taking place in the amphitheater below.

The main entrances to the large and small theaters are located at opposite ends of the pavilion, minimizing congestion and allowing the two theaters to share a common loading dock and backstage facilities. The theater entrances are announced by canopies and pedimental trusses which echo the symbolic intentions of the outdoor theater.

A continuous glazed loggia, doubling as an art gallery, connects the theater lobbies with the outdoor theater and with a potential bridge to the hotel, linking all both visually and sequentially to the harbor.

1. West elevation 2. View of northwest corner 3. Floor plan 4. View of loggia 5. View of large theater upper lobby

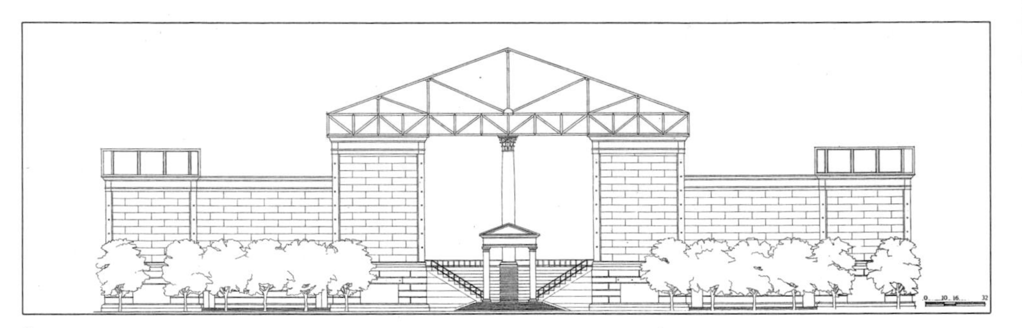

1

2

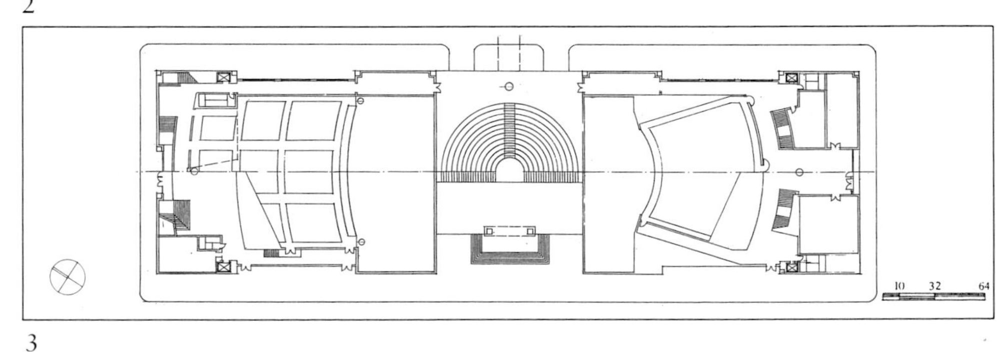

3

4

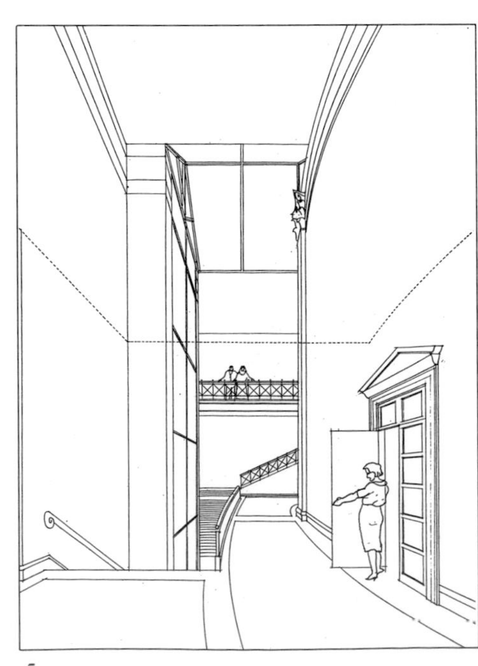

5

Penthouse Apartment
New York, New York
1984–

This penthouse apartment has terraces on three sides and expansive views to the north, east, and south along New York City's East River. Situated in an architecturally undistinguished building built in the early 1960s, the apartment interior was totally reorganized to better suit the clients' programmatic and aesthetic requirements. The clients' primary aesthetic request was that the apartment have a traditional look with stained-wood trim, paneling and cabinets. To avoid the clash of a strictly Classical interior with the realities of horizontal window openings and nine-foot ceilings, the Classicism was streamlined as it was at the beginning of this century by the Wiener Werkstätte. Piers and entablatures order almost every surface in the apartment, but the Classical orders are abstracted to the point that a simple piece of trim performs various functions, depending on its context—the same shape at the same height is used as a picture rail, a crown molding at the top of paneling or a cabinet, and sometimes as a capital for a pier.

The round entry hall and the rectangular bedroom hall create two centers in the plan—one for the bedrooms and one for the entertainment rooms. These centers provide relief from the necessarily complex circulation system. In these two rooms, stylized reeded pilasters fill the spaces between doors and cabinets. The purely decorative function of these pilasters is emphasized by their recessed location in the paneling. The round foyer is aggrandized by a low saucer dome and a false miniature lantern, a whimsical element that adds extra light into the room while giving the illusion of space above the dome.

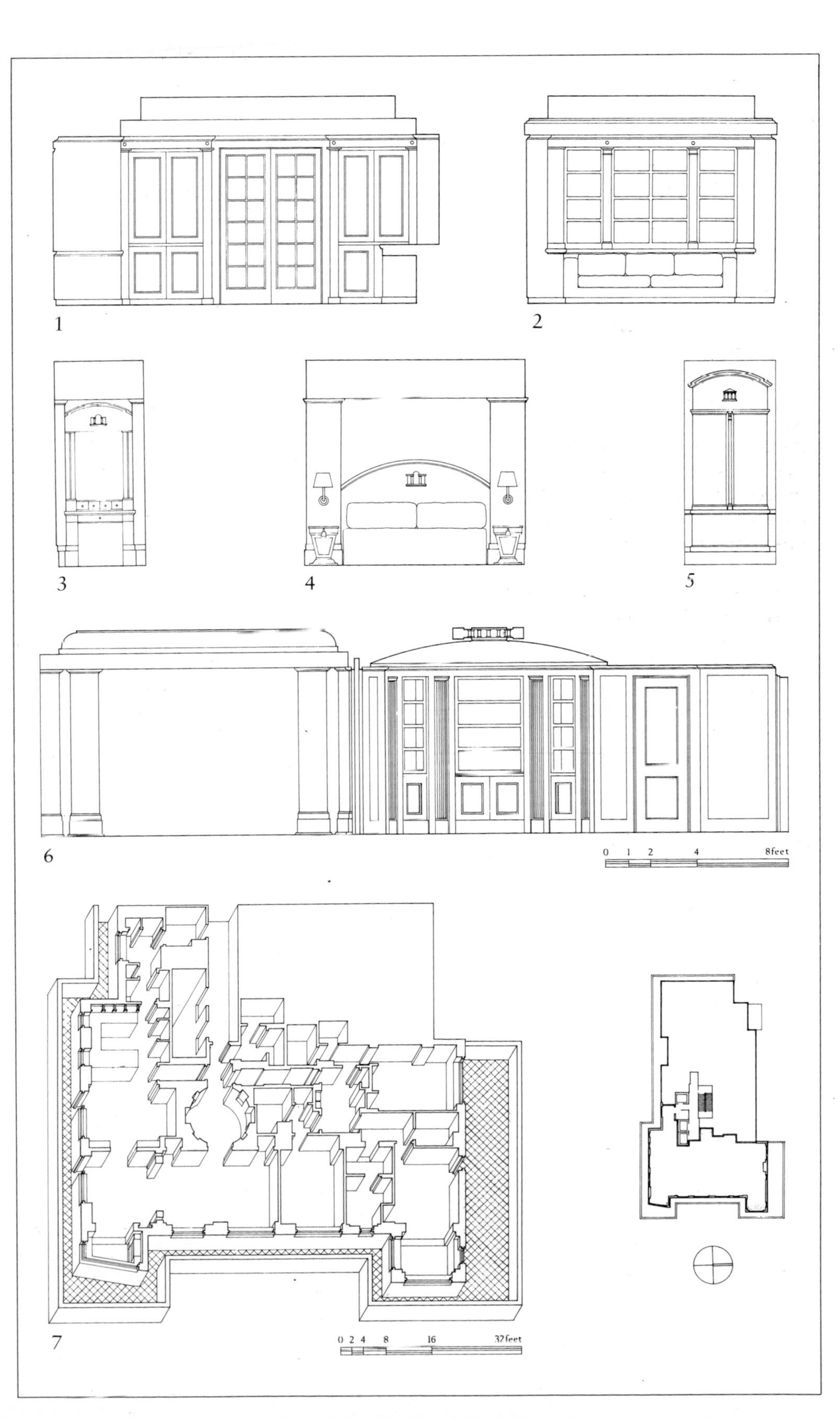

1.Family room east elevation 2.Family room north elevation 3.Master bath vanity 4.Master bed 5.China cabinet 6.Section through living room and foyer 7.Floor plan

Residence at Calf Creek
Water Mill, New York
1984–

Located along a tributary of Mecox Bay, this house consciously works within the tradition of domestic resort architecture of eastern Long Island. The picturesque massing of gambrel roof, dormer windows, and projecting bays is used in combination with more formal Classical elements such as a stylobate, Tuscan columns, and full entablatures. Raised above the ground on a rose-red brick base, the house has a traditional material palette of weathered red cedar shingles and white-painted wood trim.

Entry is through a vaulted porch, asymmetrically located in the east elevation which leads into a double-height stair hall. The plan is organized so that the more enclosed service areas are placed along the entrance facade, allowing the more formal rooms to be situated facing the view. Columns and shingled corner piers supporting the paired gambrels of the second floor at the water elevation recompose the asymmetry of the ground-floor plan while providing a large covered porch off the dining room.

Rising at the southwest corner of the house is a tower much in the manner of a shingled lighthouse. In its base is an octagonal study, indirectly lit through oculi, while at the second floor, a winding stair from a bedroom leads up to a playroom with a commanding view of the ocean.

1. East elevation 2. South elevation 3. North elevation 4. West elevation 5. Ground floor plan 6. Second floor plan 7,8. Views of model 9. Site plan 10. View from the southwest

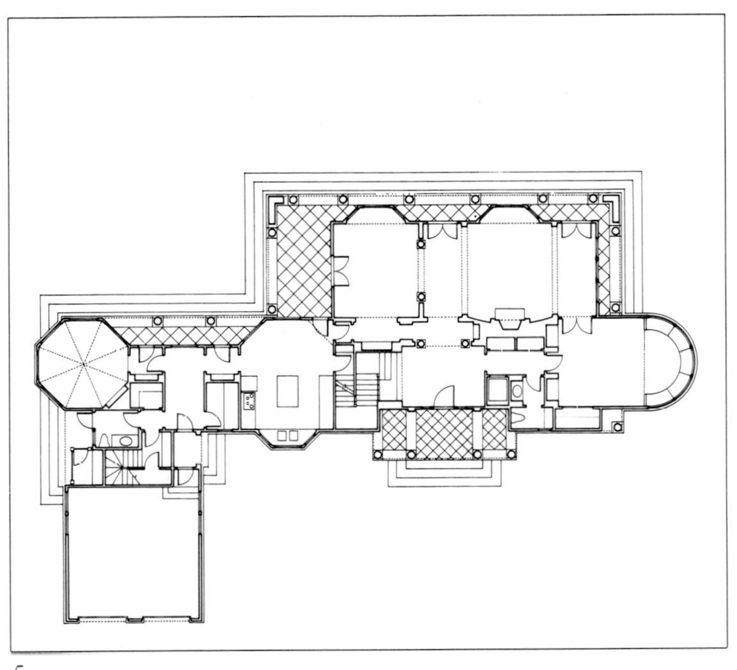

5

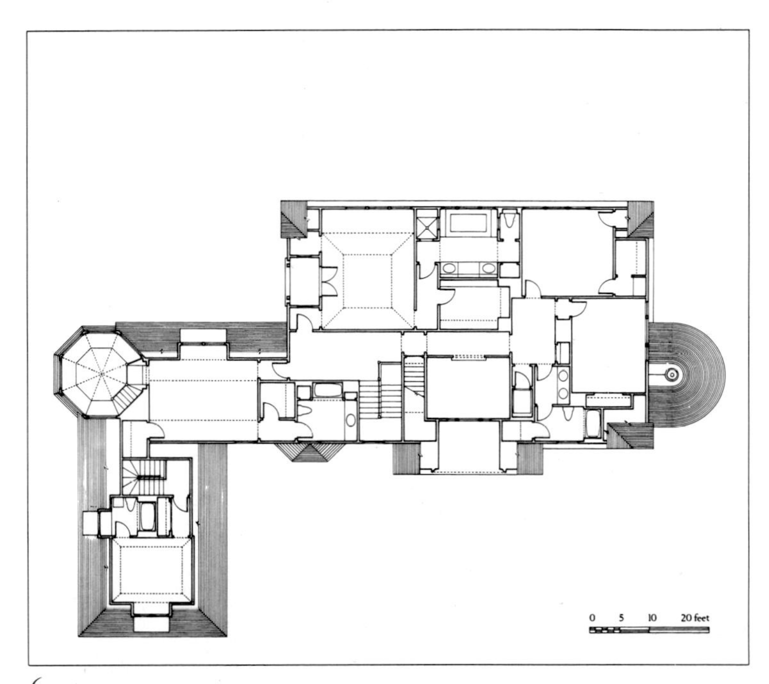

6

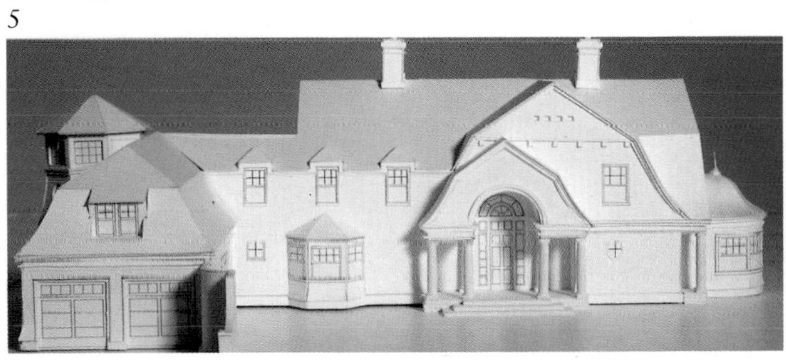

7

8

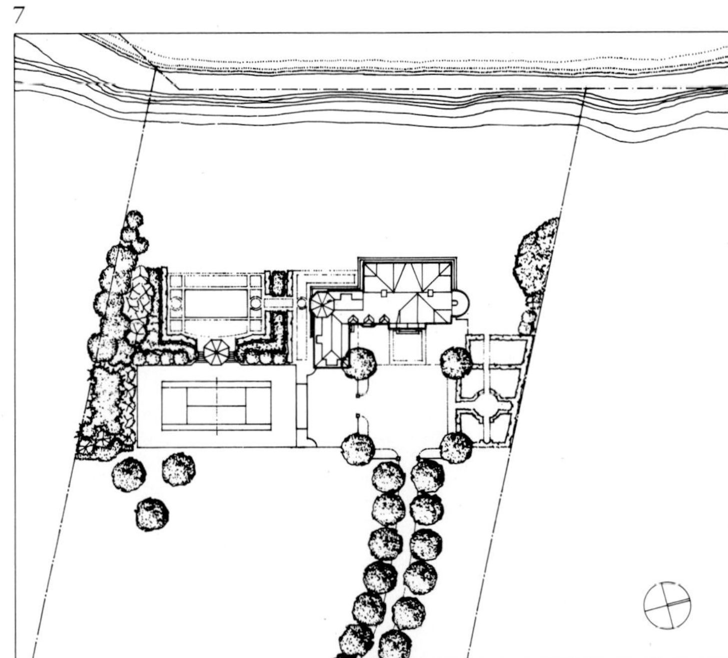

9

10

Pool Atrium

Deal, New Jersey
1984–1985

An enclosed outdoor room containing a pool and extensive terraces shaded by pergolas is connected to the main house by a path through an elaborate gateway suggestive of a triumphal arch. The atrium walls are stuccoed red to blend with the terracing and to recall the brick of the Georgian main house.

1.View from the east 2.Site plan 3.View from the west 4.Entrance pavilion 5.Plan and elevations 6.Longitudinal section

1

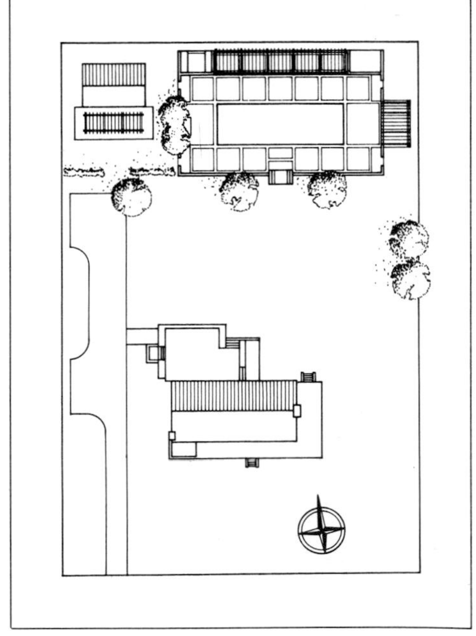

2

3

4

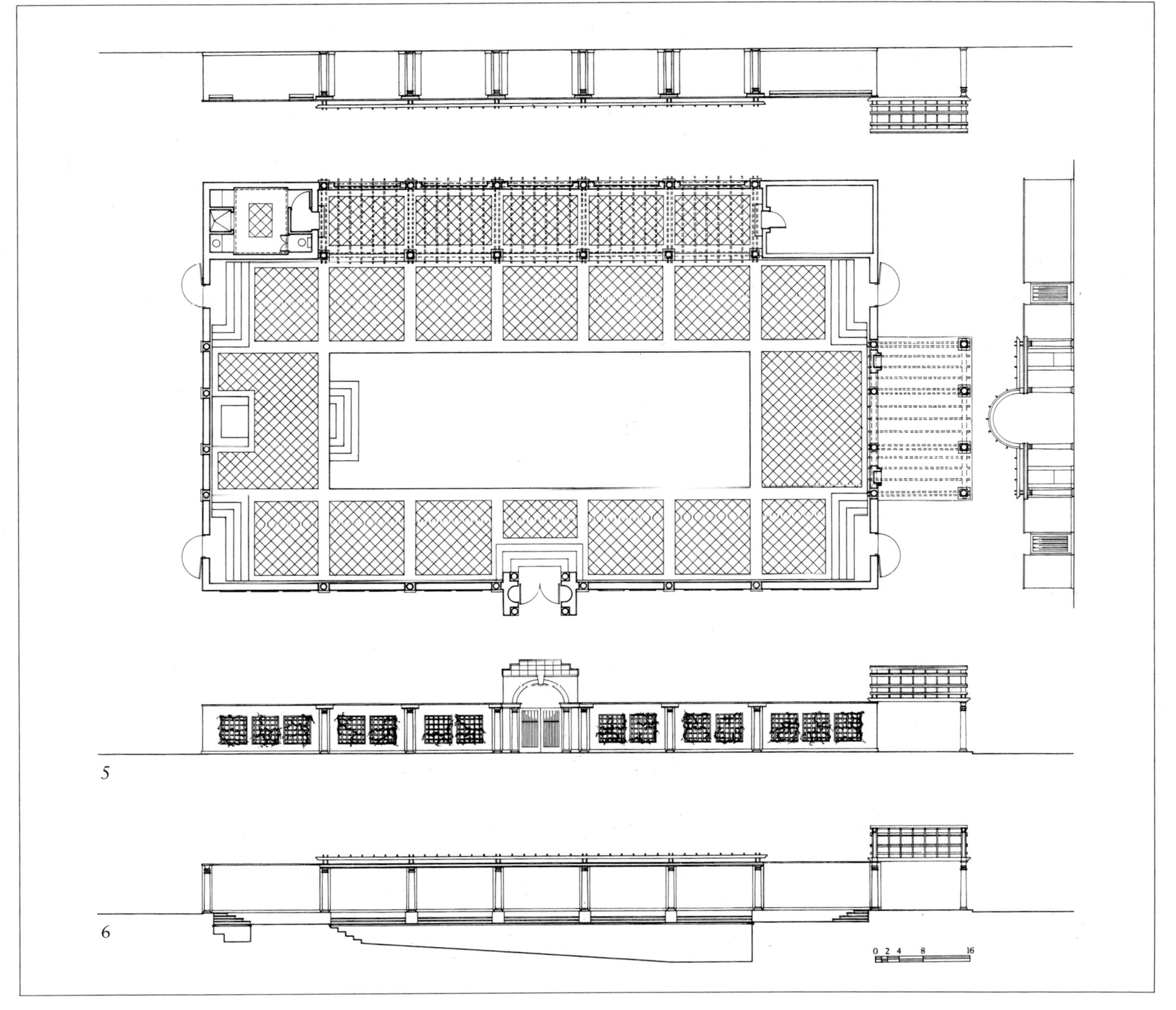

5

6

Classical Pool Pavilion
Deal, New Jersey
1984–1985

This swimming pool and pavilion elaborate on the Italo-American theme established in the main house built in the 1920s, and the tradition of Classical garden structures as established by Charles Platt. Located on a lot adjacent to the house, the pool and the pavilion relate axially to the formal rooms of the house while affording views of the ocean.

Designed to serve as the center for outdoor life in the summer, the pavilion is a tripartite composition with the center serving as a covered entertaining area open on the front and back, while the sides contain support function such as kitchen, laundry, and changing rooms. A Tennessee sandstone terrace surrounds the pool and is defined and enclosed with a hedgerow that provides privacy.

1

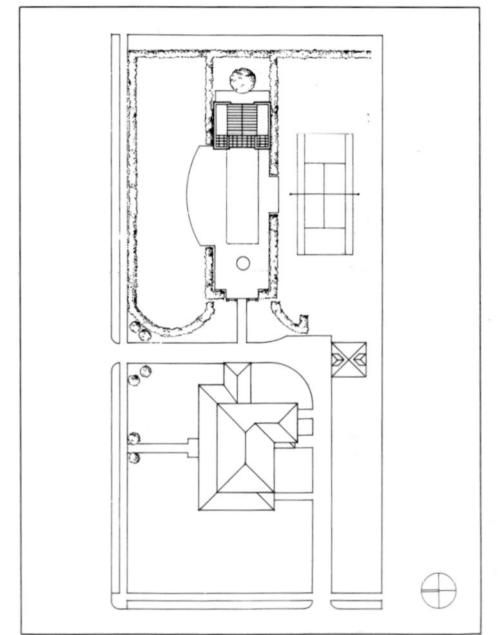

4

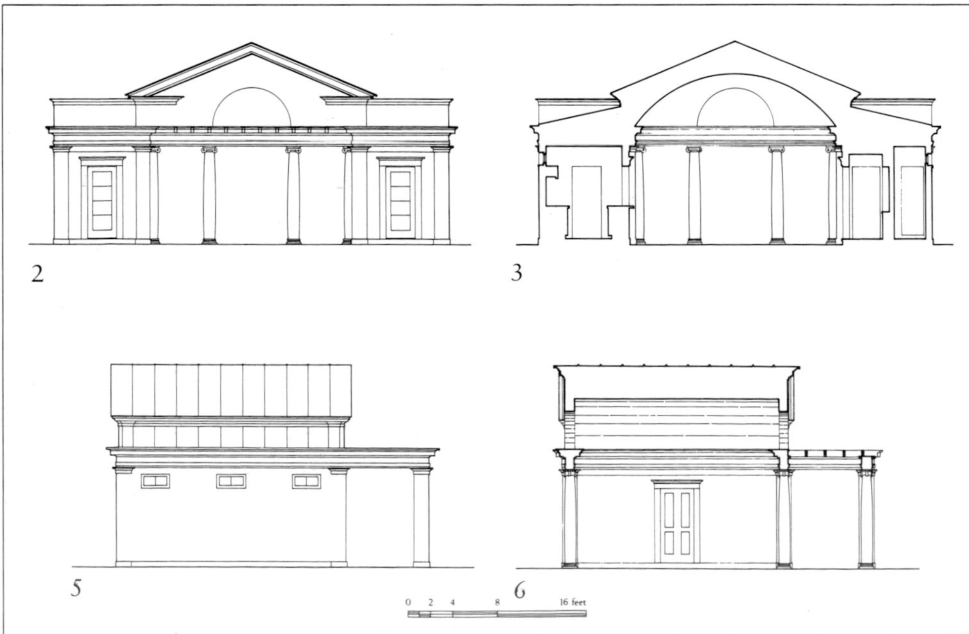

2 3 5 6

1. View from the pavilion 2. West elevation 3. Transverse section 4. Site plan 5. South elevation 6. Longitudinal section 7. View from the west 8. Floor plan

7

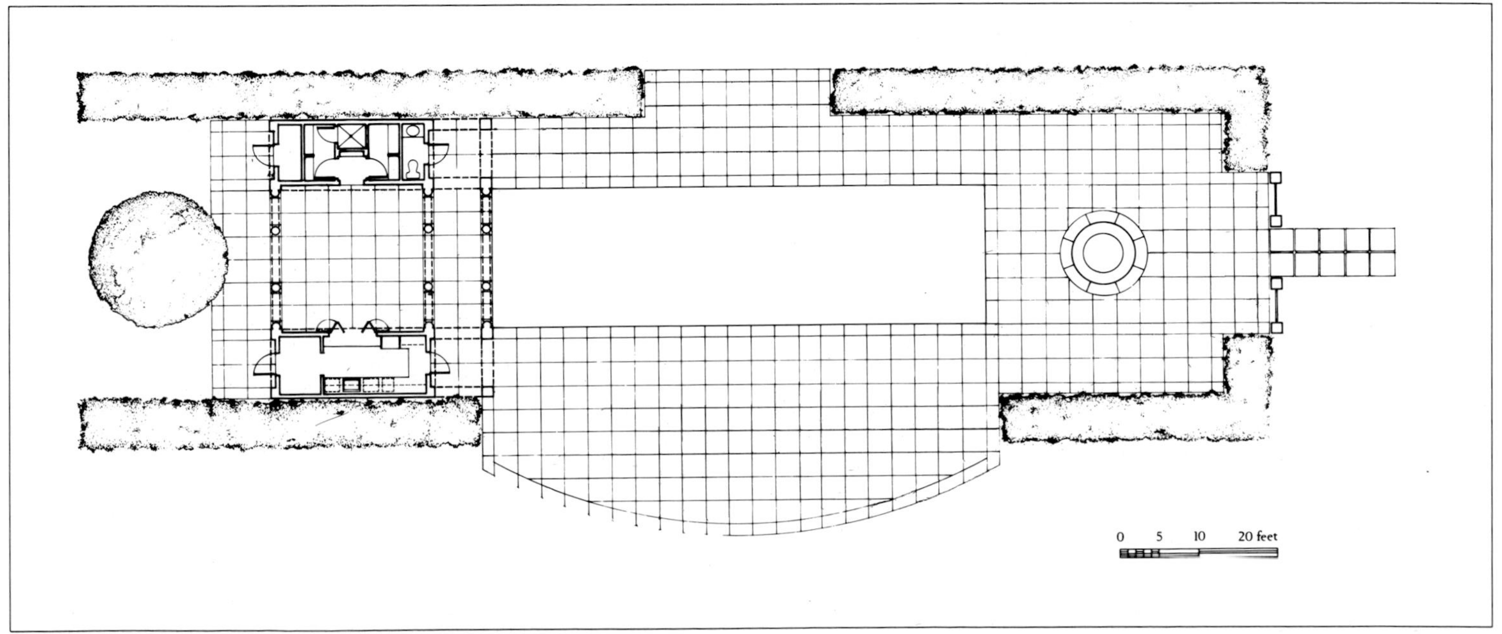

8

Farmhouse
Oldham County, Kentucky
1983

At once a farmhouse and a temple, this house in Kentucky is located on a hill with expansive views on all sides. The plan organizes a complex program into a compact square, resulting in a house that is capable of accommodating large groups of guests while remaining intimate for the owners. Most of the living spaces are on the first floor, which is zoned into three parts—the master bedroom suite to the north, the family living spaces to the south, and the formal entertainment and reception rooms in the center. The second floor contains guest rooms and galleries to display the owner's large collection of American crafts. The round gallery in the center of the second floor satisfies the expectation raised by the exterior massing, while the space between the inner and outer drum brings unexpected natural light into the center of the house. The lower floor contains service spaces and a pool in a grotto-like room that is lit by a large arched window under the living-room pergola. This lower floor also leads to garages and a sunken parking court that allow for the main pavilion to remain unobstructed in all directions.

Site development is limited to the area immediately around the house. Square planting terraces flank the house to the north and south. The grove of trees to the northeast is balanced by the lowered parking court and the screen of trees that surrounds it. To the west, planting is kept to a minimum so as not to conflict with the preferred view.

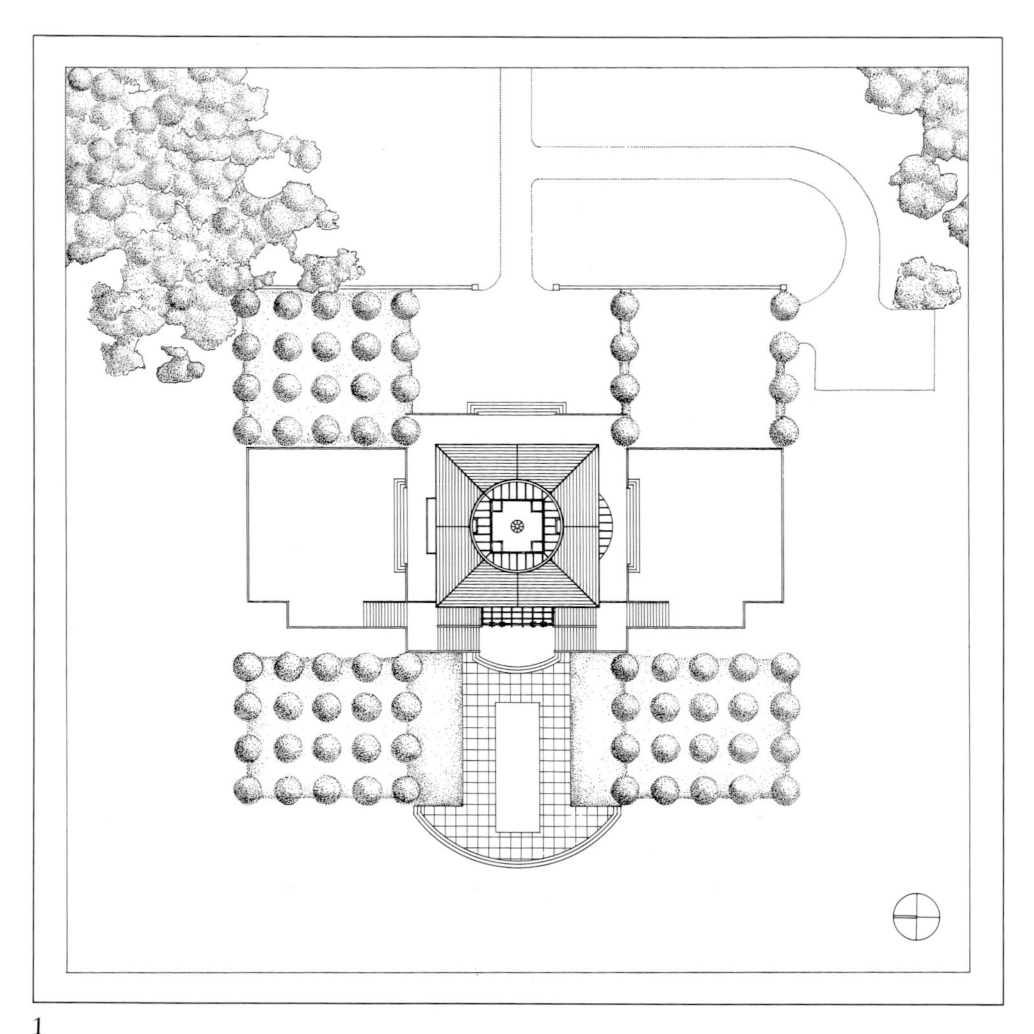

1

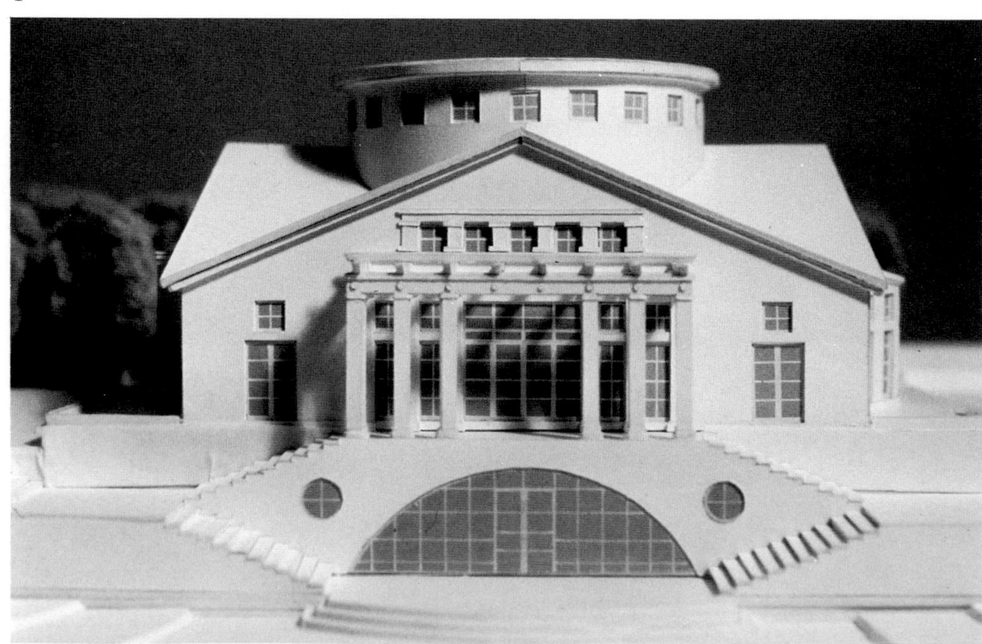

2

1.Site plan 2.View of model 3.North elevation 4.East elevation 5,6.Sections 7.South elevation 8.West elevation

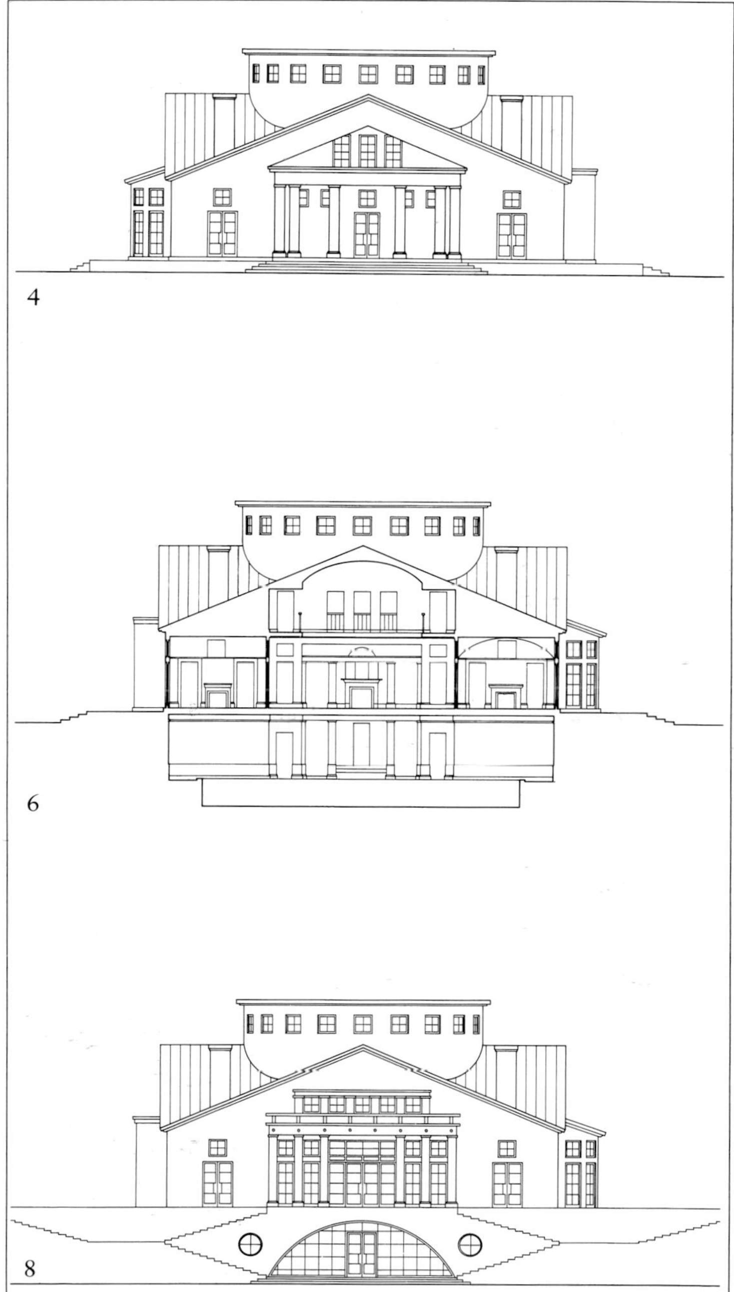

1.Second floor plan 2.Ground floor plan
3.Preliminary study of west elevation
4.View of model 5.Aerial view of model
from the southwest

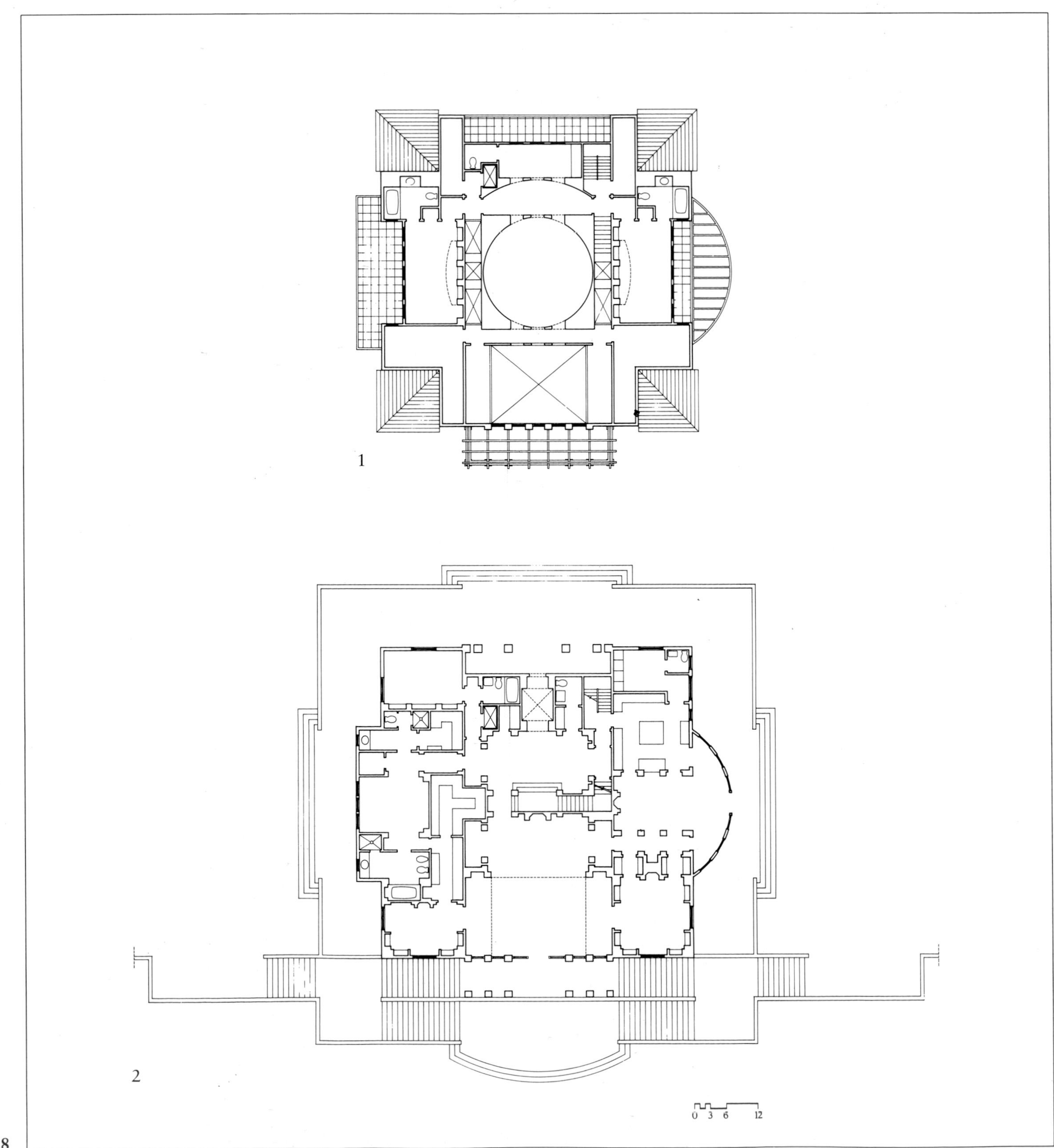

3

4

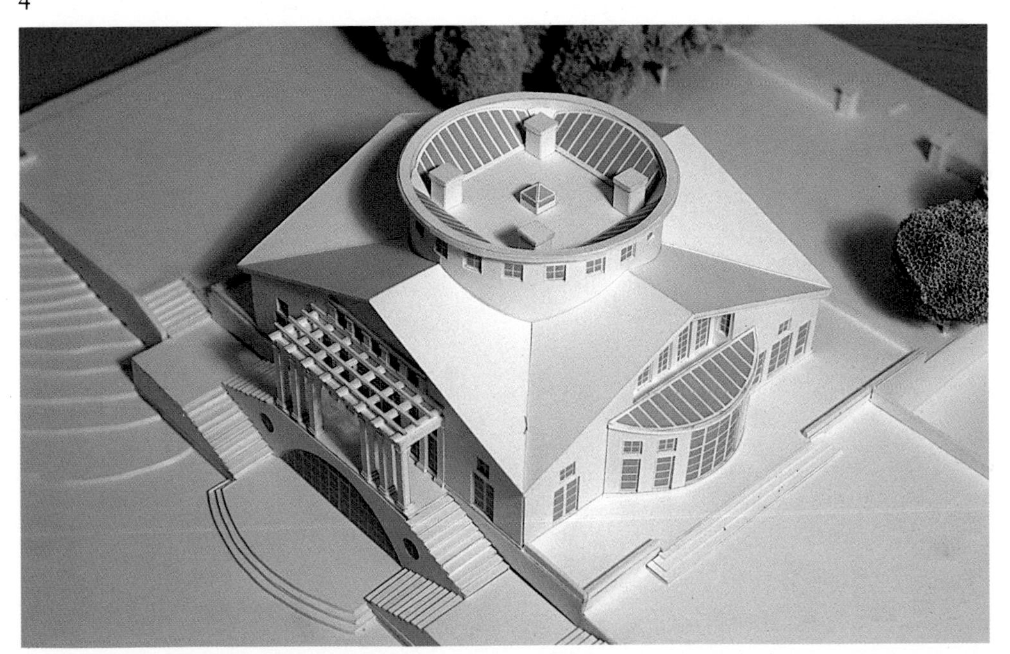
5

Addition to Congregation Shaare Zion

Brooklyn, New York
1984

This synagogue is located in an established residential neighborhood in Brooklyn. The original building, which houses the sanctuary, faces Ocean Parkway, a broad boulevard. The proposed addition faces a much narrower street lined with smallish single-family houses. Massing of the building is determined by strict residential zoning requirements and the demands of the context. Through the use of the repeated pavilion form, the design seeks to maintain the rhythm of the residential setting while uniting it to the larger bulk of the building.

The principal purpose of the addition is to provide overflow religious space for High Holy Day services and to serve as a social hall. This room, which will be one of the largest of its kind in the city, incorporates the pavilion form as a side aisle while using the interior under the main roof to increase the volume and spaciousness of the central hall.

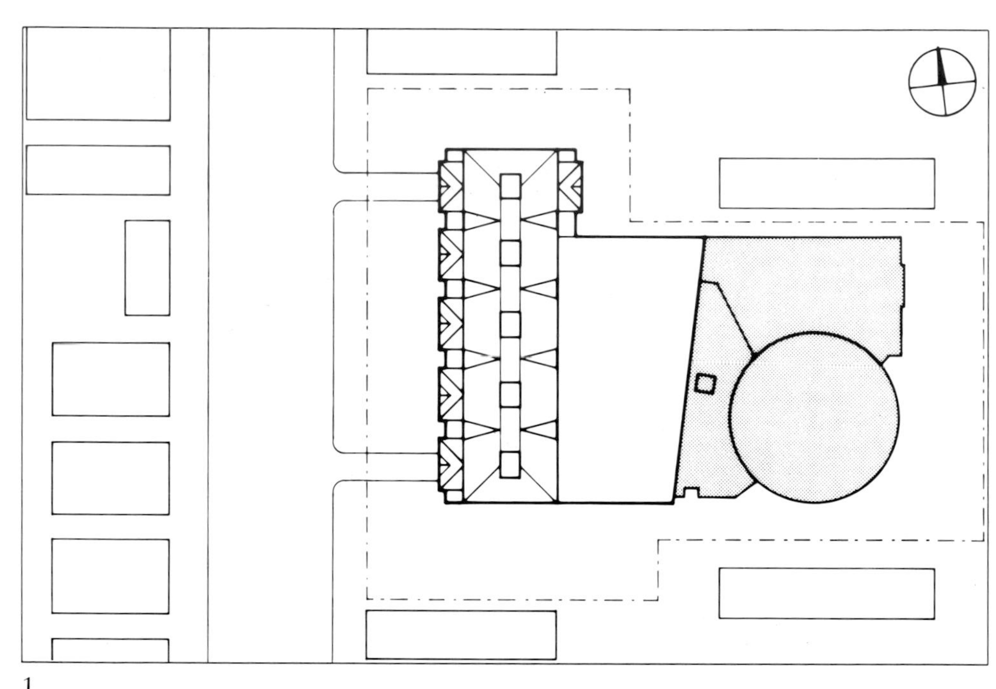

1

2

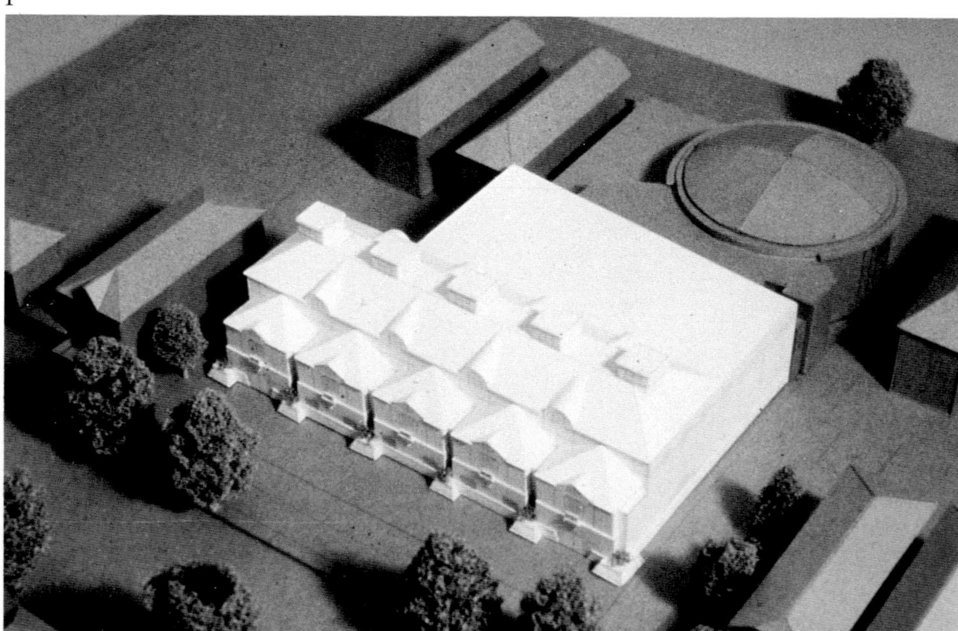

3

1.Site plan 2.Existing building 3.Aerial view of model from the southwest 4.West elevation 5.South elevation 6.North elevation 7.Section 8.Third floor plan 9.Second floor plan 10.Ground floor plan

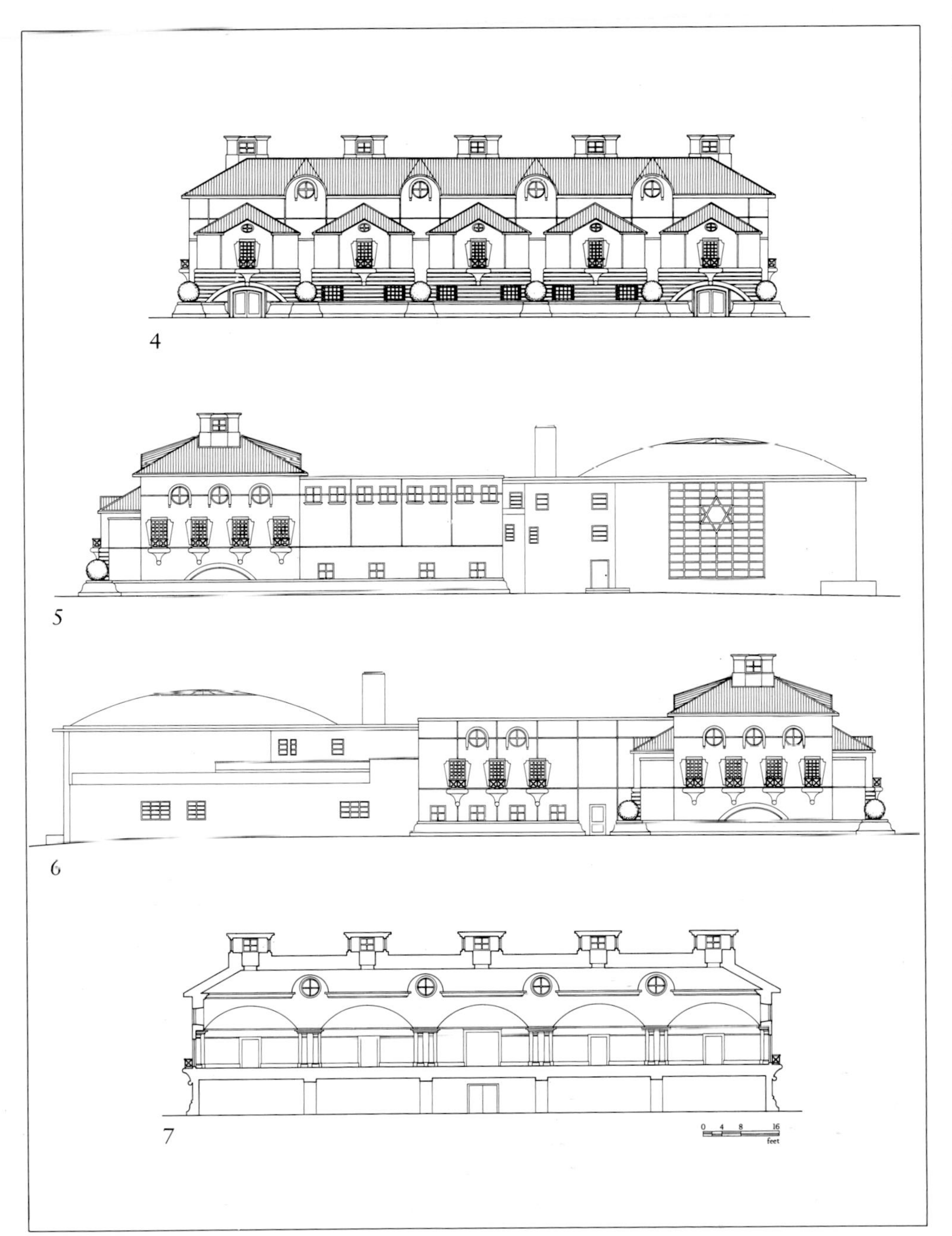

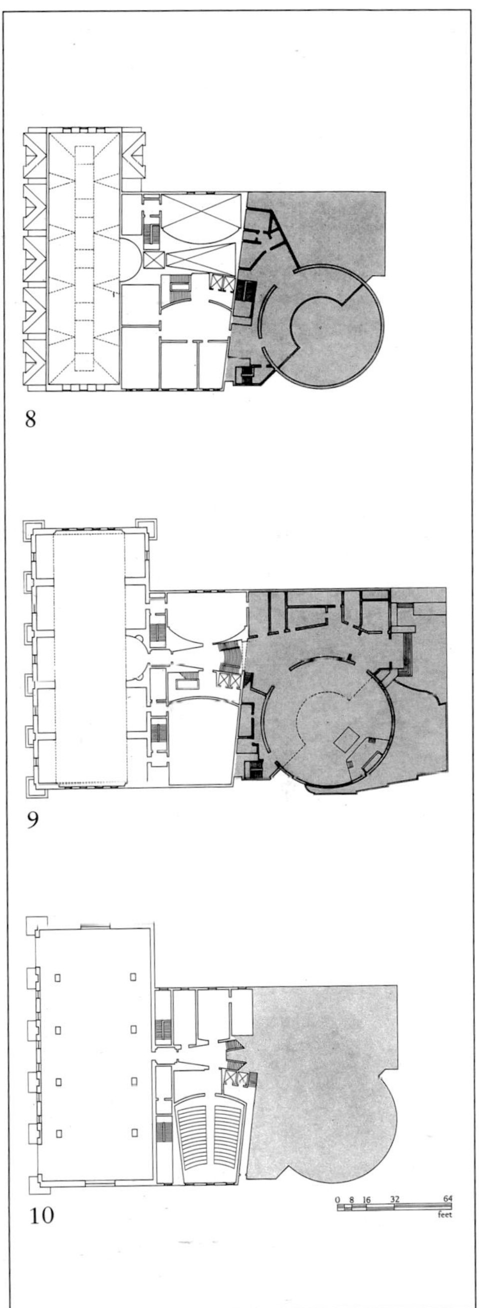

Residence at Lily Pond Lane

East Hampton, New York
1984–

Designed by Roger Bullard in 1924 and altered by Grosvenor Atterbury in 1927, this house had undergone little change for over fifty years. Inside, the house reflected the needs of a previous era which employed many servants and had many house guests, creating the need for many small bedrooms and baths. In renovating the house, some of these rooms were eliminated to create larger common rooms. At the west end of the house, an upstairs bath was removed to allow the ceiling of the solarium to follow the planes of the hipped roof outside, and lanterns of light were created within the ceiling by building small dormers outside. Similarly, the east end of the house was transformed from two servants' rooms to a barrel-vaulted family room at the edge of a new swimming pool.

The second floor alone remained filled with bedrooms for the owner, guests, and servants. The third floor, once three guest bedrooms, became a large media room, its ceilings, like the solarium, following the hipped roofline beyond.

Outside, little was done to alter the mountainous shingled roofs and their strong silhouette at the top of a beachfront bluff. A series of round windows were added, one at the center of each major axis of the house, east, west, and south. Flat-roofed dormers were replaced with hipped-roof dormers, which echoed the larger hipped roof of the house. By the pool, a new screened pavilion has a steep hipped roof which sits on massive stucco columns. These columns are repeated around the pool to hold a large lattice fence covered in beach roses, in combination creating an exterior room for the pool.

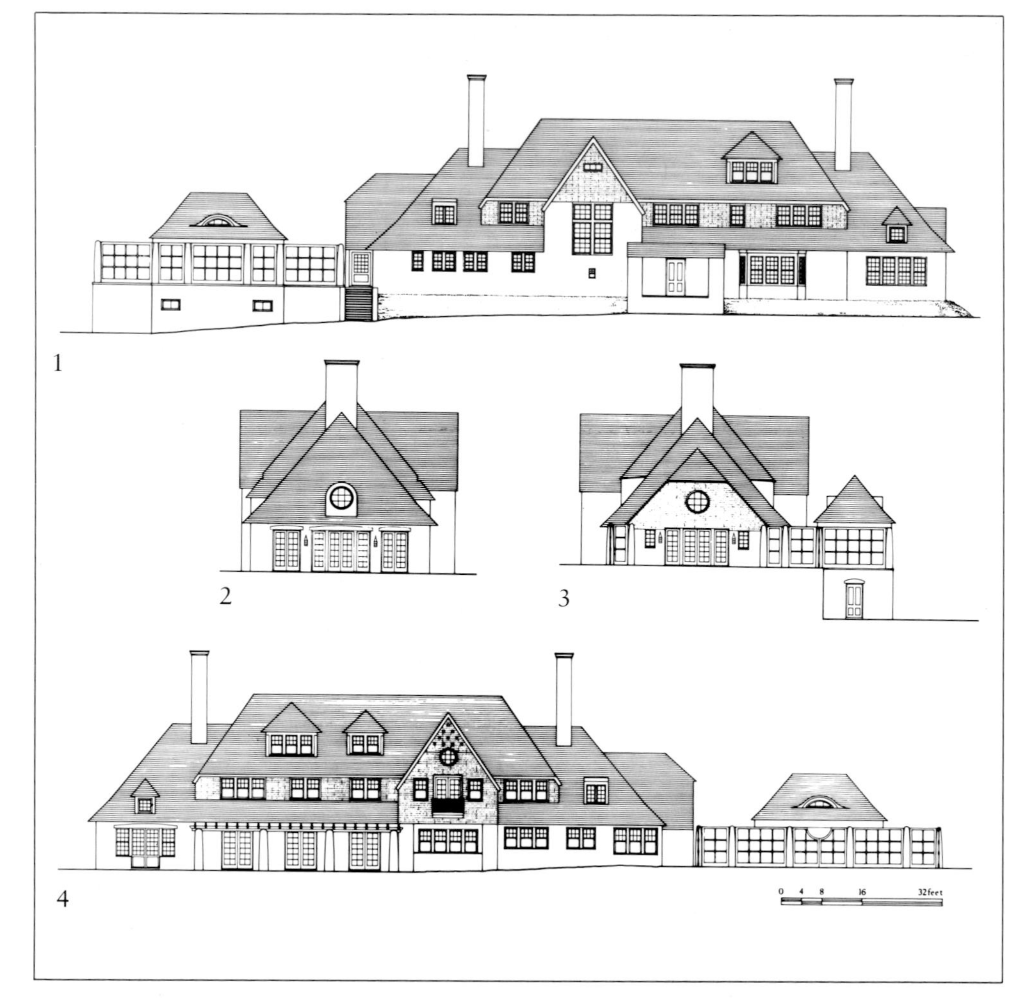

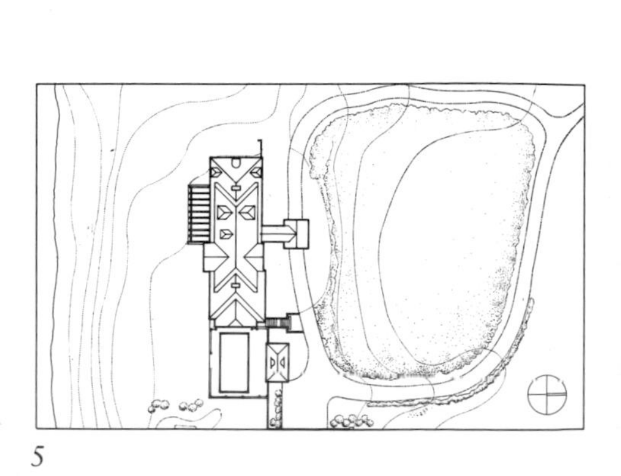

5

6

7

1.North elevation 2.West elevation 3.East elevation 4.South elevation 5.Site plan 6.View from the southwest 7.View from the northwest 8.Third floor plan 9.Second floor plan 10.Ground floor plan

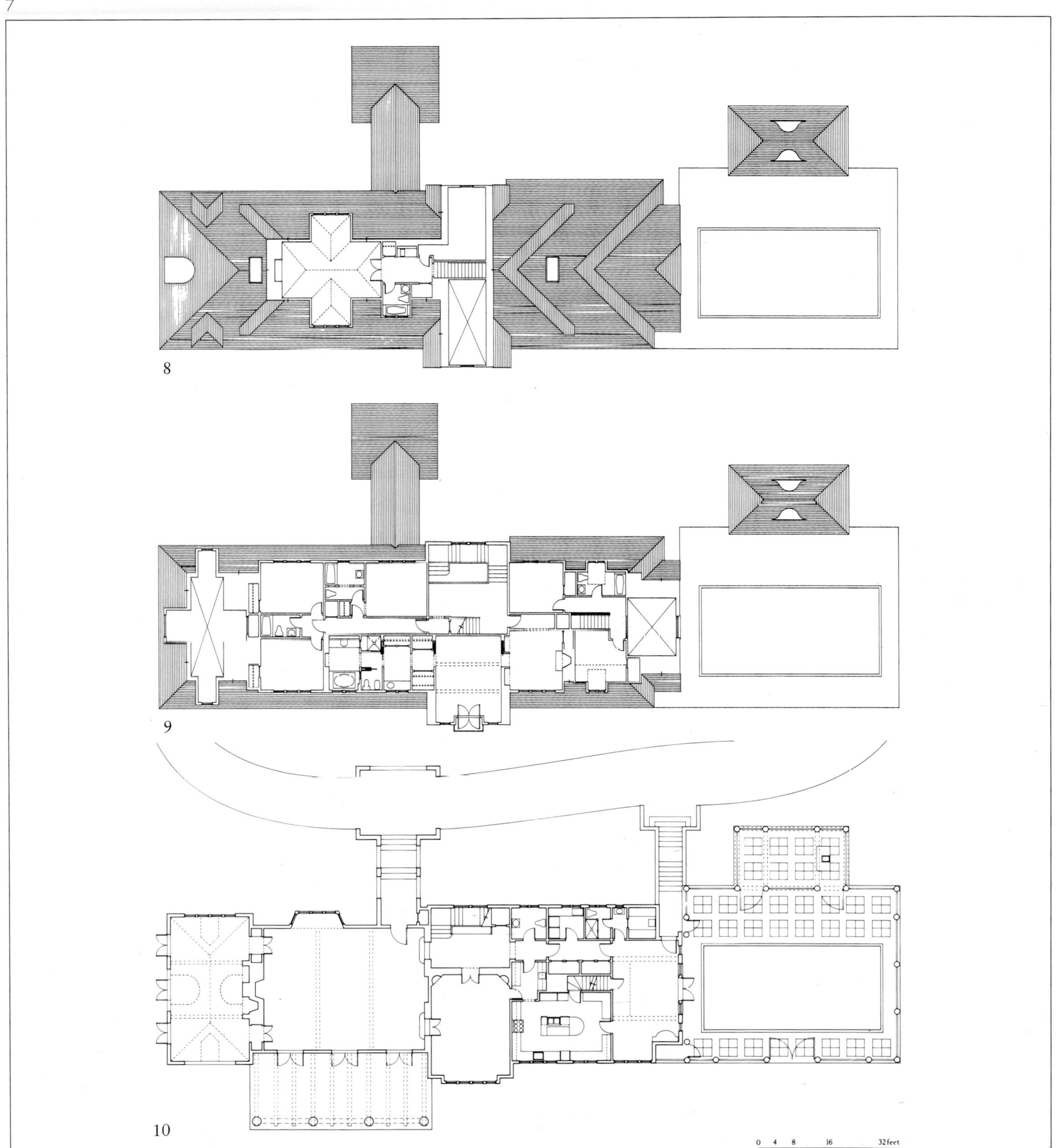

Scarsdale Heights
Thomas Street
Scarsdale, New York
1984–

Nestled in the rocky terrain of New York's Westchester County, this house is the first of nine, forming the developer-built community of Scarsdale Heights.

The brick and shingle exterior responds to the Tudoresque flavor of the 1920s Scarsdale Village. Brick jack arches and a molded water table give the house a solid, earthbound quality while the wood shingle cladding above the ground floor reinterprets the English hung-tile tradition in a typically American material.

An "L"-shaped plan creates a private, south-facing garden flanked by the living room, family room, and dining porch. The driveway, garage, and rear entrance face to the north. The second floor combines two children's bedrooms with three master suites occupied by the husband and wife, the wife's grandparents, and a brother.

1.West elevation 2.East elevation
3.North elevation 4.South elevation
5.Ground floor plan 6.Second floor plan
7.Site plan 8,9.Views of model

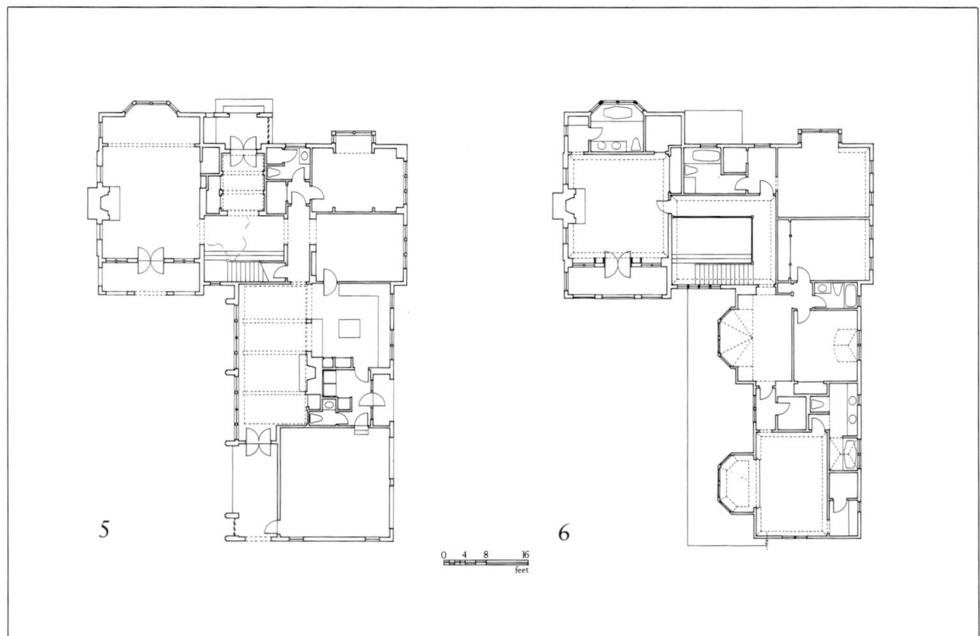

7

8

9

Greenwood Village
Bakersfield, California
1984

The plans and elevations of standard tract houses of the most modest sort have been reconfigured to enhance livability within and aesthetic appeal without. Intended for narrow lots, the reconfigured plans provide for maximum privacy from neighbors and for a greater sense of privacy and spatial coherence within the dwelling unit. With a minimum of elaborate millwork, the exteriors employ the vocabulary of Craftsman bungalows to lift the designs above the banal arrangements of the typical product.

1. Original proposal 2. New typical plan and elevation 3. Typical block

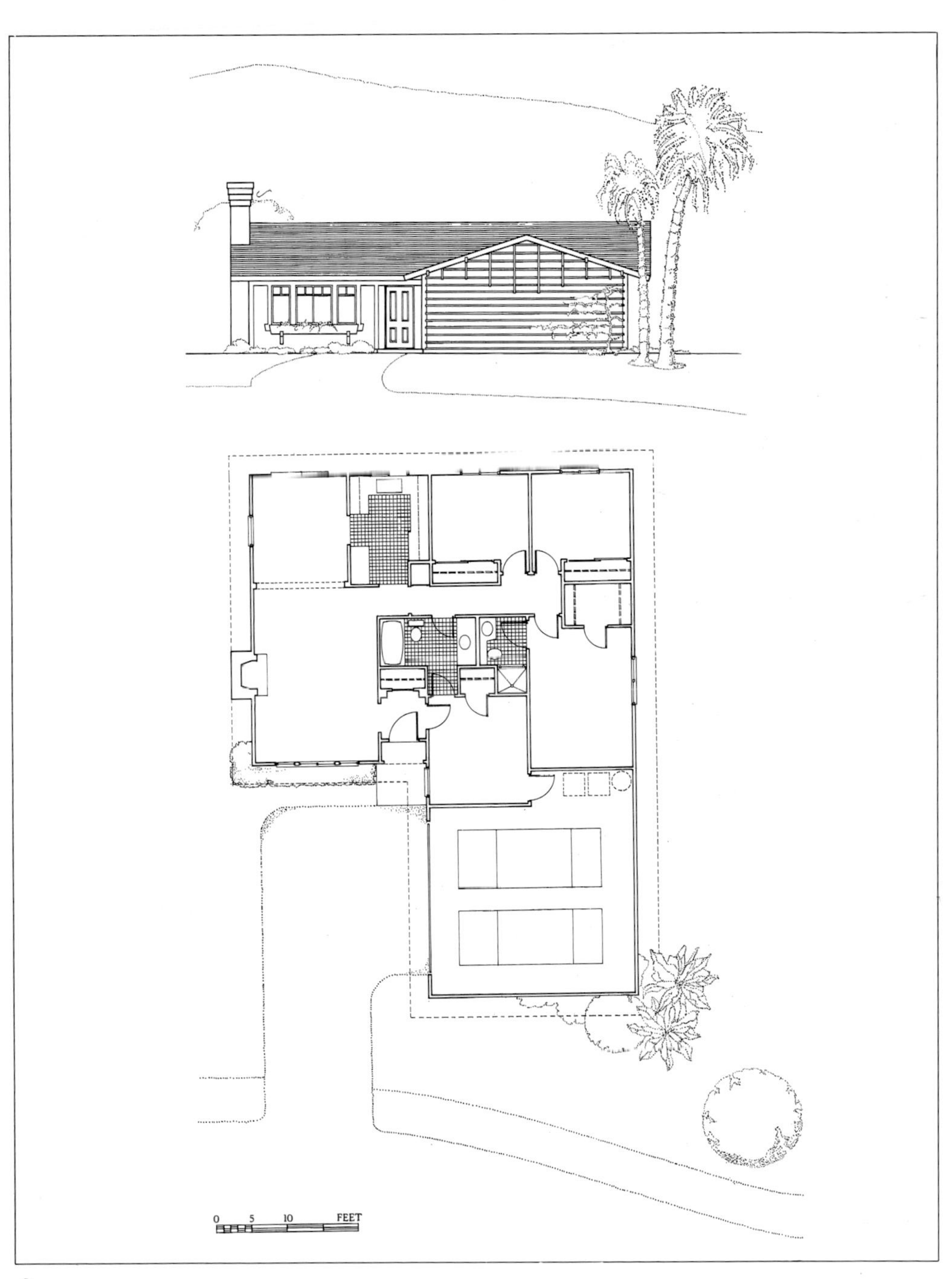

2

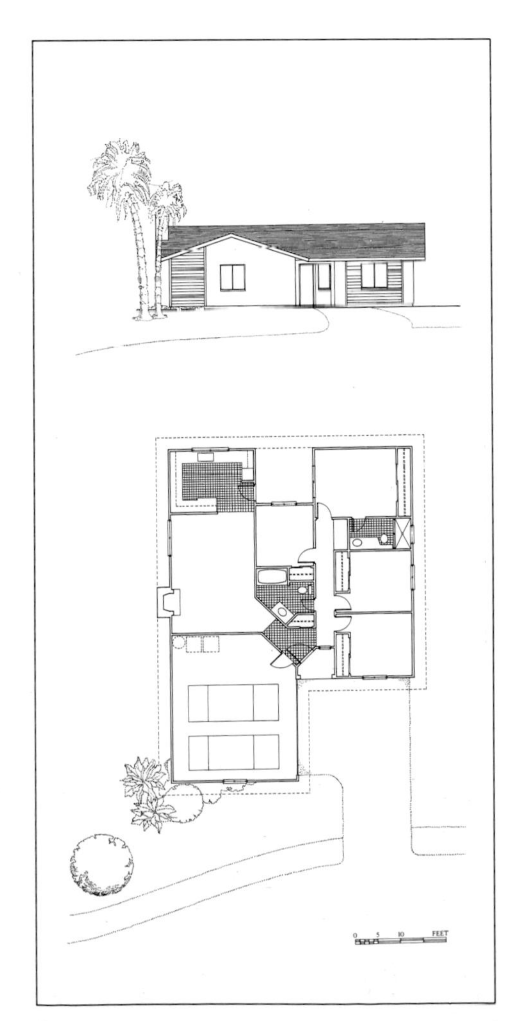

1

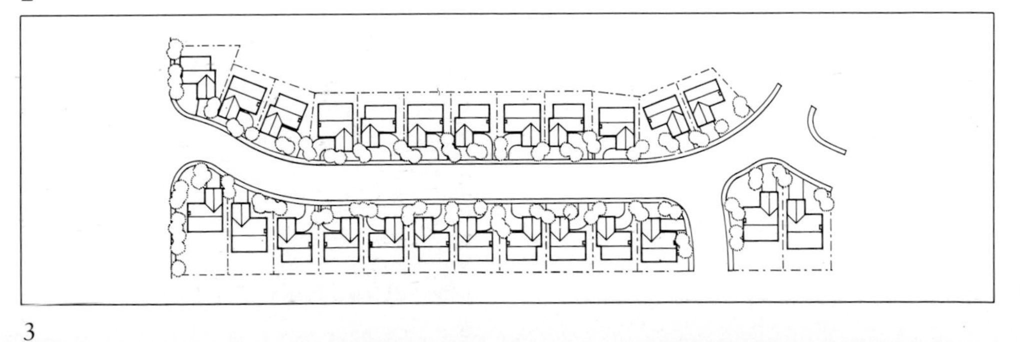

3

Hillcrest Square

San Diego, California
1984–

This 460,000-square-foot, mixed-use development in the heart of San Diego's fashionable Hillcrest neighborhood incorporates shops, restaurants, rental office space, a medical building, and 140 condominium units in a complex of buildings, open-air walkways, and courtyards. An 830-car underground parking structure is connected to the buildings above by elevators and by two sunken courtyards which provide light and air to the parking garage and a visual connection to the pedestrian walkways above.

The four-story medical building, at the north end of the site, faces Mercy Hospital across Washington Street. The remainder of the site contains four additional buildings which combine retail facilities on the ground floor with office space on the second and third floors and condominium units above. Lobbies to all of the condominium units open onto the semi-circular Palm Court which fronts on Fifth Avenue. Office lobbies are entered directly from Fifth Avenue and from the two interior courtyards. The system of pedestrian walkways recalls the mid-block alleys of Southern California but transforms them from service corridors to public paseos.

The massing, fenestration, and use of materials within the project respond to the Southern California climate and to the Spanish-Deco architectural traditions of the Hillcrest neighborhood. Cream-colored stucco walls are accented with cast stone and punctured by operable windows and balcony doors. Pitched roofs are of terra-cotta barrel tile, and rooftop terraces are shaded by vine-covered pergolas.

1.Map of San Diego showing location of site 2.Site plan 3.North elevation, Washington Street 4.East elevation, Sixth Avenue 5.South elevation, University Avenue 6.West elevation, Fifth Avenue

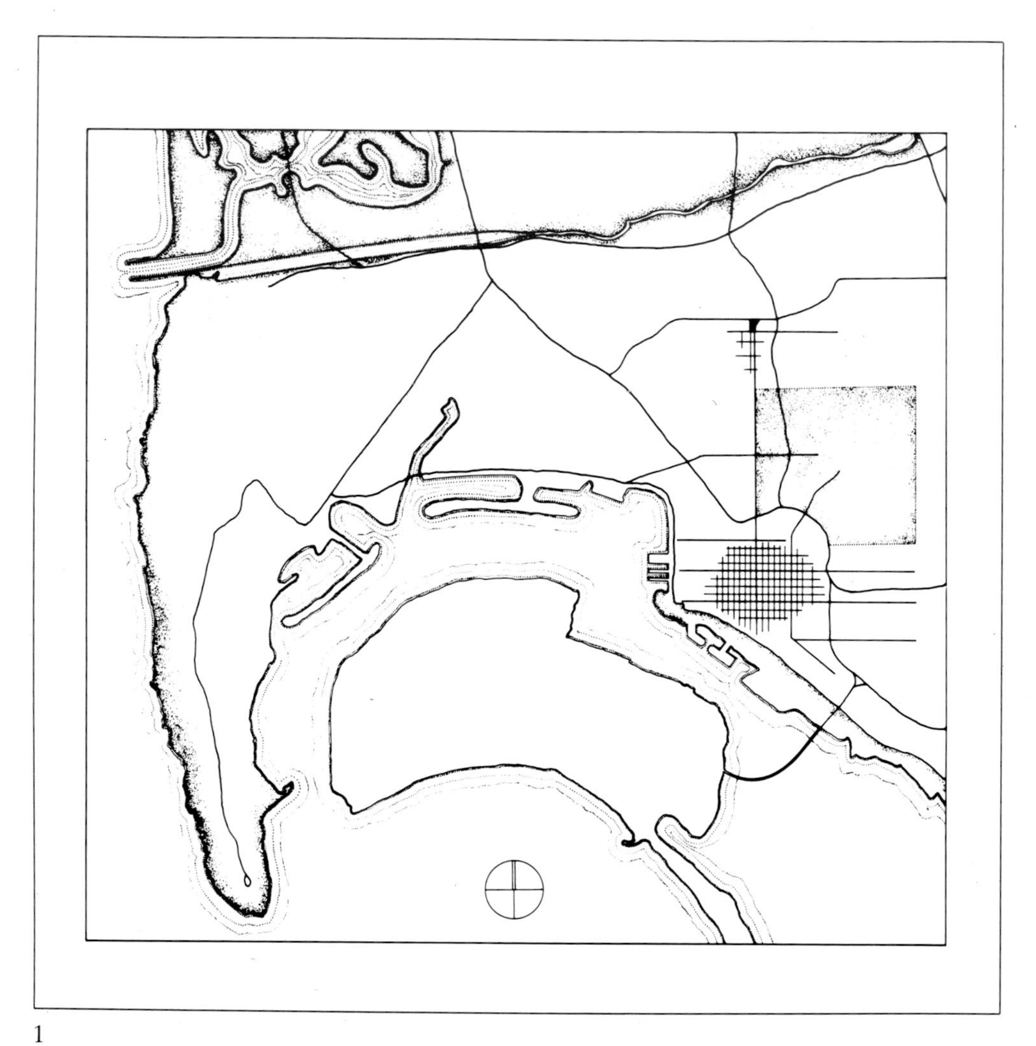

1

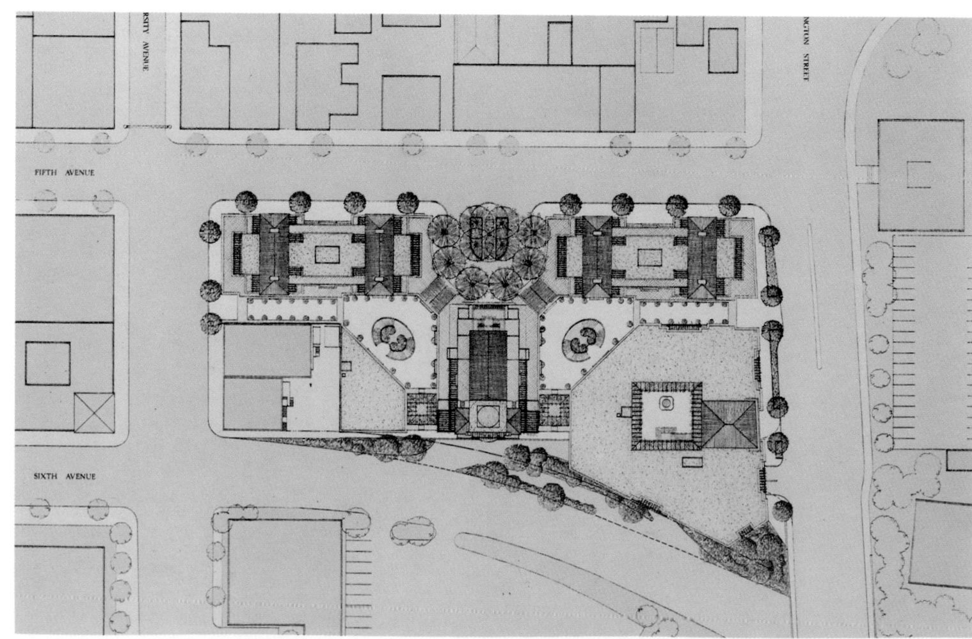

2

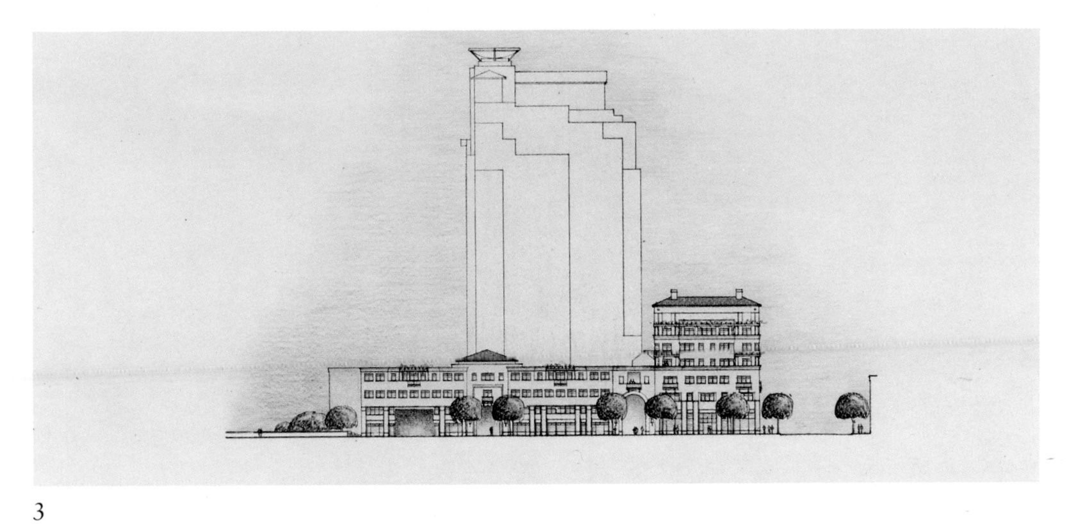

3

4

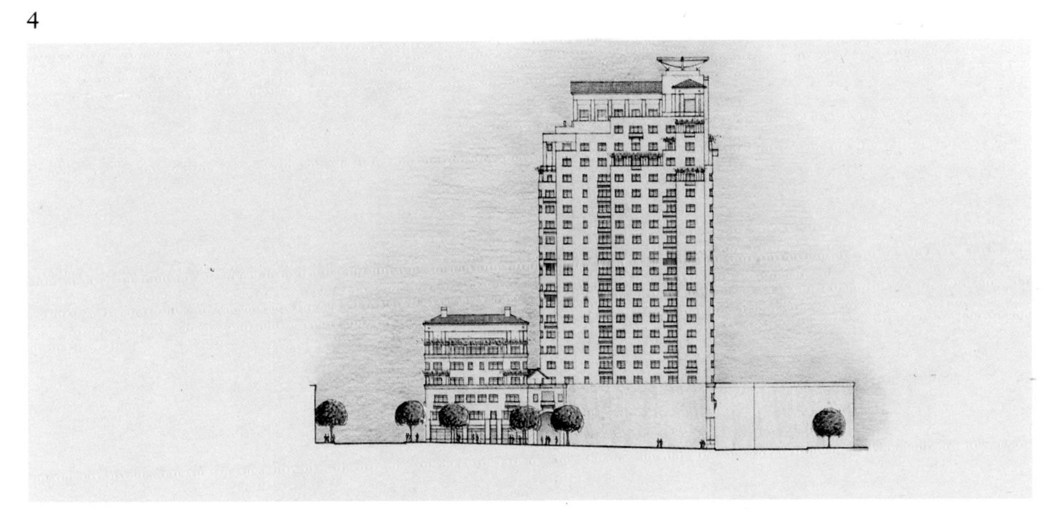

5

6

1.Second floor plan 2.Typical floor plan 3.Ground floor plan 4.Fourth floor plan 5.Longitudinal section 6.Aerial view of model from the west 7.Aerial view of model from the northwest 8.Aerial view of courtyards from the northeast

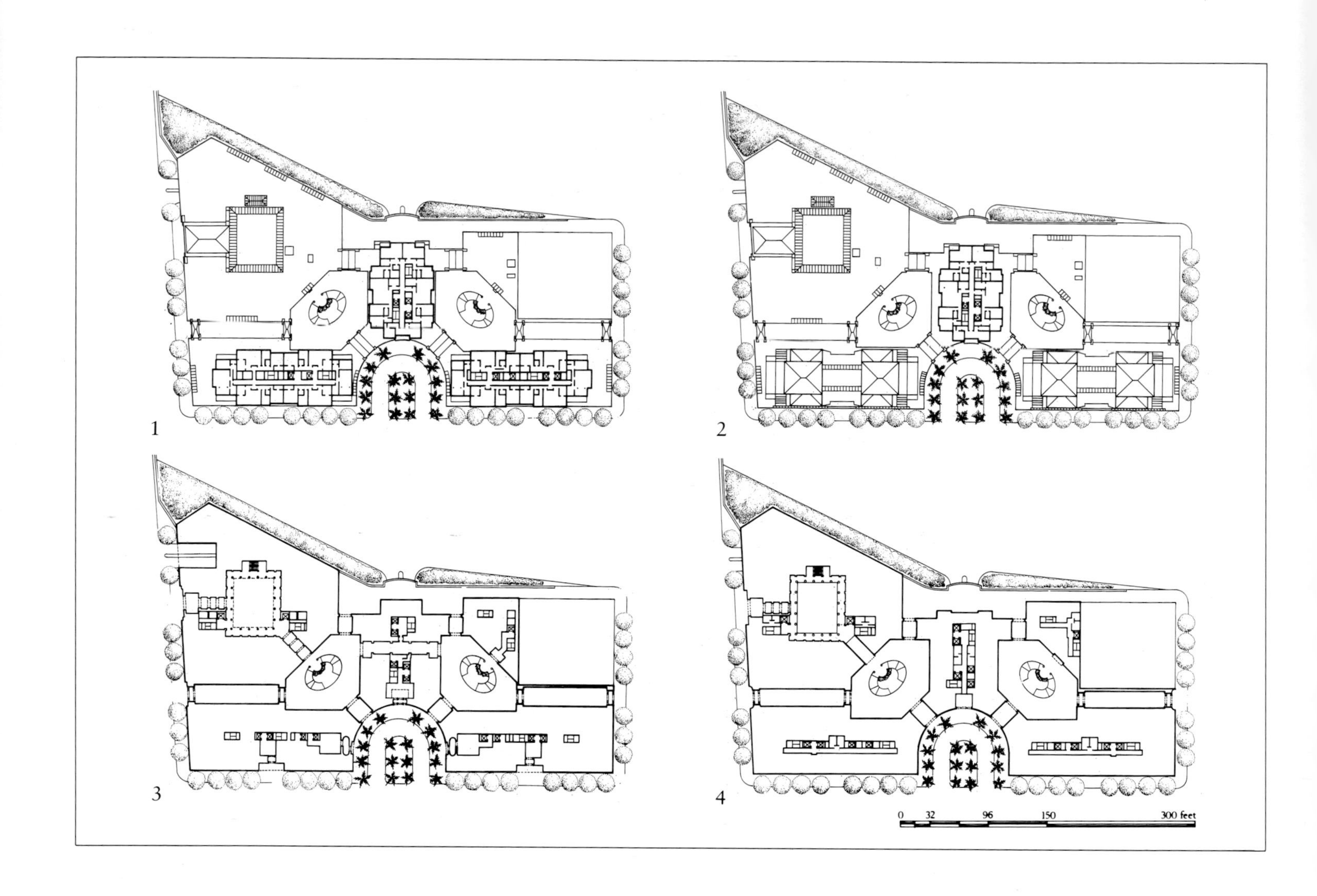

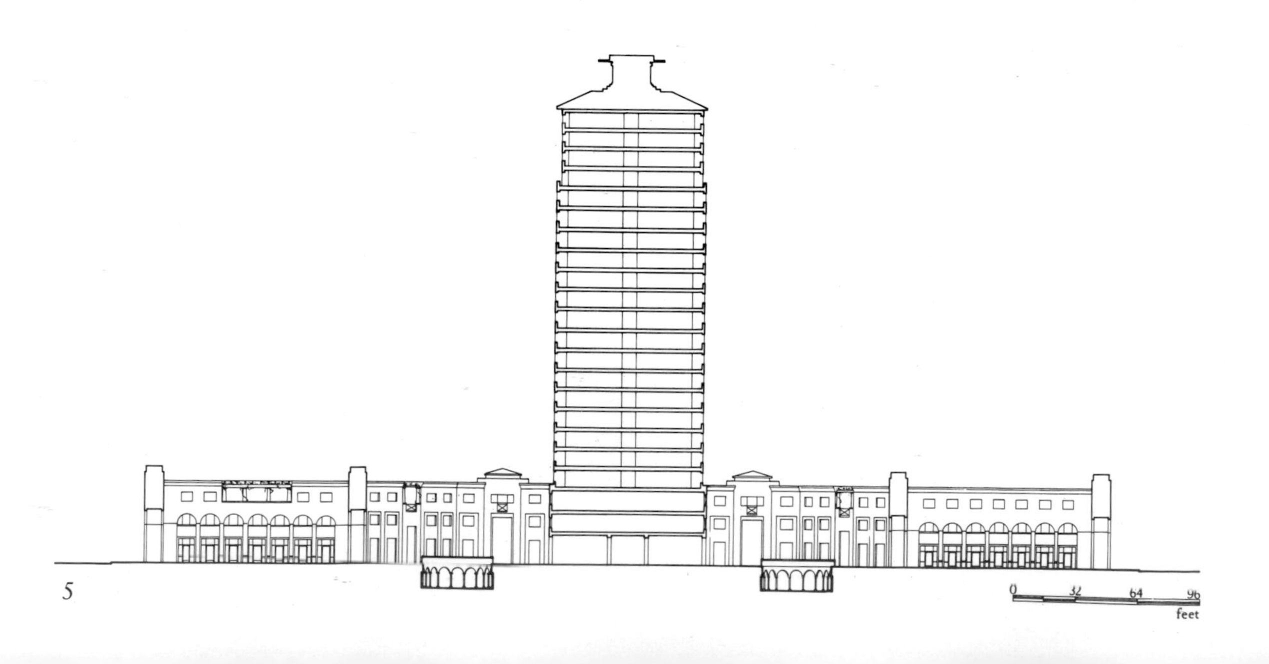

6

7

8

Civic Center
Escondido, California
1984

This project concerns itself with two issues which grow out of the program: first, the direct response to Escondido's need for a practical, flexible, and economic group of civic buildings and second, the adaptation of Southern California architectural traditions to help identify public spaces and architectural forms.

The buildings of our proposal divide into two groups organized along an open-air pedestrian walkway: a group of government buildings to the south of Grape Day Park and a group of cultural facilities to the west and north of the park. At the head of the walkway is the new city hall, surmounted by a cupola which punctuates the corner and marks the location of the skylit council chamber within.

The triple-height lobby of the city hall serves as a gateway to a public garden that creates a forecourt to the regional government facility, while providing a possible site for a second government building to accommodate future expansion. The western end of the public garden is defined by the convention hall which terminates the axis established by the city hall.

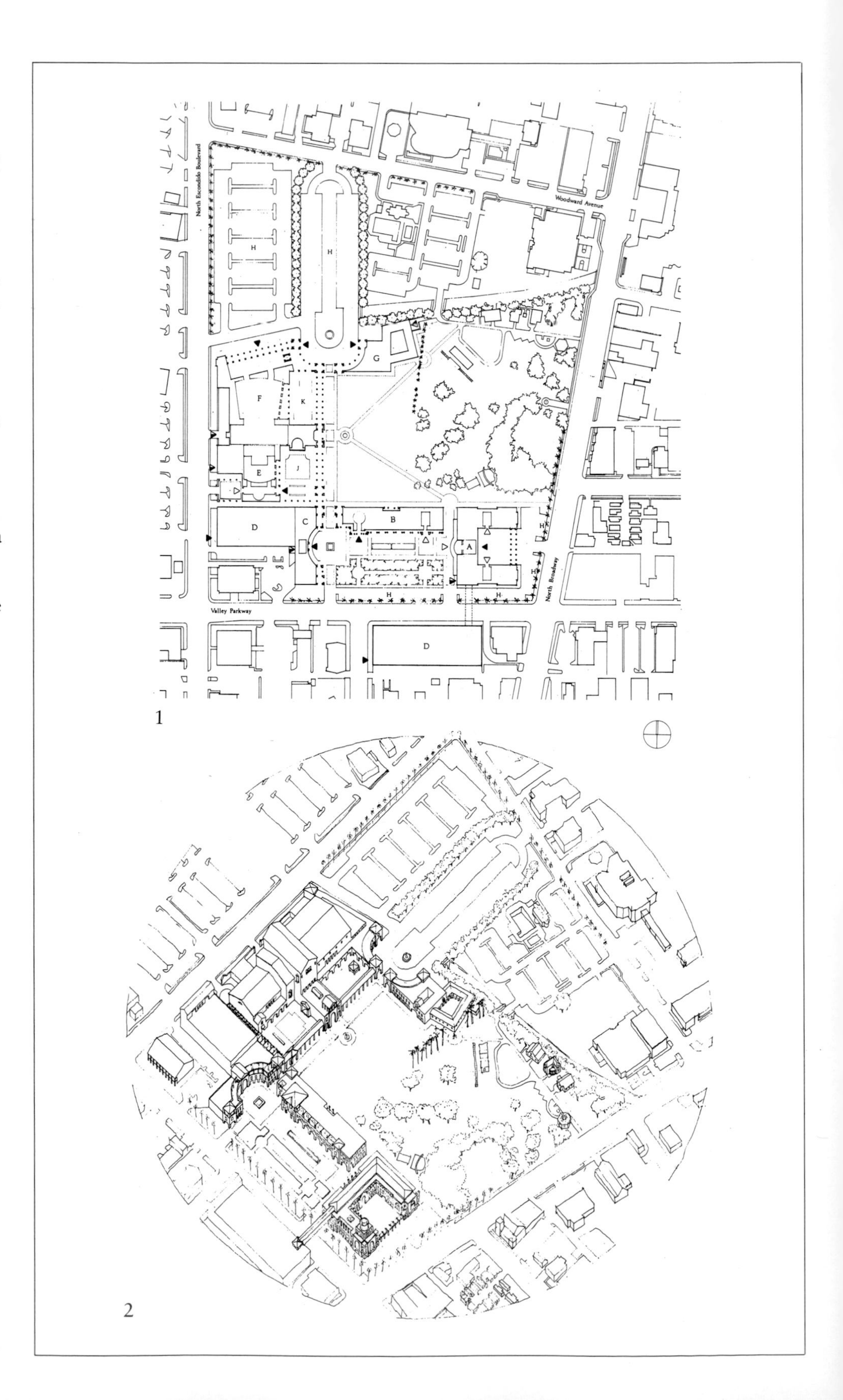

1

2

1.Site plan 2.Site axonometric 3.Perspective view of City Hall building from the southeast 4.Perspective of section through south wing 5.North Escondido Boulevard elevation 6.Valley Parkway elevation 7.Site section

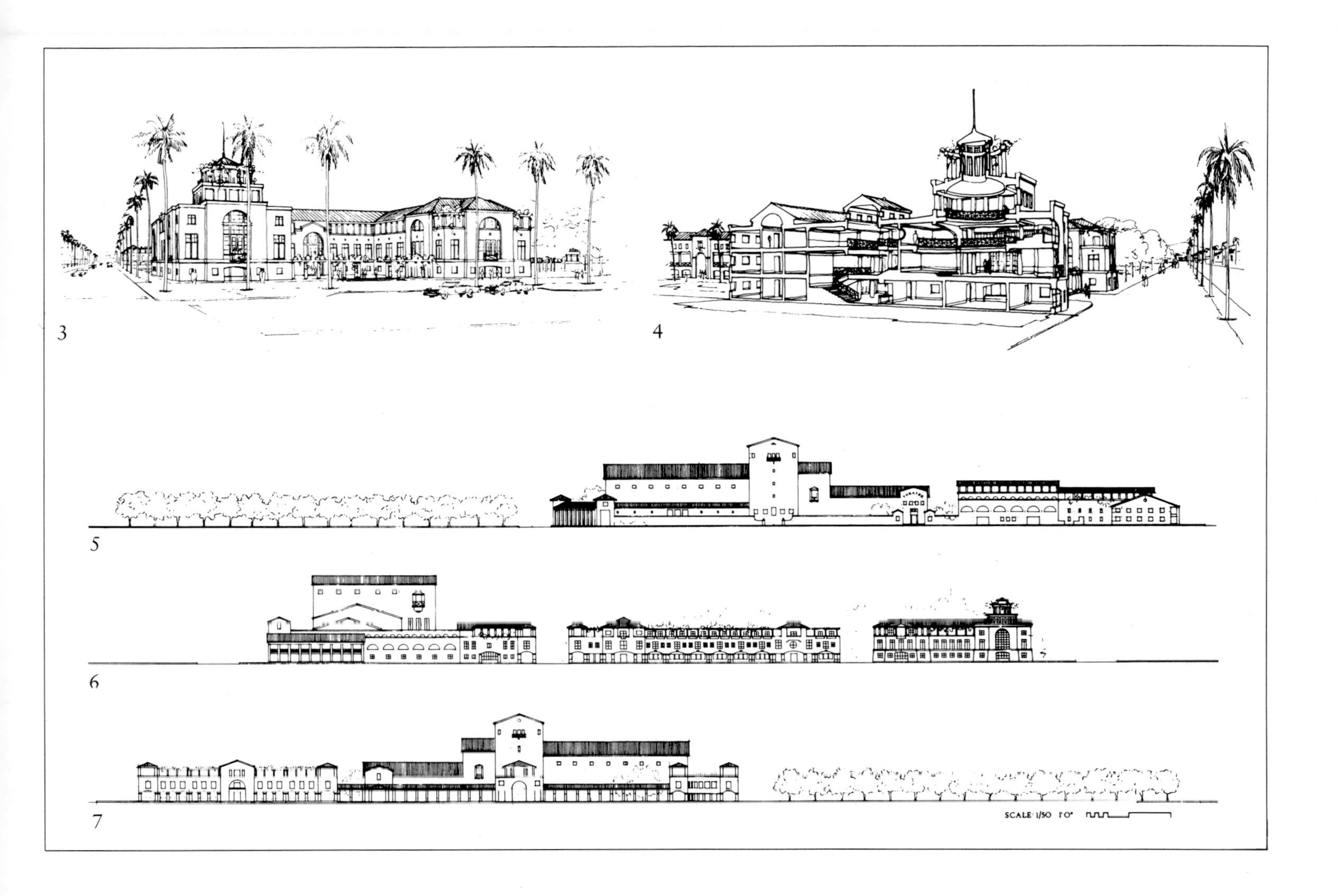

Architecture Building

Roger Williams College
Bristol, Rhode Island
1984

Our proposal for the new architecture building for Roger Williams College is oriented with a courtyard facing south to catch direct sunlight, terminate the view along the edge of the campus, and create an active forecourt for the entrance to the building.

The courtyard is lined with glass, allowing a transparency between interior and exterior, and creating a juxtaposition between the reflective openness of the building's inside and the opaque solidity of the stone wall which wraps the perimeter and relates to the stone of the existing campus buildings. Stone and glass support, and are are supported by, steel that is simply assembled in light frames to evoke the spirit of ancient artifacts through the reality of modern materials.

The process through the gateway, courtyard, and entrance is punctuated by the stair, which leads through another gateway to the rooms where both the architectural sequence and the design studio are completed in the review rooms. Connected to this sequence are the gallery and exhibition rooms which open to the courtyard and entrance, forming one large group of rooms at the entry and across the campus.

The studios, on two levels, are large open rooms oriented to take advantage of the even, indirect light. Adjacent to them are the spaces for the studio, the library model shop, the computer room, and the photography studio. The library stacks and work areas culminate in a large book-lined reading room, which looks back at the entry and across the campus.

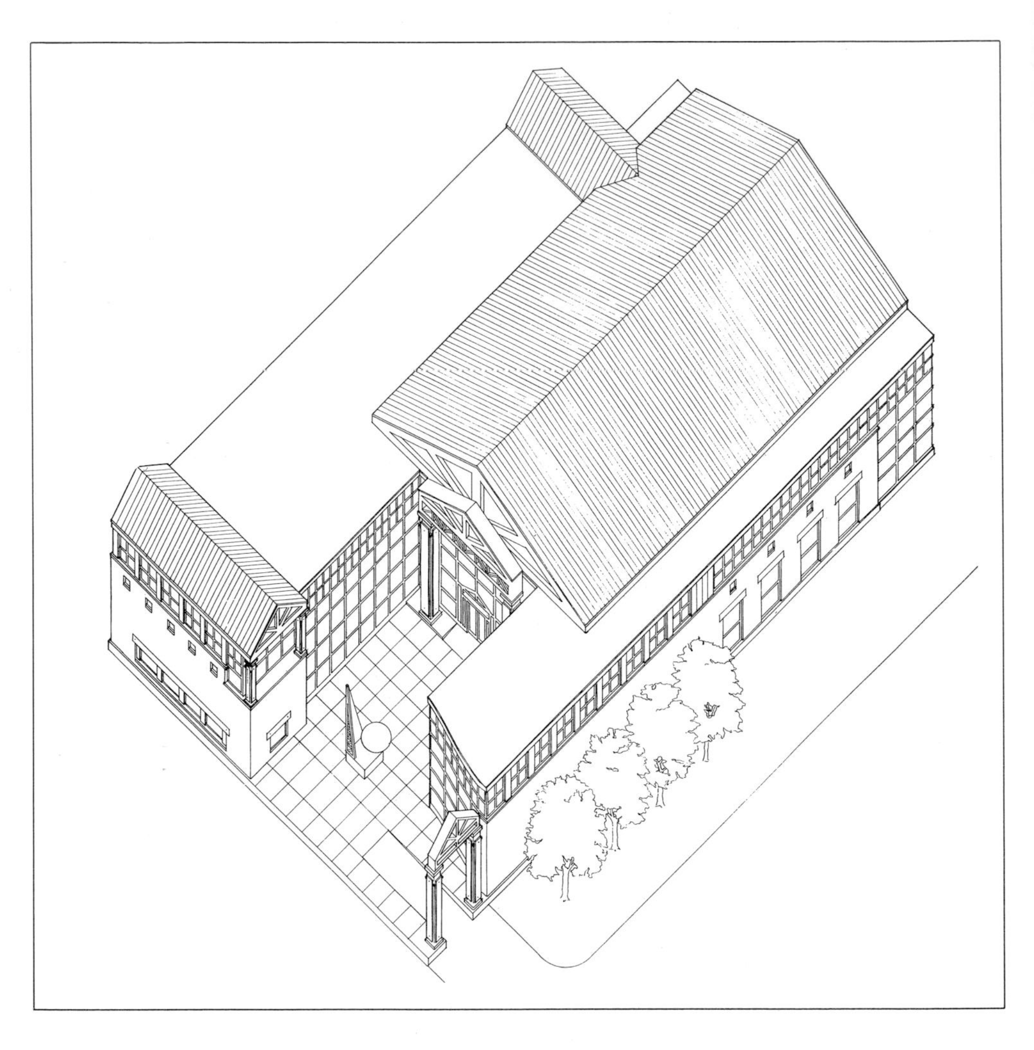

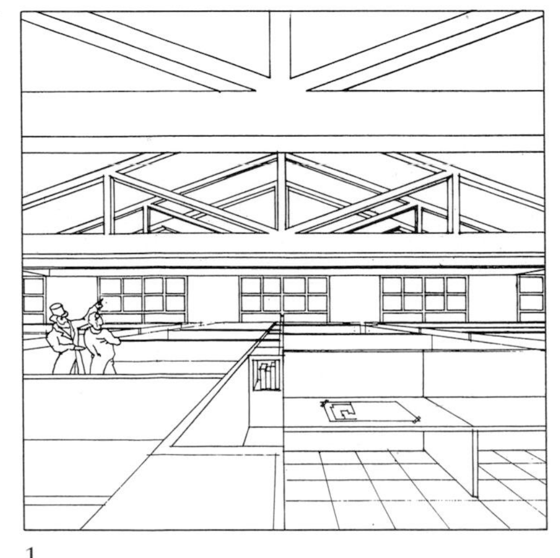

1

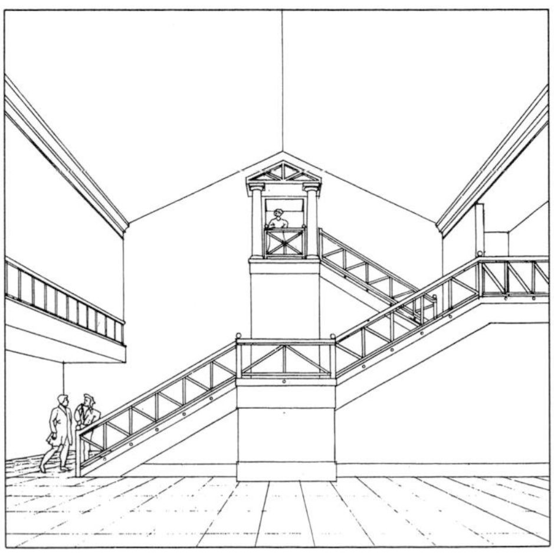

2

1.Studio space 2.Stair hall 3.North elevation 4.South elevation 5.East elevation 6.West elevation 7.Ground floor plan 8.Second floor plan 9.Third floor plan

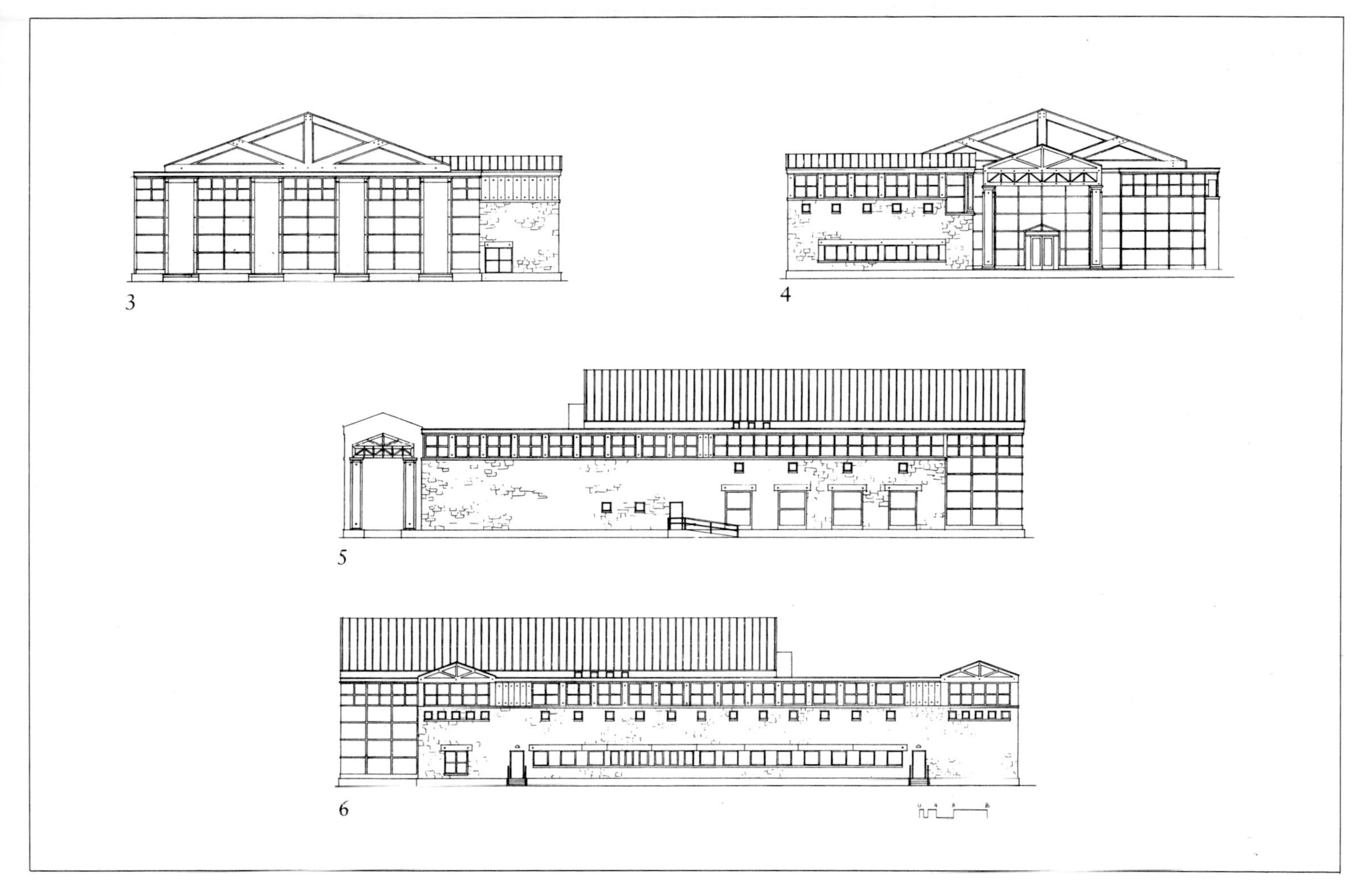

3

4

5

6

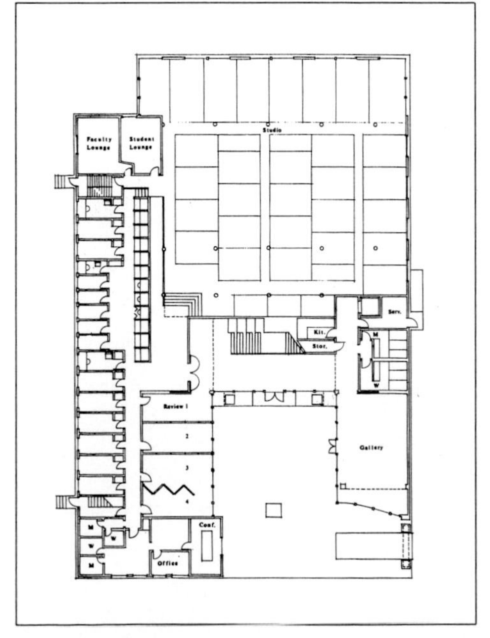

7

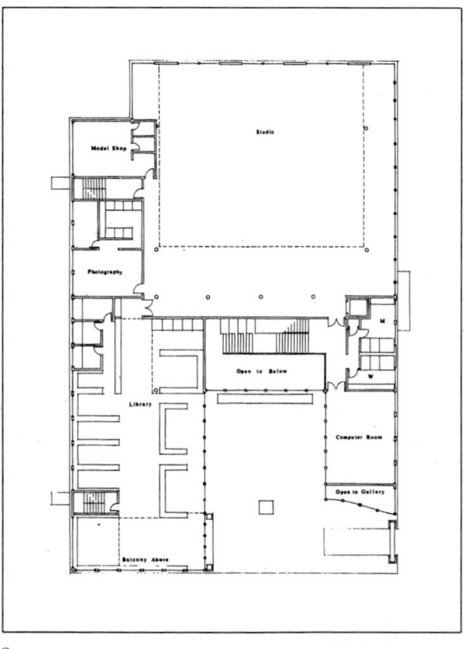

8

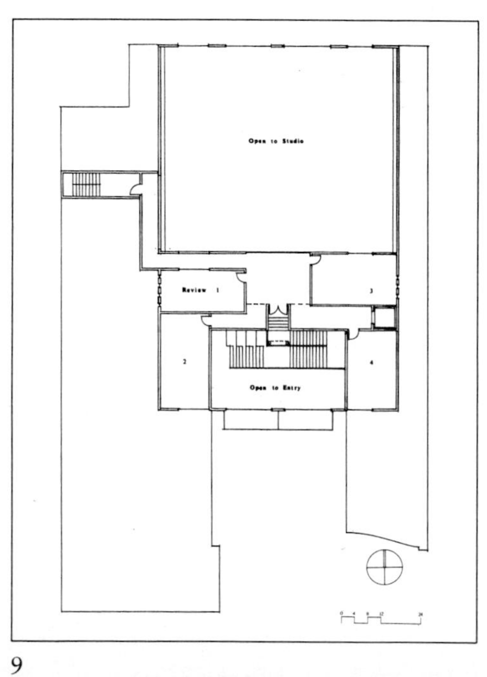

9

Residence at the Shores
Vero Beach, Florida
1984

This house at the Shores is a homage to Addison Mizner, Joseph Urban, and scores of others who evolved a regional vernacular—the Mediterranean Style—during the Florida land boom of the 1920s. Combining picturesque massing, triple-stuccoed surfaces, tiled roofs, and a sparing use of Classical detail, the Mediterranean Style conjures up images of the state's Spanish Colonial origins.

In front of the house, a curved wall hugs the shape of the roadway and screens both the service yard and a formal entrance court. Only the baroque, gabled profile of the garage rises above the wall to suggest a gatehouse. Beyond the forecourt, the house enjoys complete privacy. Its arms open outward to fill the site and embrace the view of a man-made lake. The study, family room, and double-height living room are virtually separate buildings; the aggregate massing, anchored by the stair tower, suggests a house that has been added to over time.

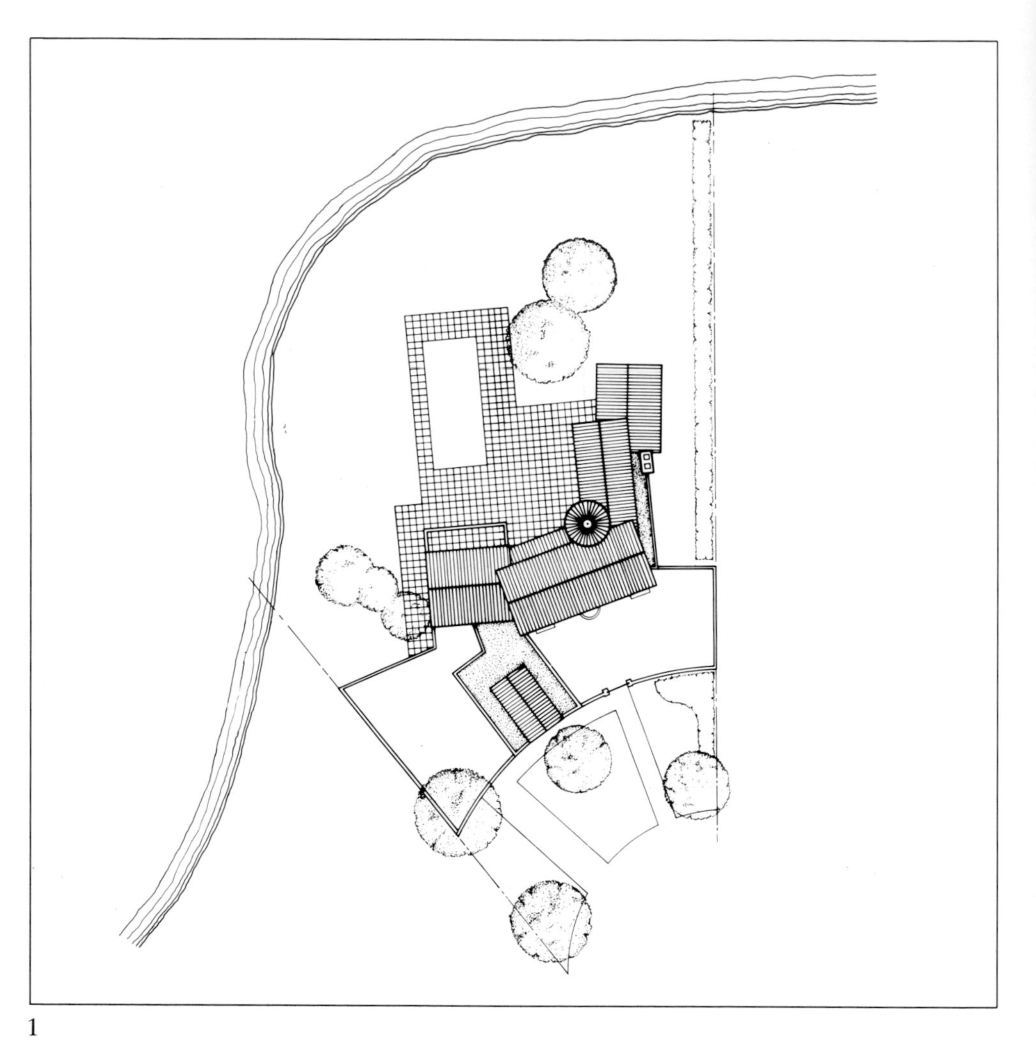

1

2

1.Site plan 2.Aerial view of model from the north 3.Entry court elevation 4.North elevation 5.South elevation 6.Aerial view of model from the south 7.Second floor plan 8.Ground floor plan

3

4

5

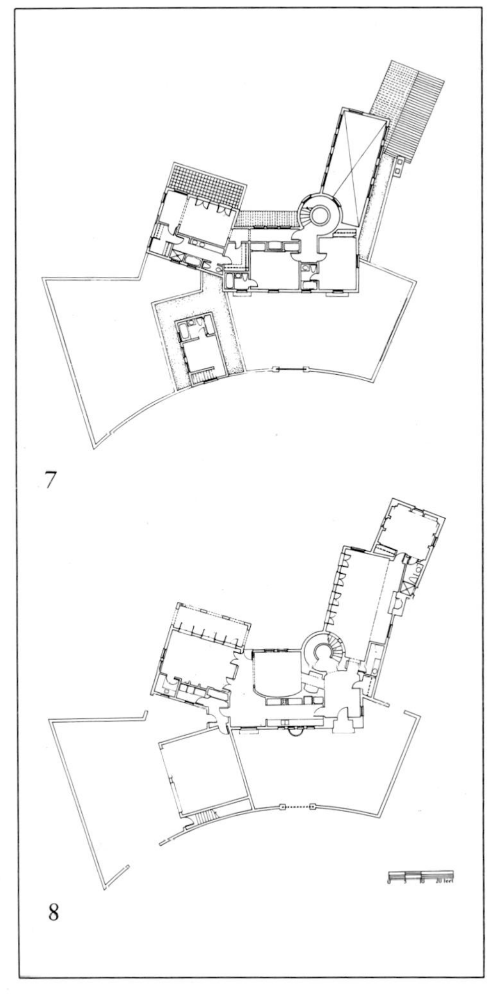

7

8

6

Municipal Center
Phoenix, Arizona
1985

Phoenix sits at a remarkable conjunction of powerful phenomena: not only is it the place where the desert landscape and the modern city meet, but where the ancient cultures of the American continent confront and meld into those of Europe. From these powerful geographical and cultural intersections, a style for Phoenix has fitfully evolved, characterized by the warm tones and muted hues of the desert, punctuated with the sparkle of copper, silver, and tiny bits of brilliant color, strong masses and solid walls, broad overhanging roofs and deeply recessed openings. Recently, the city's architecture has sacrificed the sense of place to an impersonal aesthetic of technology and abstraction. This proposal for the expansion of the city's governmental core seeks to recapture essential features of urban and natural Phoenix, and form an amalgam that reflects the diversity of the city's heritage, wedding native forms of Kiva, Pueblo, and Hogan with the urban forms that Western cultures have developed to foster pedestrian activity and human interaction. The forms of the first Americans teach us to build with the landscape rather than merely upon it; the forms of transplanted Europeans teach us to articulate the mass into the streets and spaces that describe a complex city.

1.Council chamber building 2.Aerial view of model from the northwest 3.Site plan

1

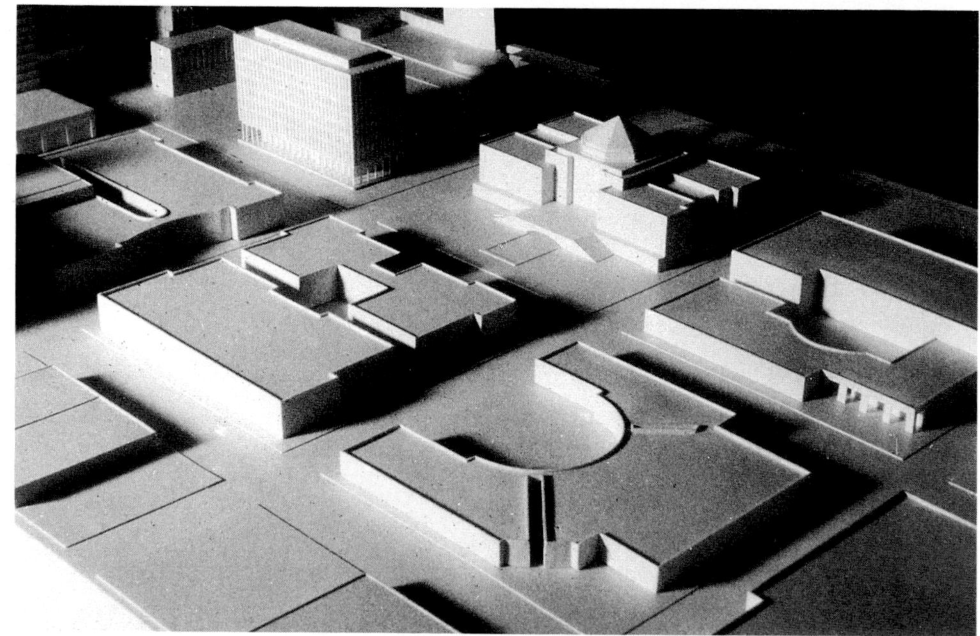

2

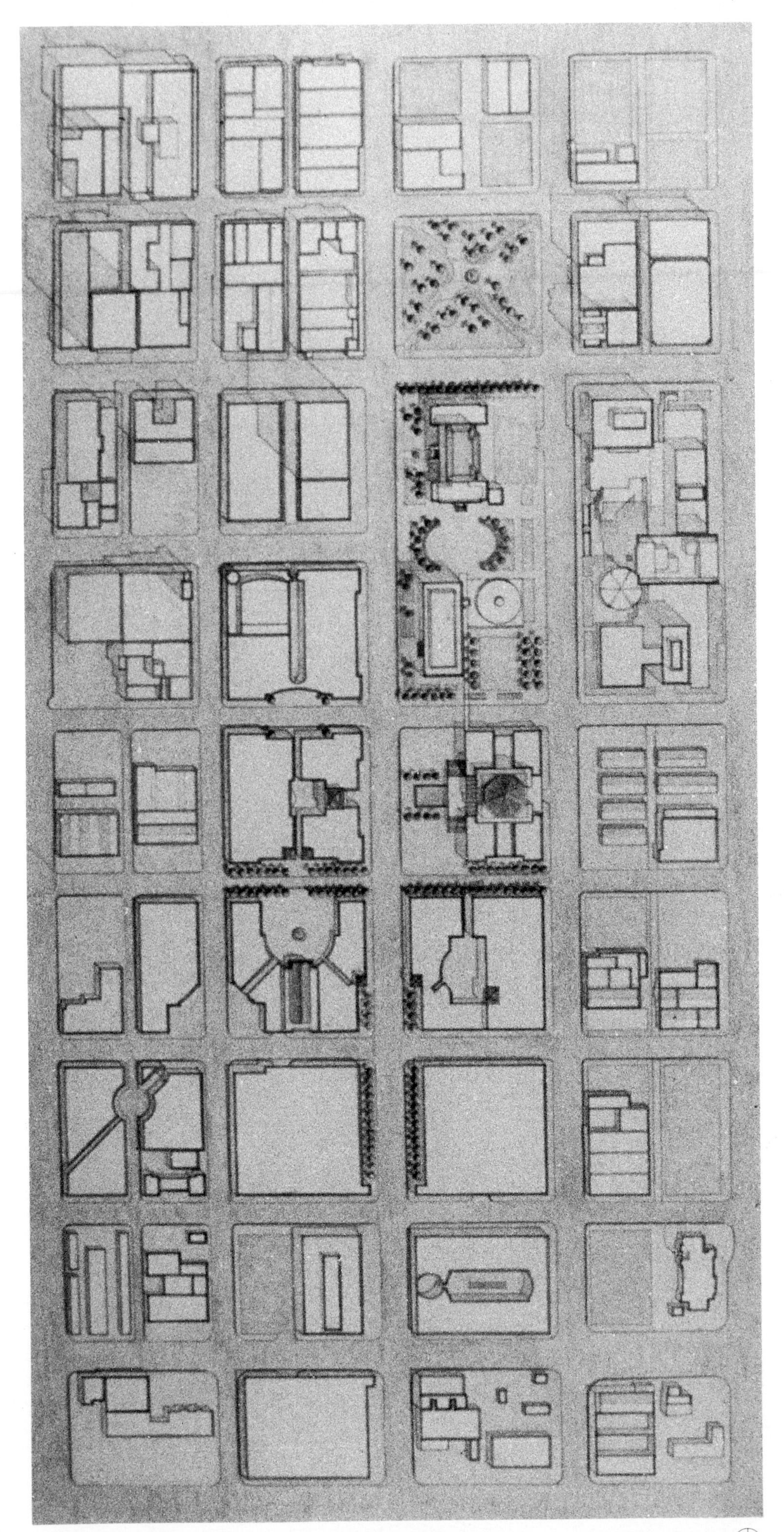

3

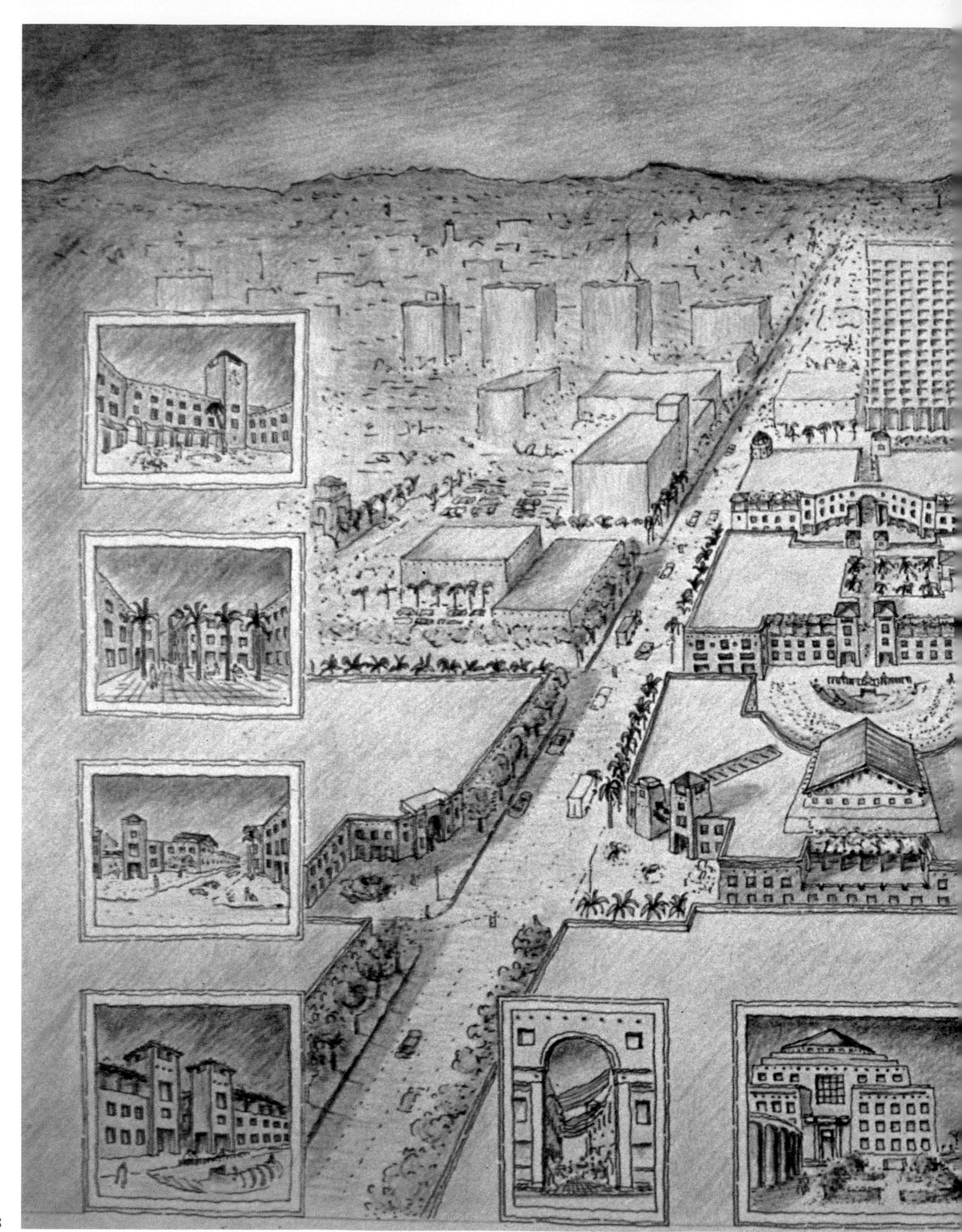

Aerial perspective of site

Residence

Marblehead, Massachusetts
1984–

Set on a steeply pitched site with northerly views towards the water, this house continues the architectural traditions refined in the stone and timber cottages that dotted Boston's North Shore as well as the rest of coastal New England at the turn of the century. As the land falls away, the house's rubble stone foundation emerges, a high base anchoring the more finely detailed and picturesquely massed shingled superstructure. Responsive as it is to the exigencies of interior planning, the massing of the house—replete with projecting bays and subsumed porches—is rendered formally sensible by a complex network of hipped roofs rising hierarchically to a unifying ridge line.

An "L"-shaped plan enhances the house's apparent compactness by lessening its perceived mass at the view side; at the front, this configuration defines an entry precinct separated by high garden walls from a service court. Within, planning centers about the interwoven planes and volumes of the cruciform living room, double-height entry hall and turreted stair to foster a relaxed architecture of the interior consonant with the exterior's relative informality.

1.Northeast elevation 2.Southeast elevation 3.Northwest elevation 4.Southwest elevation 5.Transverse section 6.Longitudinal section 7.Second floor plan 8.Ground floor plan 9.Basement floor plan 10.Site plan 11.Aerial view of model from the west 12.Aerial view of model from the northeast

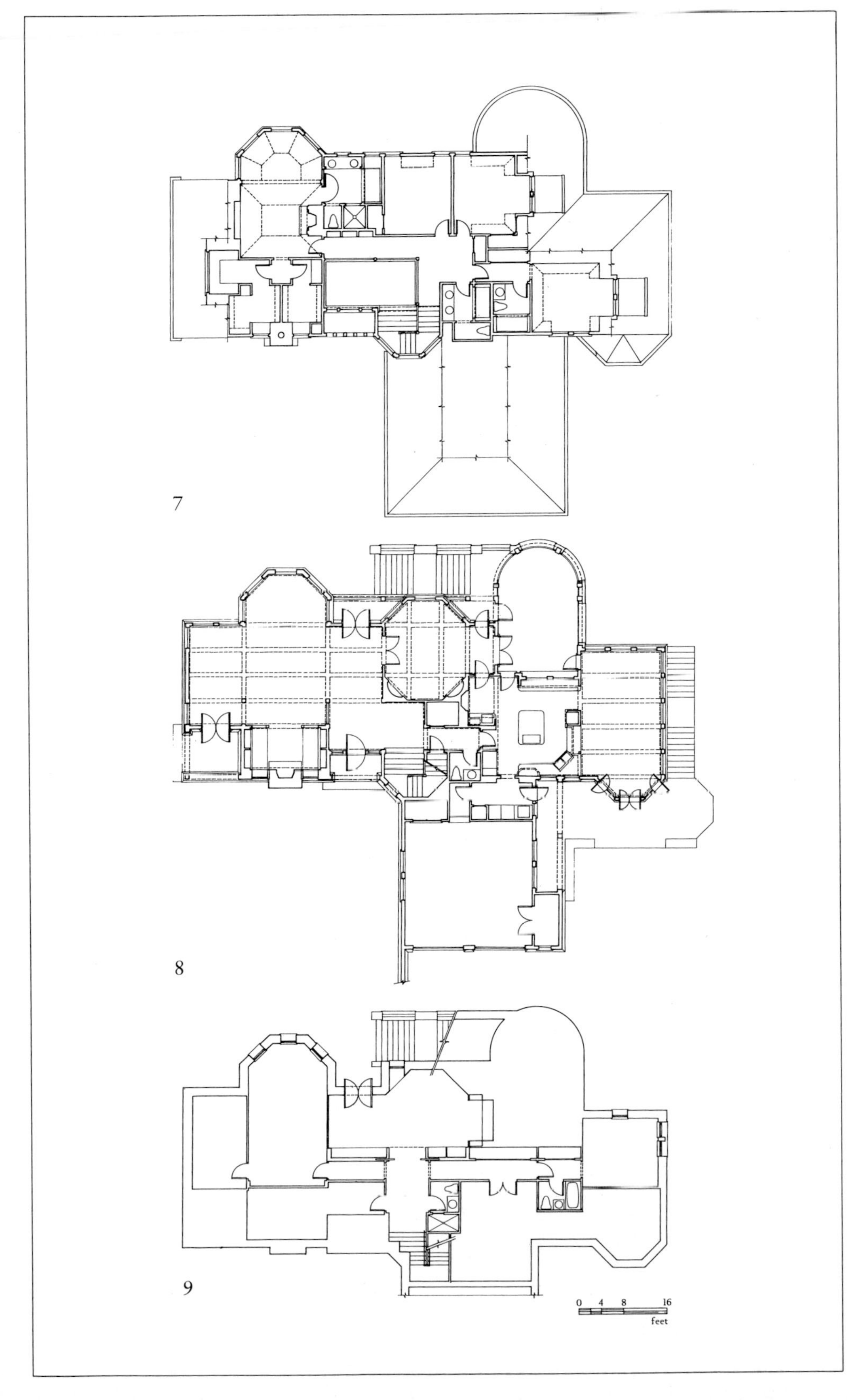

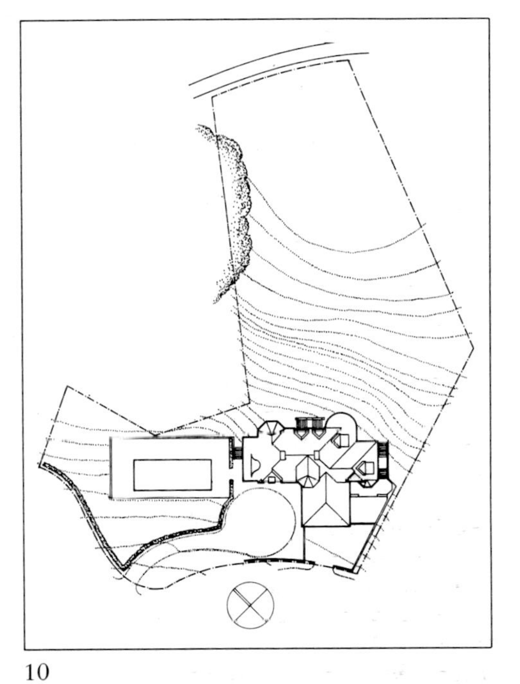

10

11

12

Temporary Clubhouse at Swan Valley

Breckenridge, Colorado
1985

A tandem structure comprising a municipal golf club and development sales office announces the first phase of a projected 1,500-unit golf-oriented resort. The site is the wooded valley of the Swan River near the mining settlement and ski resort of Breckenridge, Colorado. A temporary object, the twin prefabricated trailer structures take the form of a freestanding temple front with pediment broken to suggest a portal which frames a view of the valley with the highest peak of the snow-covered Ten Mile Range beyond. In the foreground, accommodating the activities of golfers arriving and departing from the course is a wide platform joining the two prefabricated structures housing sales office and pro shop, respectively. The architecture of the whole takes its cue from both the Arcadian structures of classical antiquity and the stylistically varied painted-wood buildings of the 1800s found in nearby Breckenridge. Rather than camouflaging man's presence in such a wild and spectacular environment, the clubhouse proposes a dialogue between the natural and the man-made.

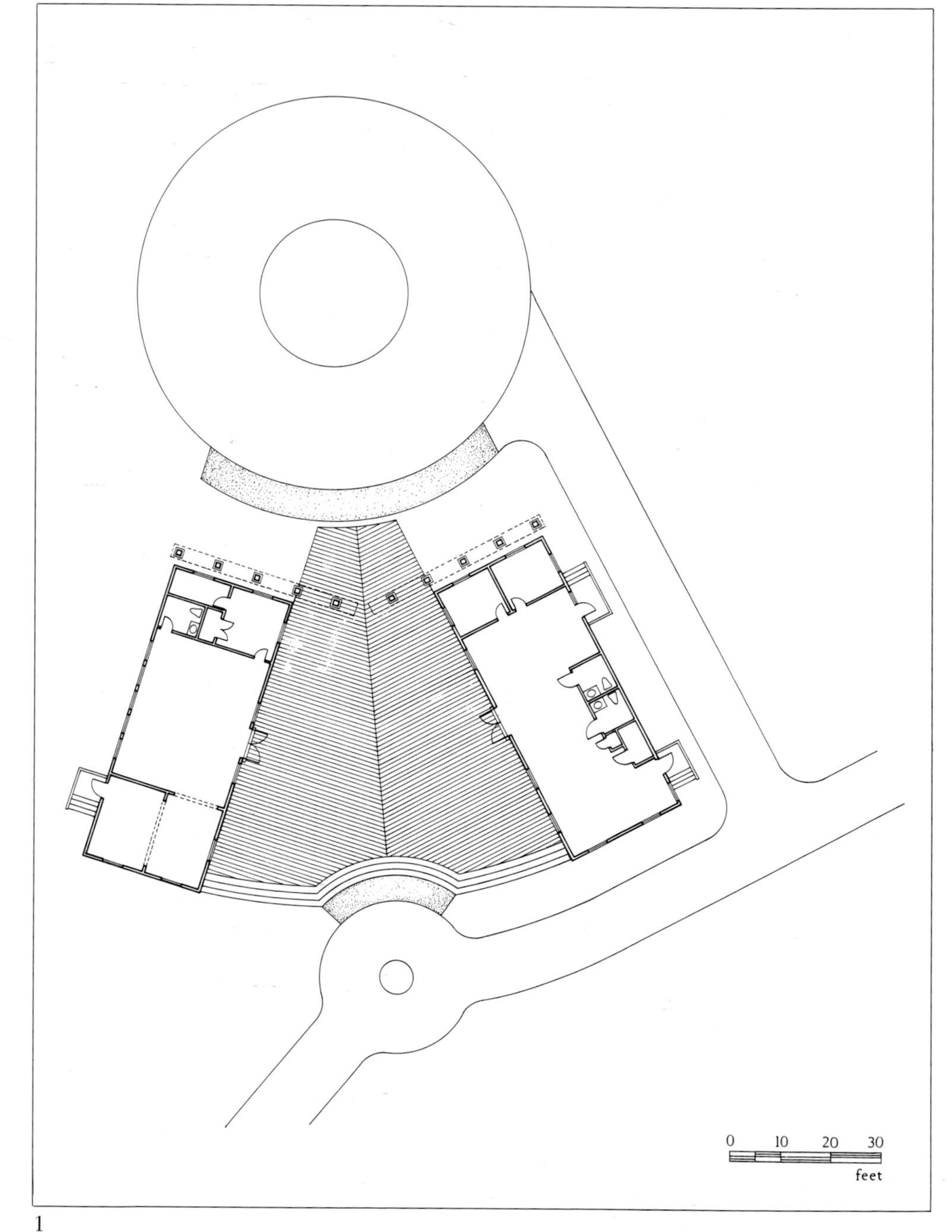

1

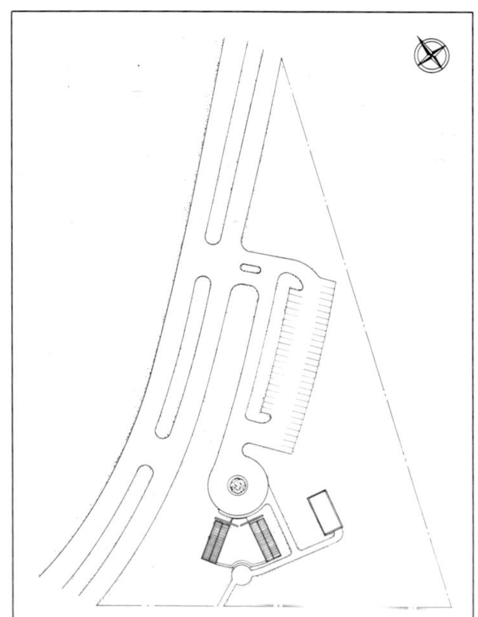

2

3

4

1.Floor plan 2.Site plan 3.View from the southwest 4.Detail of entry 5.View from the northeast 6.View from across the green

5

6

Residence
Pottersville, New Jersey
1985–

Sited on a rolling meadow in rural New Jersey, the house nestles into the brow of a low ridge. The southern side of the house has a long, low silhouette which straddles the high side of the ridge, leaving the rubble-clad basement story exposed to the north. The verticality on the north is accentuated by the juxtaposed gambrel roof and octagonal stair tower which echo the neighboring barns and silos. The house is entered from the west on the short elevation, so that rooms are open to the best views offered to the north and south.

From the entrance, a view through all of the major rooms opens up. The front hall doubles as a stage used for musical concerts sponsored by the family. The audience for such events will sit in the large living room. The east end of the house is reserved for informal family life. Small family meals and television viewing take place in the family room which opens, on one end, to the plant-filled solarium that doubles as an office. At the extreme eastern end of the house is the screened porch. Its form restates the low-pitched, temple-like entry portico. The stair tower, open through all three stories of the house, unites the basement, used for recreation and guests, with the first and second stories.

1

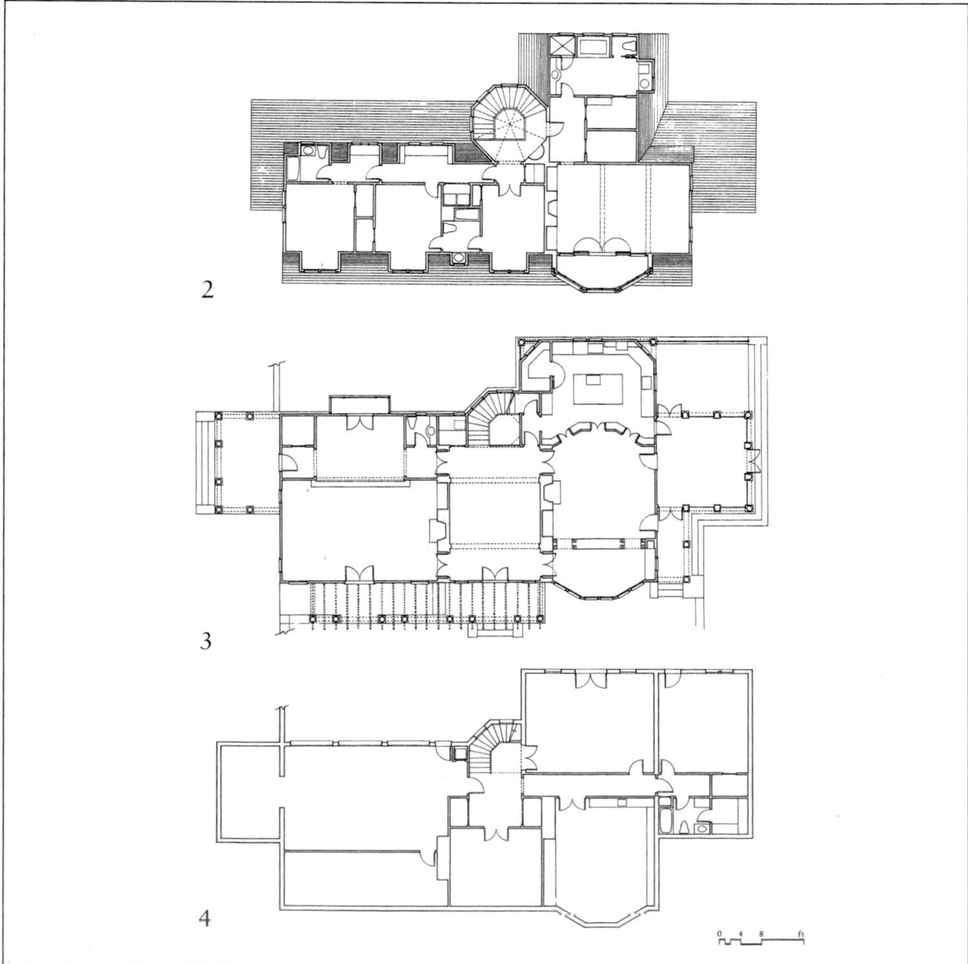

1.Perspective views of house 2.Second floor plan 3.Ground floor plan 4.Basement floor plan 5.Site plan

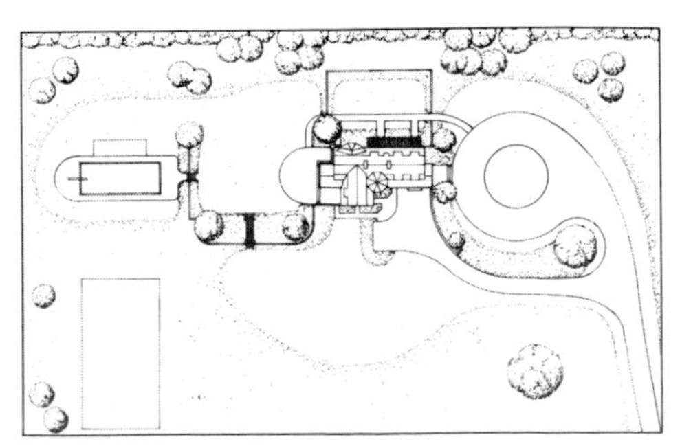

5

Park Avenue Duplex Apartment
New York, New York
1981

Located in a typical Park Avenue building, this renovation establishes a central axis that ties the living room at one end with the dining room at the other. In what was once a meanly detailed, ill-proportioned foyer, a new and grander treatment of the stair has been introduced, done in marble, as are the floors, and a series of pilasters that reveal themselves as book niches. A language of classical pilasters, a base, and a cornice unite this suite of formal rooms.

1. Library plan and elevations 2. Upper level plan 3. Lower level plan

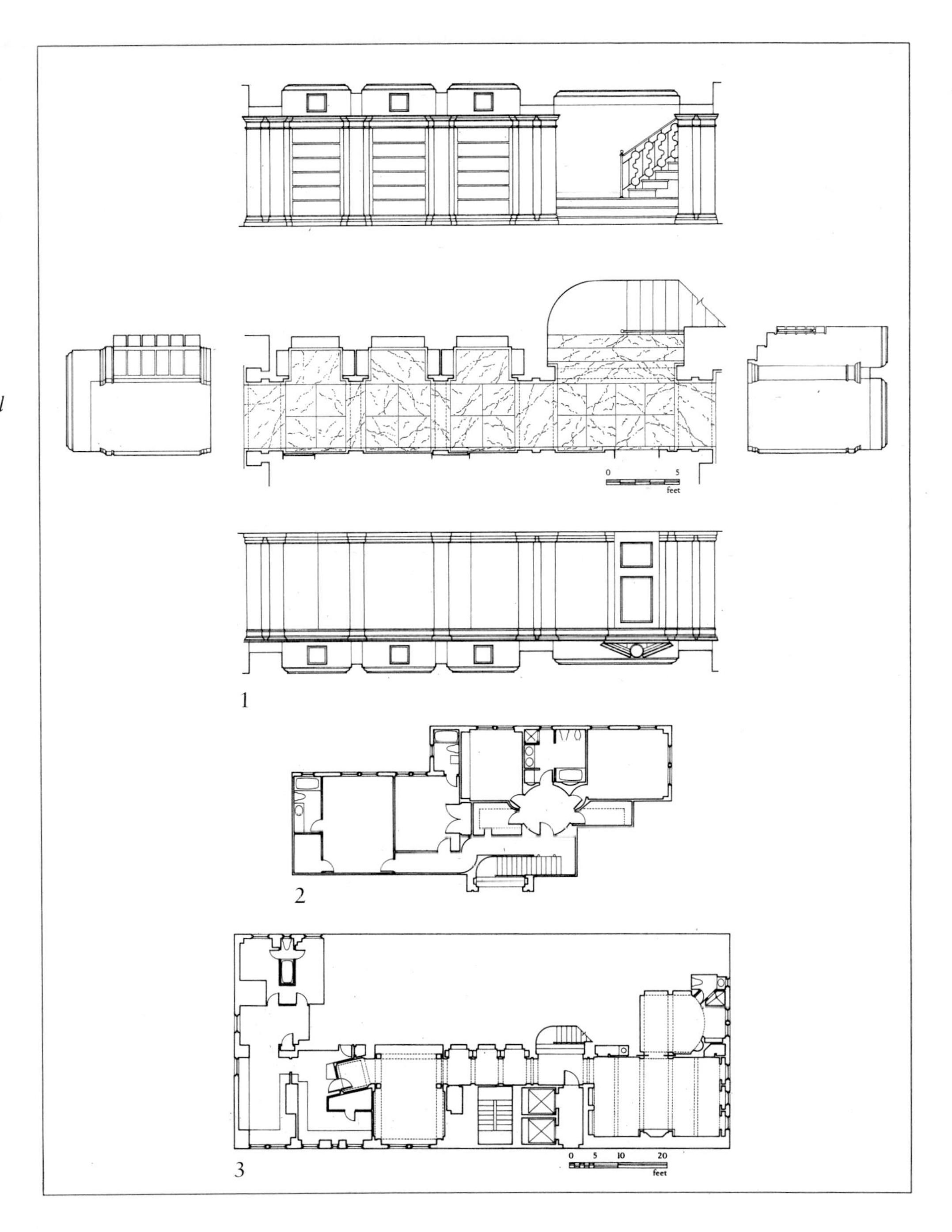

Rye Brook Park

Westchester County, New York
1985–

Rye Brook Park's two 100,000-square-foot buildings curve gently about an oval motor court to form an office campus at the heart of a thirty acre suburban site. The site is wooded along the perimeter, giving way to an open meadow at its bowl-shaped center where the three-and-one-half story buildings nestle in the natural slope of the land. Approach to the buildings is past a lake along a tree-lined allee, with parking for 660 cars in concentric terraced ovals around the buildings. The central entrance court serves as a drop-off for both buildings as it lends an urbane quality to the grouping and provides a counterpoint to the natural site. The courtyard and building entrances are enhanced through the use of classical architectural features such as a rusticated base, loggias, and a bold cornice. The palette of materials include warm earthtone bricks, buff-colored stone, and light bronze tinted glass.

The four corners of each building are articulated as pavilions rising to pitched metal roofs. Smaller pavilions modulate the curved outer wall and are suggestive of garden architecture. In essence, the collegiate spirit of the design establishes an environment that celebrates the workplace.

1

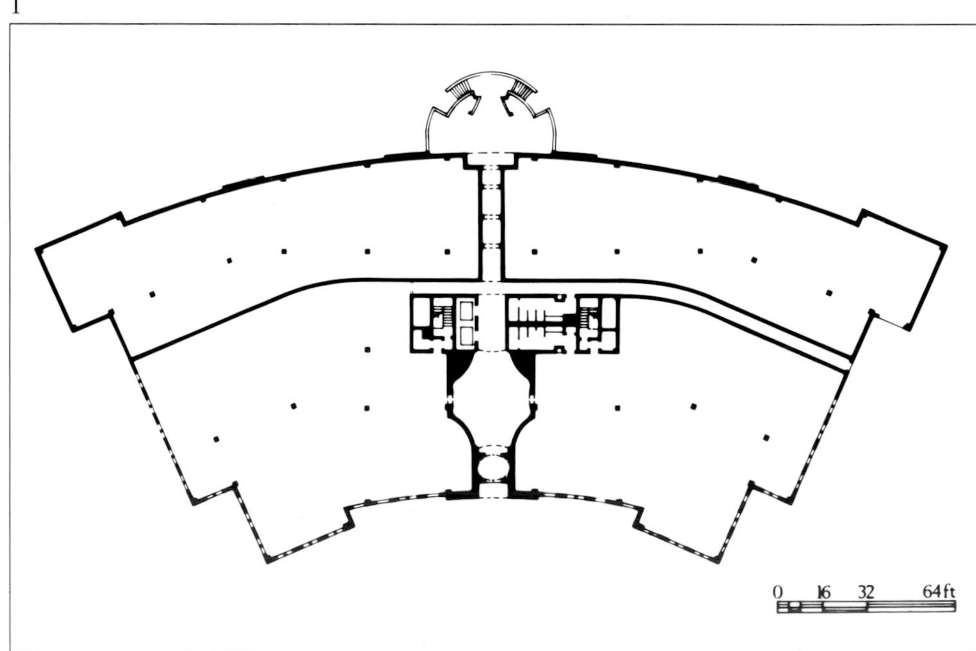

2

1.Overhead view of site model 2.Ground floor plan 3.Aerial view of model 4.Courtyard elevation 5.End elevation 6.Rear elevation

3

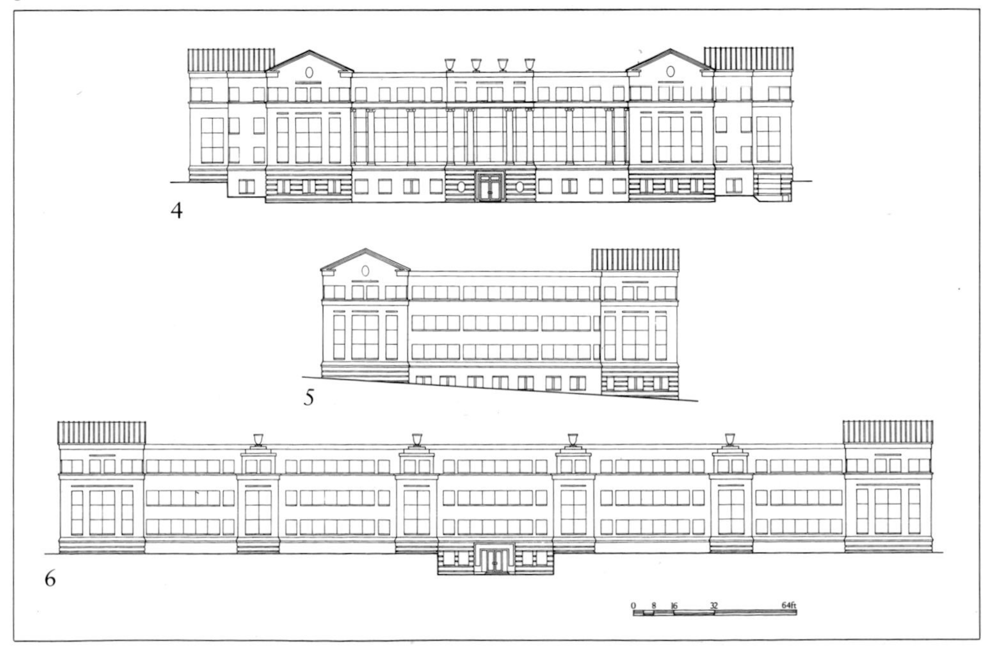

The New American Home
Dallas, Texas
1985

This project was designed for *Builder* and *Home* magazines, and for the National Council of the Housing Industry as an example of what can be built today on a typical small suburban lot. The massing strategy of the house takes its cues from the American tradition of the small classical house. The composition assembles symmetrical elements to form a picturesque effect which suggests that the house has been added onto over the years.

Situated on a long narrow corner site, the white-painted brick walls and lead-coated copper roof of the house relates to the Texas farmhouse vernacular. The house is entered from the main street on the narrow end of the lot. The entry elevation faces the most important of the two streets and is therefore the most symmetrical and formal. The center of this facade is indented to receive a compressed entry porch with a balcony above—evoking the welcoming image of the classic American front porch which for functional reasons in the automobile era has been relegated to the backyard.

To take advantage of the southern exposure, the garden elevation is perpendicular to the entry elevation. The walled rear garden is dominated by the screened-porch pavilion and the two flanking pergola-covered spaces. These elements provide the house with a zone that mediates between total interior and total exterior living while shading the dining room and family rooms from the hottest midday sun. On the north, the casual additive quality of the elevation responds to its location on a secondary street and to its use for garage and for service entries.

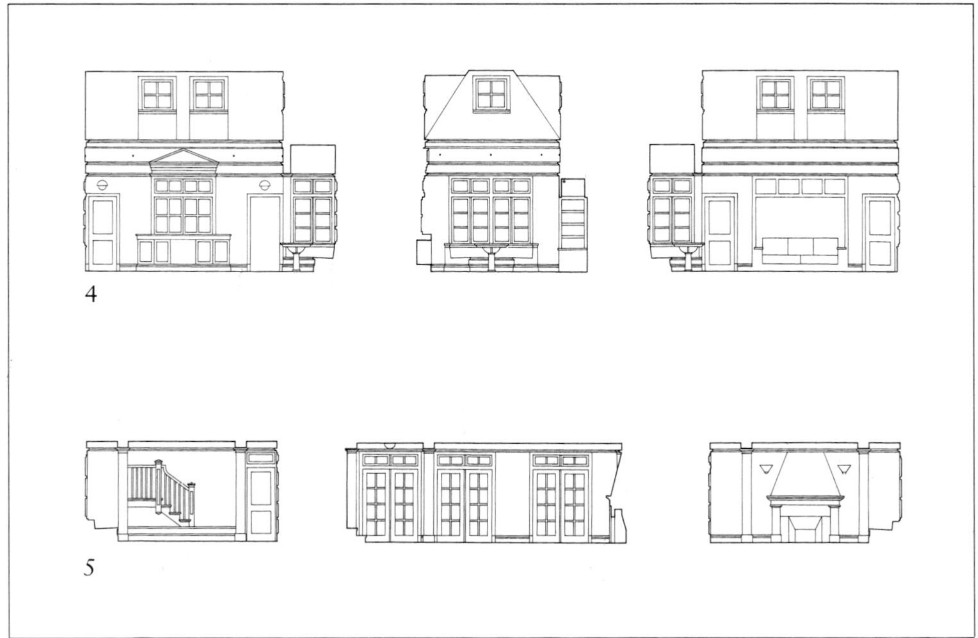

1.North elevation 2.South elevation
3.West elevation 4.Family room elevations
5.Living room elevations 6.Site plan
7.Aerial view of model from the southeast
8.Ground floor plan 9.Second floor plan

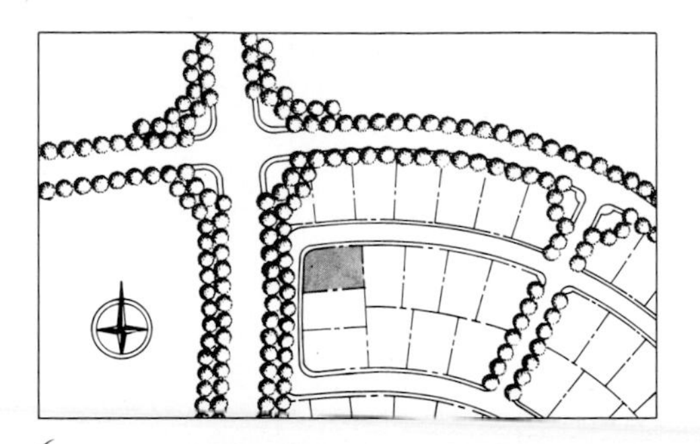

6

7

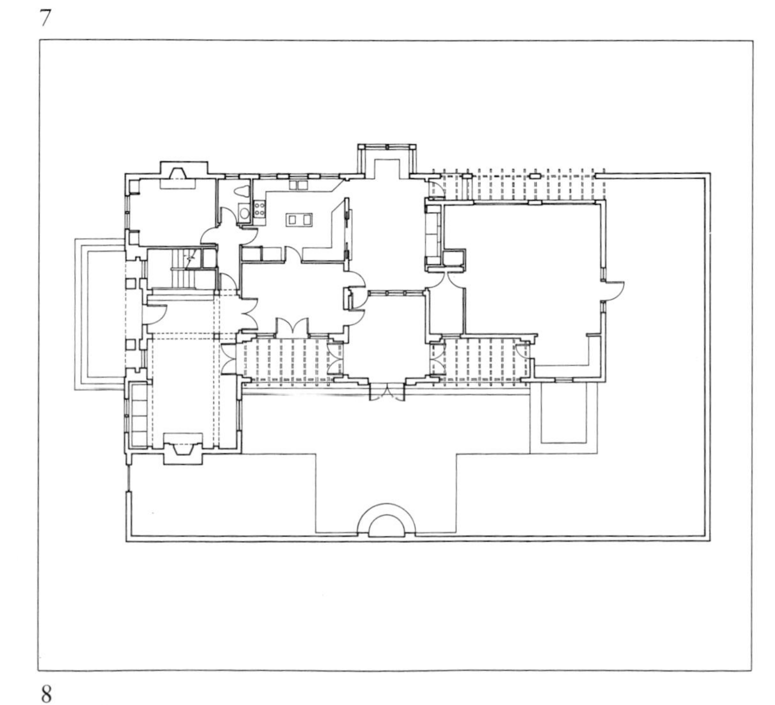

8

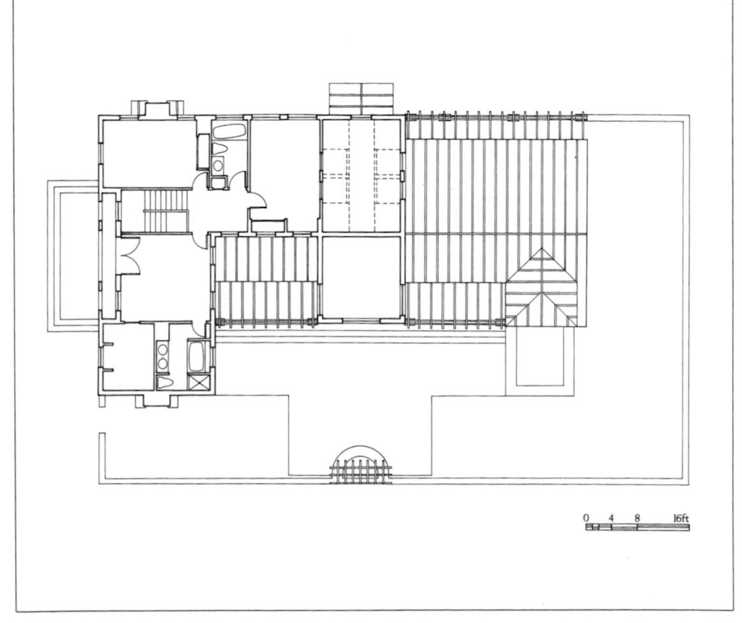

9

1.View from the southeast 2.View from the northeast 3.West facade 4.Family room 5.Screened sun room

1

2

3

4

5

Tegeler Hafen
Berlin
1985–

This urban villa is one component in the reconstruction of Tegel, a suburb of Berlin ravaged by the war and hapless post-war planning. The master plan, prepared by Moore, Ruble, Yudell in 1980, calls for the creation of three distinct areas for housing, leisure, and culture. Within the housing district, a five-story serpentine range of row houses provides the background for six freestanding urban villas. A strict set of design guidelines was established by Charles Moore and his partners and by the German building code. One of these villas is the work of Moore; the others were designed by Stanley Tigerman, Paolo Portoghesi, Antoine Grumbach, and John Hejduk.

In an effort to break with the stark impersonality of most contemporary German social housing, our solution recalls the villas of the lakeside summer community of nineteenth-century Tegel, as well as the cool Classicism of Bruno Paul. Traditional gambreled tile roofs, wrought-iron railings, and stucco walls with ceramic tile decoration are composed in symmetrical elevations. In plan, the three-story villa arranges two one-bedroom and four two-bedroom units around a shared daylit stair. All units have a double or triple exposure and all have an outdoor terrace or balcony. The unit plans maintain a balance between the desire for a light, open plan and the need for privacy. Parking and individual storage lockers are located beneath the villa.

1.North elevation 2.West elevation 3.South elevation 4.Section 5.Second floor plan 6.Roof gallery plan 7.Ground floor plan 8.Third floor plan 9.Site plan

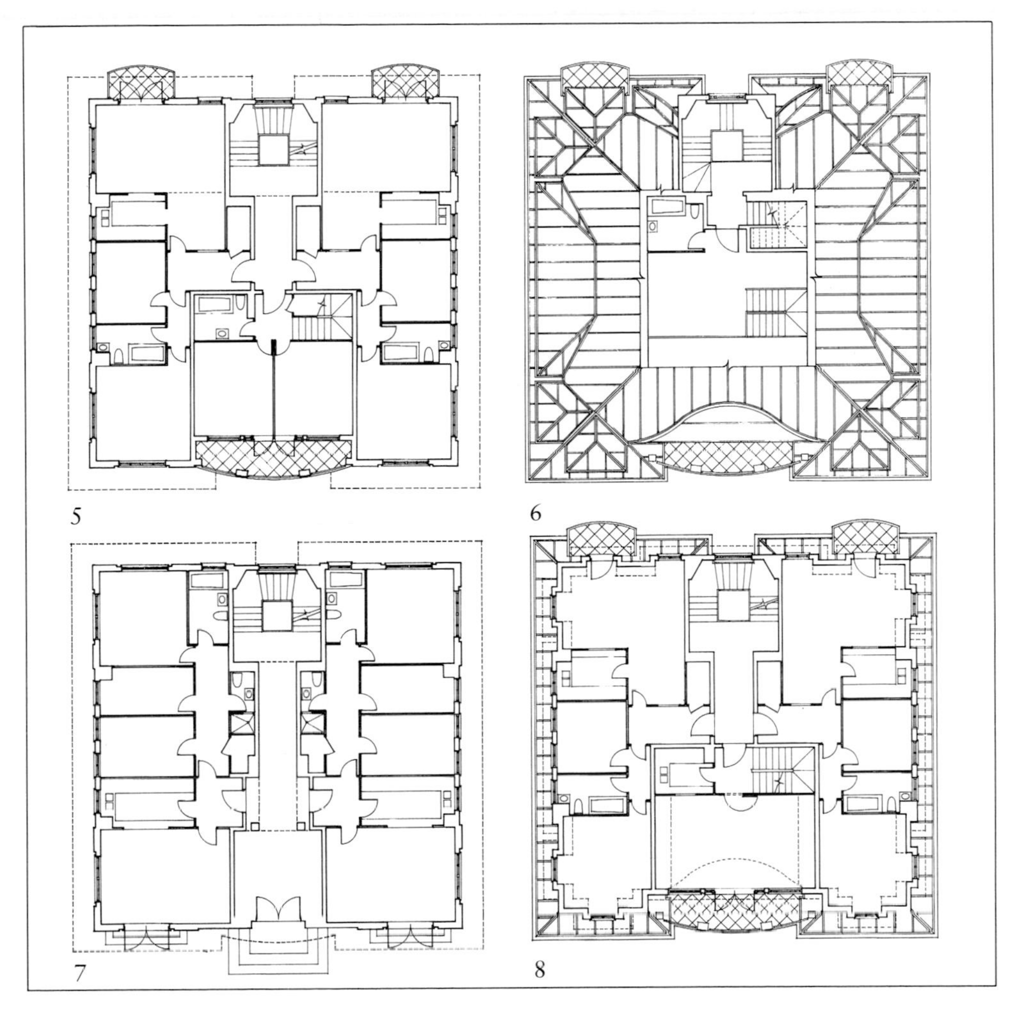

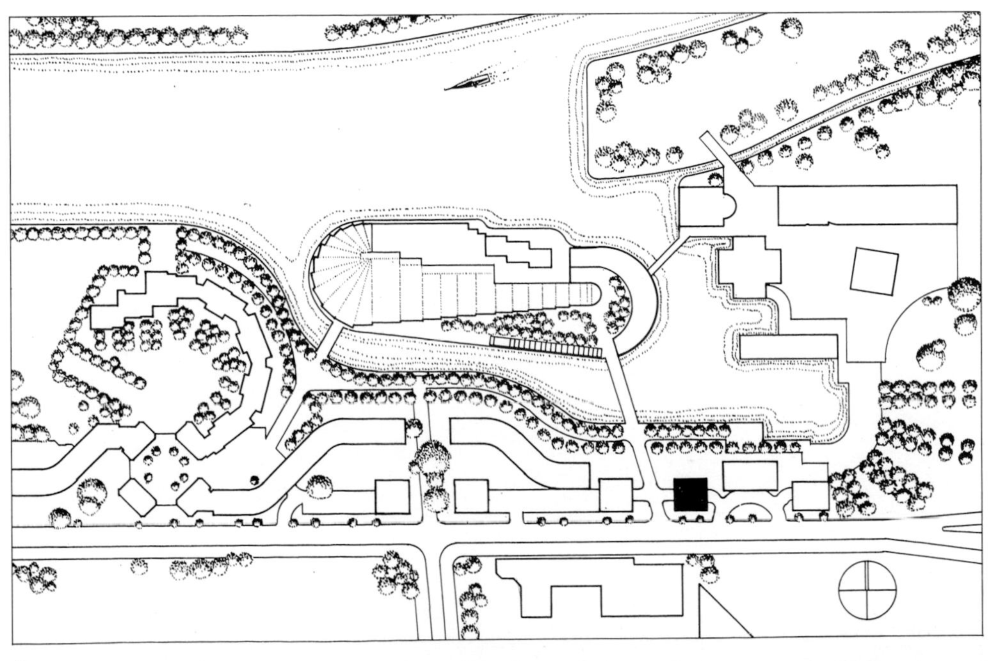

Metairie Park Country Day School

New Orleans, Louisiana

1985

This proposal for the Metairie Country Day School builds on the strengths of the existing campus. Our premise is that the original plan, with its classical references, its Jeffersonian lawn, courtyards, and covered walkways, succeeds in creating a unique sense of place; recent additions have been more haphazard. Our aim is to restore a sense of coherence by returning to the original conception of the lawn as the symbolic heart of the campus, and by sensitively echoing the vocabulary and spirit of its buildings.

The three new buildings define the now ragged eastern edge of the lawn with arcades that closely echo those already on campus. The new buildings are announced by two-story brick pavilions that provide each discipline with a focus and public identity while creating a modulated rhythm along the lawn.

1

2

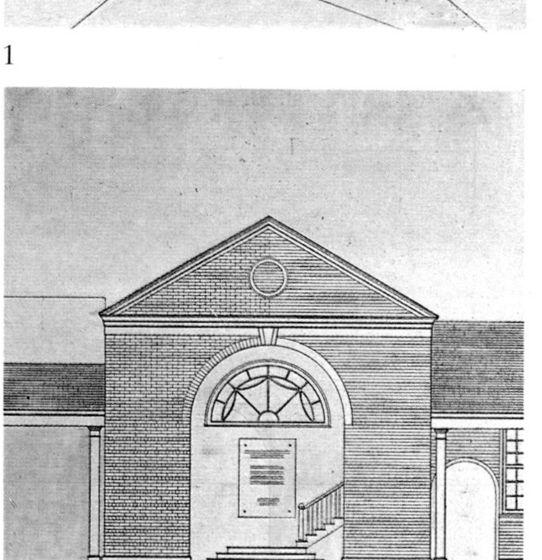

3

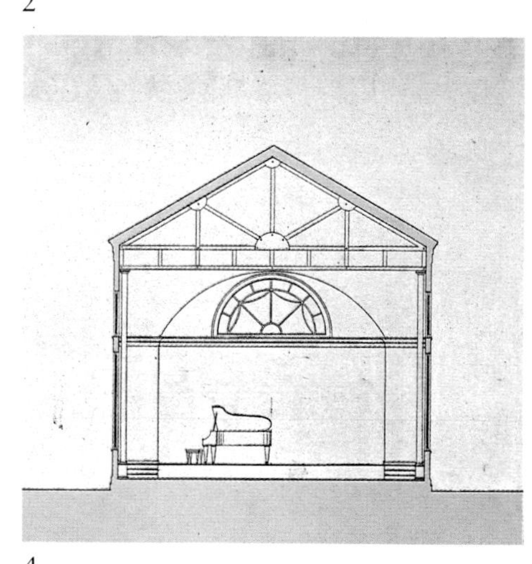

4

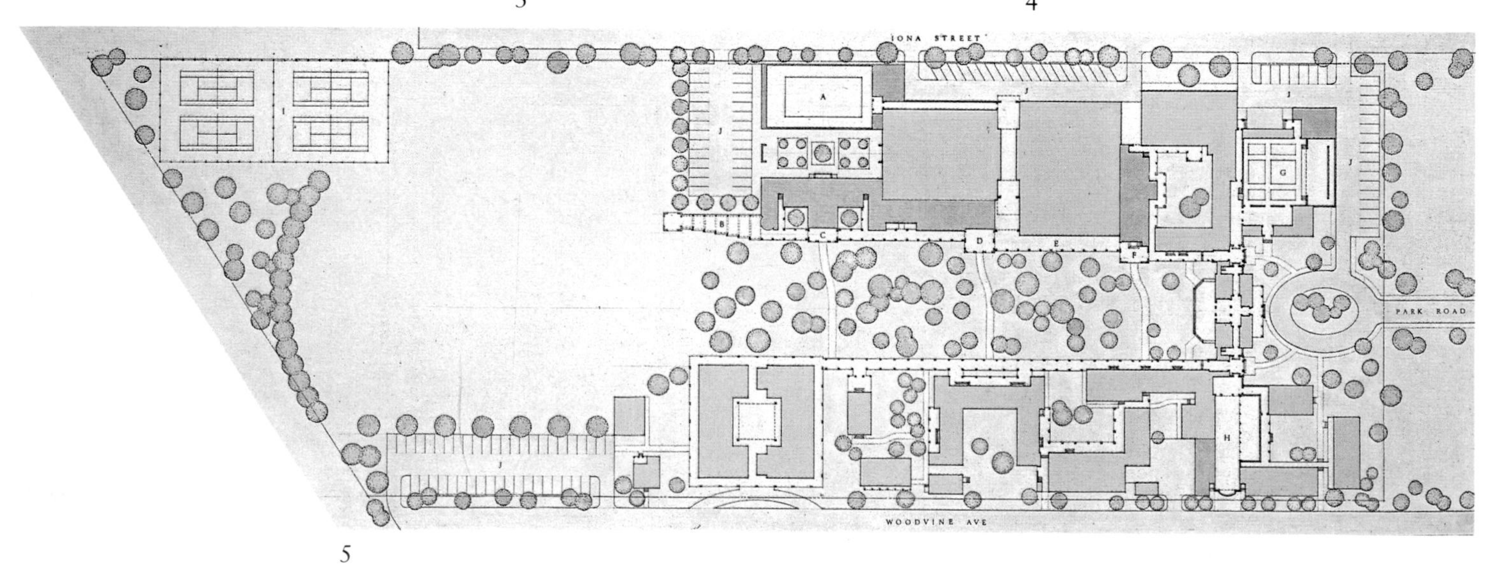

5

1. View of the Music Building 2. View of Upper School Building 3. Upper School Building, west elevation 4. Section through Recital Hall 5. Site plan 6. West elevation: A. Music B. Activities C. Classrooms 7. Building sections 8. Ground floor plan 9. Music Building, second floor plan 10. Upper School Classroom Building, second floor plan

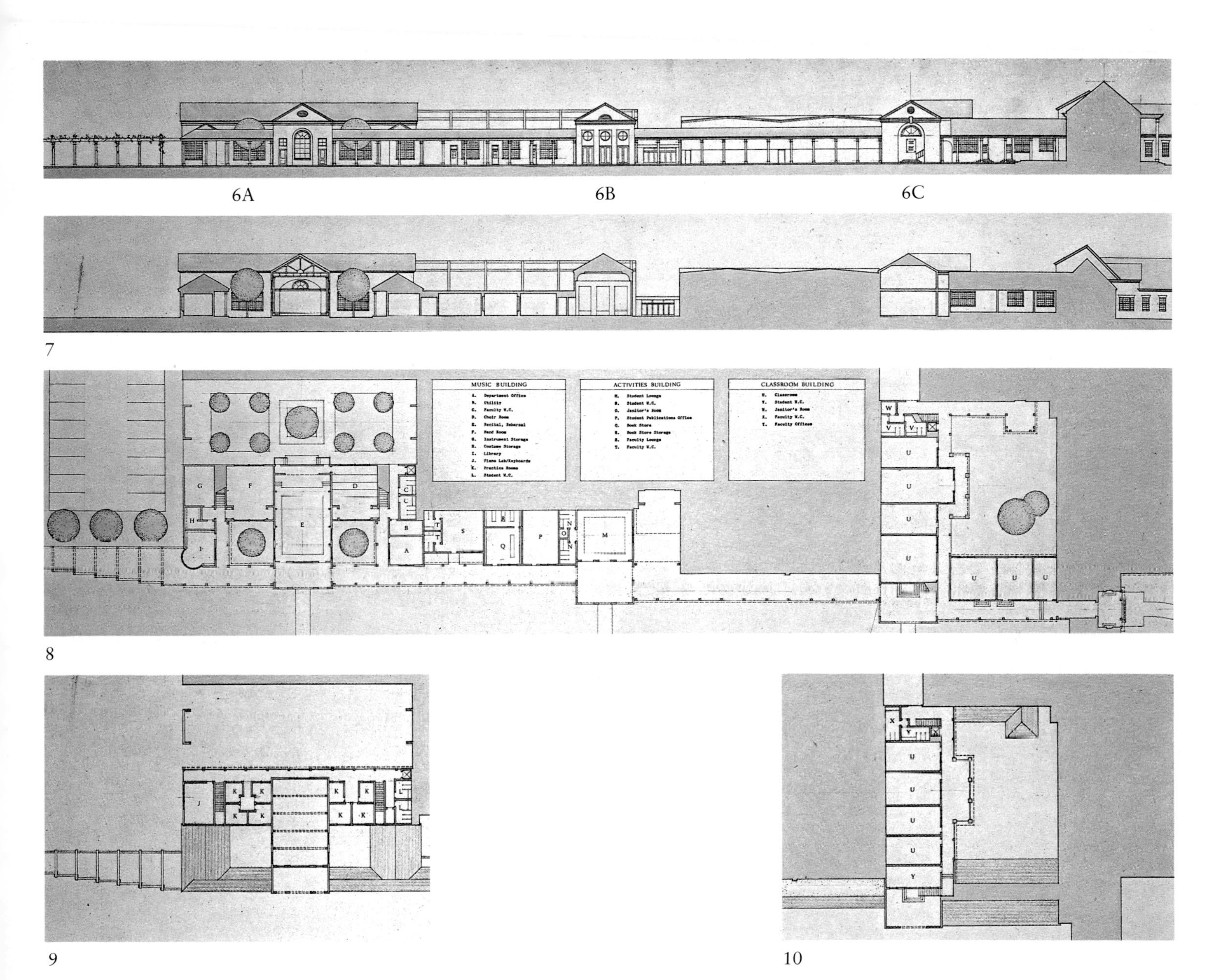

Congregation Kol Israel

Brooklyn, New York
1985–

This synagogue for a growing congregation occupies a corner site in an established residential neighborhood. The massing is arranged to present a civic scale along the major avenue and more intimate entrance front on the residential cross street. The brick, stone, and tile exterior adapts the Mediterranean vocabulary of the surrounding houses to the public scale and use of the new structure.

To accommodate an otherwise oversized congregation and conform to stringent zoning setback and height limitations, the entire site has been excavated to allow for a large sanctuary level below grade. The building is entered at a half level; congregants either walk up a level to the balconies or walk down to the main sanctuary level.

1.South elevation 2.Transverse section 3.Longitudinal section 4.East elevation 5.Mezzanine level plan 6.Entry level plan 7.Congregation level plan 8.Site plan

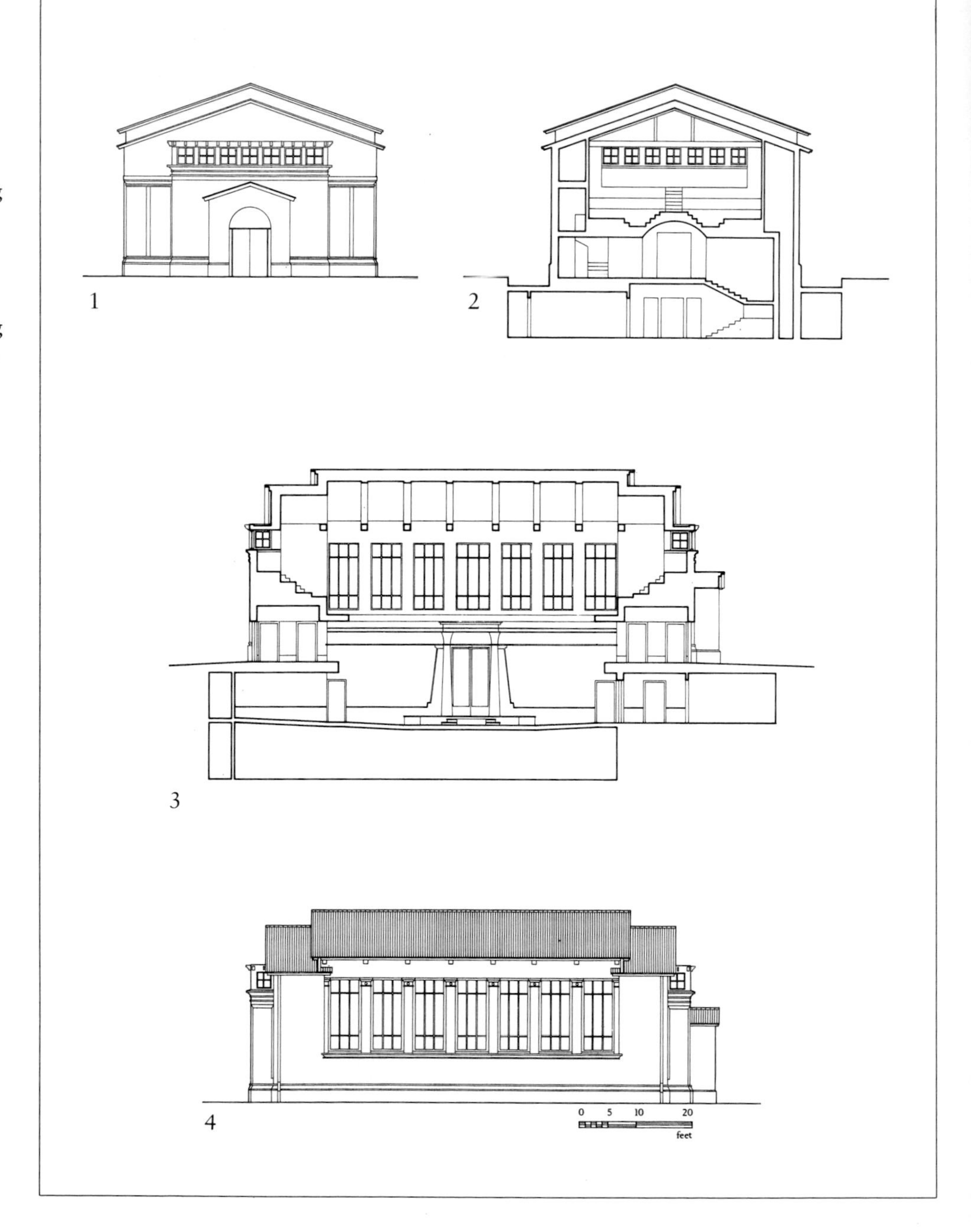

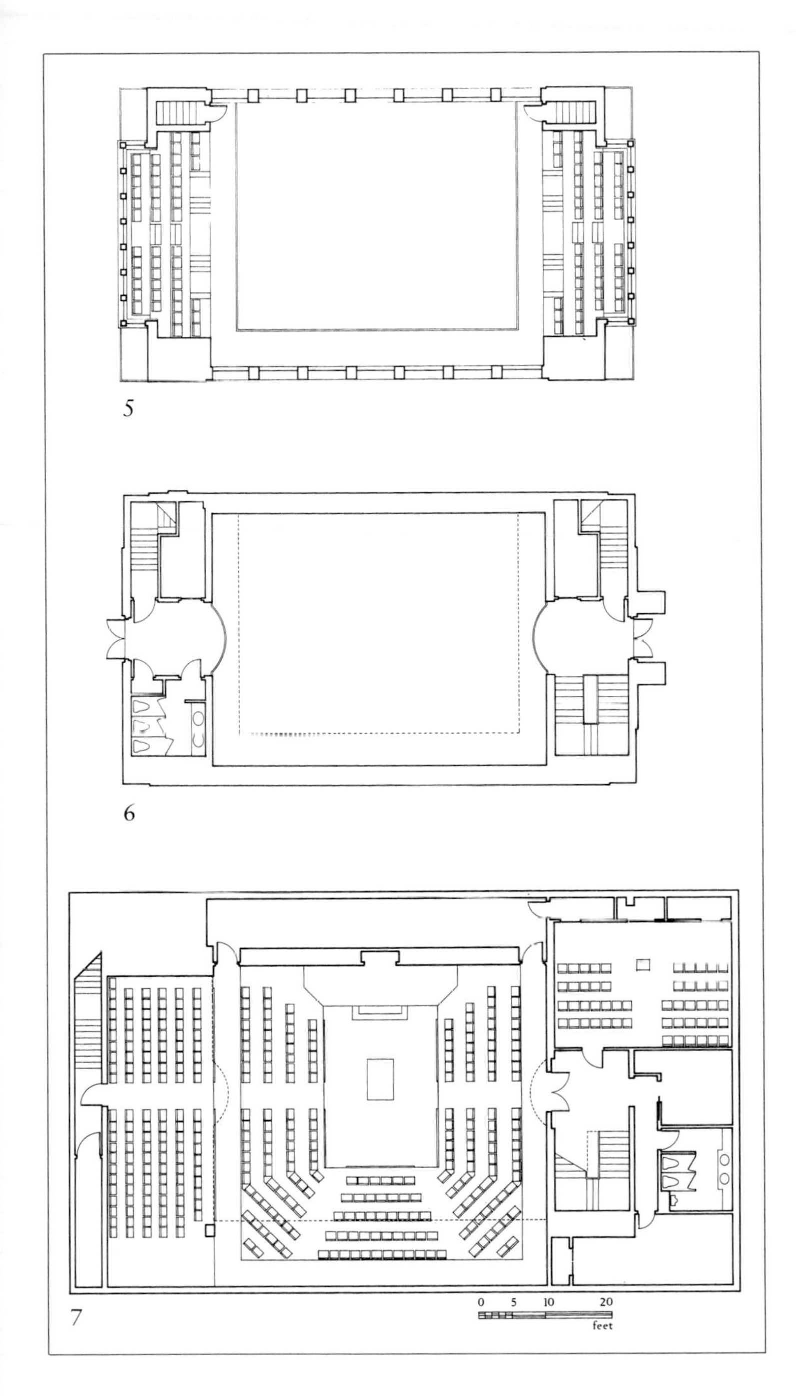

5

6

7

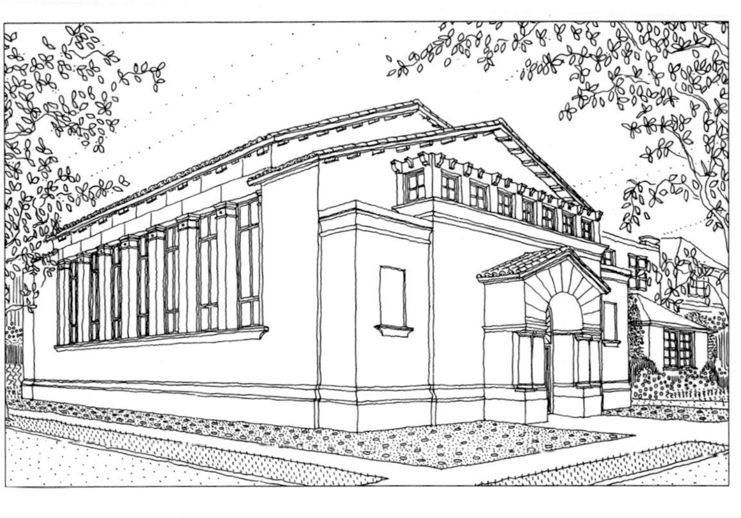

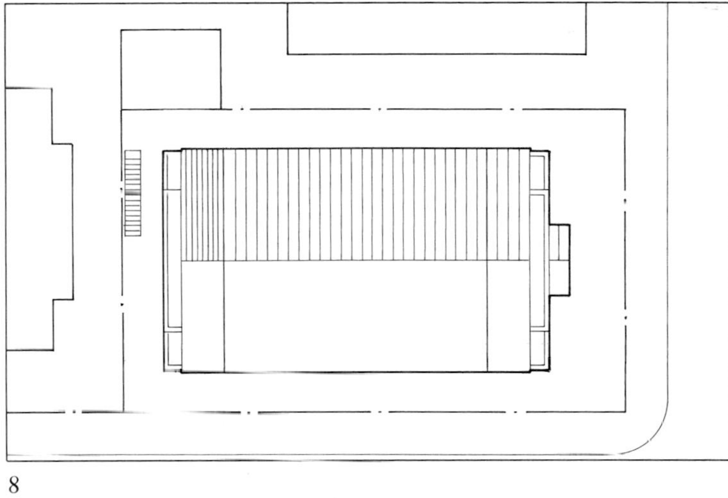

8

The Shops at Primrose Brook

Bernardsville, New Jersey
1985–

The Shops at Primrose Brook sit alongside both the highroad, traveled since Colonial times between Morristown and Bernardsville, and the recently constructed Interstate highway. The design for the center grows out of an American tradition which adapts historical building types to contemporary functions. Here five separate buildings sit in a clearing surrounded by trees. In place of typical shopping centers that produce a single building or enclosure, this spatial arrangement, inspired by Ancient Greek planning principles, combines building and landscape to form a shopping precinct amidst the helter skelter of roadside development.

Each shop building adopts either a simple temple- or a stoa-like form, with slight variations in detail as well as in specific store-front design. Each shop building, given a singular position on the exterior court, contributes to the formation of eddy-like spaces at the edge. The food hall breaks with the temple and stoa forms to create a more complex cross-axial composition on two levels.

The Shops at Primrose Brook reestablish a precedent in shopping-center design where innovation results from respecting the authority of historical architecture and planning rather than producing anonymous boxes and spaces that rely solely on seasonal marketing display for variation.

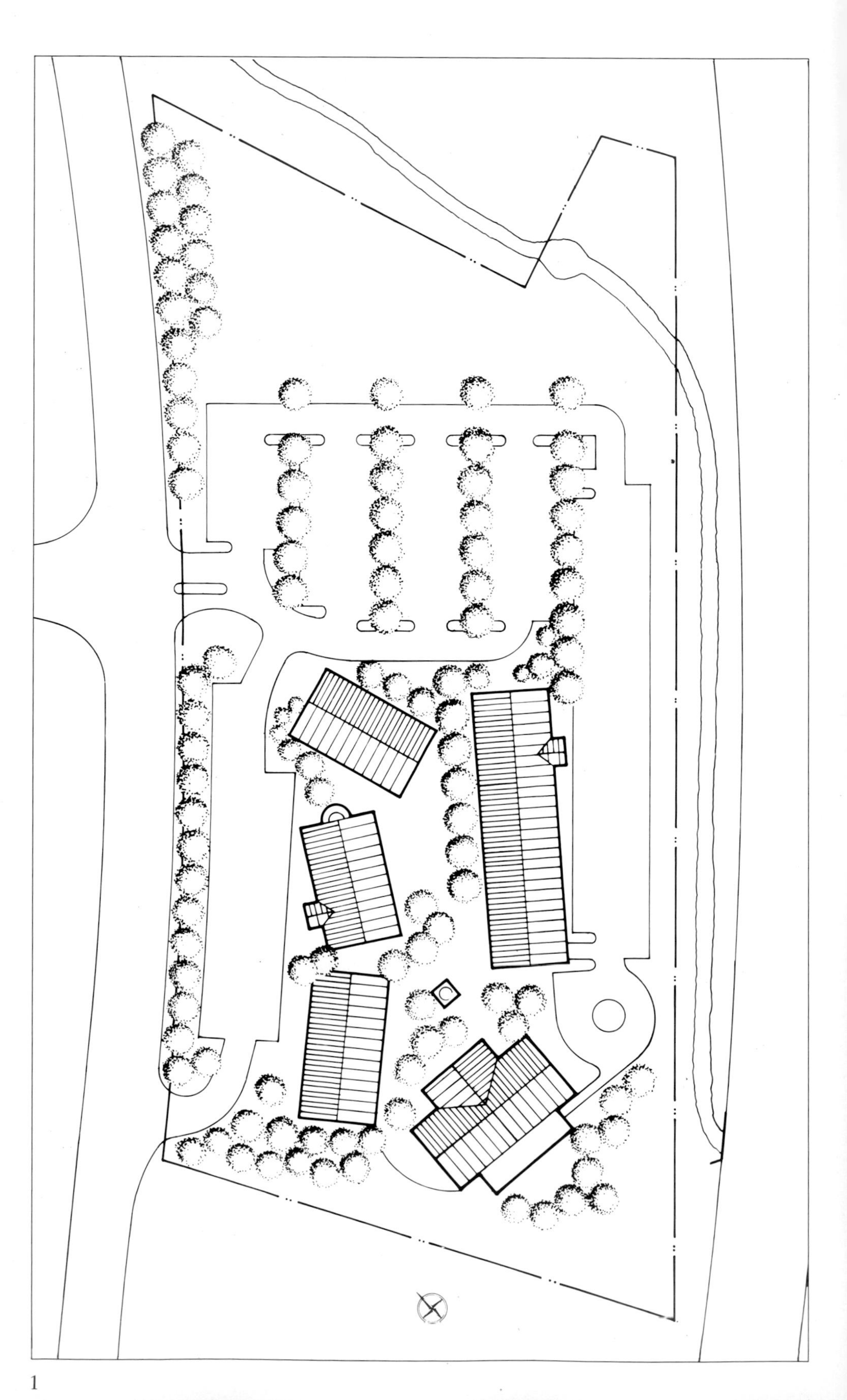

1

1.Site plan 2.View of Building B model 3.Building B: A.East elevation B.North elevation C.West elevation 4.Aerial view of site model from the south 5.Building B, partial storefront plan and elevation

2

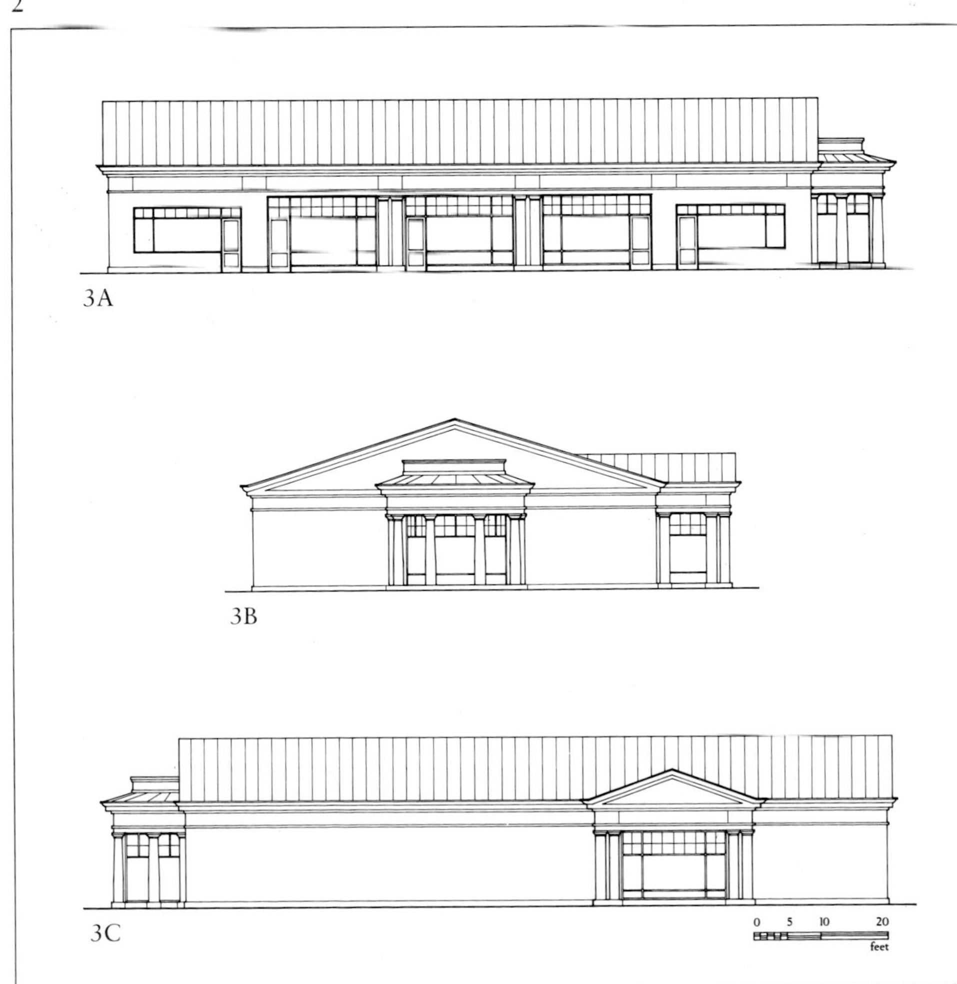

3A

3B

3C

4

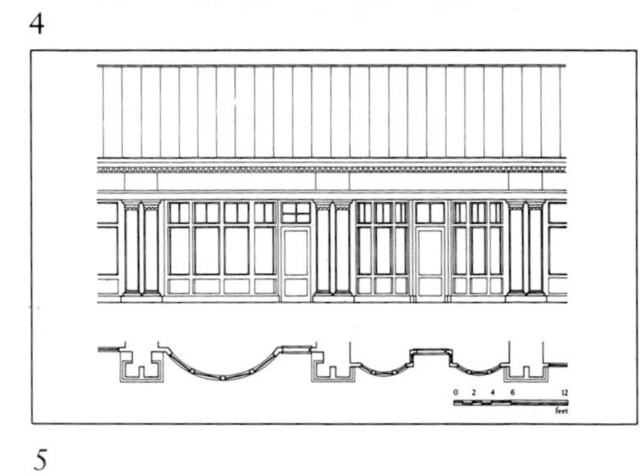

5

House in the Highlands

Seattle, Washington
1985–

From a bluff overlooking Puget Sound, this house commands panoramic views of the water and distant mountains. Entered from the corniche-type road above, the driveway leads down to the flat shelf that forms the house site. The tight composition of main house and outbuildings, enclosed garden and terraces imposes a formal order upon the naturally lush Pacific Northwest landscape.

The main house adopts a vocabulary of massing and detail previously explored by McKim, Mead and White and by Julia Morgan: intricacies of internal planning are subsumed and disguised by a symmetrical, low-slung shingled roof. While the twin pedimented wings on the motor-court elevation inflect towards the main entrance, the gently arced and distended western facade recognizes and embraces a view of 180 degrees. Classical Ionic detailing and proportions endow the house with a formality befitting its commanding site, without ever overwhelming the more casual and cottage-like nature of its low profile and shingled mass.

Interior planning of the main house orients largely about a double-height stair hall off which the living and dining rooms open and, in turn, establish an enfilade along the west-facing edge. This zone of circulation for formal entertainment culminates at the northwest in a projecting octagonal family room from which views to the north and south might be enjoyed. Concurrently, a secondary service zone winds through the center and along the eastern edge of the house towards the garage and servants' quarters to the north.

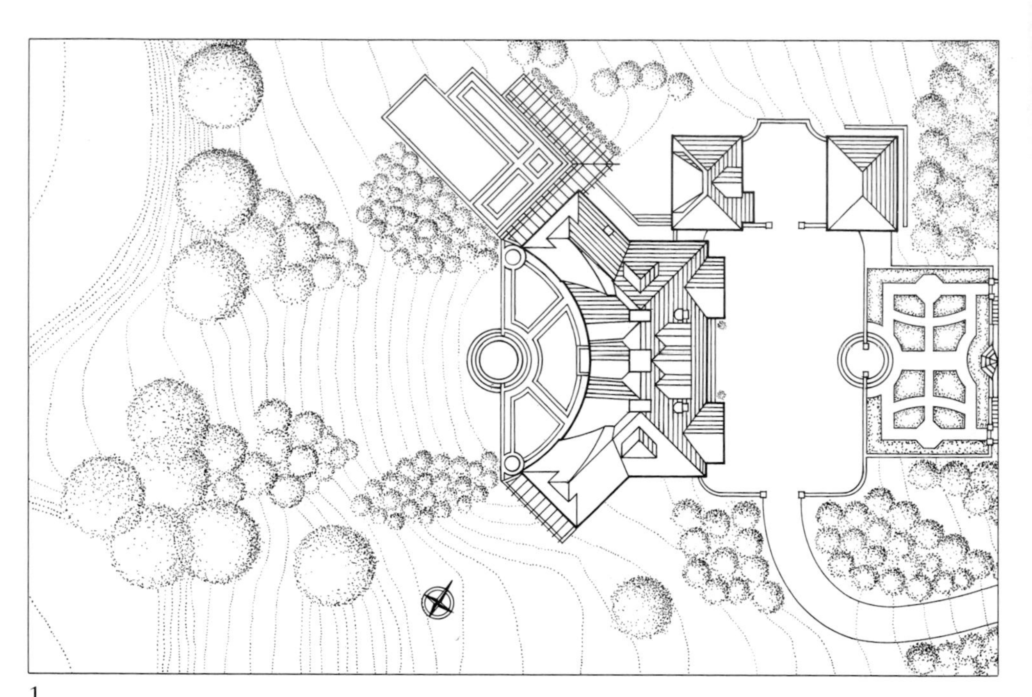

1

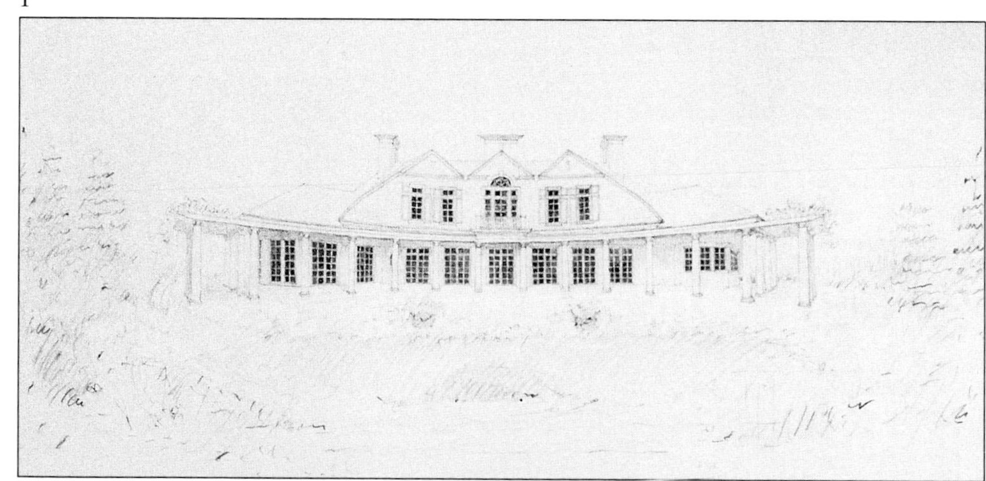

2

3

1.Site plan 2.Southwest elevation 3.View from the southeast 4.View of model from the south 5.Second floor plan 6.Ground floor plan

4

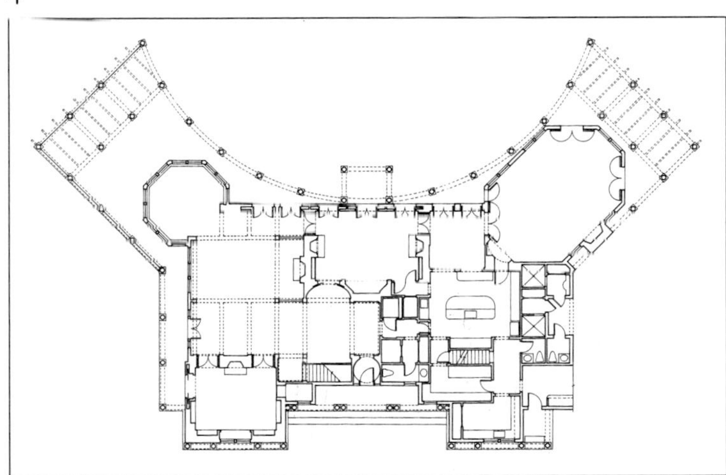

5

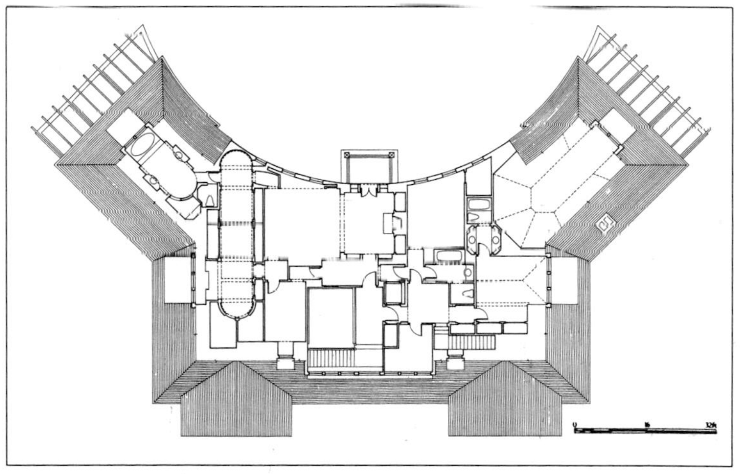

6

Residence at Cove Beach

East Marion, New York
1985

The shingled houses of Long Island's North Fork traditionally have assumed a lower architectural profile than have their grander cousins in the resort towns to the south. Therefore, this house on 100 acres near Orient Point recalls the horizontal, meandering farmhouses and seaside cottages of such architects as Wilson Eyre, rather than the more stately villas of McKim, Mead and White. Set low to the ground on wood plank decks, this house turns its principal ridge parallel to the shoreline; secondary, projecting gambreled- and hip-roofed wings, combined with repetitive dormers, lend a syncopated rhythm to the long mass and establish a fictive scenario of an original farmhouse that has been added to over time.

Internal planning of the main house emphasizes an informal flow between rooms and from individual rooms to the subsumed and projecting porches which, in turn, establish an easy transition from house to ground. In order to maximize the penetration of direct sunlight without sacrificing the north-facing vistas across the Sound, the rather open plan also orients rooms to the south, east, and west, as well as to the principal view. From without, the plan creates a series of enclosed and semi-enclosed courtyards for entrance, pool, and garden, whose formal order stands in marked contrast to the alternately windswept and heavily wooded surrounding landscape.

As it fulfills the utilitarian functions of shelter and security, the gatehouse/stable complex serves as a symbolic entry to the site at large. Here the suppressed area through which one must pass actively recalls the similar motif at the main house, while the flanking picturesque grouping of shingled and gambreled forms sets the architectural tone for the project.

1

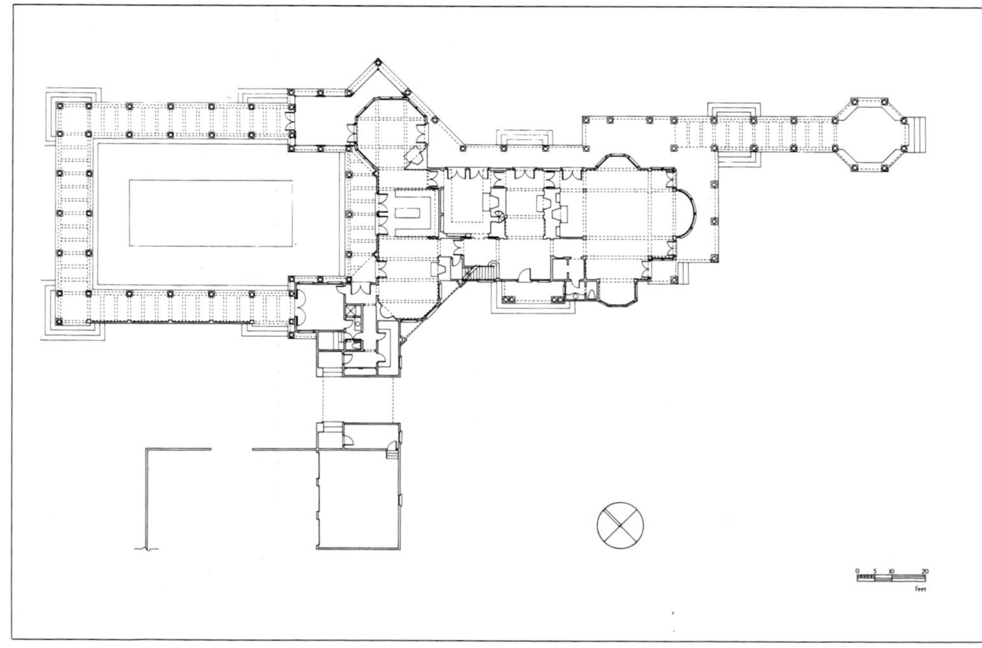

2

3

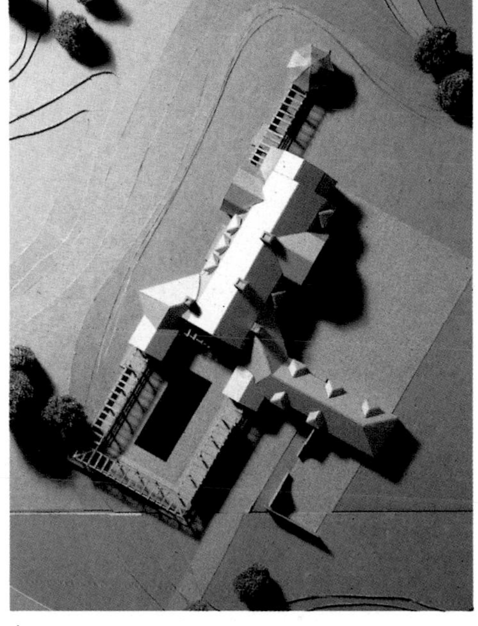

4

1.Perspective views of main house 2.Ground floor plan 3.Aerial view of model from the north 4.Overhead view of model 5.View of model from the northwest 6.Model of gatehouse and stable 7.View of entrance elevation

5

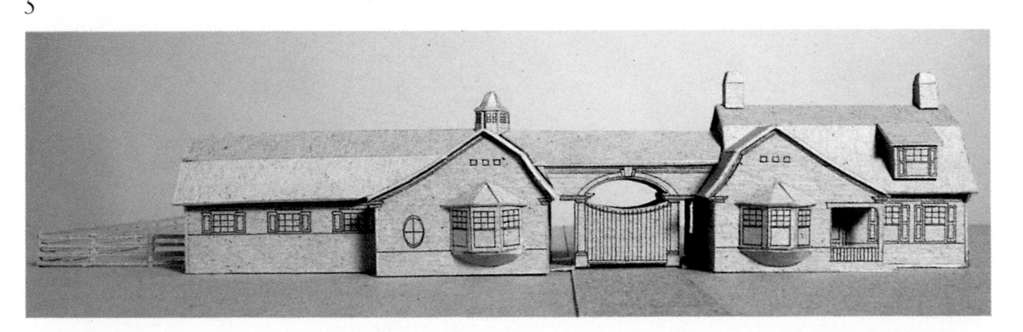

6

7

House in Cold Spring Harbor
Long Island, New York
1985

Set on a hillside commanding a view of Cold Spring Harbor, this house continues the traditions of New England domestic architecture in general, and the houses of the great whaling centers in particular.

The colossal pillared portico at the front provides a porch for the piano nobile and a scale commensurate with the sweeping views of the harbor and Long Island Sound beyond. The approach first reveals this aspect of the house, then bends around and is terminated by a motor court and the entry facade that responds to the scale of the individual. The sequence from the enclosed north court through the relatively dark entry hall, and the ascent through the skylighted central stair, creates a prelude to the principal floor with its dramatic views of the harbor. The rooms on this floor have large doors which slide into pockets in the walls, creating a sense of openness and connection to the shore as well as actual connection to terraces and the swimming pool, at the top of the hillside garden at the back.

1.West elevation 2.North elevation 3.South elevation 4.East elevation 5.Site plan 6.Second floor plan 7.Third floor plan 8.Ground floor plan

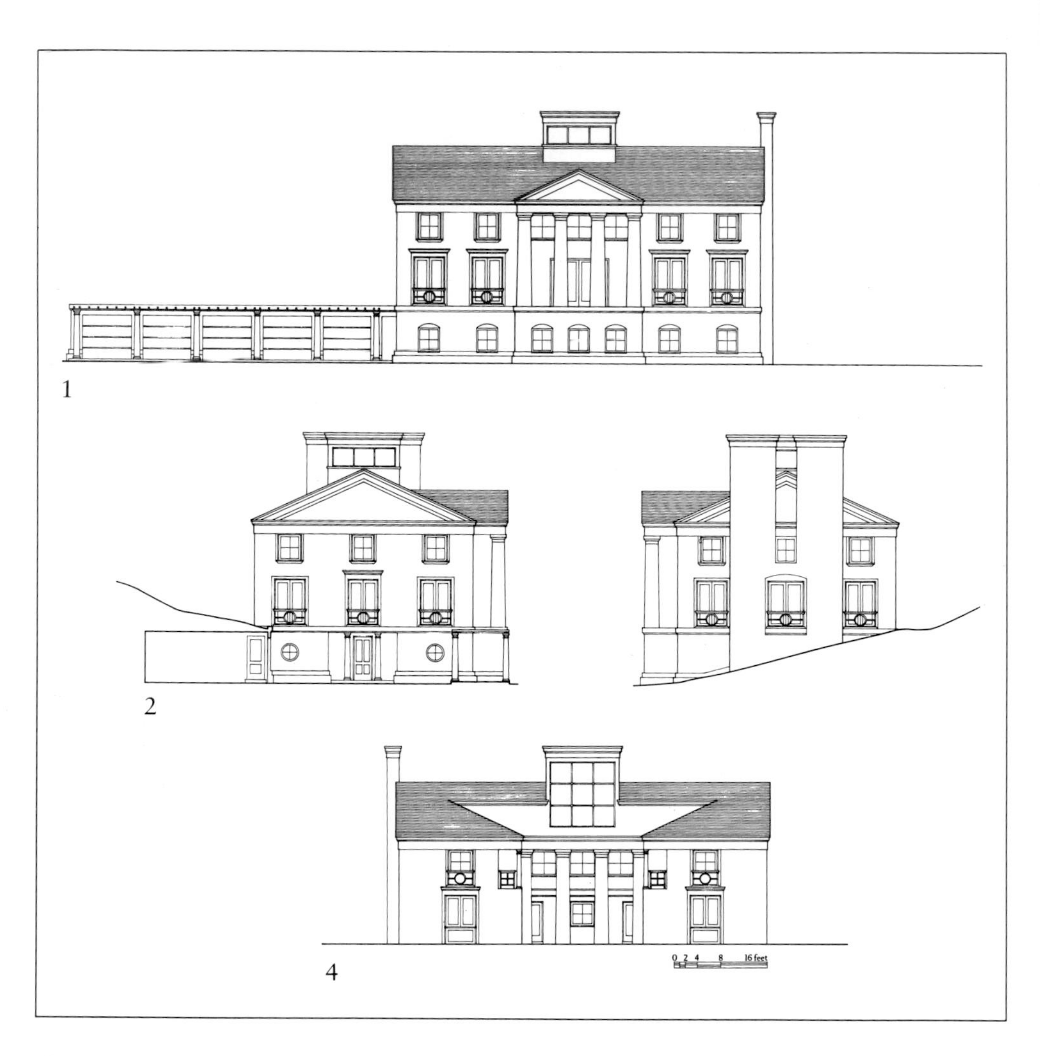

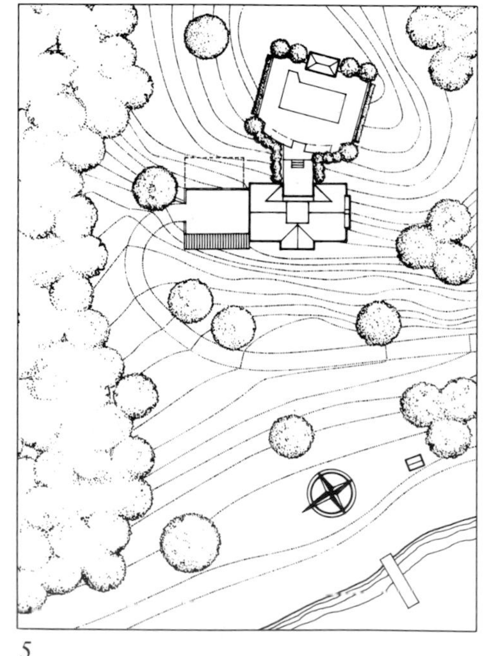
5

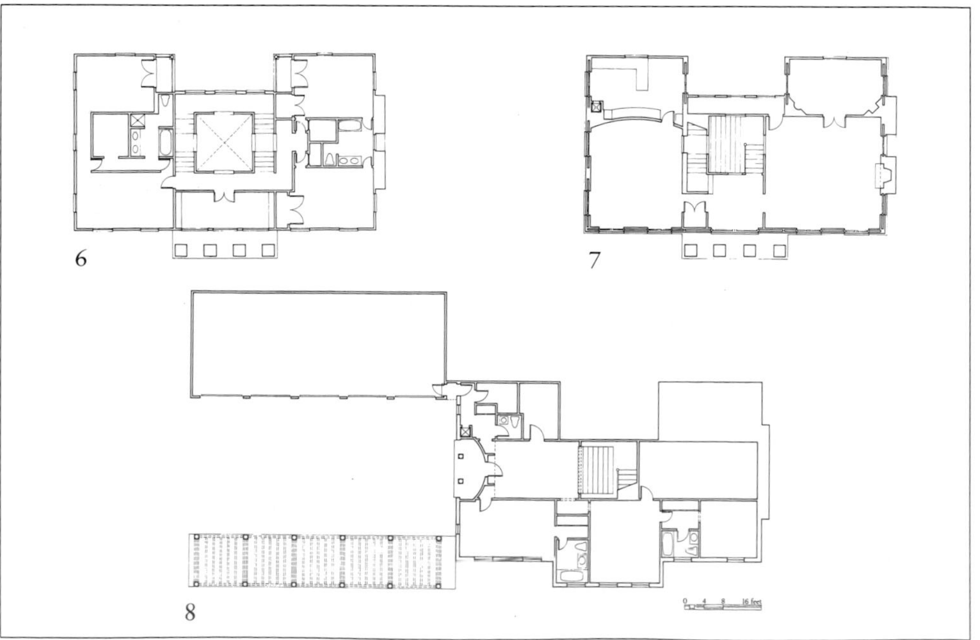

Residence on Russian Hill

San Francisco, California
1985-

This extensive reconstruction and expansion of one of the oldest houses on Russian Hill consists of two significant compositional moves: a picturesque tower located asymmetrically at the northwest corner, where it forms a dramatic entry, and a straight run of stairs that cuts across the building to lead visitors to the principal living rooms, which are located at the top. Although the austere shingled idiom of the original house is retained in this reconstruction, with few clues given to the intricate play of planes and volumes that occur on the interior, the prominent corner tower clearly announces the reinvigorating transformation of the original house.

1.North elevation 2.West elevation 3.South elevation 4.East elevation 5.Site plan 6.Second floor plan 7.Third floor plan 8.Ground floor plan

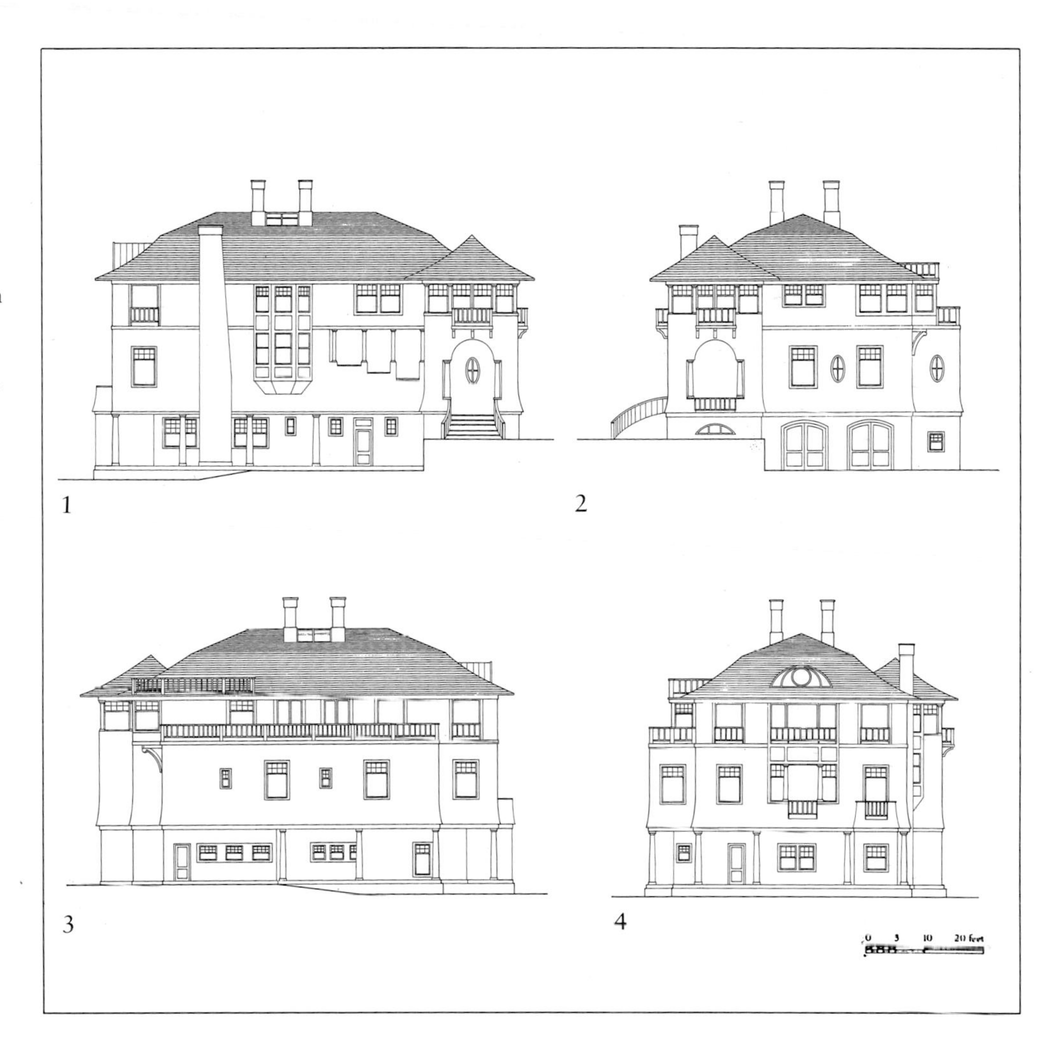

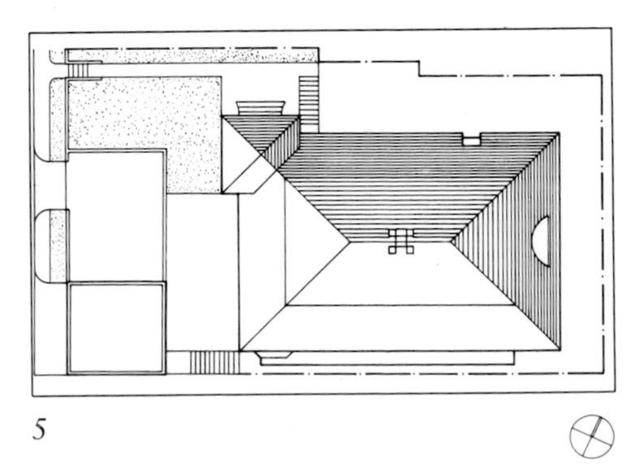

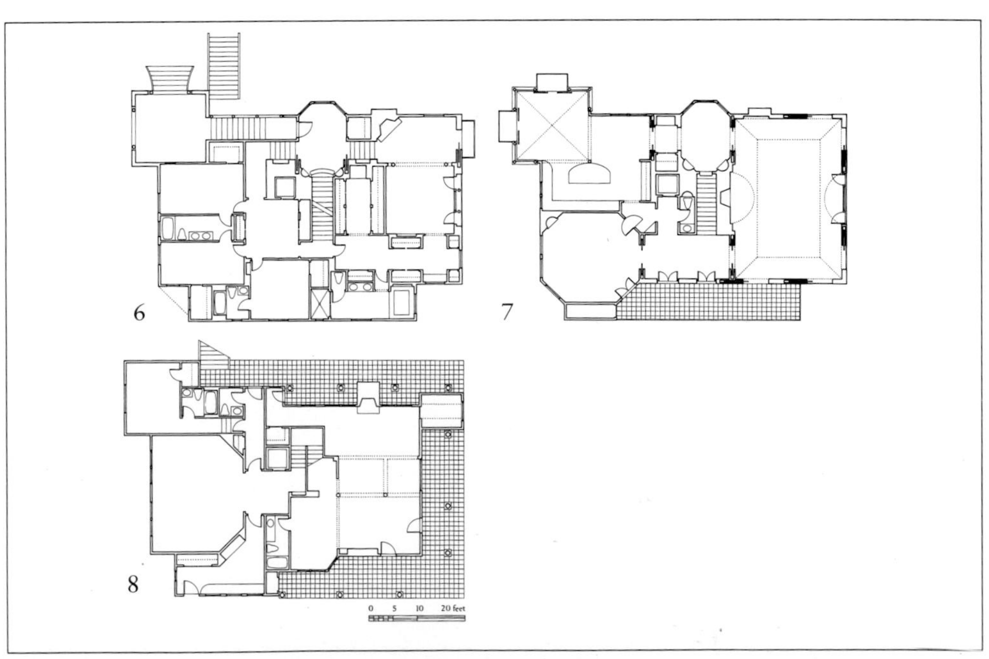

McGee Farm

Holmdel, New Jersey
1985

A mixed-use proposal as an alternative to high-density office development on approximately 100 acres of agricultural land near the village of Holmdel, the design for McGee Farm preserves both existing landscape and architectural features while incorporating them into a larger planned suburban form. Small office buildings are restricted to a corner of the site which allows the bulk of the former farmland to accommodate clusters of luxury condominium residences arranged in terraces, modulating the open space of the residential area into a meaningful succession of streets and squares. The close spacing of the units permits them to be designed as larger domestic structures, while the changes in plan geometry accommodating the requirements of outdoor circulation result in exteriors and interiors of unusual interest and character. The arrangement of these residences on the site leaves large areas of the former farm landscape intact, incorporating the historic farmsteads for reuse as small shops and restaurants. The proposal suggests two alternative stylistic models, either of which would be suitable to a rural surrounding.

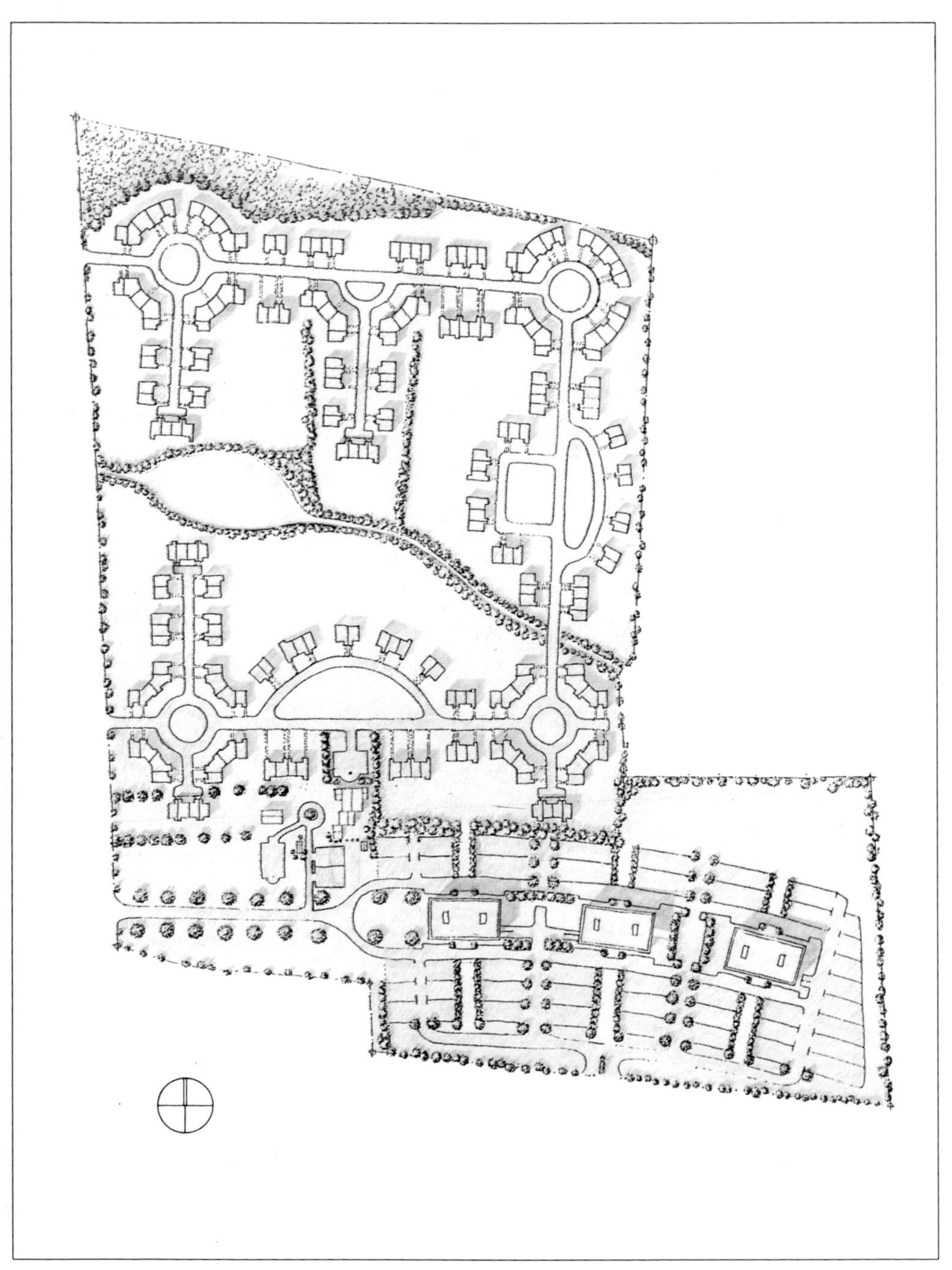

1

1.Site plan 2.The Munstead, typical three-unit cluster: A.Principal elevation B.Ground floor plan C.Second floor plan 3.The Millbrook, typical three-unit cluster: A.Principal elevation B.Ground floor plan C.Second floor plan

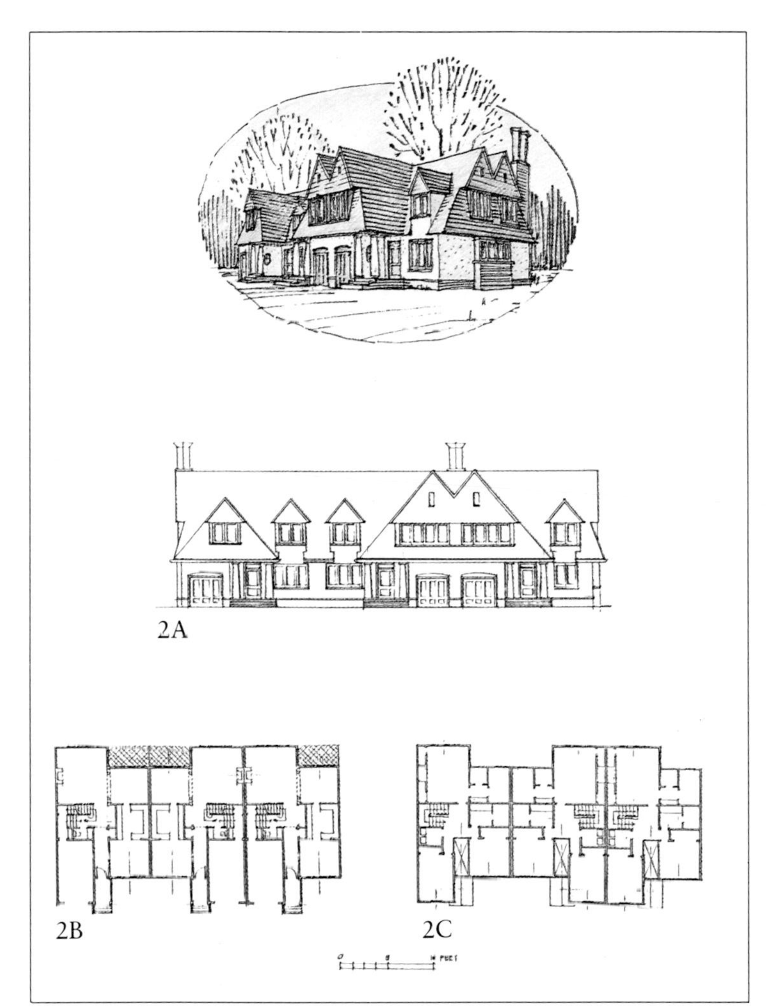

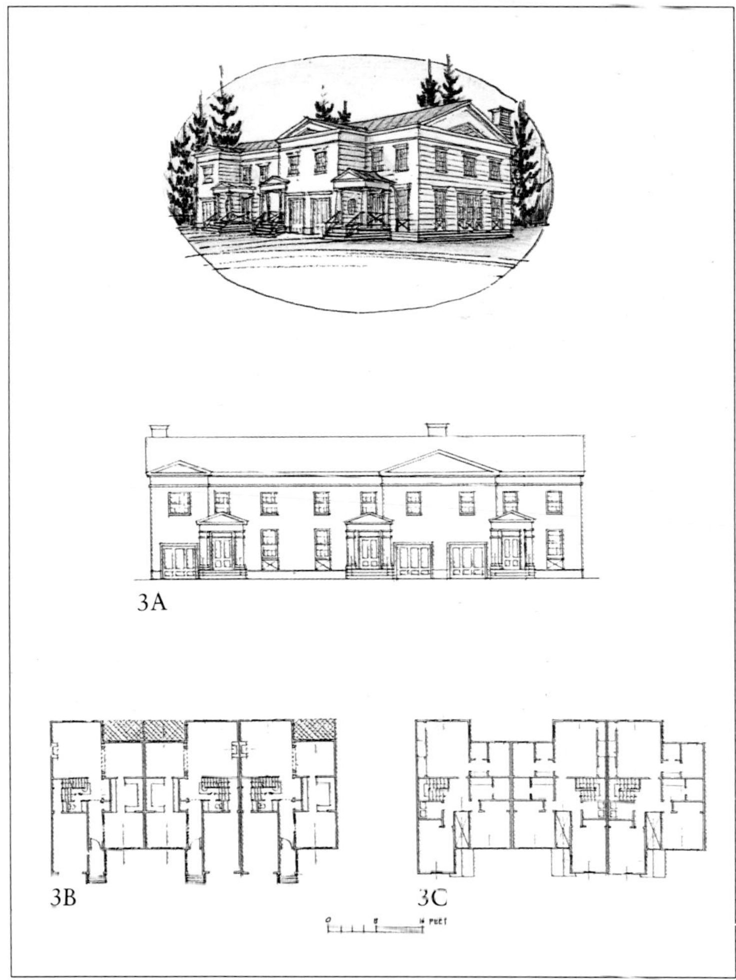

1. The Circle, Munstead style

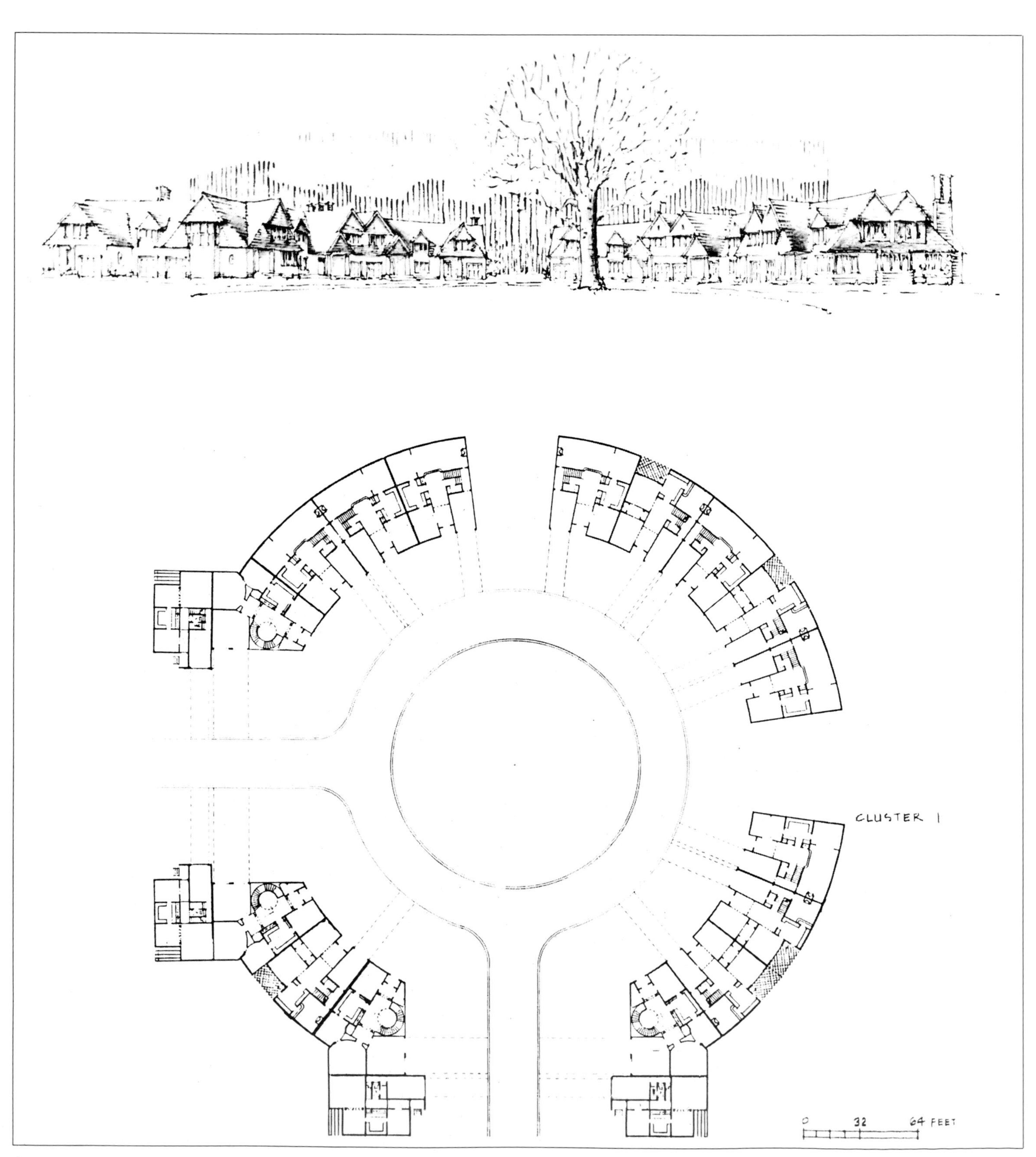

1

2.The Octagon, Millbrook style

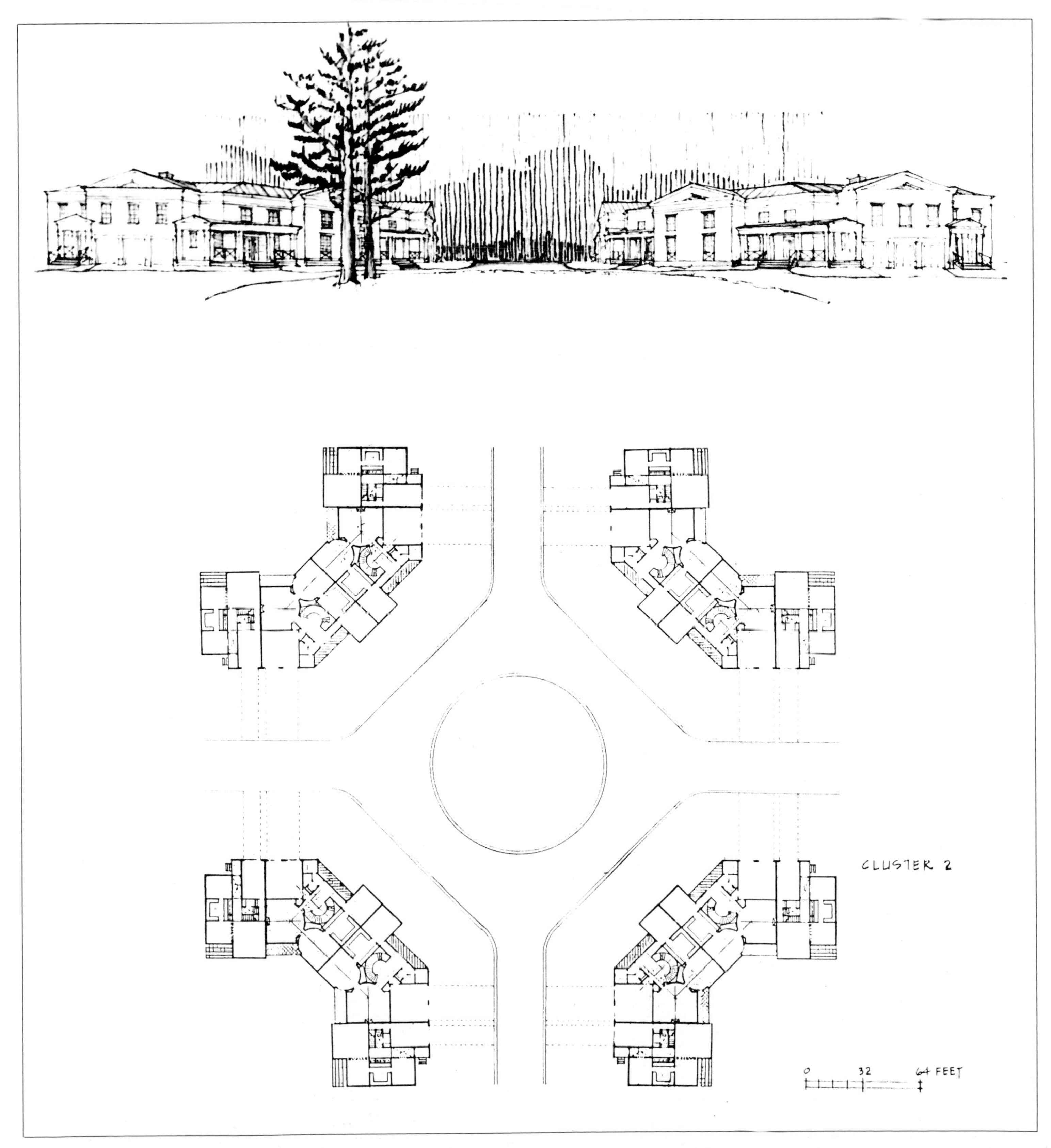

The Hamptons
Lexington, Massachusetts
1984 –

This development groups six Shingle Style houses along a newly created cul-de-sac in one of Boston's affluent bedroom communities. A consistent vocabulary is established employing shingled walls and roofs, bays, turrets, and covered porches that allows each individual house to vary considerably from its neighbor with regard to massing and floor plan while remaining integral to the development as a whole. Each 3,500-square-foot house is designed specially for its location on the street, taking advantage of considerable topographical variety in the site as well as sight lines and real or implied arcs. The assemblage is designed to appeal to a variety of homeowners seeking to accommodate contemporary life-styles in a traditional architectural environment.

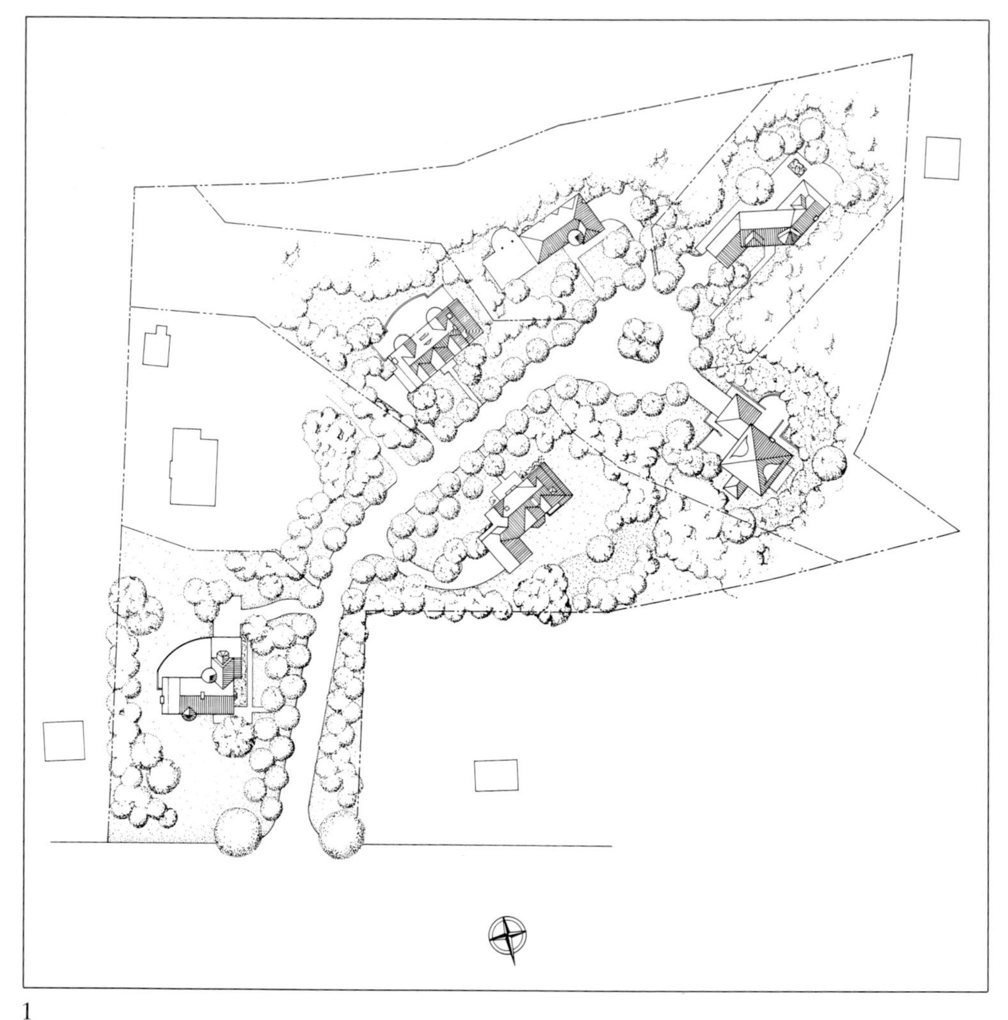

1

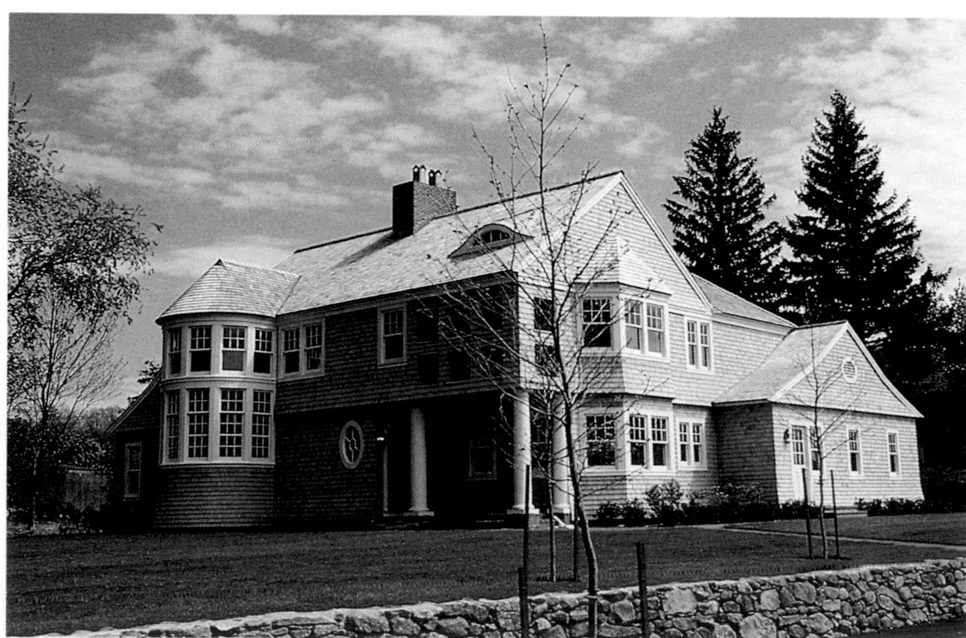

4

1.Site plan 2.House 1: A.North elevation B.East elevation C.South elevation D.West elevation E.Ground floor plan F.Second floor plan G.Site plan 3.House 3: A.North elevation B.East elevation C.West elevation D.South elevation E.Ground floor plan F.Second floor plan G.Site plan

4.House 1, view from the northwest 5.House 1, view from the southeast 6.House 1, detail of stair tower

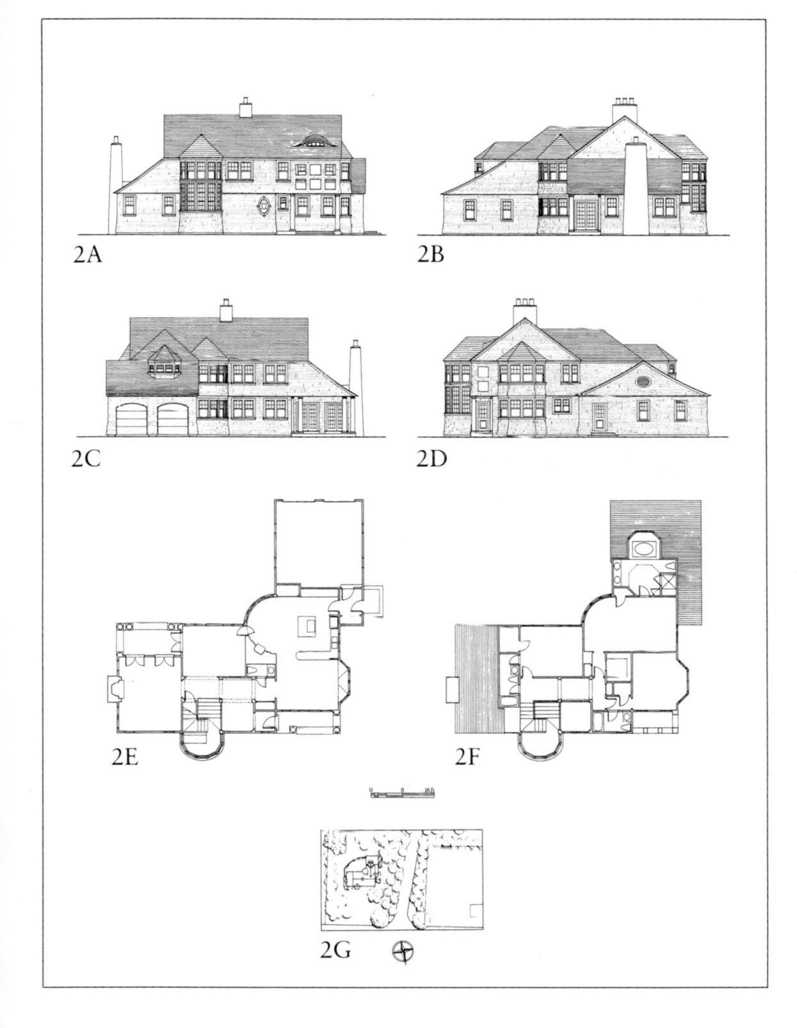

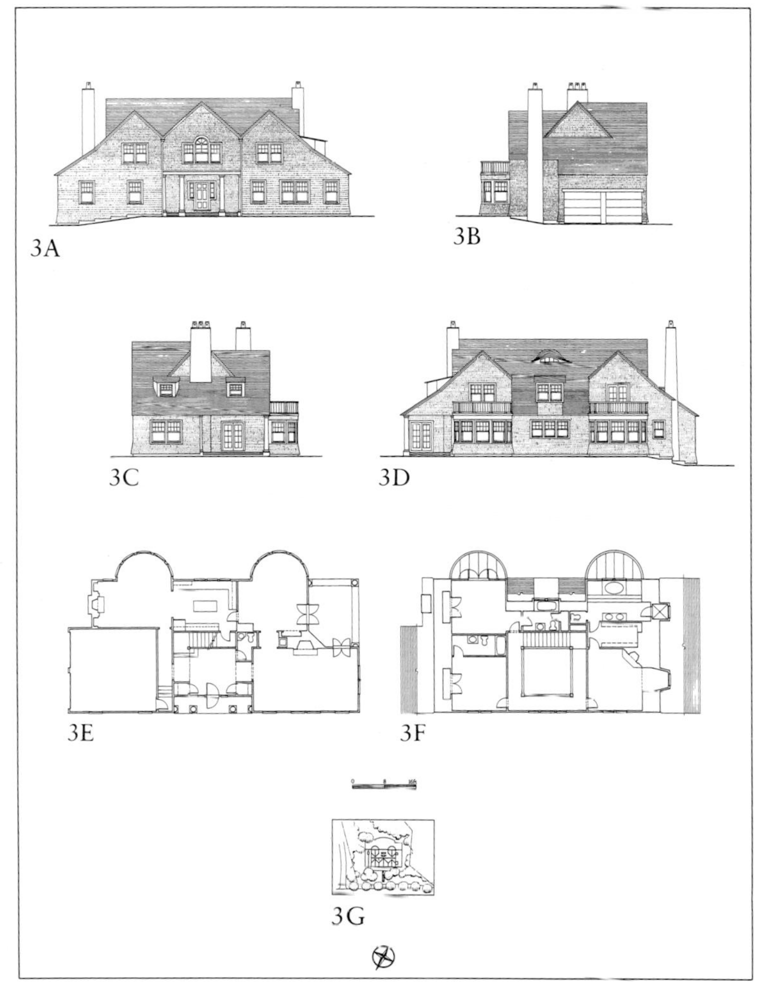

5

6

4.House 4: A.North elevation B.East elevation C.West elevation D.South elevation E.Second floor plan F.Ground floor plan G.Site plan 5.House 5: A.North elevation B.South elevation C.Second floor plan D.Ground floor plan E.Site plan

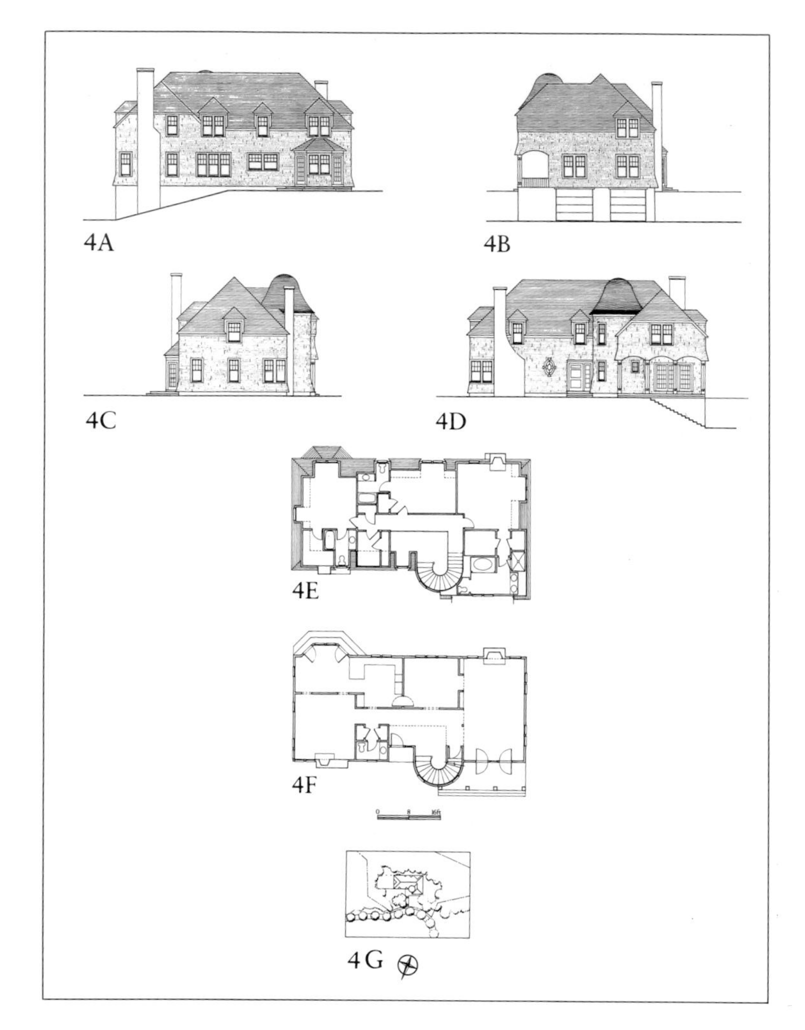

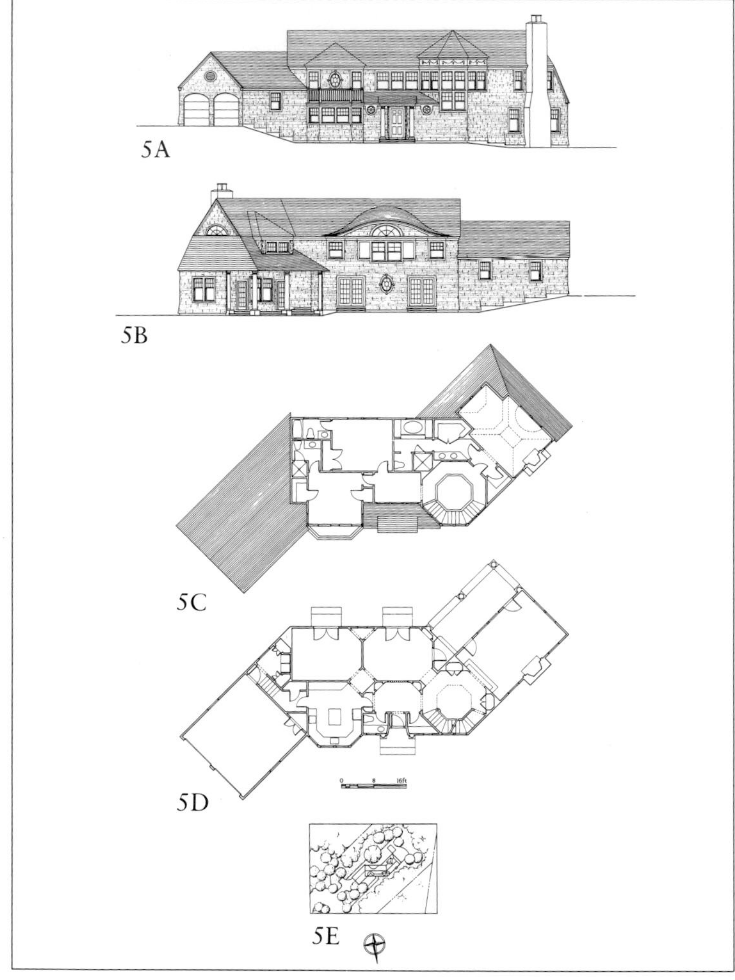

6.House 6: A.North elevation B.East elevation C.West elevation D.South elevation E.Ground floor plan F.Second floor plan G.Site plan

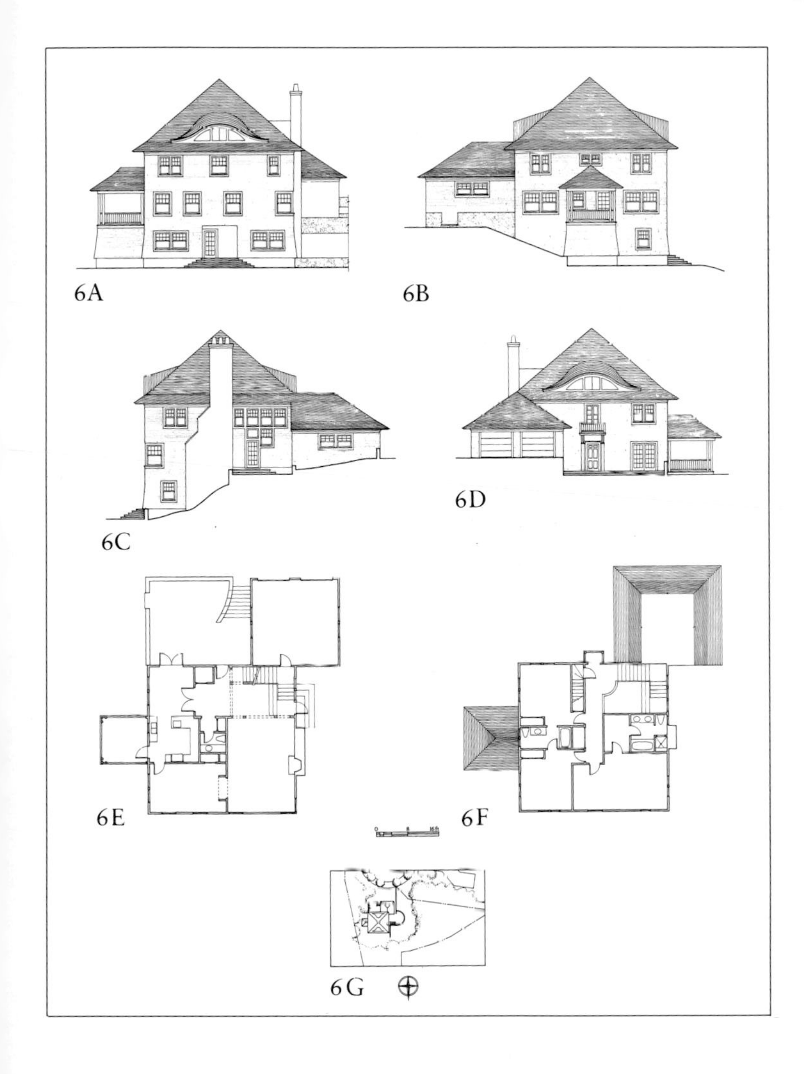

Other Projects

Alterations to the Schmertz Residence
East Hampton, New York, 1980

Project Architects: John Krieble, Roger H. Seifter
Assistant: Gregory Bader

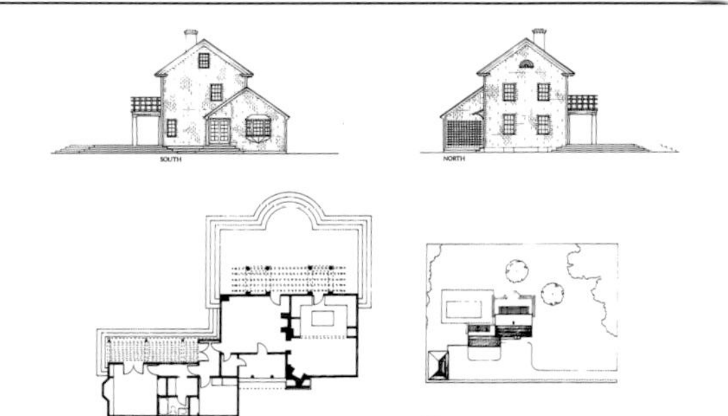

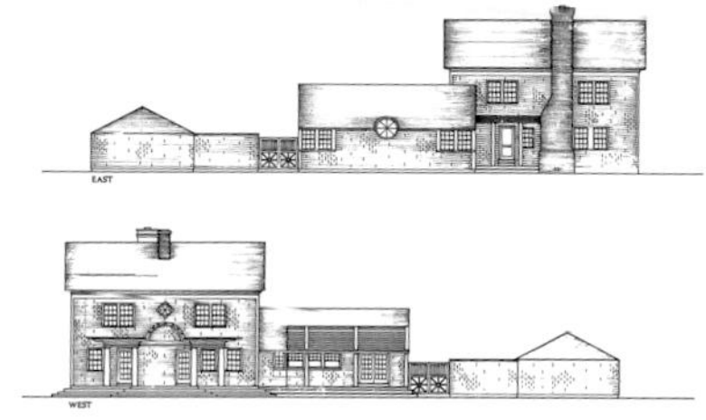

Bedroom Suite
Deal, New Jersey, 1980

Project Architect: Mark Mariscal

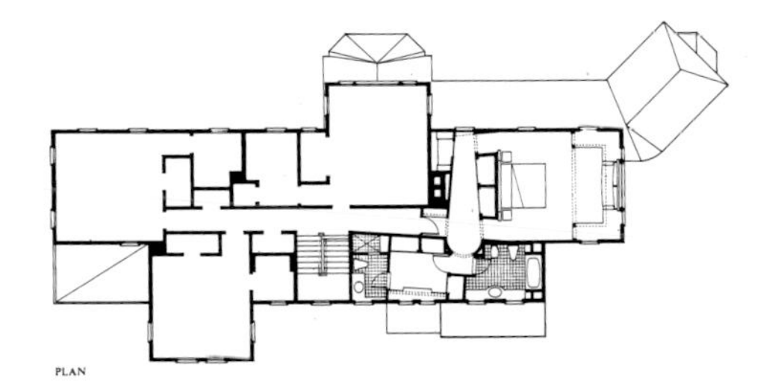

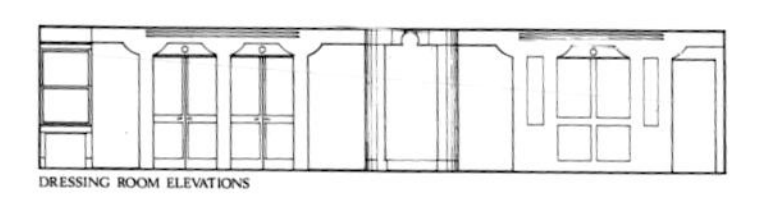

Stone Douglass Residence
East Hampton, New York, 1981

Project Architect: John Claggett

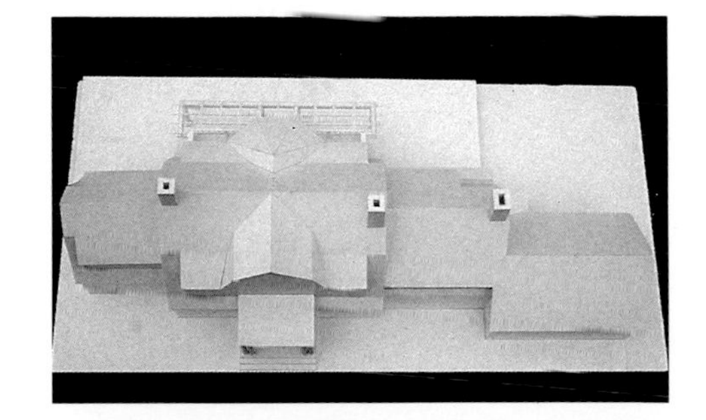

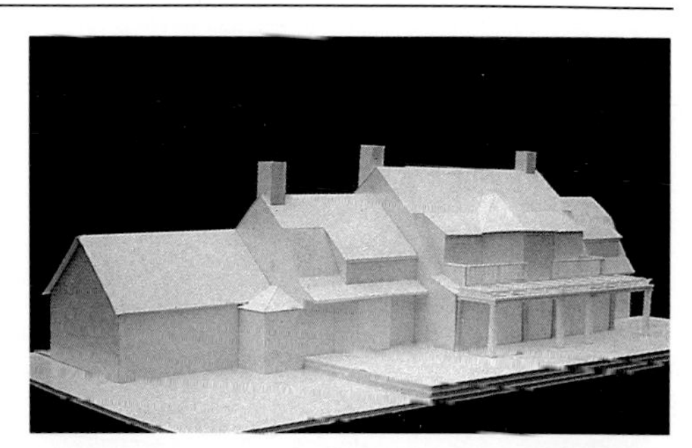

Residence
Ram Island, New York, 1981

Project Architect: John Ike

Residence
Greenwich, Connecticut, 1981

Project Architect: John Ike

Television Room at International House
New York, New York, 1981

Project Architect: John Krieble

House in New Canaan
Connecticut, 1982

Project Architect: Charles D. Warren
Assistant: Anthony Cohn

Interiors for the Yacht Ondine VI
Ondine Yacht Charters, 1982–1983

Project Architect: Thomas P. Catalano
Assistant: John M. Massengale

Borden Stable Renovation
Rumson, New Jersey, 1982

Project Architect: Thomas A. Kligerman
Assistant: Randy Correll

Silvera Apartment
New York, New York, 1982

Project Architect: Randy Correll

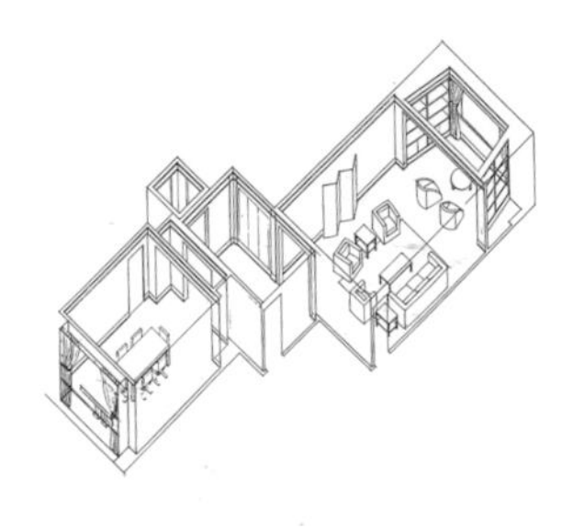

Residence Renovation
Bridgehampton, New York, 1983

Project Architect: Thomas Nohr

Meltzer House Renovation
Pound Ridge, New York, 1983

Project Architect: Randy Correll
Assistant: Kerry Moran

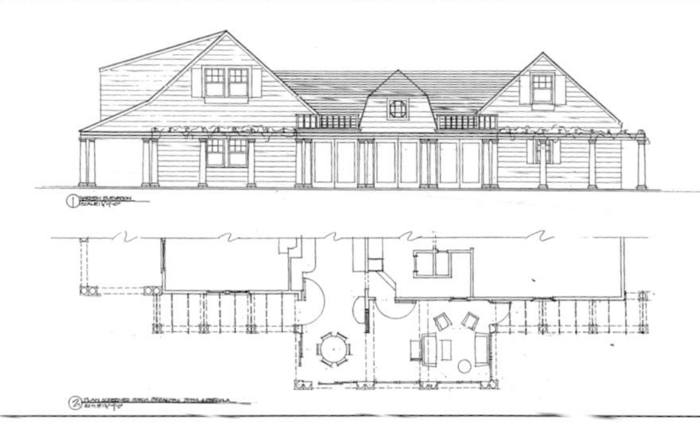

Residence at Briar Patch
East Hampton, New York, 1983

Project Architect: Randy Correll
Assistant: Kerry Moran

East Hampton Poolhouse
New York, 1983–1985

Project Architect: Roger H. Seifter
Assistant: Kerry Moran

Park Avenue Bedroom Suite
New York, New York, 1984

Project Architect: Charles D. Warren

Residence at Cow Bay
Martha's Vineyard, Massachusetts, 1984

Project Architect: Paul L. Whalen
Interiors: Ronne Fisher

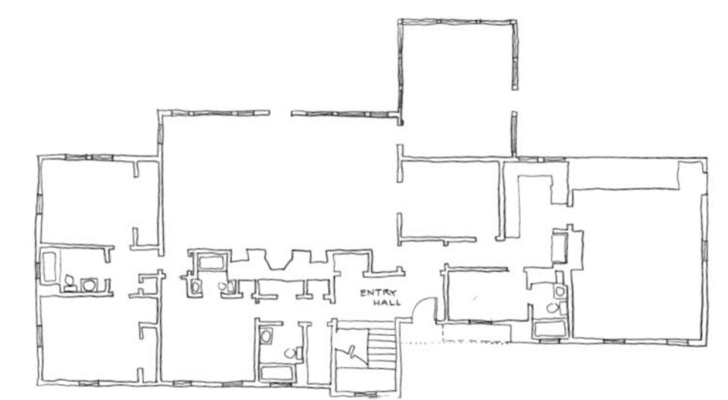

Saint Andrews Clubhouse
Hastings-on-Hudson, New York, 1984–

Project Architects: Thomas P. Catalano, Anthony Cohn, Re Hagele

Ronald McDonald House
New York, New York, 1985

Project Architect: Anthony Cohn

Residence Renovation
Green's Farm, Connecticut, 1985

Project Architects: Alan Gerber, John Ike

Pitkin Bargain Center
Brooklyn, New York, 1985

Project Architect: John Ike

Executive Suite
The Druker Company
Boston, Massachusetts, 1985–

Project Architect: John Ike
Assistants: Victoria Casasco,
William Nolan, Deirdre O'Farrelly

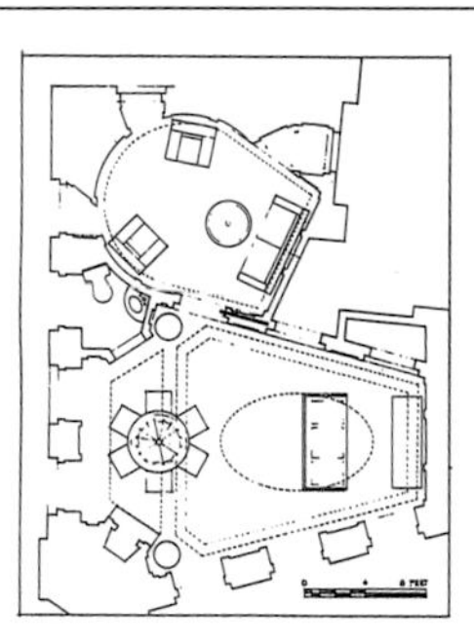

Chronological List of Buildings and Projects*

Residence in Quogue
Long Island, New York, 1979–1981
Project Architect: John Averitt
Assistants: Terry Brown, John Krieble, Charles D. Warren

Residence
Llewellyn Park, New Jersey, 1979–1981
Project Architect: Anthony Cohn
Assistants: Ethelind Coblin, Alan Gerber, Gavin MacRae-Gibson

Residence at Chilmark
Martha's Vineyard, Massachusetts, 1979–1983
Project Architect: Roger H. Seifter
Assistants: Alan Gerber, John Krieble

Alterations to the Schmertz Residence
East Hampton, New York, 1980
Project Architects: John Krieble, Roger H. Seifter
Assistant: Gregory Bader

Bedroom Suite
Deal, New Jersey, 1980
Project Architect: Mark Mariscal

Classical Duplex Apartment
New York, New York, 1980–1982
Project Architect: Gavin MacRae-Gibson
Assistants: Terry Brown, Alan Gerber

House at Farm Neck
Martha's Vineyard, Massachusetts, 1980–1983
Project Architect: Roger H. Seifter
Assistant: John Krieble
Interiors: Ronne Fisher

Residence
East Hampton, New York, 1980–1983
Project Architect: Terry Brown
Assistant: Roger H. Seifter
Interiors: Ronne Fisher

Park Avenue Duplex Apartment
New York, New York, 1981
Project Architect: Alan Gerber
Assistants: Anthony Cohn, John Ike

Lincoln Squash Club
New York, New York, 1981
Project Architect: John Ike
Assistant: Mark Mariscal

Offices for Obstetric and Gynecologic Associates
New York, New York, 1981
Project Architect: Anthony Cohn
Assistants: Peter Pennoyer, Whitney Sander

Alterations to the Former Woodhouse House
East Hampton, New York, 1981
Project Architect: John Krieble
Assistant: Terry Brown

Raymond Hood Exhibit
The Institute for Architecture and Urban Studies
New York, New York, 1981
Assistant: Thomas P. Catalano

Residence
Napeague, New York, 1981
Project Architect: Perry Kulper
Assistant: Thomas P. Catalano

Residence
Ram Island, New York, 1981
Project Architect: John Ike

Residence
Greenwich, Connecticut, 1981
Project Architect: John Ike

Stone Douglass Residence
East Hampton, New York, 1981
Project Architect: John Claggett

Kalamazoo Center
Kalamazoo, Michigan, 1981
Competition
Project Architect: John Ike

Television Room
International House
New York, New York, 1981
Project Architect: John Krieble

Showroom for Shaw-Walker, Inc.
Chicago, Illinois, 1981–1982
Project Architect: Roger H. Seifter
Assistants: Traci Aronoff, Ronne Fisher, Mark Mariscal, Paul L. Whalen

Two Houses
Aspen, Colorado, 1981–1982
Project Architect: Perry Kulper

House for Corbel Properties
Cove Hollow Farm, New York, 1981–1982
Lot 13
Project Architect: Roger H. Seifter

House for Corbel Properties
Cove Hollow Farm, New York, 1981–1983
Lot 10
Project Architect: Roger H. Seifter
Interiors: Randy Correll

Residence in Mill Neck
Long Island, New York, 1981–1983
Project Architect: Charles D. Warren
Assistants: Alan Gerber, John Ike

San Remo Apartment
New York, New York, 1981–1983
Project Architect: Paul L. Whalen
Assistants: Traci Aronoff, Thomas P. Catalano, Charles D. Warren

Mecox Fields
Bridgehampton, New York, 1981–
Project Architects: Randy Correll, Roger H. Seifter
Assistants: Armand LeGardeur, W. Jude LeBlanc, Thomas Nohr

Showroom for Shaw-Walker, Inc.
Los Angeles, California, 1982
Project Architect: Thomas A. Kligerman
Assistants: Rives Taylor, Johanna Vanderbulche

"Classical Corner"
For *House and Garden Magazine*
1982
Assistant: Alan Gerber

Anthony Fisher Residence
Napeague, New York, 1982
Project Architect: Roger H. Seifter
Assistant: Randy Correll

Faulkner House Apartments
University of Virginia
Charlottesville, Virginia, 1982
Competition
Project Architect: Roger H. Seifter

House at Seaview
Amagansett, New York, 1982
Project Architect: John Ike

Tableware for Swid Powell
1982–1985
Assistants: Randy Correll, Ronne Fisher

House in New Canaan
Connecticut, 1982
Project Architect: Charles D. Warren
Assistant: Anthony Cohn

Borden Stable Renovation
Rumson, New Jersey, 1982
Project Architect: Thomas A. Kligerman
Assistant: Randy Correll

Silvera Apartment
New York, New York, 1982
Project Architect: Randy Correll

Interiors for the Yacht Ondine VI
Ondine Yacht Charters, 1982–1983
Project Architect: Thomas P. Catalano
Assistant: John M. Massengale

Showroom for Shaw-Walker, Inc.
Washington, D.C., 1982–1983
Project Architect: John Ike
Assistant: John M. Massengale

Showroom for Shaw-Walker, Inc.
New York, New York, 1982–1983
Project Architect: John Ike
Assistants: Thomas A. Kligerman, John M. Massengale

Sprigg Lane Dormitories
University of Virginia
Charlottesville, Virginia, 1982–1984
Project Architect: Roger H. Seifter
Assistant: John Ike
Associate Architects: Marcellus Wright, Cox & Smith, P.C.

Observatory Hill Dining Hall
University of Virginia
Charlottesville, Virginia, 1982–1984
Project Architect: Roger H. Seifter
Assistant: Thomas A. Kligerman
Associate Architects: Marcellus Wright, Cox & Smith, P.C.

Residence
New Jersey, 1982–1984
Project Architect: John Ike
Assistant: Thomas A. Kligerman
Interiors: Ronne Fisher

St. Andrews
A Jack Nicklaus Golf Community
Hastings-on-Hudson, New York, 1982–
Project Architects: Thomas P. Catalano, Robert Dean, Re Hagele
Assistants: Anthony Cohn, Joseph W. Dick, Peter Dick, David Eastman, Preston Gumberich, Kerry Moran, Thomas Nohr, William Nolan, Diane Smith, Pat Tiné

Reading Room
International House
New York, New York, 1983
Project Architect: Paul L. Whalen
Assistant: Peter Pennoyer

"Dinner at Eight" Carpet
For Furniture of the Twentieth Century
1983
Assistant: Randy Correll

San Remo Carpet
1983
Assistant: Randy Correll

Cherry Creek Housing Development
Denver, Colorado, 1983
Project Architect: Thomas P. Catalano
Assistants: Victoria Casasco, Alex Lamis, Graham S. Wyatt
Associate Architects: Michael Barber Architects

Residence on Lake Agawam
Southampton, New York, 1983
Project Architect: Roger H. Seifter
Assistants: Caroline Hancock, Barry Goralnick

Residence at West Tisbury
Martha's Vineyard, Massachusetts, 1983
Project Architect: Paul L. Whalen
Assistant: Gregory Gilmartin

Fox Hollow Run
Chappaqua, New York, 1983
Project Architect: Thomas P. Catalano
Assistants: Victoria Casasco, John M. Massengale

Performing Arts Center
Anchorage, Alaska, 1983
Competition
Project Architect: John Ike
Assistants: Charles Felton, Bonnie Glasser, Graham S. Wyatt

Additions to the New Orleans Museum of Art
New Orleans, Louisiana, 1983
Competition
Project Architect: Gregory Gilmartin
Assistant: Oscar Shamamian

Residence
Pound Ridge, New York, 1983
Project Architect: Randy Correll
Assistant: Alex Lamis

Farmhouse
Oldham County, Kentucky, 1983
Project Architect: Paul L. Whalen
Assistants: Gregory Gilmartin, Oscar Shamamian, Mark Wade

Urban Villa
Brooklyn, New York, 1984
Project Architect: Alan Gerber

Residence Renovation
Bridgehampton, New York, 1983
Project Architect: Thomas Nohr

Meltzer House Renovation
Pound Ridge, New York, 1983
Project Architect: Randy Correll
Assistant: Kerry Moran

Residence at Briar Patch
East Hampton, New York, 1983
Project Architect: Randy Correll
Assistant: Kerry Moran

Schweber Apartment
The Dakota
New York, New York, 1983
Project Architect: Alan Gerber
Assistants: Gregory Gilmartin, Luis F. Rueda, Oscar Shamamian, Graham S. Wyatt

Point West Place Office Building
Framingham, Massachusetts, 1983–1985
Project Architect: John Ike
Assistants: Stephen Falatko, Peter Merwin, Thai Nguyen, Mariko Takahashi, Graham S. Wyatt
Associate Architects: Drummey Rosane Anderson, Inc.

House for Corbel Properties
Cove Hollow Farm, New York, 1983–1984
Lot 14
Project Architect: Armand LeGardeur

Prospect Point Office Building
La Jolla, California, 1983–1985
Project Architects: Thomas A. Kligerman, Graham S. Wyatt
Associate Architects: Martinez/Wong Associates, Inc., and Wheeler/Wimer Architects

East Hampton Poolhouse
New York, New York, 1983–1985
Project Architect: Roger H. Seifter
Assistant: Kerry Moran

Treadway House
Southampton, New York, 1983–1985
Project Architect: Randy Correll
Assistants: Joseph W. Dick, David Eastman

Residence at Hardscrabble
East Hampton, New York, 1983–1985
Project Architect: Armand LeGardeur
Assistants: Robert Ermerins, Kaarin Taipale
Interiors: Ronne Fisher

Residence
Brooklyn, New York, 1983–
Project Architect: Alan Gerber
Assistants: Anthony Cohn, David Eastman, Robert Ermerins, William T. Georgis, Jens Happ, Kristin McMahon

Villa in New Jersey
1983–
Project Architect: Thomas A. Kligerman
Assistants: Augusta Barone, Victoria Casasco, Robert Ermerins, William T. Georgis, Natalie Jacobs
Interiors: Ingrid Armstrong

Residence in Massachusetts
1983–
Project Architect: Edward R. Mudd
Assistants: Randy Correll, Thomas Gay, Gregory Gilmartin, Warren A. James, Alex Lamis, Armand LeGardeur, Richard Manion, Kerry Moran, Luis F. Rueda, Mario Sampaio, Roger H. Seifter, Oscar Shamamian, Graham S. Wyatt

Colfax at Beden's Brook
Skillman, New Jersey, 1983–
Project Architect: Alex Lamis
Assistants: David Eastman, Robert Ermerins, Barry Goralnick, Caroline Hancock, William Nolan
Interiors for House #23: Ronne Fisher, Lisa Goldman

Copperflagg Corporation Residential Development
Staten Island, New York, 1983–
Project Architect: Stephen Falatko
Assistants: Keller A. Easterling, Robert Ermerins, Natalie Jacobs, Warren A. James, W. Jude LeBlanc, John M. Massengale, Kerry Moran, Thai Nguyen, Deirdre O'Farrelly, Paul L. Whalen, Paul B. Williger

Student Pub
International House
New York, New York, 1984
Project Architect: Paul L. Whalen
Assistants: Victoria Casasco, Luis F. Rueda
Murals: Paul L. Whalen

1992 Chicago World's Fair
With a National Design Team organized by SOM
Chicago, 1984
Project Architect: Graham S. Wyatt
Assistant: Charles D. Warren

CityPlace
Providence, Rhode Island, 1984
Project Architect: Alan Gerber
Assistants: Barry Goralnick, Alex Lamis, W. Jude LeBlanc, Timothy Lenahan

Addition to Congregation Shaare Zion
Brooklyn, New York, 1984
Project Architect: Alan Gerber

Sephardic Study Center
Brooklyn, New York, 1984
Project Architect: Alan Gerber

Private High School
Brooklyn, New York, 1984
Project Architect: John Ike
Assistants: Victoria Casasco, Stephen Falatko

Greenwood Village
Bakersfield, California, 1984
Project Architect: Graham S. Wyatt

Architecture Building
Roger Williams College
Bristol, Rhode Island, 1984
Competition
Project Architect: Charles D. Warren

Civic Center
Escondido, California, 1984
Competition
Project Architect: Paul L. Whalen
Assistants: Augusta Barone, Thomas A. Kligerman, Deirdre O'Farrelly, Graham S. Wyatt

Park Avenue Bedroom Suite
New York, New York, 1984
Project Architect: Charles D. Warren

Residence at Cow Bay
Martha's Vineyard, Massachusetts, 1984
Project Architect: Paul L. Whalen
Interiors: Ronne Fisher

Seaside Hotel
Seaside, Florida, 1984
Project Architects: John Ike, Paul L. Whalen
Assistant: Stephen Falatko

Residence at the Shores
Vero Beach, Florida, 1984
Project Architect: Paul L. Whalen
Assistant: Barry Goralnick

Newport News Cultural Arts Pavilion
Newport News, Virginia, 1984
Competition
Project Architect: Charles D. Warren
Assistant: Richard Del Monte

Preakness Hills Country Club
Wayne, New Jersey, 1984
Project Architects: Thomas P. Catalano, Graham S. Wyatt
Assistants: Alex Lamis, Constance Treadwell

Pool Atrium
Deal, New Jersey, 1984–1985
Project Architect: John Ike
Assistants: William T. Georgis, Grant Marani

Classical Pool Pavilion
Deal, New Jersey, 1984–1985
Project Architect: John Ike
Assistant: Armand LeGardeur

Saint Andrews Clubhouse
Hastings-on-Hudson, New York, 1984 –
Project Architect: Thomas P. Catalano, Anthony Cohn, Re Hagele

Residence
Marblehead, Massachusetts, 1984–
Project Architect: Roger H. Seifter
Assistants: Caroline Hancock, Kaarin Taipale

Hillcrest Square
San Diego, California, 1984–
Project Architect: Graham S. Wyatt
Assistants: Victoria Casasco, Ellen Coxe, William T. Georgis, Re Hagele, Grant Marani, Luis F. Rueda
Associate Architects: Wheeler / Wimer Architects

Residence
Quogue, New York, 1984–
Project Architect: Randy Correll
Assistants: Thomas Nohr, Constance Treadwell

Scarsdale Heights
Scarsdale, New York, 1984–
Project Architect: Graham S. Wyatt
Assistants: Barry Goralnick, Caroline Hancock

Two Newton Place
Newton, Massachusetts, 1984–
Project Architect: John Ike
Assistants: Victoria Casasco, Alex Lamis, Jeff Schofield, Graham S. Wyatt
Associate Architects: Drummey Rosane Anderson, Inc.

Residence
Hewlett Harbor, New York, 1984–
Project Architect: Charles D. Warren
Assistants: Robert Ermerins, Re Hagele, Armand LeGardeur, Grant Marani, Jenny W. Peng
Interiors: Lisa Goldmann

Residence at Lily Pond Lane
East Hampton, New York, 1984–
Project Architect: Randy Correll
Assistant: Oscar Shamamian

The Hamptons
Lexington, Massachusetts, 1984–
Project Architect: John Ike
Assistants: Thomas P. Catalano, Anthony Cohn, Joseph W. Dick, Natalie Jacobs, Graham S. Wyatt

Penthouse Apartment
New York, New York, 1984–
Project Architect: Paul L. Whalen
Assistants: David Eastman, Barry Goralnick, Caroline Hancock, Grant Marani
Interiors: Ronne Fisher, Ingrid Armstrong

Residence at Calf Creek
Watermill, New York, 1984 –
Project Architect: Armand LeGardeur
Assistants: Robert Ermerins, Barry Goralnick, Luis F. Rueda
Interiors: Lisa Goldmann

McGee Farm
Holmdel, New Jersey, 1985
Project Architect: Stephen Falatko
Assistants: Victoria Casasco, Ellen Cox, Keller A. Easterling, Alex Lamis

Residence at Cove Beach
East Marion, New York, 1985
Project Architect: Roger H. Seifter

Metairie Park Country Day School
New Orleans, Louisiana, 1985
Competition
Project Architect: Charles D. Warren
Assistant: Armand LeGardeur

New American Home
Dallas, Texas, 1985
Project Architect: Paul L. Whalen
Assistant: Joseph W. Dick
Interiors: Alan Gerber

Temporary Clubhouse at Swan Valley
Breckenridge, Colorado, 1985
Project Architect: Stephen Falatko
Assistants: Ellen Coxe, Alex Lamis
Associate Architects: Baker & Hogan Associates Architects

Municipal Center
Phoenix, Arizona, 1985
Competition
Project Architect: Charles D. Warren
Assistants: John DiGregorio, William T. Georgis, Timothy Lenahan, Richard Maimon, Kenneth McIntyre-Horito, Deirdre O'Farrelly

House in Cold Spring Harbor
Long Island, New York, 1985
Project Architect: Charles D. Warren

Ronald McDonald House
New York, New York, 1985
Project Architect: Anthony Cohn

Residence Renovation
Green's Farm, Connecticut, 1985
Project Architects: Alan Gerber, John Ike

Pitkin Bargain Center
Brooklyn, New York, 1985
Project Architect: John Ike

Tegeler Hafen
Berlin, 1985–
Project Architect: Graham S. Wyatt
Assistants: Ellen Coxe, W. Jude LeBlanc

Executive Suite
The Druker Company
Boston, Massachusetts, 1985–
Project Architect: John Ike
Assistants: Victoria Casasco, William Nolan, Deirdre O' Farrelly

Congregation Kol Israel
Brooklyn, New York, 1985–
Project Architect: Thomas A. Kligerman
Assistants: Augusta Barone, Victoria Casasco, Caryl Kinsey, Timothy Lenahan

Rye Brook Park
Westchester County, New York, 1985–
Project Architect: John Ike
Assistants: Alex Lamis, Kenneth McIntyre-Horito, Richard Maimon, Jeff Schofield

House in the Highlands
Seattle, Washington, 1985–
Project Architect: Roger H. Seifter
Assistants: Robert Ermerins, Caroline Hancock, Timothy Lenahan, Elizabeth Thompson, Paul B. Williger

Residence
Pottersville, New Jersey, 1985–
Project Architect: Randy Correll
Assistant: Deirdre O'Farrelly

The Shops at Primrose Brook
Bernardsville, New Jersey, 1985–
Project Architect: Anthony Cohn
Assistant: Keller A. Easterling

Residence on Russian Hill
San Francisco, California, 1985–
Project Architect: Alan Gerber
Assistants: Sarah Hunnewell, Warren A. James, Kristin McMahon, Elizabeth Thompson, Paul B. Williger

* This list represents all projects in progress between 1981 and 1985, including buildings begun before but not completed until after 1981, and projects begun before 1981 still incomplete at the end of 1985.

Biography

Robert A. M. Stern was born on May 23, 1939 in New York City. After receiving a B. A. degree from Columbia University in 1960 he enrolled at Yale University where he received his Master of Architecture degree in 1965. After graduation, he returned to New York City and began his professional career as the first J. Clawson Mills Fellow of the Architectural League of New York. In 1966 he worked in the office of Richard Meier and between 1967 and 1970 he was a special assistant for design in the Housing and Development Administration of the City of New York. In 1969, he and John Hagmann established Stern & Hagmann Architects, a partnership that lasted until 1977, when the firm became Robert A. M. Stern Architects.

An educator as well as a practicing architect, Robert A. M. Stern is a Professor at the Graduate School of Architecture, Planning and Preservation at Columbia University. In addition, in 1984 he was appointed the first Director of Columbia's Temple Hoyne Buell Center for the Study of American Architecture. Robert A. M. Stern has also been associated with the Institute for Architecture and Urban Studies. Between 1973 and 1977 he was president of the Architectural League of New York.

Robert A. M. Stern's work has been included in numerous exhibitions and has been published in several monographs. The firm has received numerous awards for design including: the first place award in the national competition for 1,000 units of housing on Roosevelt Island (1975); National Honor Awards of the American Institute of Architects (1980, 1985); the Distinguished Architecture Award of the New York Chapter of the AIA in 1982, 1984, and 1985. Mr. Stern is a Fellow of the American Institute of Architects and received the Medal of Honor of the New York Chapter of the AIA in 1984.

As a writer and an editor Robert A. M. Stern has produced important articles and books, the most recent being *New York 1900,* which he co-authored with Gregory Gilmartin and John M. Massengale, and *New York 1930* with Gregory Gilmartin and Thomas Mellins. In the spring of 1986, he presented "Pride of Place: Building the American Dream," a television documentary on American architecture prepared for Mobil Oil Corporation and the Public Broadcasting System.

Bibliography

Articles by Robert A. M. Stern in Books and Periodicals

"Architecture, History, and Historiography at the End of the Modernist Era," in John E. Hancock, editor, *History in, of, and for Architecture* (New York: Rizzoli International Publications, Inc., 1981), pp. 34–43.

"Exhibition of Work by Members of the Chicago Architectural Club," *The Chicago Architectural Journal* (New York: Rizzoli International Publications, Inc., 1981), pp. 76–94.

"Gideon's Ghost," book review, *Skyline* (October 1981), pp. 22–25.

"Modernismus und Postmodernismus," *Design Ist Unsichtbar* (Vienna: Locker Verlag, 1981), pp. 259–271.

"Notes on Post-Modernism," *Yale Seminars in Architecture* (New Haven, Connecticut: Yale University Press, 1981), pp. 1–35.

"Human Scale at the End of the Age of Modernism," *Collaboration: Artists & Architects* (New York: Whitney Library of Design, 1981), pp. 114–115.

"Setting the Stage: Herts and Tallant," with John M. Massengale and Gregory Gilmartin, *Skyline* (December 1981), pp. 32–33.

"Toward an Urban Suburbia, Once Again Suburban Enclaves," *Cities* (1982), pp. 32–33, 79.

"International Style: Immediate Effects," *Progressive Architecture* (February 1982), pp. 106–109.

"Beginnings," *A + U* (July 1982 Extra Edition), pp. 13–16.

"Stern Chase in Chicago," *Inland Architect* (July/August 1982), pp. 2, 4, 6–7.

"Las Duplicidades del Postmodernismo," *Arquitectura* (September/October 1982), pp. 26–29, 68–75; a translation of "Doubles of Post-Modern," *Harvard Architectural Review* (Spring 1980), pp. 74–87.

"Kampf dem Raster: Die Vision von New York als einer schonen Stadt," in Karl Schwartz, ed., *Die Zukunft der Metropolen: Paris, London, New York, Berlin* 1 (Berlin: Katalog zur Ausstellung in der Technischen Universitat Berlin, (1984)), pp. 196–203.

"On Style, Classicism, and Pedagogy," *Precis: The Journal of the Graduate School of Architecture and Planning, Columbia University in the City of New York* 5 (Fall 1984), pp. 16–23.

"After the Modern Period," *Forum 29,* No. 2, Amsterdam, (1984–1985), pp. 54–55.

"Four Towers," *A + U* (January 1985), pp. 49–58.

"Robert A. M. Stern," in Jaquelin Robertson, ed., *The Charlottesville Tapes* (New York: Rizzoli International Publications, Inc., 1985), pp. 48–55.

Books by Robert A. M. Stern

With John M. Massengale, *The Anglo-American Suburb* (London: Academy Editions, 1981).

Guest Editor, "American Architecture After Modernism," *A + U* (March 1981 Special Issue).

With Thomas P. Catalano, *Raymond Hood* (New York: Institute of Architecture and Urban Studies and Rizzoli International Publications, Inc., 1982).

With Clay Lancaster and Robert Hefner, *East Hampton's Heritage: An Illustrated Architectural Record* (New York: W.W. Norton & Company, Inc., 1982).

With John M. Massengale and Gregory Gilmartin, *New York 1900* (New York: Rizzoli International Publications, Inc., 1983).

Editor, *International Design Yearbook 1985/86* (Amsterdam/Brussels: B. V. Uitgeversmaatschappij Elsevier, 1985) and (New York: Abbeville Press, 1985).

Interviews and Profiles of Robert A. M. Stern

Betty Dillard, "Viewpoint," *Texas Homes* (January 1981), pp. 149–151.

"Interview with Robert A. M. Stern," *Dimensions* (January 1981), pp. 6–10.

Charles K. Gandee, "Behind the Facades: A Conversation with Robert A. M. Stern," *Architectural Record* (March 1981), pp. 108–113.

Daralice Donkervoet Boles, "An Interview with Robert Stern," *Crit 9, The Architectural Student Journal* (Spring 1981), pp. 19–21.

Monica Meenan, "At Home: Soaring to New Architectural Heights," *Town and Country* (September 1981), pp. 238–239.

Barbaralee Diamonstein, "Robert A. M. Stern," *Interior Design: The New Freedom* (New York: Rizzoli International Publications, Inc., 1982), pp. 160–175.

Barbaralee Diamonstein, "The Temple of Love and Other Musings: A Conversation with Robert A. M. Stern," *Historic Preservation* (September–October 1982), pp. 28–31.

"Robert A. M. Stern: One Architect's Decidedly Developed Style," *Home* (June 1983), pp. 52–57.

Katherine Dolgy, "Interviews," *The Fifth Column, Canadian Student Journal of Architecture* (Autumn 1983), pp. 33–36.

Carol Vogel, "Robert A. M. Stern on Avoiding the Architectural Zoo," *Architectural Digest* (January 1984), pp. 22–30.

Suzanne Stephens, "The Fountainhead Syndrome," *Vanity Fair* (April 1984), pp. 40–45.

Beverly Russell, "The Stern Conversations," *Interiors* (September 1984), pp. 160–161, 176, 180, 182, 184; (October 1984), pp. 138–139, 154, 158; (November 1984), pp. 142–143, 148, 150.

Sarah Williams, "More is More," *Art News* (January 1985), pp. 11, 13.

Michael Walker, "Chief Architect of the Post-Modern House," *Metropolitan Home* (February 1985), pp. 24, 136.

R. Douglas Hamilton, "The Language of Modernism: An Interview with Robert A. M. Stern," *The Columbia Art Review* (Spring 1985), pp. 3–6.

John Arthur, "Alternative Space—Robert A. M. Stern," *Art New England* (April 1985), pp. 8–9.

Manuela Cerri Goren, "Architetti U.S.A.," *Vogue Italia* (April 1985), pp. 206, 218–219.

Warren A. James, "As Others See Us: An Interview with Robert A. M. Stern," *The San Juan Star: Sunday Magazine* (April 7, 1985), pp. 2–4.

Daniel Lorber, "Action," *The Three Village Herald,* East Setauket, New York (May 29, 1985), p. 3.

Christina Farnsworth, "Interview with Custom Architect Robert Stern," *Professional Builder* (Mid-June 1985), pp. 37–38.

"Heart and Mind Essential in Design: Stern," *F. W. Dodge Construction News* (July 26, 1985), pp. 14–15.

Gerald Adams, "Architects Tour City's Backwoods," *San Francisco Examiner* (August 14, 1985), p. ZA–1.

Sherri Dalphonse, "A 'Modern Traditionalist,'" *Hamptons Newspaper/Magazine* (August 20, 1985), pp. 33–34.

Benita Feurey, "Man of the Hour, Robert A. M. Stern is Wanted Everywhere," *House in the Hamptons International* (September 1985), pp. 9–10, 61.

Kay Kaiser, "A Stern View of San Diego," *The San Diego Union* (September 8, 1985), pp. F1, F13–14.

Mark Gill, "Avenue Update," *Avenue* (October 1985), p. 127.

Linda Mandeville, "Robert A. M. Stern: Custom of the Country," *Columbia* (December 1985), cover, pp. 16–23.

Critical Discussions of Work in Books and Periodicals

"Robert A. M. Stern: Die Moderne Architektur Nach dem Modernismus," *Design Ist Unsichtbar* (Vienna: Locker Verlag, 1981).

Helen Searing, *Speaking a New Classicism: American Architecture Now* (Northampton, Massachusetts: Smith College Museum of Art, 1981), pp. 50–52.

Idea As Model (New York: The Institute of Architecture and Urban Studies and Rizzoli International, Inc., 1981), pp. 92–93.

Christopher Wilk, "Renovating Columbia Interiors," *Skyline* (January 1981), p. 20.

Barclay Gordon, "Reminted in the Coin of Post-Modernism," *Architectural Record* (Mid-February 1981), pp. 74–75.

"San Juan Capistrano Public Library Design Competition," *Architectural Record* (March 1981), p. 47.

Carol Lawson, "How Art and Architecture Look at the 80's," *New York Times* (March 6, 1981), p. C22.

Douglas Davis, "Mixed Marriages of Art," *Newsweek* (March 16, 1981), p. 71.

Martin Filler, "'Collaboration: Artists and Architects' at the New-York Historical Society," *Art in America* (May 1981), p. 139.

Charles K. Gandee, "Robert A. M. Stern/Points of View, Mount Desert Island, Maine," *Architectural Record* (Mid-May 1981), p. 139.

"Of Artists and Architects," *Cultural Post,* National Endowment for the Arts, (May/June 1981), p. 27.

Charles Jencks, "Stern and Post-Modern Space," *Architectural Design News Supplement* (July 1981), pp. 1, 6–7.

David Bourdon, "Collaboration: Artists and Architects," *Vogue* (July 1981), pp. 43–44.

"Buildings for Best Products (The exhibition at the Museum of Modern Art)," *Space Design* (August 1981), p. 43.

"Robert Stern," *Parametro* (August/September 1981), pp. 50–51.

Vincent Scully, "Robert Stern: Perspecta to Post-Modernism," *Architectural Design* (December 1981), pp. 98–99.

Charles Jencks, ed., "Free Style Classicism," *Architectural Design* (January/February 1982), pp. 18, 72–75.

Paolo Portoghesi, *After Modern Architecture* (New York: Rizzoli International Publications, Inc., 1982), pp. 7–13.

Paul Goldberger, "The Maturing of Robert Stern," *The New York Times* (April 4, 1982), pp. D31, D34.

Charles Jencks, "On the Edge of Content: Charles Jencks Reviews Robert Stern's Oeuvre," *Skyline* (June 1982), pp. 28–29.

Douglas Brenner, "A Villa in Three Acts," *Architectural Record* (June 1982), pp. 120–125.

Stanley Tigerman, "The Kaleidoscopically Wonderful R.A.M.S.," *The Residential Works of Robert A. M. Stern, A + U* (July 1982 Extra Edition), pp. 149–151.

Allan Greenberg, "Recent Houses by Robert Stern," *The Residential Works of Robert A. M. Stern, A + U* (July 1982 Extra Edition), pp. 155–156.

Thomas S. Hines, "Citizen Stern: A Portrait of the Architect as Entrepreneur," *The Residential Works of Robert A. M. Stern, A + U* (July 1982 Extra Edition), pp. 227–231.

Benjamin Forgey, "The Union of Art and Architecture," *The Washington Post* (July 3, 1982), pp. B1–B2.

Lance Knobel, "Interior Design: Three Interiors by Robert A. M. Stern," *Architectural Review* (July 1982), pp. 52–57.

Pilar Viladas, "Dressed to Sell: Shaw-Walker Showroom, Chicago, Illinois," *Progressive Architecture* (September 1982), pp. 214–217.

Susan Grant Lewin, "Robert A. M. Stern Expresses American Architecture with a Sense of Wit," *House Beautiful* (September 1982), pp. 102–107.

"Robert A. M. Stern," *G.A. Houses* (October 1982), pp. 16–29.

"Brighton Lively," *House & Garden* (January 1983), pp. 106–115.

Lance Knobel, "Interior Design: Showroom, Chicago," *The Architectural Review* (March 1983), pp. 66–67.

Ross Miller, "Architecture: Robert A. M. Stern," *Architectural Digest* (April 1983), pp. 111–121.

Daniel Solomon and Anne Fougeron, "Raymond Hood," *Design Book Review* (Summer 1983), pp. 26–27.

Philip Jodidio, "La Decoration N'est Pas Un Crime," *Connaissance des Arts* (May 1983), cover, pp. 74–81.

Doris Chevron, "Architektur, die Geschichten Erzahlt," *Ambiente* (June /July 1983), pp. 22–34; reprinted in "Une Architecture Inspiree De L'Histoire," *First International Ligne Decoration* (October /November 1983), pp. 80–91.

Roy Strickland and James Sanders, "Project for Northtown Extension," *At Home In The City: Housing in New York 1810–1983* (June–July 1983), p. 48.

"Robert Stern," *Beaux Arch I: A Hamptons Architectural Exposition* (July 1983), unpaginated.

Charles Jencks, "Abstract Representation," *Architectural Design* (July /August 1983), pp. 66–69.

"Sulla spiaggia," *Ville Giardini* (October 1983), pp. 12–15.

Carleton Knight III, "Post-Modern What?," *Builder* (November 1983), pp. 72–79.

Edie Cohen, "Not Quite Traditional," *Interior Design* (December 1983), pp. 150–153.

Carter Wiseman, [book review] "City Dreams," *New York* (December 5, 1983), pp. 154–155.

Helio Pinon, *Arquitectura de las Neovanguardias* (Barcelona: Editorial Gustavo Gili S.A., 1984), pp. 174–175.

Charles Jencks and Maggie Keswick, *The Language of Post Modern Architecture* (New York: Rizzoli International Publications, Inc., 1984), pp. 118–119, 155.

David Mackay, *La Casa Unifamiliar /The Modern House* (Barcelona: Editorial Gustavo Gili, S.A., 1984), pp. 150–153.

Hal Foster, "(Post) Modern Polemics," *Perspecta 21: The Yale Architectural Journal* (1984), pp. 144–153.

"Robert A. M. Stern: Residence at Chilmark, Martha's Vineyard," *Architectural Design* (1984), pp. 70–71.

Constance Regnier, "Sentimentale Reise zuruch in die sonnige Jugendzeit. Der Architekt Robert Stern machte sie moglich," *Ambiente* (December–January 1984), pp. 167–170.

Howard Kissel, [book review] "New York 1900," *Women's Wear Daily* (January 10, 1984), p. 23.

Digby Diehl, [book review] " 'New York 1900' Studies Foundation of Urban Age," *Los Angeles Herald Examiner* (February 8, 1984), p. B2.

Paul Goldberger, [book review] "A Noble Vision In Stone," *The New York Times Book Review* (March 18, 1984), pp. 11–12.

Douglas Brenner, "Bozzi House: East Hampton, New York by Robert A. M. Stern Architects," *Architectural Record* (Mid-April 1984), pp. 108–111.

Alessandra Mauri, "Il Giocco Dello Stile," *Gran Bazaar* (April 1984), pp. 110–113.

Geoffrey C. Ward, "Book Reviews: 'New York 1900: Metropolitan Architecture & Urbanism, 1890–1915'," *Americana* (May /June 1984), pp. 33–36.

Paul Goldberger, "Shingle Style Again," *House and Garden* (June 1984), pp. 168–177, 211.

Hideaki Haraguchi, "A Comparative Analysis of Twentieth-Century Houses, *Toshi-Jutaku* (June 1984), pp. 64, 74.

Vincent Scully, "Architecture: Robert A. M. Stern," *Architectural Digest* (June 1984), pp. 136–141, 164, 166; reprinted Japanese Edition (September 1984), pp. 64–69.

Douglas Brenner, "Is There a Hamptons Style?," *Beaux Arch II: Houses by the Sea* (July 1984), p. 5.

"East Hampton Residence," *Beaux Arch II: Houses by the Sea* (July 1984), pp. 52–53.

"New Jersey . . . Pool House," *Domus* (July /August 1984), pp. 42–47.

Maeve Slavin, "Out on the Table," *Interiors* (August 1984), pp. 152–155.

"PM By Any Other Name . . . ," *Progressive Architecture* (September 1984), pp. 26–27.

"In Progress: Prospect Point Office Building, La Jolla, Calif.," *Progressive Architecture* (September 1984), p. 45.

William H. Jordy, [book review] "The Renaissance in New York: The Buildings of McKim, Mead & White," *The New Criterion* (October 1984), pp. 49–60.

"Production Housing," *Builder* (October 1984), pp. 154–156.

Aaron Betsky, "Designs for Living," *Horizon* (November 1984), pp. 49–54.

Warren A. James, [book review] "Books: 'New York 1900—Metropolitan Architecture and Urbanism 1890–1915' (Robert A. M. Stern, Gregory Gilmartin, and John M. Massengale)," *Architectural Record* (November 1984), p. 75.

Joseph Masheck, "Judy Rifka and 'Postmodernism' in Architecture," *Art in America* (December 1984), pp. 148–163.

Douglas Davis, [book review] "Deck the Shelves with Books Aplenty," *Newsweek* (December 10, 1984), p. 89.

"Rigoureux Avec Couleurs," *Maison Francaise* (December 1984 / January 1985), pp. 116–125.

"Tradition Revised: Grandma's House Revisited," *Better Homes and Gardens* (Winter 1984 /1985), pp. 52–59.

G. Simeoforidis, "U.S.A. Post-war Architecture," *Architecture in Greece* (1985), p. 135.

Gavin MacRae-Gibson, "Scenography and the Picturesque," *The Secret Life of Buildings: An American Mythology for Modern Architecture* (Cambridge, Massachusetts: MIT Press, 1985), pp. 98–117.

Carol Vogel, "The Trend-Setting Traditionalism of Architect Robert A. M. Stern," *The New York Times Sunday Magazine* (January 13, 1985), pp. 40–49.

Karin Tetlow, "Temple of Entertainment," *Interiors* (January 1985), pp. 174–175.

"Robert A. M. Stern: Point West Place, Framingham, Massachusetts," *Architectural Design* (January /February 1985), pp. 38–43.

Carleton Knight III, "Making Peace," *Builder* (February 1985), pp. 122–125.

Carl W. Condit, [book review] "American Architecture And Urbanism: Robert A. M. Stern, Gregory Gilmartin, and John M. Massengale, 'New York 1900: Metropolitan Architecture and Urbanism 1890–1915'," *Journal of the Society of Architectural Historians* (March 1985), pp. 77–79.

Kurt Gustmann, "Great Architects: Robert A. M. Stern," *Hauser* (March 1985), pp. 59–70.

Kaarin Taipale, "Erään Klassisismin tarina: Robert A. M. Stern," *Arkkitehti*, Finland (March 1985), pp. 88–91.

Leland M. Roth, "Book Reviews: Robert A. M. Stern, Gregory Gilmartin, and John M. Massengale. 'New York 1900: Metropolitan Architecture & Urbanism, 1890–1915'," *Winterthur Portfolio* (Spring 1985), pp. 98–100.

Aaron Betsky, [book review] " 'New York 1900: Metropolitan Architecture and Urbanism 1890–1915'," *Journal of Architectural Education* (Spring 1985), pp. 31–32.

Paolo Portoghesi, ed., "Il Progetto," *Eupalino* (April 1985), pp. 6–11.

Thomas Vonier, "Six Architects Show: But is it Art?," *Progressive Architecture* (April 1985), pp. 30, 32.

Robert Campbell, "Shingle Style Reinvented: Residence at Chilmark: Robert A. M. Stern," *Architecture* (May 1985), pp. 262–267; reprinted in *Architecture Quarterly* (Fall 1985), pp. 18–23.

Hugh Newell Jacobsen, "Architecture: Robert A. M. Stern," *Architectural Digest* (May 1985), pp. 210–219.

Andrew Saint, "Myopia Biographica [book review]: Raymond Hood, by Robert A. M. Stern," *AA Files* (Summer 1985), pp. 102–104.

Scott Gutterman, "Architect Designed Tableware," *Art & Design* (July 1985), pp. 10–11, back cover.

Sally Woodbridge, "Seaside Starts Commercial District," *Progressive Architecture* (July 1985), p. 77.

"Architect-Designed Objects for the Home Swid Powell Collection," *SD* (August 1985), pp. 77–79.

Gavin MacRae-Gibson, "Robert A. M. Stern and the Tradition of the Picturesque," *A + U* (August 1985), pp. 83–90.

Toshio Nakamura, ed., "Recent Works of Robert A. M. Stern," *A + U* (August 1985), pp. 75–114.

"Robert A. M. Stern Architects: Residence at Farm Neck," *Global Architecture Houses* (August 1985), pp. 130–141.

Robert Guenther, "Resort developer breaks rules in quest to do project 'right'," *The Wall Street Journal* (October 30, 1985), pp. 31–32.

Douglas Brenner, "A Classical Education," *Architectural Record* (November 1985), pp. 110–115.

Stanley Tigerman, "Villa with a View: Melding Traditions on Oyster Bay," *Architectural Digest* (November 1985), pp. 132–141.

Susan Zevon, "Building the American Dream," *House Beautiful* (November 1985), pp. 70–75.

Mark A. Hewitt, [book review] "The Emerging Metropolis: Its Visionaries, Builders, and Critics," *Cite* (Winter 1985), pp. 6–7.

Yvonne V. Chabrier, "Home or Office?," *Boston* (December 1985), pp. 161–164.

Carleton Knight III, "Mr. Jefferson and His Succesors," *Architecture* (December 1985), pp. 62–70.

Vincent Scully, [book review] "Epoch Architecture—From Times Square to Red Square," *Architectural Digest* (December 1985), pp. 206–210.

Monographs of Architectural Work

David Dunster, ed. (introduction by Vincent Scully), *Robert Stern* (London: Academy Editions, 1981).

Peter Arnell and Ted Bickford, eds., *Robert A. M. Stern, Buildings and Projects 1965–1980,* (New York: Rizzoli International Publications, Inc., 1981).

Toshio Nakamura, ed., "The Residential Works of Robert A. M. Stern," *A + U*, (July 1982 Extra Edition).

Exhibitions of Work

"Post-Modernism Comes to England: Robert A. M. Stern /Six British Architects," Architectural Design Gallery, London, 1981.

"The House as Image: Louisiana Museum for Moderne Kunst," Humlebaek, Denmark, 1981.

"Architectural Fantasies: Creative Alternatives," American Institute of Architects Foundation, Washington, D.C., January 1981.

"City Segments," Neuberger Museum, State University of New York at Purchase, January 18–March 15, 1981.

"Collaboration: Artists and Architects," The Architectural League of New York Centennial Exhibition, New-York Historical Society, March–June 1981.

"Speaking a New Classicism: American Architecture Now," Smith College Museum of Art, Northampton, Massachusetts, April 30–July 12, 1981; Sterling and Francine Clark Art Institute, Williamstown, Massachusetts, July 25–September 8, 1981.

"Robert A. M. Stern: Modern Architecture After Modernism," Neuberger Museum, State University of New York at Purchase, March–June 1982.

"Similar Spaces, Island Houses," Art and Architecture Gallery, Vineyard Haven, Massachusetts, August 1982.

"Drawings of Works in Progress," Form and Function Gallery, Atlanta, Georgia, May 1983.

"At Home in the City: Housing in New York 1810–1983," The Municipal Art Society of New York and the Graduate School and University Center of the City University of New York, New York, June–July 1983.

"Beaux Arch I: A Hamptons Architectural Exposition," Bridgehampton, New York, July 1983.

"Chicago and New York: Architectural Interaction," the New-York Historical Society, Fall 1983; Art Institute of Chicago, March 8–July 29, 1984.

"Ornamentalism: The New Decorativeness in Architecture and Design," Hudson River Museum, Yonkers, New York, May 1983; Fendrick Gallery, Washington, D.C., June–August 1983; Archer M. Huntington Art Gallery, University of Texas, Austin, September–October 1983.

"Old Buildings, New Places," Municipal Art Society, Urban Center, New York, January 1984.

"A Tribute to Contemporary Architecture," University Place Gallery, Cambridge, Massachusetts, May 1984.

"Beaux Arch II," Bridgehampton Day School, Bridgehampton, Long Island, New York, July 1984.

"The International Exhibition XVth U.I.A. Congress," International Union of Architects, Center of Art and Communication, Buenos Aires and Cairo, January 1985.

"Ideas / Ideal /Deal /Real: Design Histories," University of Maryland, College Park, Maryland, February 6–March 15, 1985.

"Architects for Social Responsibility," benefit auction, Max Protetch Gallery, New York, June 1985.

"Homo Decorans–Man Who Decorates," Louisiana Museum for Moderne Kunst, Humlebaek, Denmark, June–September 1985.

"Beaux Arch III," Bridgehampton Day School, Bridgehampton, New York, July 1985.

"High Styles: Twentieth Century American Design," Whitney Museum of American Art, New York, September 1985–February 1986.

"Selection Three," Design and Architecture Collection, Esther Annenberg Simon Gallery, The Metropolitan Museum of Art, October 1985–January 1986.

Exhibitions Organized by Robert A. M. Stern

"Suburbs," Cooper-Hewitt Museum, New York, Fall 1982.

Awards

Distinguished Architecture Award, New York Chapter, American Institute of Architects, 1982. For Residence, Llewellyn Park, New Jersey.

Lumen Award, given by the New York Section Illuminating Engineering Society and the International Association of Lighting Designers, 1982. For Residence, Llewellyn Park, New Jersey.

Interiors Award, Recreation /Entertainment Design Section, 1982. For Lincoln Squash Club.

Lumen Award, given by the New York Section Illuminating Engineering Society and the International Association of Lighting Designers, 1983. For Classical Duplex Apartment.

Research Grant, National Endowment for the Arts, 1983. For *Suburbs* book.

Distinguished Architecture Award, New York Chapter, American Institute of Architects, 1984. For Residence in East Quogue, New York.

Distinguished Architecture Award, New York Chapter, American Institute of Architects, 1984. For Residence in Chilmark, Martha's Vineyard, Massachusetts.

Merit Award, Competition. For Newport News Cultural Arts Pavilion, Newport News, Virginia, 1984.

Medal of Honor, New York Chapter, American Institute of Architects, June 1984.

Builder Magazine, Grand Award for Unit Design, Honorable Mention for Overall Development, 1984. For St. Andrews.

First Honor Award, Westchester/Mid-Hudson Chapter, American Institute of Architects, 1984. For St. Andrews.

Record House 1984, *Architectural Record* (Mid-April 1984). For Residence, East Hampton, New York.

Interiors Award, Recreation and Entertainment Design, 1985. For Student Pub, International House, New York, New York.

National Honor Award, American Institute of Architects, 1985. For Residence at Chilmark, Martha's Vineyard, Massachusetts.

Distinguished Architecture Award, New York Chapter, American Institute of Architects, 1985. For Residence, East Hampton, New York.

Award for Excellence in Design, New York State Association of Architects, Inc., American Institute of Architects, 1985. For Point West Place Office Building.

Award for Excellence in Design, New York State Association of Architects, Inc., American Institute of Architects, 1985. For Observatory Hill Dining Hall, University of Virginia.

Award for Excellence in Design, New York State Association of Architects, Inc., American Institute of Architects, 1985. For Residence at Farm Neck, Martha's Vineyard, Massachusetts.

Award, Unbuilt Projects Awards, New York Chapter, American Institute of Architects, 1985. For Residence, Brooklyn, New York.

Award, Unbuilt Projects Awards, New York Chapter, American Institute of Architects, 1985. For Villa in New Jersey.

Project Credits

Models are an important tool in our design process, and the following people have made important contributions:

Traci Aronoff
David Baer
Mark Devlin
Joseph W. Dick
John DiGregorio
John R. M. Fowler
Scott Harmon
Charles Lopez
Robert Lucero
Richard Maimon
Kenneth McIntyre-Horito
Kristin McMahon
Peter Merwin
Thai Nguyen
Deirdre O'Farrelly
Luis F. Rueda
Mario Sampaio
Whitney Sander
Mariko Takahashi
Rives Taylor
Constance Treadwell
Johanna Vanderbulche
Mark Wade

Photographic Credits

All photographs by Robert A.M. Stern Architects except for the following:

Peter Aaron, Copyright ESTO, Mamaroneck, New York: p.11-3; p.14-2; p.16-1,2; p.17-3,4; p.18-1; p.21-3; p.22-1; p.23-4,5; p.24-1,2,3; p.25-5; p.27-3,4,5,6,7; p.29-5,6,7,8; p.30-1,2,3; p.31; p.33-5; p.34-1,2,3; p.35-4,5; p.73-3,5; p.74-1,2; p.75-3,4;

Courtesy of *Architectural Digest:* p.50-2; p.51-10; p.52-1,2; p.53-3,4; p.54-1,2; p.55-3,4,5;

Courtesy of *Progressive Architecture:* p.69-3,4; p.70-1,2,3,4,5; p.71-6,7,8,9;

Courtesy of *Interior Design Magazine:* p.77; p.78; p.79-1,3.

Jaime Ardiles-Arce, New York; courtesy of *Architectural Digest:* p.106-1; p.108-1,2; p.109-3,4; p.111-8,9.

Antoine Bootz, New York; courtesy of Furniture of the Twentieth Century: p.94.

"Classical Corner" photographs courtesy of *Metropolitan Home,* Copyright Meredith Corporation 1983: p.66-1,2; p.67-3,4,5.

Langdon Clay, New York; courtesy of *House & Garden,* Copyright 1984, Conde Nast Publications, Inc.: p.38-2; p.39-3,7,9; p.41-7,8.

Whitney Cox, Richmond, Virginia; courtesy of *Architectural Record:* p.98-1,2; p.99; p.100-2; p.101-5,6; p.102; p.103.

Y. Futagawa & Associated Photographers, Copyright Retoria: p.20-2; p.21-12; p.22-2,3; p.23-6; p.24-2; p.25-6,7.

R. Greg Hursley, Austin, Texas; courtesy of *Builder Magazine* & *Home Magazine:* p.260-1,2; p.261-3,4,5.

Timothy Hursley, The Arkansas Office; courtesy of *Architectural Record:* p.104-3; p.127-2,3; p.129-7,8; p.130-1; p.131; p.133-2,3; p.134-2. Also photographs on front and back covers.

Tom Lamb, Laguna Beach, California: p.252-3,4; p.253-5,6.

Jon Naar, New York; courtesy of *Interiors Magazine:* p.197-2,3,4,5.

Roberto Schezen, New York: p.37-2; p.38-1; p.39-4,5,6,8; p.41-9.

Steven Simpson, California: p.142-1,2; p.143-3,4,5.

Tony Soluri, Chicago, Illinois; courtesy of *Architectural Digest:* p.114-1; p.116-2; p.117-3,4; p.118-1,3; p.119-5,6.

Edmund Stoecklein, New York; courtesy of *Interior Design Magazine:* p.46-1,2; p.47-3. Also: p.11-4,5; p.15-3,4,5,6,7,8; p.19-3,4; p.43-3,4,5,6,7,8; p.45-5,6.

Peter Vanderwerker, West Newton, Massachusetts: p.134-1; p.135-3.

Paul Warchol, New York; courtesy of Swid Powell: p.83-1,2,3,4.

Acknowledgments

Renderings

p.204-1; p.205-2,3,4,5 by Carlos Deniz.
p.213-6,7 by Jeffrey George.

Watercolors

p.114-2; p.118-2 by Chuck Felton.
p.151-5A,5B,5C; p.193-6; p.209 by William T. Georgis.
p.201-3 by Timothy E. Lenahan

Karen Lazar deserves particular thanks for the long hours she spent typing and revising the text. A battery of draftsmen worked with me in preparing the drawings, among them Augusta Barone, Arthur Chabon, Mark Devlin, Karen Fairbanks, Eric Fang, Kristin Johann, Robert Lucero, Richard Maimon, Deirdre O'Farrelly, Joel Rosenberg, Whitney Sander, Eric Schiller, Oscar Shamamian, Nicholas Stern, Hailim Suh, Mariko Takahashi, Paul Williger, and Brian Yeley.

My thanks to Alessandro Franchini and Clark Candy, and to the staff of Rizzoli, particularly to Solveig Williams who supervised the project from beginning to end. I am also grateful to the many photographers and publications that contributed material, which through their kindness, I have been able to incorporate in this book.

Finally, a note of special gratitude to Gregory Gilmartin for his valuable editorial advice, and to Eileen Emmet for her inestimable help in researching and putting together the bibliography.

L. F. Rueda
May, 1986

Index to Buildings and Projects